in 10·03·2020

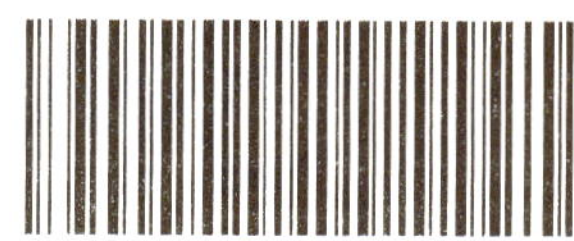

See page 180
Repose

MASTERPIECES OF AMERICAN PAINTING

MASTERPIECES OF AMERICAN PAINTING IN THE METROPOLITAN MUSEUM OF ART

by MARGARETTA SALINGER

with a foreword by JOHN K. HOWAT

The Metropolitan Museum of Art
Random House

NEW YORK

PUBLISHED BY
The Metropolitan Museum of Art, New York,
and Random House, New York

Bradford D. Kelleher, *Publisher, The Metropolitan Museum of Art*
John P. O'Neill, *Editor in Chief*
Barbara Burn, *Project Coordinator*
Margot Feely and Brenda Gilchrist, *Editors*
Peter Oldenburg, *Designer*
Stephen S. Sechrist, *Production Coordinator*

LIBRARY OF CONGRESS CATALOGING-IN-PUBLICATION DATA
Salinger, Margaretta M., 1907–1985.
Masterpieces of American painting in the Metropolitan Museum of Art.
Bibliography: p. 193
1. Painting, American—Catalogs. 2. Painting, Modern—United States—Catalogs. 3. Painting—New York (N.Y.)—Catalogs. 4. Metropolitan Museum of Art (New York, N.Y.)—Catalogs. I. Metropolitan Museum of Art (New York, N.Y.) II. Title.
ND205.S33 1986 759.13'074'01471 86.8793

ISBN 0-87099-472-2 (MMA)
ISBN 0-394-55491-4 (Random House)

The photographs for this volume were taken by The Photograph Studio, The Metropolitan Museum of Art, with the exception of those on the following pages, which were taken by Geoffrey Clements: 16, 17, 23, 24–25, 26, 27, 34, 35, 42, 43, 48, 49, 54, 66, 67, 68–69, 70–71, 76–77, 78, 79, 90–91, 92–93, 99, 108–9, 126, 134, 134–35, 146, 147, 149, 150, 156, 157, 183, 190–1.

Composition by Cardinal Type Service, Inc.
Printed and bound by Grafiche Milani, Italy

Foreword

THIS BOOK is the happy product of the labors of Margaretta Salinger begun some years ago in preparation for opening the new American Wing of The Metropolitan Museum of Art. A decision was made that the American paintings to be shown in the Joan Whitney Payson Galleries of the American Wing were each to be accompanied by a brief discursive label—called a "chat" label by museum people—which would provide basic information about the artist and painting. The hope was to achieve a clear, understandable, and evocative presentation of information that would be well received by visitors to the galleries. The Metropolitan Museum attracts many "publics," from the youngest children to the most sophisticated of art scholars, and there are specific kinds of publications which can be used to reach these different groups. We wished to produce labels that would be sensible to the widest possible range of thoughtful visitors. In this effort the Department of American Paintings and Sculpture was extremely fortunate in being able to persuade Miss Salinger to undertake the demanding task of preparing the hundreds of labels needed. Later, because the results were so well received by the public, the suggestion was made and accepted by Miss Salinger that she select one hundred paintings and accompanying texts for publication in book form. Accordingly, and supplemented by a brief introduction and bibliography, here are the plates and texts, amended in some cases to fit a new format.

To select one hundred paintings from among almost one thousand and to present them, in effect, as the "cream of the crop" is always a risky business: people will invariably agree to disagree over what is "good" or "better," and certainly over what is "best" within the world of art. However, choices must be made here as elsewhere, and there is a broad consensus as to which are the greatest of the Metropolitan's greatest American pictures. In addition, Miss Salinger brought a fine and wonderfully trained eye to the task, since she knew what made a great picture as well as what the reader and museumgoer would like.

The history of acquisition of these one hundred paintings is reflective of the larger history of building all the Metropolitan's collections during the 116 years since the Museum's founding: approximately twenty percent were bequeathed, another forty percent were donated, and some forty percent were purchased with funds received from donors and endowments. The collection stands as a proud monument both to the generosity of donors and to the wise policies of our government to encourage such donations. The periods of greatest acquisition activity for American pictures were the first three decades of this century—certainly a remarkable period of great economic and cultural growth in America—and the past twenty-five years, a period of prosperity and introspection when Americans have been eager to rediscover the beauties of their nation's art.

This book appears after the completion of a long and distinguished career at the Metropolitan Museum. Miss Salinger graduated *cum laude* from Bryn Mawr College in 1928, and after completing a Bryn Mawr Fellowship at the University of Munich she joined the staff of the Department of Paintings (which then included American paintings) in 1930. Beginning as a special cataloguer, she rose through a series of increasingly more demanding research and curatorial positions until the Metropolitan trustees elected her curator in the Department of European Paintings in 1970 and curator emeritus in 1972. Thereafter Miss Salinger continued to work on various publications until she undertook the American paintings label project, which was completed in 1980, capping a career of fifty years with the Metropolitan Museum.

A superb and animated speaker, Miss Salinger gave many individual lectures and lecture series at the Metropolitan Museum. She also taught at Barnard College, the Columbia Graduate School, the School of Adult Education at New York University, and the Juilliard School of Music. She was a regular contributor to *The Metropolitan Museum of Art Bulletin* and was author of *The Flower Piece in European Painting* and co-author of *Early Flemish, Dutch, and German Painting in the Metropolitan Museum of Art* and *French Painting of the 19th and 20th Centuries in the Metropolitan Museum of Art*. Sadly, Miss Salinger died in March, 1985.

In all of her work, whether spoken or written, Margaretta Salinger strove to express her perceptive ideas with precision and grace. I hope the reader will agree that she succeeded once again with this, her last book.

JOHN K. HOWAT

The Lawrence A. Fleischman Chairman
of the Departments of American Art
The Metropolitan Museum of Art

Introduction

THIS GROUP of one hundred American paintings—representing about a tenth of the Metropolitan Museum's holdings of eighteenth, nineteenth, and early twentieth-century paintings in the American field—has been selected to provide an attractive and fair impression both of these holdings and of American painting in general. Although no book based on a specific collection could claim to offer an accurate review of the history of American painting, because of inevitable gaps in any collection—as exemplified here by the slight representation of folk or naive painting—the overall breadth and strength of the Metropolitan collection are not only remarkable but also serviceable for suitably displaying the history and range of American painting.

Here, then, are one hundred American paintings, reproduced in the best color possible, each with a short commentary that gives a very brief record of the artist's life and training and remarks on the picture itself.

The problem of choosing an arrangement for these pictures was complex. A chronological sequence seems to be the most obvious, although it presents its own drawbacks. Long-lived artists often change very much in the course of their careers and early works by them may look very different from late ones, but it is surely desirable to keep them together. Strict grouping into such categories as patriotism and history, landscape and fantasy, and genre and the related portrait in its own interior would have been hopelessly confusing and really useless unless a careful (and tedious) treatise had been intended.

Actually, an ordering of pictures roughly according to the years when they were painted reveals wide, general similarities in the subject matter artists chose to treat during the same years. Colonial painting through the eighteenth century dealt with the engrossing matter of the age—the making of history, the attainment of autonomy as a new nation. There are battle scenes, and among the subjects for portraits are the men who led the battles and the statesmen who shaped the policies. By the end of the first quarter of the nineteenth century, well-being and security had calmed the spirits. Artists looking about their ordinary surroundings found undemanding objects, such as vegetables and slices of cake, worthy material for pictures. Around the mid-1800s, fanciful subjects like flower girls and allegories of spring appeared, and modest, unpretentious subjects from everyday life like cider-making were painted with gratifying truthfulness. Still life, fantasy, and genre have continued to this day. In the 1830s there was also a great surge of lofty feelings of admiration and awe toward the landscape of America. Cole and his many followers studied and sketched the merest details of the near scene and marveled at the distant views, combining them in wide, heroic landscapes.

From the period of the Civil War on, it is less easy and even more dangerous to hazard these overbroad generalizations. Painters of very different tastes and abilities were turning out pictures of many different kinds, all at the same moment, exploring whatever interested them. International trade and opportunities for foreign travel widened their choices. No artists came back from their travels totally unchanged. A little group, chiefly Whistler, Sargent, and Cassatt, found the foreign scene so sympathetic that they, like the writer Henry James, became true expatriates and remained abroad. Even Homer and Eakins, who more deeply and consistently than any other American painters immersed themselves in America, had visited Europe. Eakins indeed spent several years at the Beaux-Arts school in Paris.

The last quarter of the nineteenth century and the opening years of the twentieth, up to World War I, saw two general tendencies that touched the art of many and varied artists, but were marked enough in a few of them to constitute a "school." French Impressionism, which dropped a bomb on Parisian sensibilities in 1874, horrified and revolted visiting Americans perhaps even more. But shock is not a sustained reaction. By 1885, when the movement had peaked and was already being transformed in France, a number of American artists, including John Twachtman, Theodore Robinson, and William Merritt Chase, had incorporated in their paintings, especially their landscapes, so much devotion to the study of light that we speak now of a school of American Impressionists.

As to the other "school," in the early years of the new century a total dedication to intense realism so dominated a group of painters in the New York area that they came to be called the Ashcan School. In their search for the essence of the life they witnessed around them, these artists, conscious of the sociological implications, chose to paint the dreariest aspects of the urban scene. The leaders of this cult of ugliness among the "have-nots" were Henri, Sloan, and Glackens, who were also members of the little coterie that banded itself together as The Eight.

Most of the painters whose works make up this volume are represented by no more than one or two pictures, although the galleries and reserves of the Museum may boast many others. Seven artists present themselves in greater numbers: Copley, Cole, and Cassatt have three paintings; Sargent, four; Stuart and Eakins, five; Homer, with much justification, seven. There are many reasons why these decisions were made. In most cases the determinant was the fact that the Metropolitan is especially rich in the works of those artists who are the outstanding painters of America, works that are strong in quality and variety.

John Singleton Copley and Gilbert Stuart are two of the best colonial portrait painters. Copley was an American by birth and worked successfully in New York, Philadelphia, and Boston until he was thirty-six. At that point he packed up and went to England, where he remained more than four decades until his death in 1815. The settlers in the colonies had found no artistic heritage in their new land on which to build a native style, and the English artists who came to work there gave young Americans their traditions of style and technique. But this very lack of a ready-made, homegrown formula accounts for the great strength of the American work. Artists had to dig deep for their basic understanding of structural effects, and fine artists like Copley, as soon as they could, enhanced what they took from English artists with a vigorous approach based on their own vision and experiments. Here are three of Copley's splendid portraits—likenesses of a young American boy; an admirable, strong-minded, and actively intelligent American woman; and a second youth, an English boy, done after the artist had left the United States for good.

If Copley was the strongest artist the colonies produced, Stuart was probably the most accomplished and polished. He is probably also the most generally known, largely because his portraits of George Washington and their innumerable copies and replicas are the basis of the popular image of the first president. Very few schoolbooks of American history lack a reproduction of one of Stuart's portraits of him, and more often than not the one chosen is the Museum's painting seen in this book. This artist's career is a curious one. After a precocious beginning as a portraitist in America he became the pupil of a Scottish painter with whom he worked for two years in Scotland. In 1775, three years after returning to America, he decided to go back to Britain and there he worked for eighteen years. His considerable professional success in London was sadly marred by extravagant living and the threat of debtors' prison, and in 1793 he came back home. The ensuing thirty-five years were an active and productive period in which he took the lead among American artists. The second half of the eighteenth century in England had produced one of the world's great schools of portraiture, and Stuart had certainly profited by seeing the works of Raeburn, Romney, Lawrence, and, especially, Gainsborough. This artist's fresh, breezy style, which combines ease and naturalness with great refinement and elegance, had apparently made a lasting impression on the young American painter, and dashing impressionistic passages in many of Stuart's works recall Gainsborough. All the Stuart portraits in this book except one date from the last ten years of the eighteenth century. Within that span of a decade they exhibit a remarkable variety. The portrait of George Washington is lofty and idealized, a little more than life size in conception. Horatio Gates, on the other hand, looks like a much more worldly human being, regarding the spectator with the tolerant, even amused, expression of a rich and satisfied retiree. He had fought under Washington and no one could guess from his bearing that his troops had suffered a crushing defeat, which had led to his being relieved of his command. The Vicomte de Noailles is an aristocrat, a brother-in-law of Lafayette. He was also a soldier and had fought with the French in the American Revolution. The artist has made the Vicomte a very impressive figure, without concealing the fact that he was apparently small in stature, with slender feet in fine boots and slim round arms in elegantly tailored sleeves. Stuart's great success as a painter of portraits depends in large part on the diversity and sensitivity of his awareness of human variety. Another of his eighteenth-century portraits represents neither a statesman nor a soldier, but a sixteen-year-old young woman. She was an American by birth, married to a young Spanish diplomat pushing his way upward toward an ambassadorship. Matilda de Jaúdenes is dressed, one might almost say bedizened, in a showy style of jewels and headdress affected at the Spanish court. She has been careful not only to dress well in the taste of her time but also to leave a book open beside her, as if she had been reading until the painter arrived, a symbol of the eighteenth-century woman's learning and intellectuality.

A new chapter in American history, of national consolidation and independence, was being enacted when Stuart made the portrait of James Monroe, fifth president of the United States (1817–1825). Monroe's short-cropped hair is the major difference in physical appearance of this statesman of the new age, but there seems to be also an assertive, forthright attitude on the part of the sitter. This alert air of purpose and decision is altogether different from the timeless leisure that characterized the eighteenth-century portrait, even when the subject was known to be a man of action and responsibilities.

In this new age, the American school of landscape painting began to flourish. Awareness of their own national character and identity opened the eyes of painters to the majesty and beauty of their country. Artists such as Cole and Church, who felt the grandeur and sweep of great vistas, turned out heroic landscapes, large in scale and filled with wonderment and admiration. Others, such as William Sidney Mount and George Caleb Bingham, found the scenery of a particular locale more accessible, but also emotionally appealing and just as worthy of recording.

Thomas Cole was the chief painter of the Hudson River School of landscape painting, drawing his subjects from the scenery of the great river valley in New York State, but working also in New England. Cole had come to America from England when he was about seventeen. Later, a lengthy stay in England, France, and Italy gave him a knowledge of the great classic landscapes by Poussin, Claude, and the Italian and Dutch artists of the seventeenth century. Using this foundation and his natural predilection for the grand and awesome in scenery, Cole made even his painting of a particularized Italian motif, for example the aqueduct near Tivoli, with its wide, lonely background of the Sabine Hills, universal and impressive. His taste for myth and allegory led him to compose a man-diminishing landscape as a setting for his theme in *The Titan's Goblet.*

Cole had many followers, and an active group of landscape painters carried on the traditions of the Hudson River School for more than a generation. But a number of artists who had begun their careers painting Cole-like scenery of the Catskills and the Hudson valley branched out into very different kinds of work that today is associated with their names and styles. The art of John Kensett, Jasper Cropsey, and Albert Bierstadt, so dissimilar from Cole's in character, is rooted in the same tradition.

Frederic Church was Cole's pupil and followed his lead in the general trend of the Hudson River School of landscape painting. He was deeply involved in the investigation of distant places, traveling widely, studying and sketching, and choosing as settings grandiose vistas of mountains and forests in Central America. There were many other kinds of landscape painting practiced by the American painters. A few, unusually original in their way of seeing and exceptionally personal in their stylized expression, Fitz Hugh Lane, Martin Johnson Heade, and later Albert Pinkham Ryder, create a separate category among landscapists Then there are a number of artists who painted as poets, and their pictures are widely differing expressions of their individual feelings. They range in emotional content from the grateful appreciation of nature's gifts, as we find it in George Inness, through such gentle mood paintings as Homer Martin's *Harp of the Winds,* to the fiercely passionate, violent views of the Maine coast that Winslow Homer painted toward the end of his career.

Winslow Homer's prime importance in American painting cannot be denied or diminished. The catchall of the quality of Americanness, with all its varied and contradictory implications, can surely be applied to Homer. No other country, no other set of circumstances could have produced him. In his diversity, in his simplicity, in his independence, and in his truthfulness, he is the most American of painters. He began his career as an illustrator. An illustrator culls his material from his observations, drawing upon a stock of impressions from which he chooses. Throughout his life Homer remained an acutely sensitive and active observer. For at least half of his working life the subjects of his pictures could be classified as genre. Genre pictures are scenes from everyday life, showing people engaged in some activity to which they are accustomed, or that is the common experience of many other people. The nature of that activity has the quality of being usual; special or rare events would make it narrative. With Homer, however, even three young women on a bathing beach, or children outside their schoolhouse playing an age-old game, are so intensely and accurately observed, so skillfully depicted, that they go beyond the category of genre. We feel more than the undemanding pleasure of saying "How true!" but go on to ask about the permanent significance of these people and their world.

In 1862 Homer went to the Civil War as an artist-reporter, and the war furnished him with many themes that he expanded afterward. His skill increased constantly, and he developed an extraordinary facility in the handling of watercolor. He left a matchless record of life in the old South and painted typical country ways and sports. His interests gradually settled on nature in its varying moods, and he adapted his style to his changing interpretations. Although he continued to do figure paintings, people become less and less important in them. Homer's views of the sea painted at Prouts Neck, Maine, are pure proclamations of nature's inescapable power.

The art of Winslow Homer could never be confused with that of Thomas Eakins, though both are so-called realist painters and have much in common. Eakins was eight years younger than Homer, and they lived through approximately the same passage in American history. Both painted their fellow countrymen, engaged in the ordinary activities of everyday life and shown in their customary settings. In their approach to rendering real life and the real world, however, there is a vast difference. No work of Homer's is without some affective tone—some feeling, or some emotion. In the Civil War scenes there is always pathos and sympathy; in *Snap the Whip,* sheer pleasure in well-being, in sunshine, and in health; in the *Northeaster,* awe and fear; and in the tragic *Gulf Stream,* pure terror augmented by the hopeless apathy of the victim. Eakins, on the other hand, attacked his subjects with scientific objectivity. This artist, who is said to have considered becoming a surgeon, whose greatest claim to fame rests on his two clinic paintings of operations in progress in the teaching theaters of Doctors Gross and Agnew, betrays neither pity nor fear. The horror engendered by the blood and the intimate involvement of the spectator in an abhorrent scene were certainly felt by the Philadelphia public, but not by Eakins. There is equal avoidance of empathy in his early paintings of the sports he enjoyed. Complete detachment marks the figure of his young friend Max Schmitt resting his oars; the same detachment is found in the trees and their reflections along the river bank and in the dazzling accuracy of the metal bridge across the Schuylkill River.

Eakins's beautiful, sober portraits are all devoid of any concern with flattery or approval. They are too serious, too searching, too accurate to please. Many of the best of them are of family and intimate friends. Several very fine ones of his wife make us ponder a little how she felt about them: one recalls the young subject of one of Manet's stunning works who confesses, "I wept that he had made me so ugly."

Eakins's fierce and unrelenting pursuit of truth places him at the opposite pole from John Singer Sargent, who is the very epitome of the popular and fashionable portrait painter. A just appraisal, however, of Sargent's vast abilities must include a consideration of his small portraits of peasant women, which are so moving in their quiet interpretation, and painted with so much tender feeling, that it is hard to believe they are the creations of the artist who produced the theatrical *Madame X* and the opulent, exuberant *Wyndham Sisters.* Our *Padre Sebastiano* is another painting where his sympathetic understanding of a human being, whom he knew personally, dominates a setting as brilliantly executed and as dashing in technique as any of his works.

Sargent received his warmest admiration and his best commissions from wealthy Americans and Britons. Having set himself up in a studio in Paris, he was led by disappointment, a bad press, and lack of orders, after three years, to transfer to London, where he worked with general success and acclaim for the rest of his life. French taste has always inclined toward the classic values of measure and restraint, and Sargent's most famous works undeniably have a quality that can only be described as excess. This artistic extravagance pleased his Anglo-Saxon audience and for it he was well paid.

Sargent and James McNeill Whistler both had succumbed to the alluring scent of intellectual sophistication that pervaded the arts in London and Paris in the second half of the nineteenth century. Much of this fragrance, which occasionally became heavy enough to approach decadence, was wafted from the literary and artistic circle of Henry James, another expatriate, who lived and wrote in London.

Mary Cassatt, who also spent most of her working life abroad, never took up the idiom of sophistication. Working in Paris, and in the nearby countryside where she ultimately settled in a country house of her own, in close touch with her family, who lived abroad more than at home in Philadelphia, she painted the pleasant scenes of a gentlewoman's daily life. She made of these agreeable subjects, however, very distinguished works of art. Cassatt had not only looked at the paintings of the French Impressionists, she had actually joined their group, invited by Degas, her friend and champion. She exhibited with them and responded to the same stimuli, especially to the influence of Japanese prints. In spite of this complete absorption in French life and art, Cassatt remains clearly an American painter.

A critic writing of another of the arts describes the spirit Europeans associate with America, a spirit of optimism, practicality, and freedom from the freight of European culture. Not all of the best-traveled American artists became expatriates. Most of them did their major work at home. They went to Europe, sometimes for fairly lengthy stays. They traveled and studied. The marvel is that they never lost their own souls. They came back home to evolve styles and paint pictures that were better drawn, better constructed, and better painted as a result of their experience abroad. But the styles are basically their own, and American to the core. They found the material around them rich and satisfying, and there is a wholesomeness about their lack of embarrassment and self-consciousness when expressing feeling, often strong and deep, sometimes tender and even occasionally sentimental. If there is one quality that characterizes the best American artists, it is probably an honesty and sturdy integrity.

MASTERPIECES OF AMERICAN PAINTING

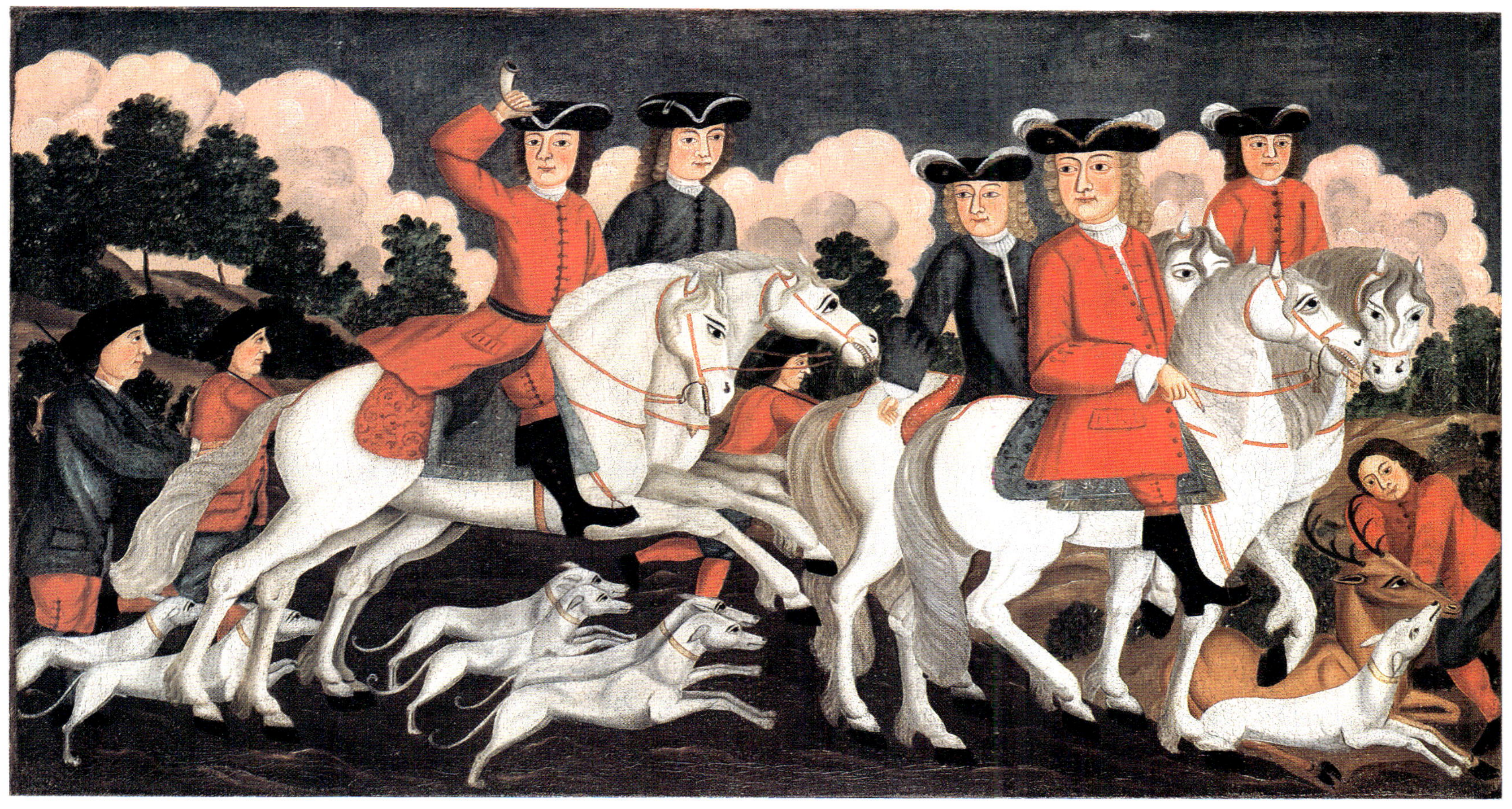

Unknown American Painter

The Hunting Party—New Jersey

Oil on canvas
25¾ x 47⅛ in. (65.4 x 119.7 cm.)
Late 17th or early 18th century
Gift of Mr. and Mrs. Samuel Schwartz, 1979 (1979.299)

THIS HUNTING SCENE, designed to serve the semiutilitarian purpose of decorating the empty wall space above a fireplace, is probably the oldest painting in the Museum's American Wing. There is good reason to believe that it was painted at the end of the seventeenth century, or at the beginning of the eighteenth, in New Jersey, where it remained for many years in its original location, ornamenting a mantel in a farm house. The pictured horses and riders are separated into two groups, one slightly in advance of the other, and glimpsed between them is the profile of a running beater. The pack of small, lean, identical, and determined hounds courses under the hooves of the steeds. At the right edge a henchman leans over a fallen stag, which stares ahead with a strangely human gaze. In fact the eyes and eyebrows of all the horses are rendered in a fashion so similar to the depiction of the human eye that the equines have taken on an anthropomorphic look of purpose and anxiety. The naive artist did not neglect his decorative effects, and the trees on the hillside are echoed in the banks of scalloped clouds that form the background of the scene.

The tradition of the English aristocratic hunting party, along with innumerable other customs, came to the colonies with the early settlers. The untamed country, however, replete with animals of all sorts, and a markedly simpler way of life, produced many changes in the sport, but a picture such as this reveals the colonists' tenacity in attempting to cling to traditional costumes and practices.

Attributed to Pieter Vanderlyn ca. 1687–1778

Young Lady with a Rose

Oil on canvas
32½ x 27 in. (82.6 x 68.6 cm.)
1732
Inscribed at lower left: [illegible] / Geschil [dered] [painted] 1732
Gift of Edgar William and Bernice Chrysler Garbisch, 1962 (62.256.1)

THIS SEVERE PORTRAIT of a young woman is similar to several other likenesses thought to have been painted by Pieter Vanderlyn, an artist who came to this country from Holland in 1718 and worked in the region around Kingston, New York. The subject's mien is solemn, but her somber dress is stylish, and she wears earrings, a necklace, and a ring on the fourth finger of each hand. Although the outlines are overstated and the drawing awkward, the artist has shown a genuine interest in depicting human character. In her disproportionately large right hand, the woman holds out a stylized rose in a gesture so explicit that it seems to offer a clue for identifying her, which, however, no one has yet been able to do.

OVERLEAF:

John Smibert 1688–1751

Francis Brinley

Oil on canvas
50 x 39¼ in. (127 x 99.7 cm.)
1729
Rogers Fund, 1962 (62.79.1)

JOHN SMIBERT, who was born in Scotland, painted this portrait and that of the sitter's wife and son, shown on the facing page, in 1729, the year he arrived and began his work in the colonies. This was the best moment of his art. His fresh memories of the way eighteenth-century painters in England presented rich and influential country squires undoubtedly helped him to achieve this smooth and impressive image of a colonial grandee. Francis Brinley (1690–1765), heir to a considerable fortune, built himself a lavish residence in Roxbury, Massachusetts. Smibert has shown him here, relaxed and satisfied, posed in a handsome armchair outdoors, with a view of Boston in the distance and his own hayfields and extensive landholdings in the foreground.

John Smibert 1688–1751

Mrs. Francis Brinley and Her Son Francis

Oil on canvas
50 x 39¼ in. (127 x 99.7 cm.)
1729
Rogers Fund, 1962 (62.79.2)

MRS. BRINLEY (1698–1761), born Deborah Lyde, was a young woman of social prominence when she married. She ultimately bore her husband seven children. The infant on her lap in this picture is young Francis, born the year the picture was painted, when his mother was thirty-one. The decorative orange tree in the sculptured urn at her side is characteristically in fruit and flower at the same time. Customarily a symbolic allusion to purity, marriage, and fertility, the tree is also evidence of the wealth and luxury that its cultivation required. In the late seventeenth century, following the fashion set by Louis XIV when he built the giant orangery at Versailles, a demand for this delicate bloom was created among European society. Smibert's inclusion of the tree—which was a rarity in eighteenth-century Massachusetts—in Mrs. Brinley's portrait links this colonial matron with the aristocratic ladies of Great Britain.

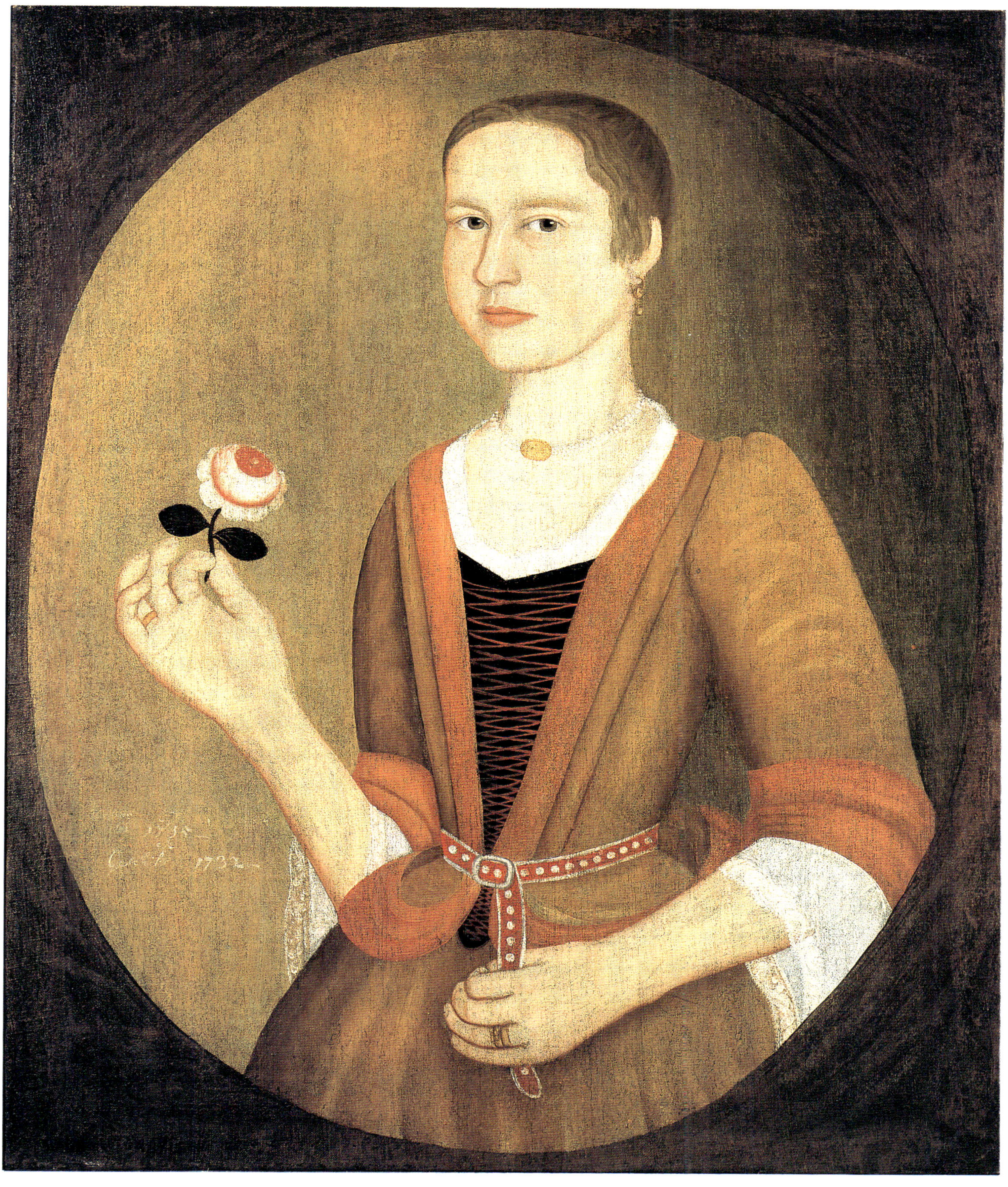

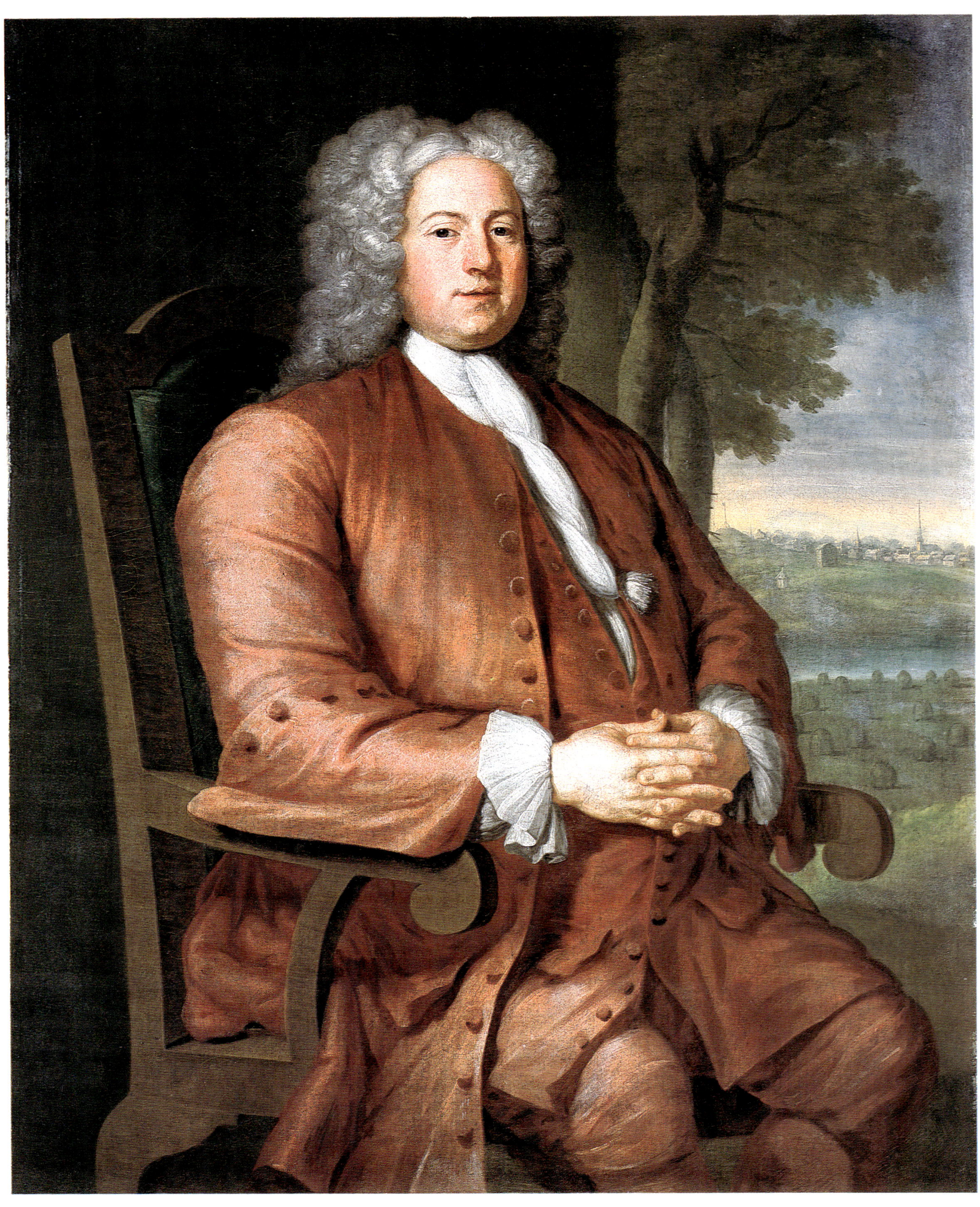

John Smibert: *Francis Brinley*

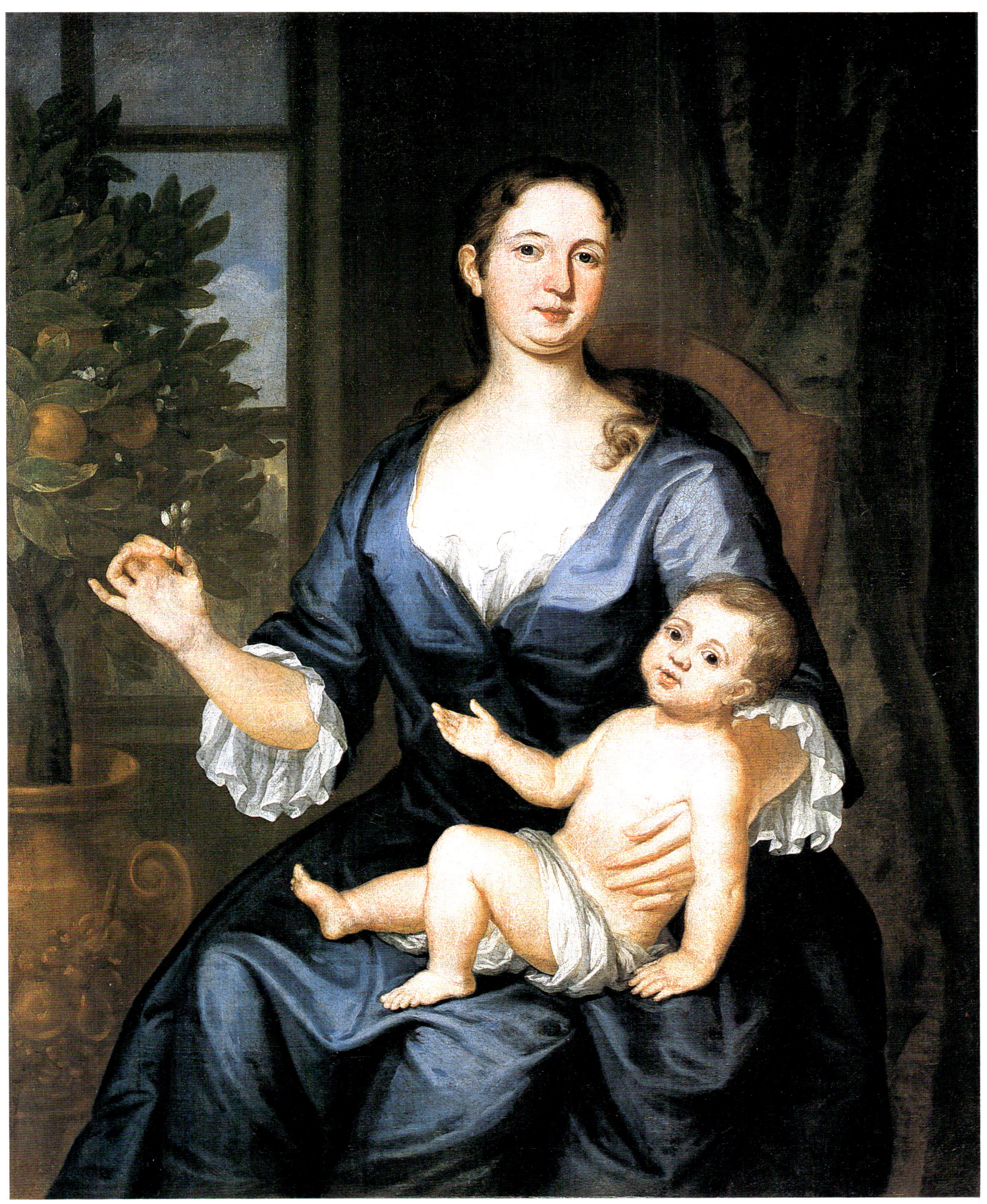

John Smibert: *Mrs. Francis Brinley and Her Son Francis*

Robert Feke
ca. 1708–ca. 1751

Tench Francis

Oil on canvas
49 x 39 in. (1245 x 99.1 cm.)
1746
Signed and dated at lower right:
R. Feke/Pinx 1746
Maria DeWitt Jesup Fund, 1934 (34.153)

BORN IN IRELAND, the son and grandson of Anglican clergymen, Tench Francis (1690?–1758) was educated in the law in London and emigrated to the colonies before 1720. After living for many years in Maryland, in 1738 he settled in Philadelphia, where he spent the rest of his life and where Robert Feke painted this portrait. At the age of about fifty-six, Tench Francis became attorney general and undisputed leader of the bar in Pennsylvania; he was gifted as an orator and respected for his extensive knowledge of the law. He is represented here as both a dignified and an attractive figure.

Feke was a prominent colonial portrait painter. Although the details of his early career are scarce, he left a sizable body of work, done in Philadelphia, Boston, Newport, and his native Long Island. At the time he was painting *Tench Francis*, he was at the height of his powers as a portraitist. His earnings were substantial, for his many portraits were all of high quality, rich in realism and expressiveness.

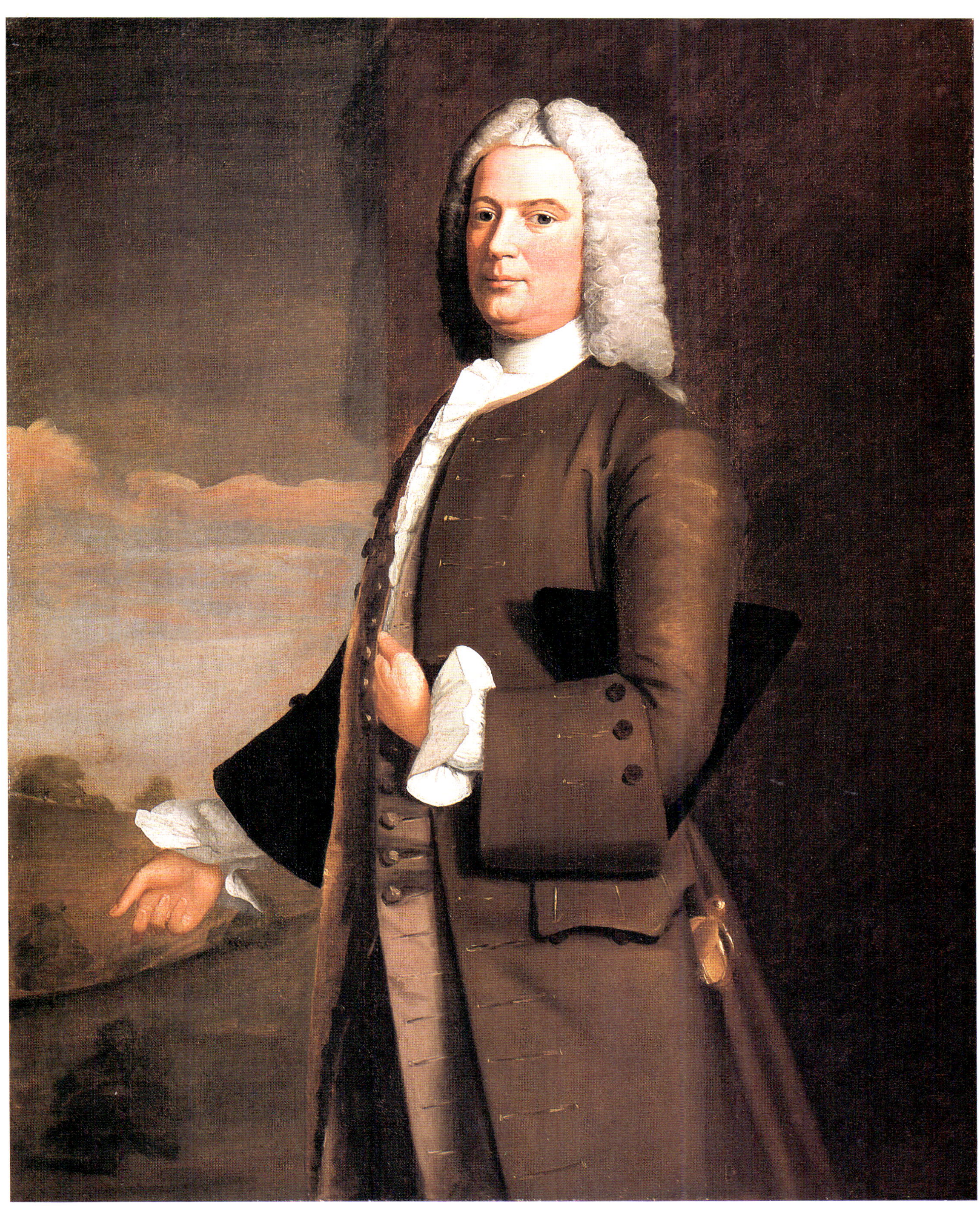

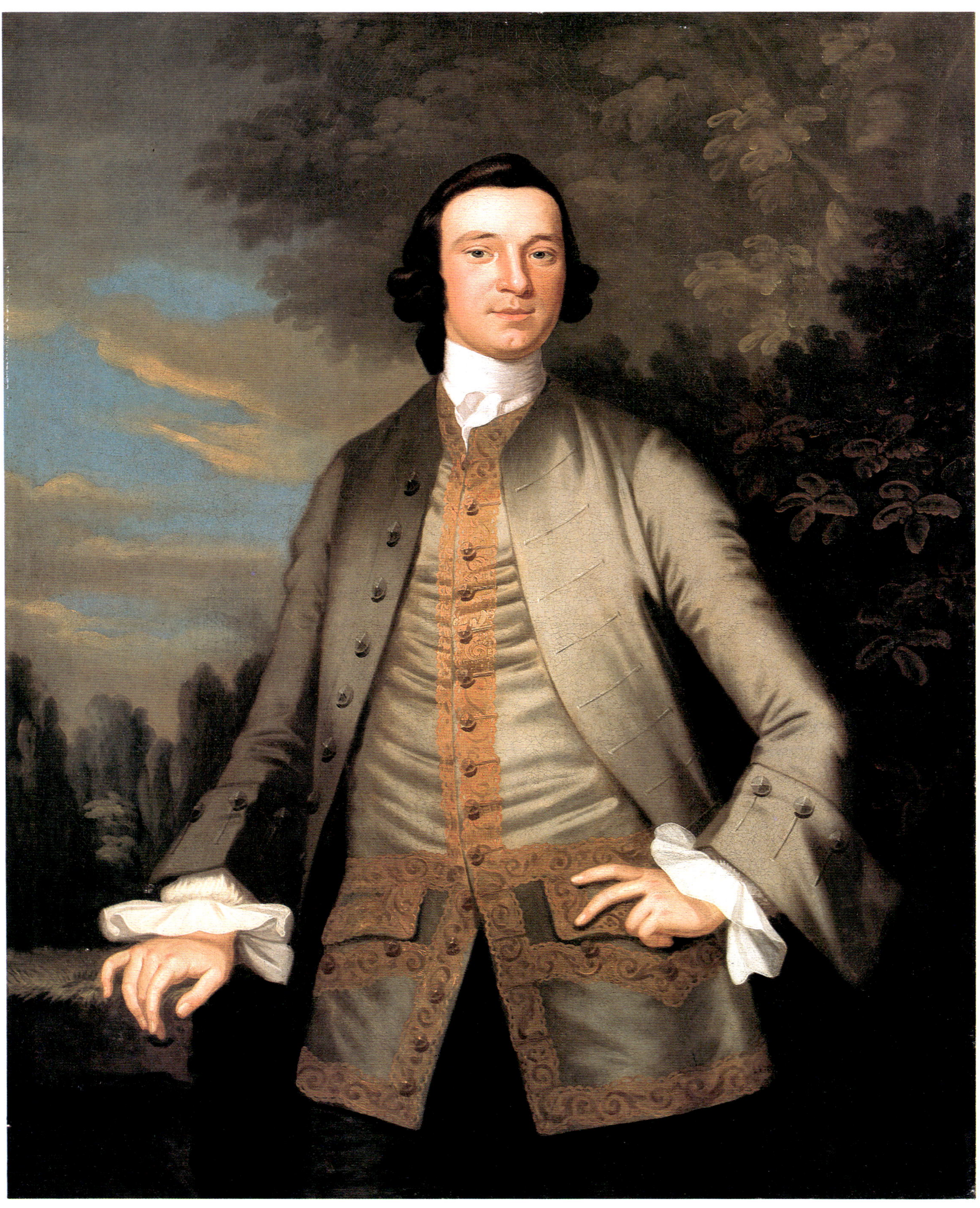

John Wollaston
active 1733–1767

Colonel William Axtell

Oil on canvas
50 x 40 in. (127 x 101.6 cm.)
ca. 1750
Gift of Clarence Dillon, 1976 (1976.23.1)

WILLIAM AXTELL (1719/20–1795), born in the West Indies to a landowning family, came north to New Jersey about the age of twenty-seven. Himself a monied merchant and landowner, he married a member of the prominent De Peyster family and acquired two properties, one in New York and the other, a country estate, in Flatbush, Long Island. His loyalties during the Revolution, however, were firmly committed to England. After the fall of New York he was appointed colonel of a Long Island corps in the British army, a lucrative post he held until the colonial forces regained control. At that point Axtell lost all his American holdings and fled, first to Nova Scotia, and eventually to England, where he remained until his death.

John Wollaston, an English portrait painter, was a stylish artist who was very popular in the colonies. He worked in New York from 1749 to 1752 and it was doubtless during this period that Axtell posed for this large and somewhat self-satisfied likeness. The stately, spacious outdoor setting reflects the status of the subject, who directs a cool, almost challenging gaze toward the spectator. His bearing is assured, without warmth, enthusiasm, or commitment. Wollaston has achieved a perfect envelope for conveying the untroubled well-being of a man content with himself and his world.

OVERLEAF:

William Williams
1727–1791

Portrait of a Boy, probably of the Crossfield Family

Oil on canvas
52¼ x 35¾ in. (132.7 x 91 cm.)
ca. 1770–1775
Victor Wilbour Memorial Fund, 1965 (65.34)

WILLIAM WILLIAMS was born in England, the son of a mariner. He lived through shipwreck and adventure in the Caribbean before arriving in Philadelphia at the age of twenty, by which time he was already earning a livelihood as a painter. He worked in New York from 1769 to 1776, the year he returned to England, where he died fifteen years later in an almshouse.

It has long been believed that the solemn young man represented in this portrait is a member of the Crossfield family. He holds the equipment for the game of battledore and shuttlecock, a decorous eighteenth-century version of badminton. In this picture, one of Williams's best, the rendering of the rocks, the verdure, and the distant view reminds us that the artist was also a painter of theatrical scenery; the dog, with the stare and the pose of a stage prop, sits beside the well-dressed boy in the great English tradition of faithful attendant.

John Durand
active in America
1766–1782

Boy of the Crossfield Family, possibly Richard Crossfield

Oil on canvas
50¼ x 34½ in. (127.6 x 87.6 cm.)
ca. 1770
Gift of Edgar William and Bernice Chrysler Garbisch, 1969 (69.279.2)

ALTHOUGH THIS PORTRAIT is not signed or dated, in style it closely resembles a series of children's portraits completed by John Durand in New York in 1766. The identification of the young sitter rests on a long tradition in the Crossfield family. It is possible that he was the older brother of the boy in the painting by William Williams shown on the facing page. The open book in the boy's hand and the volumes on the shelf behind him are surely meant to affirm the importance of liberal education in colonial times. The massive column rising in the background heightens the elegance of the youthful figure, and the flashing light on the drapery and table cover draws attention to the opulence of the setting. Neither the technical awkwardness in the rendering of the costume's details nor the boy's stilted pose negates the overall effect of self-confidence and sophistication.

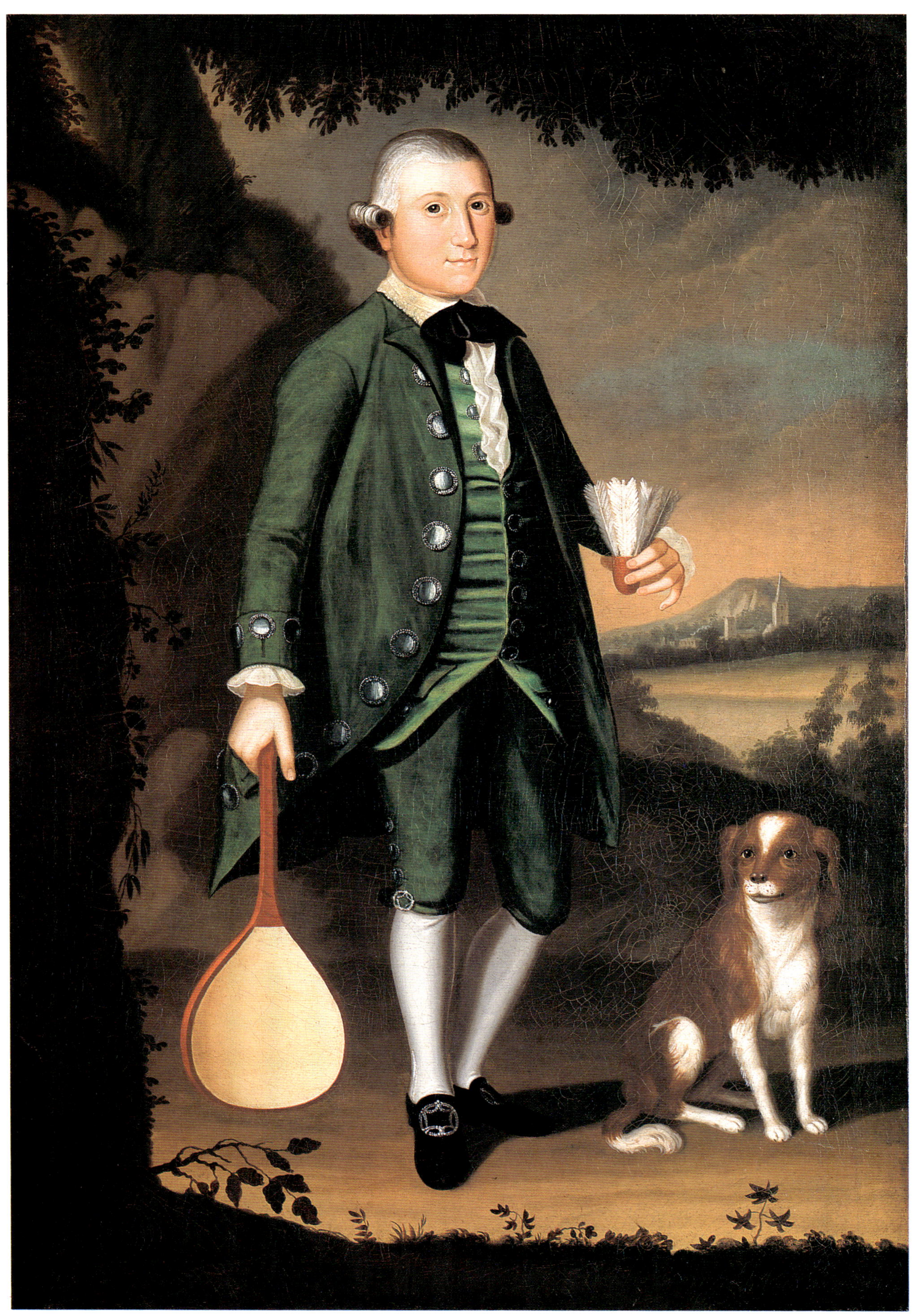

William Williams: *Portrait of a Boy, probably of the Crossfield Family*

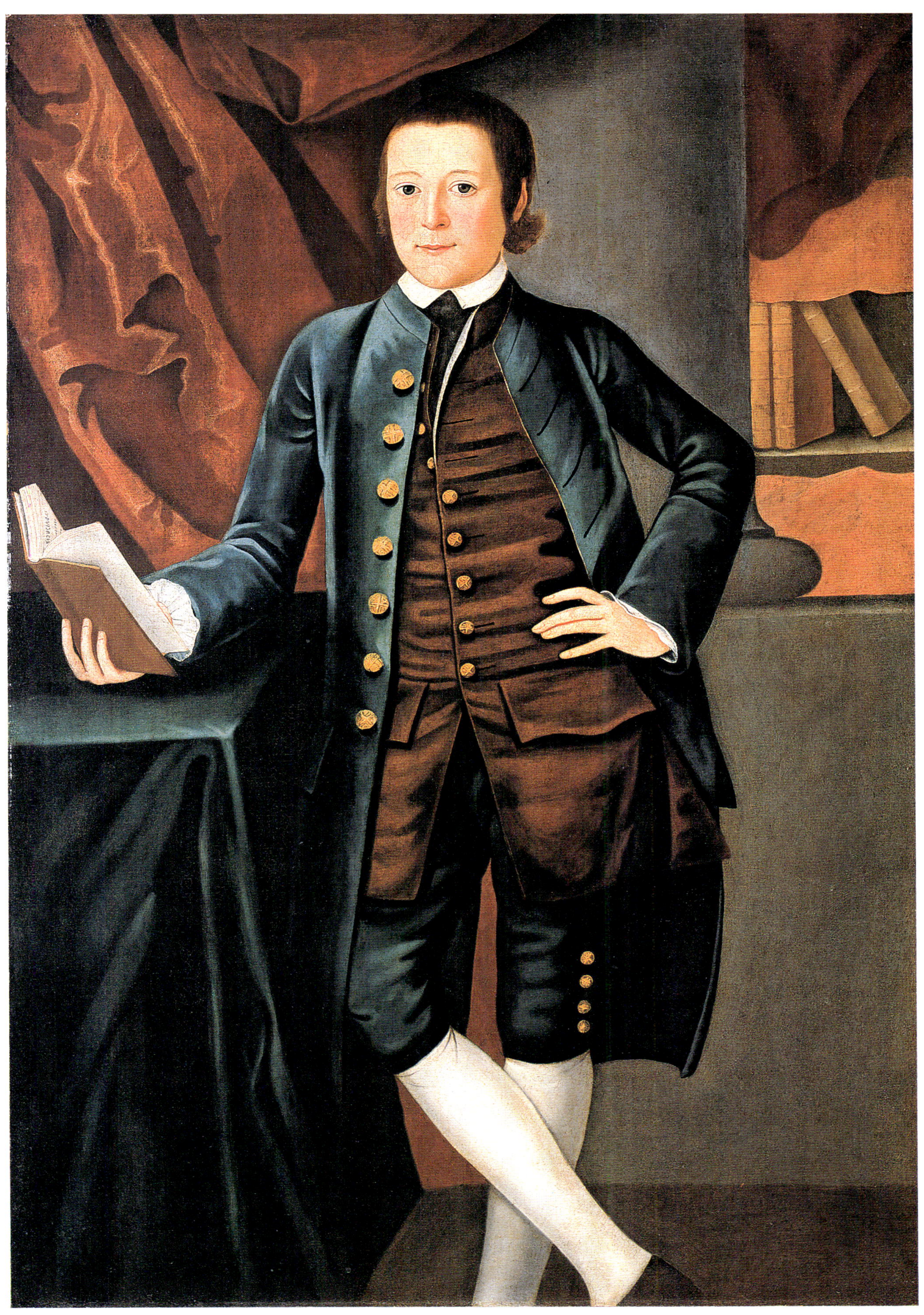

John Durand: *Boy of the Crossfield Family, possibly Richard Crossfield*

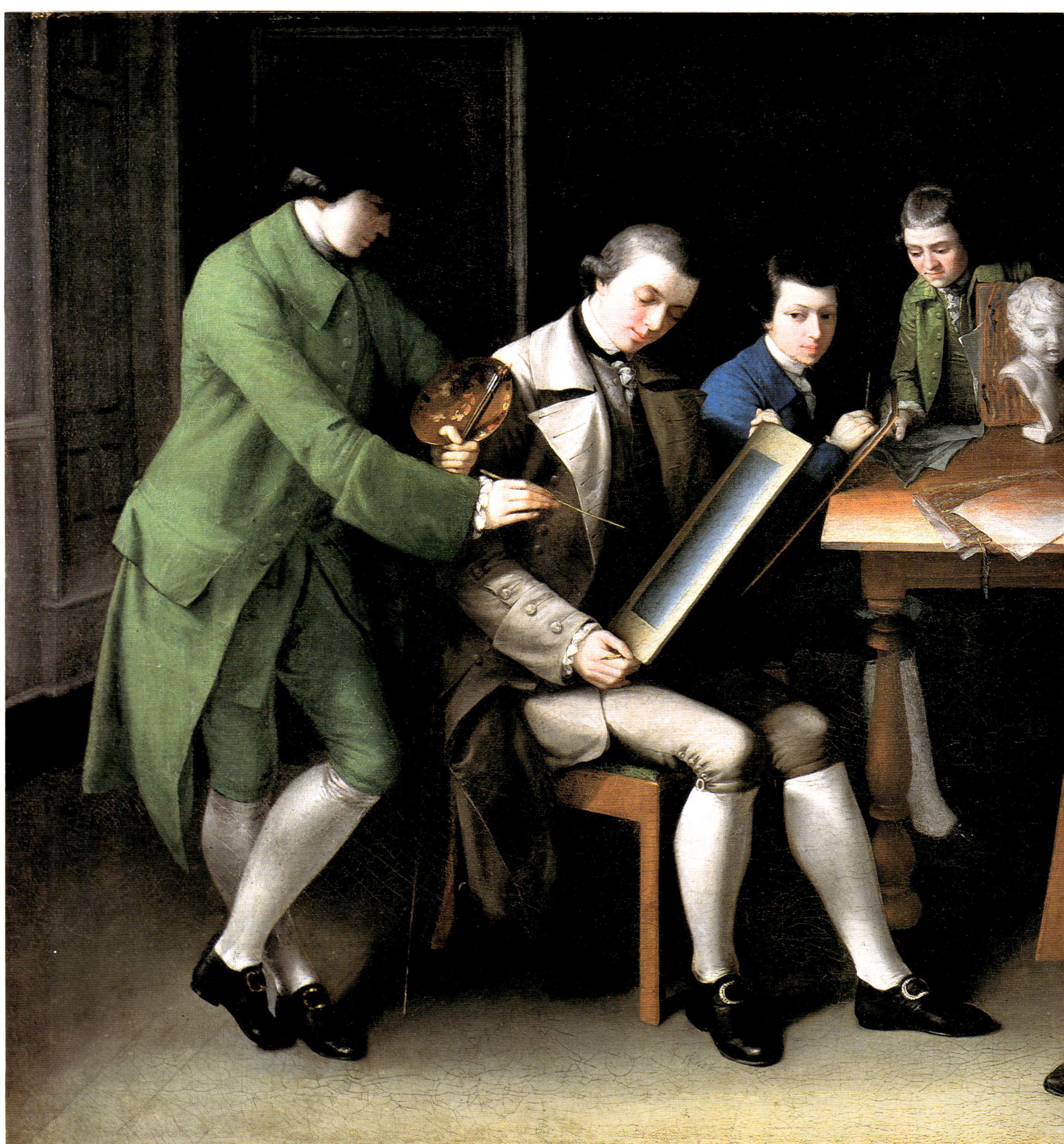

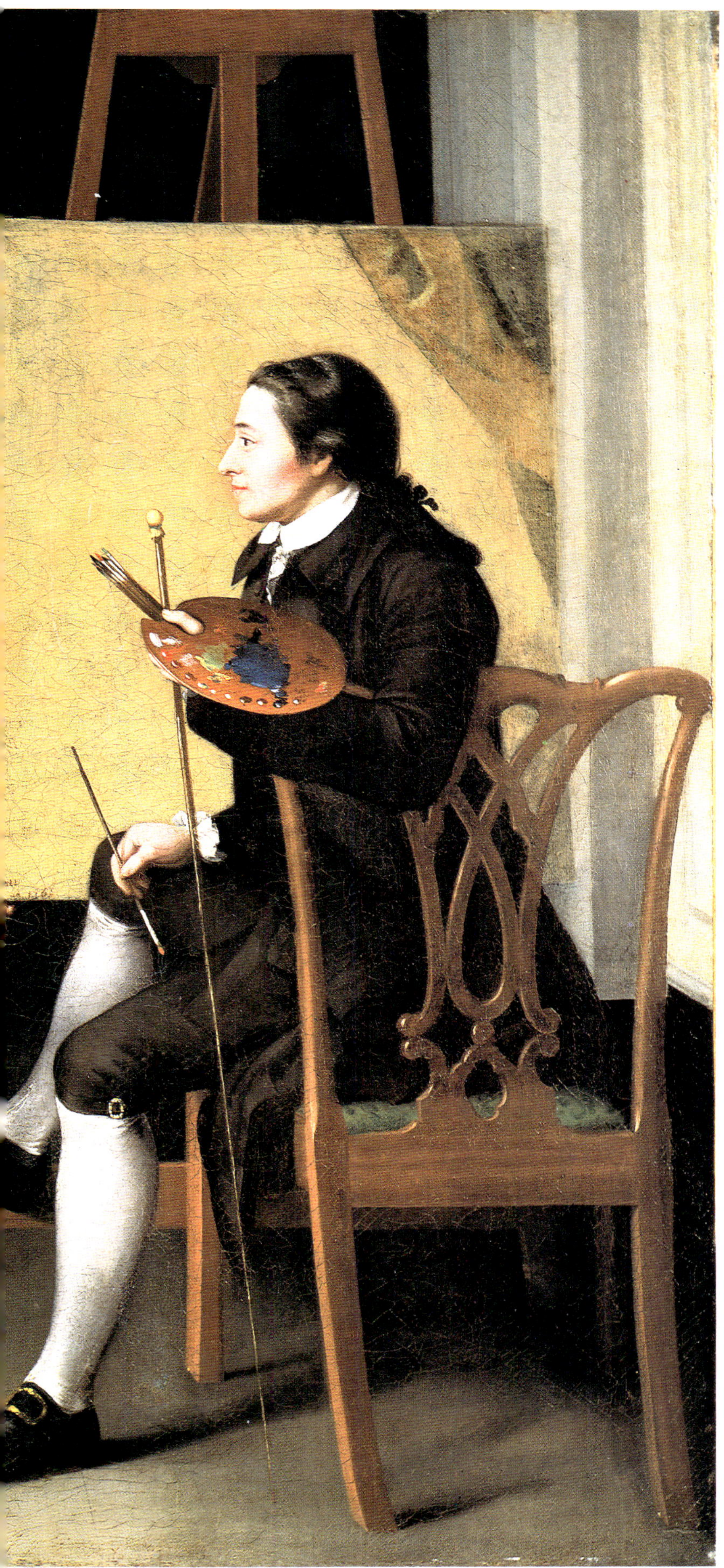

Matthew Pratt
1734–1805

The American School

Oil on canvas
36 x 50¼ in. (91.4 x 127.6 cm.)
1765
Signed and dated at lower left of the painting on the easel:
M. Pratt/ed. 1765
Gift of Samuel P. Avery, 1897 (97.29.3)

WHEN MATTHEW PRATT went to London in 1764, he was welcomed by his slightly younger compatriot Benjamin West. West had been practicing there for only a year but was already well on the way to success; young American painters were beginning to seek him out for instruction and advice. Although these young artists from the colonies had gone to London to learn about European traditions, they sturdily maintained their national character. The figure standing at the left is believed to be West himself, and the figure seated beside him, receiving criticism and instruction, a self-portrait of Pratt. The three other attentive students have unfortunately not been satisfactorily identified. Pratt had set himself a difficult task in composing this rather unwieldy group. His artistic embarrassment shows in the disparate proportions and in a certain stiffness, suggesting that he was working from lay figures, or jointed artist's models.

Benjamin West
1738–1820

Omnia Vincit Amor, or The Power of Love in the Three Elements

Oil on canvas
70⅜ x 80½ in. (178.8 x 204.5 cm.)
1809
Signed and dated at lower right:
B. West—1809—
Maria DeWitt Jesup Fund, 1923 (95.22.1)

"LOVE TRIUMPHS OVER EVERYTHING," in Latin *omnia vincit amor,* is a quotation from Virgil's *Eclogues. The Triumph of Love over Animated Nature,* another title to be found in early lists, probably refers to the same picture. Venus, the goddess of love, is shown at the left with her attributes the doves and with her small son, Amor, armed with bow and arrows, clinging to her draperies. A young deity, presumably Hymen, god of marriage, brandishes a flaming torch in his right hand and grasps in his left cords that leash an eagle. The eagle, usually the attribute of Jove, here symbolizes all the creatures living in the element Air; the hippocampus stands for those in Water and the lion for those on Earth. The fourth element, Fire, especially the Fire of Love, is implicit in the goddess herself, in the winged Amores, or little Loves, and, most particularly, in Hymen's flaming torch.

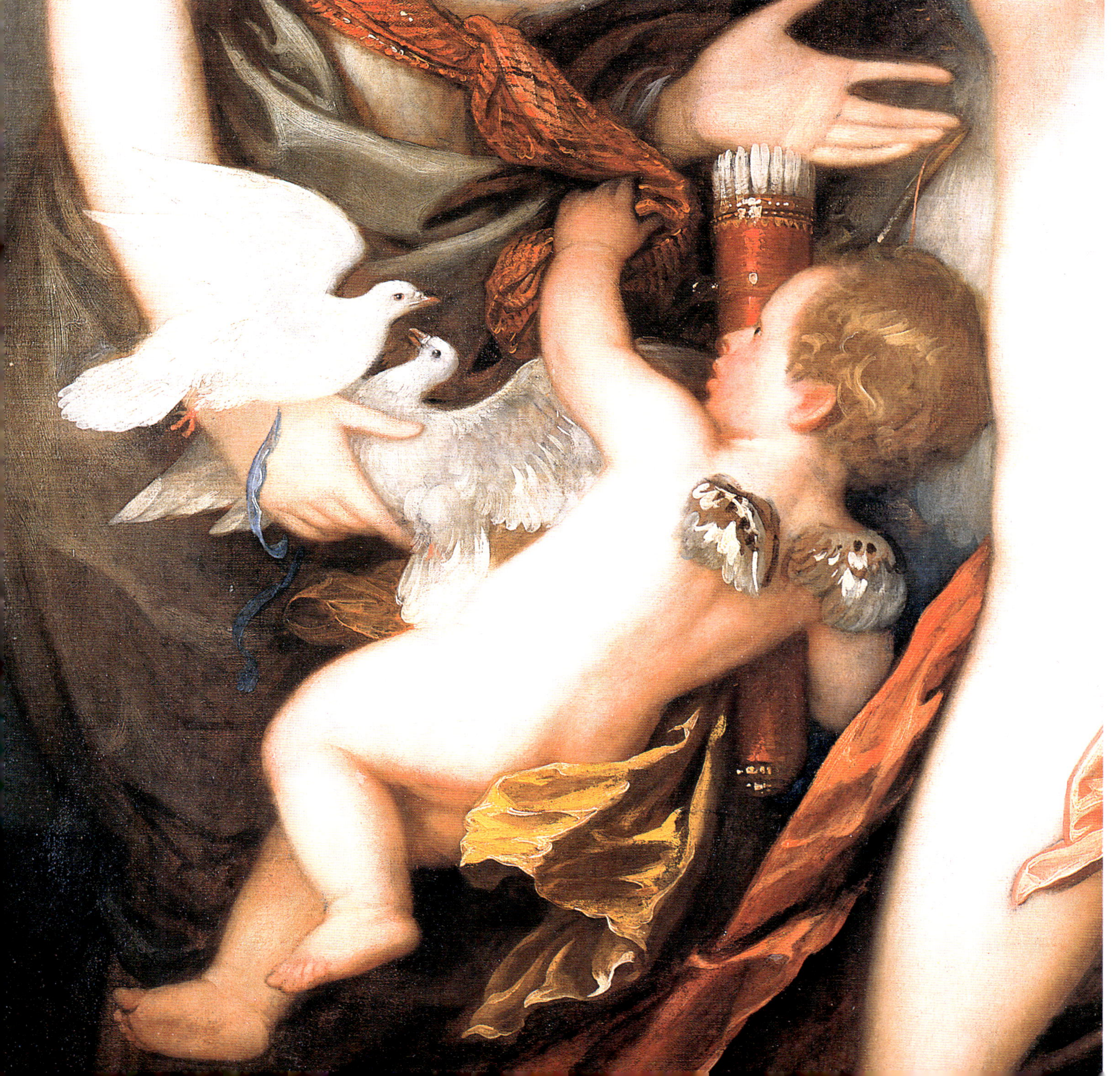

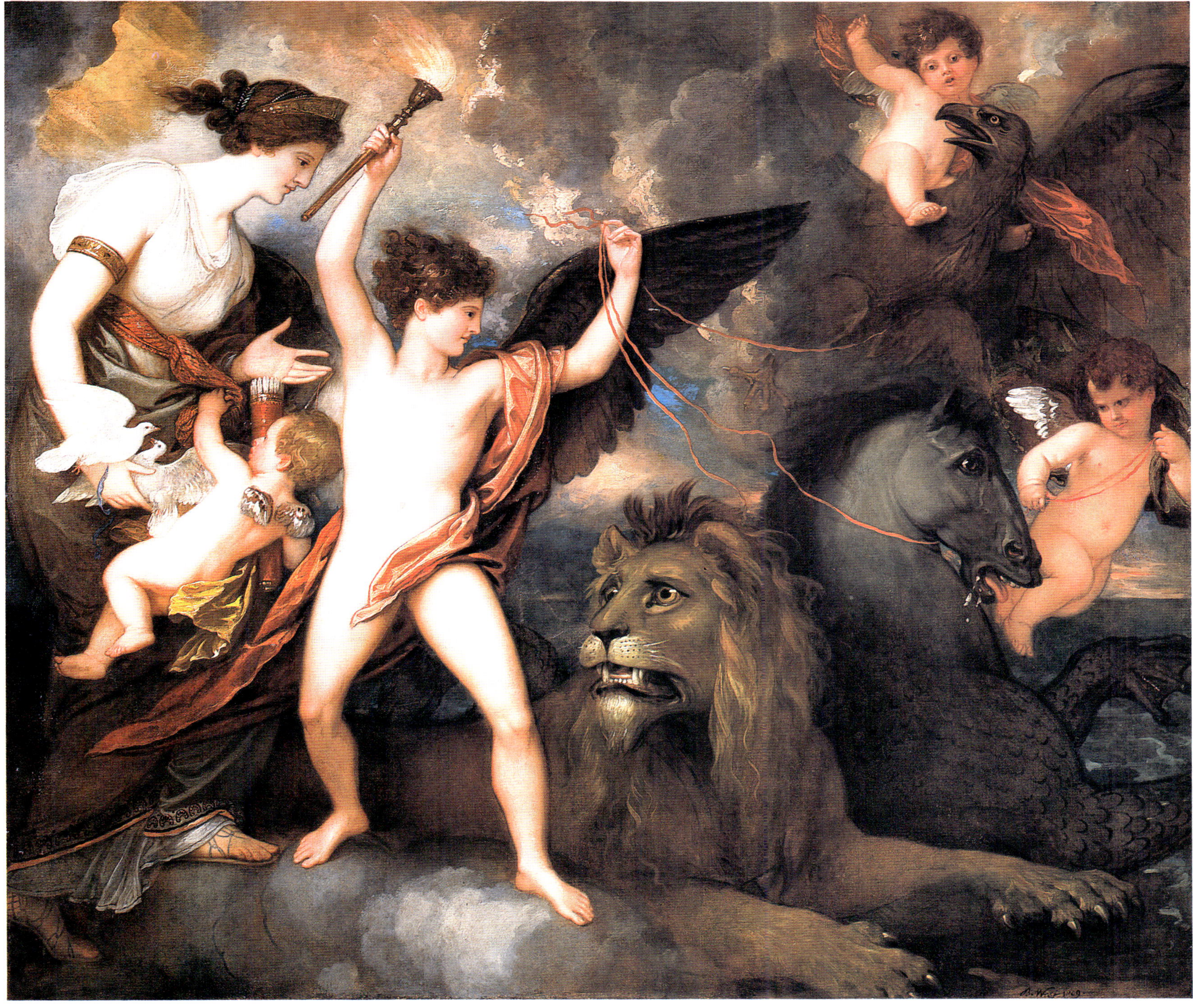

Benjamin West was an American painter who from 1763 until his death worked and taught in London. He exerted an enormous influence on the generations of American students who flocked to him there, and he made a deep impression on the development of late eighteenth-century art in Europe. A charter member of the Royal Academy and official history painter to King George III, his friend and patron, West was held in such high esteem at the time of his death, in 1820, that he was honored by burial in London's Saint Paul's Cathedral.

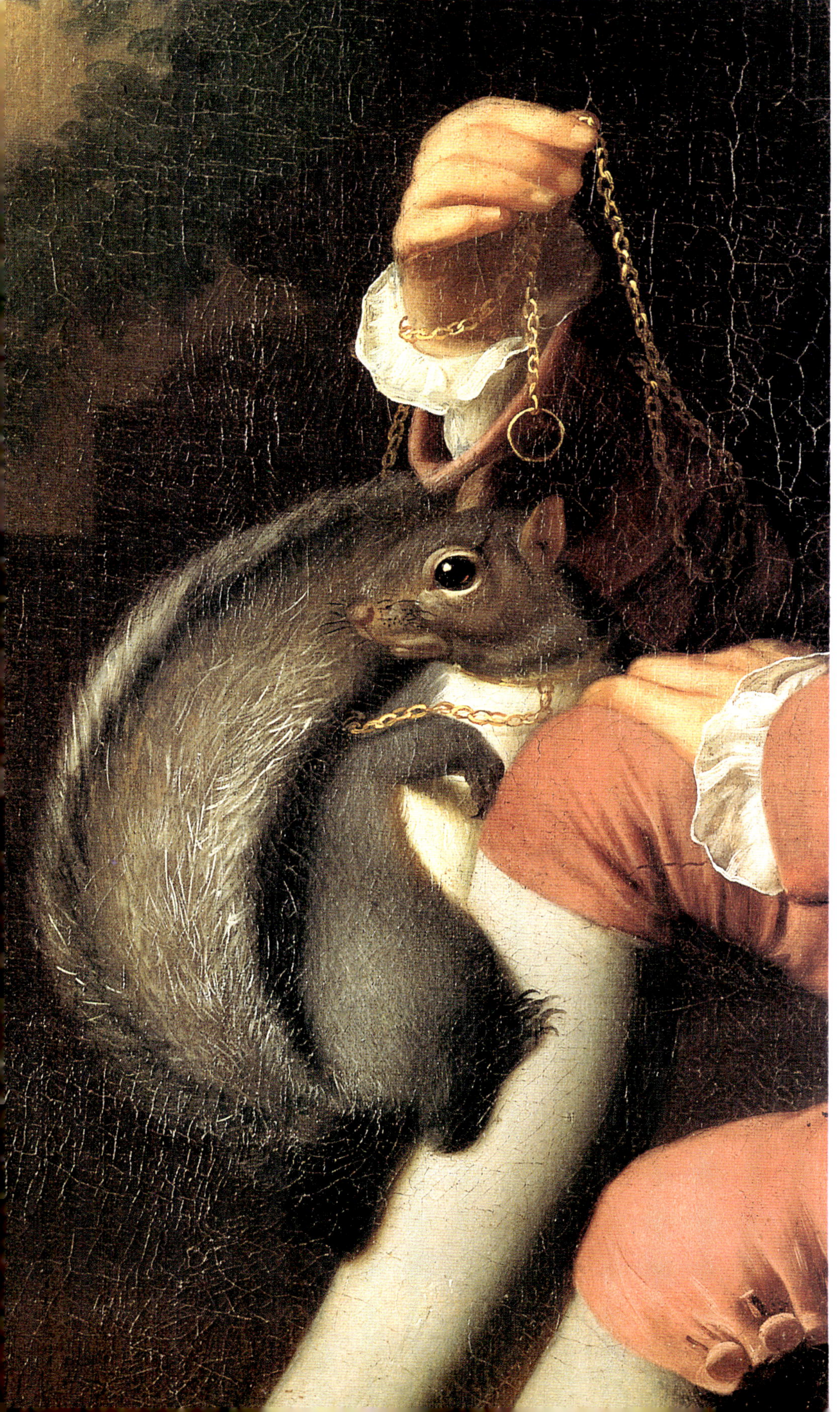

John Singleton Copley
1738–1815

Daniel Crommelin Verplanck

Oil on canvas
49½ x 40 in. (127.3 x 101.6 cm.)
1771
Gift of Bayard Verplanck, 1949 (49.12)

JOHN SINGLETON COPLEY, who is believed to have been born in Boston, began, after a brief training, a successful career as a painter of portraits in Boston, New York, and Philadelphia. In these portraits, early adherence to the English style soon gave way to the attainment of a personal fusion of realistic vision and clear brilliant technique.

A pet squirrel on a golden leash was a motif he used several times in his portraits of young people. He sent one of these portraits in 1765 to London, where it earned warm praise from Sir Joshua Reynolds and Benjamin West. Not surprisingly Copley reverted to this theme six years later in New York when called upon to paint Samuel Verplanck's eldest son, nine-year-old Daniel (1762–1834). Unlike the other members of the Verplanck family painted by Copley, Daniel is shown outdoors; he sits before a grandiose portico with a monumental column behind him. There is a sunset glimpse of a picturesque landscape, which is traditionally held to be a part of his father's country estate at Fishkill, New York. In spite of the child's position on the low step and his playful gesture with the pet, his face and bearing are serious, as if he were already conscious of his inheritance of wealth, aristocratic status, and moral responsibility.

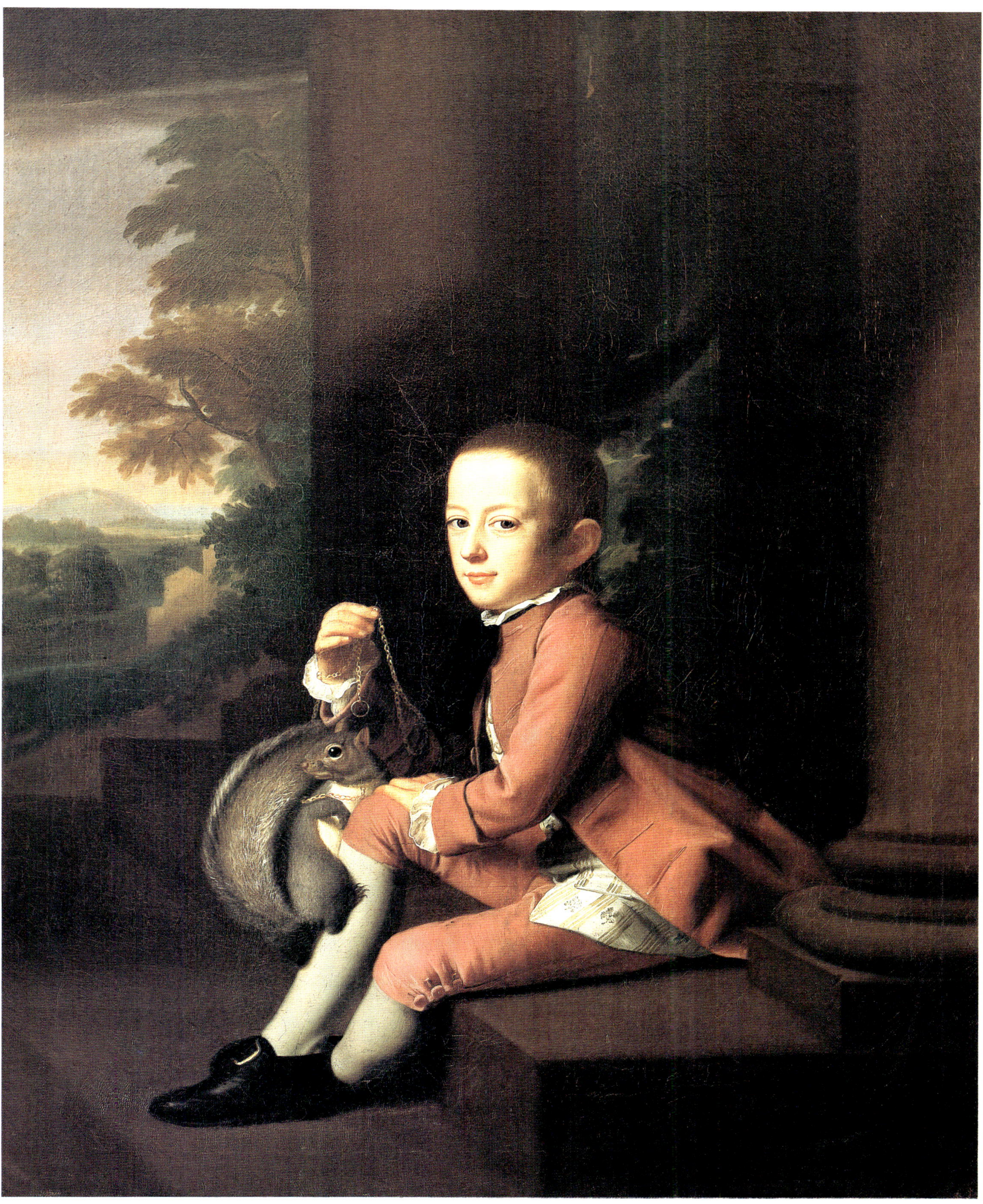

John Singleton Copley
1738–1815

Mrs. John Winthrop

Oil on canvas
35½ x 28¾ in. (90.2 x 73 cm.)
1773
Morris K. Jesup Fund, 1931 (31.109)

John Singleton Copley enjoyed great prosperity in the colonies until shortly before the Revolution. In 1774, with conditions unsettled and his commissions declining, he emigrated to England, where he spent the rest of his life. This portrait of Mrs. John Winthrop (1727–1790) was one of the last he painted before he left. The subject, whose strong and candid personality comes through so vividly, was born Hannah Fayerweather. She was forty-six when Copley painted her, and married to her second husband, John Winthrop, a professor at Harvard. America's first prominent astronomer, he carried out important investigations of sunspots and earthquakes.

As a great portraitist Copley had two aims: to recreate on canvas a particular human being and to use with artistic determination every means in the painter's power—color, line, texture, light and shadow, and composition—to the end of making a beautiful picture. Here, the calculated design of the hands and their reflection in the polished tabletop add to the interest aroused by the rich variety in costume and pose.

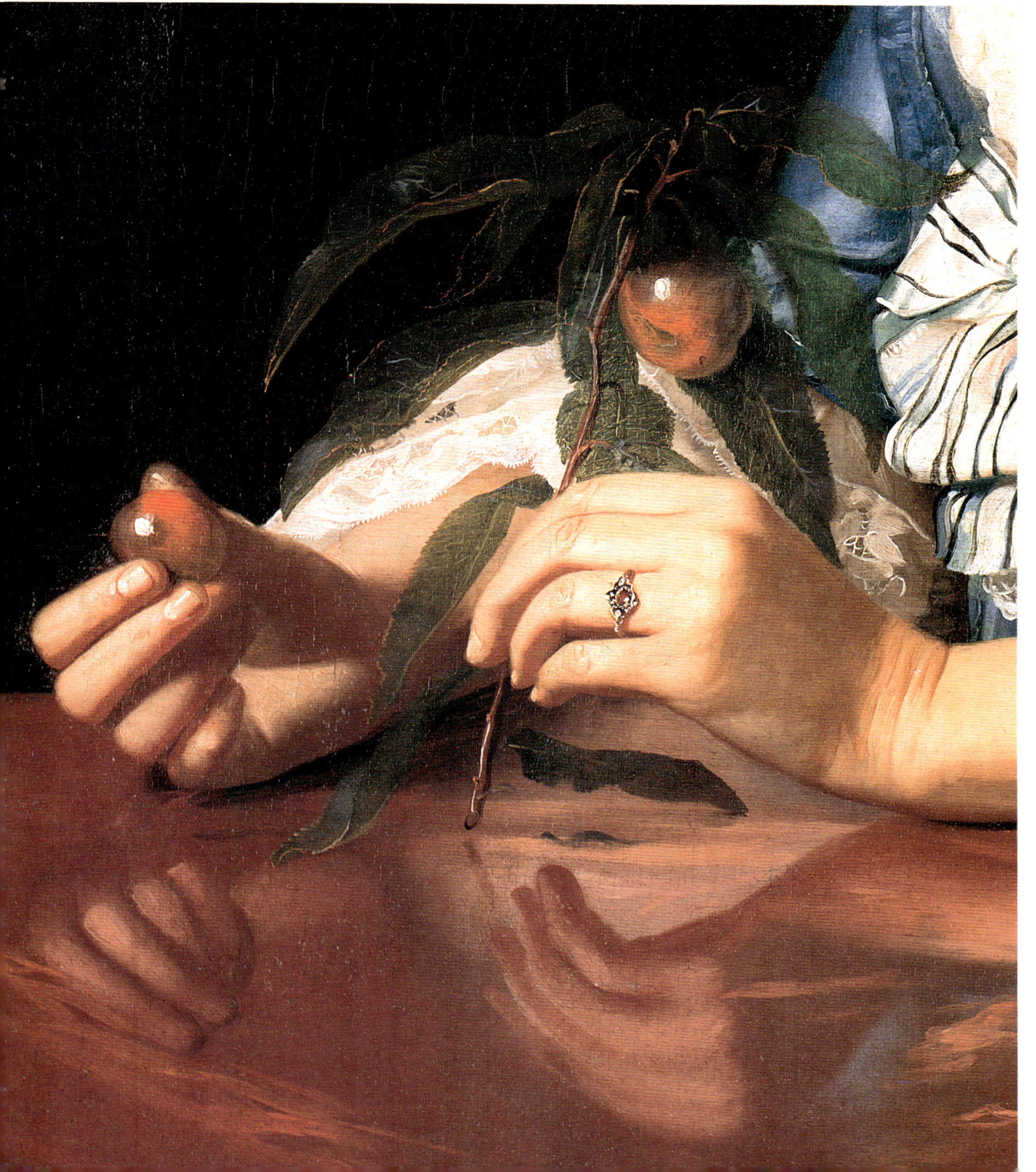

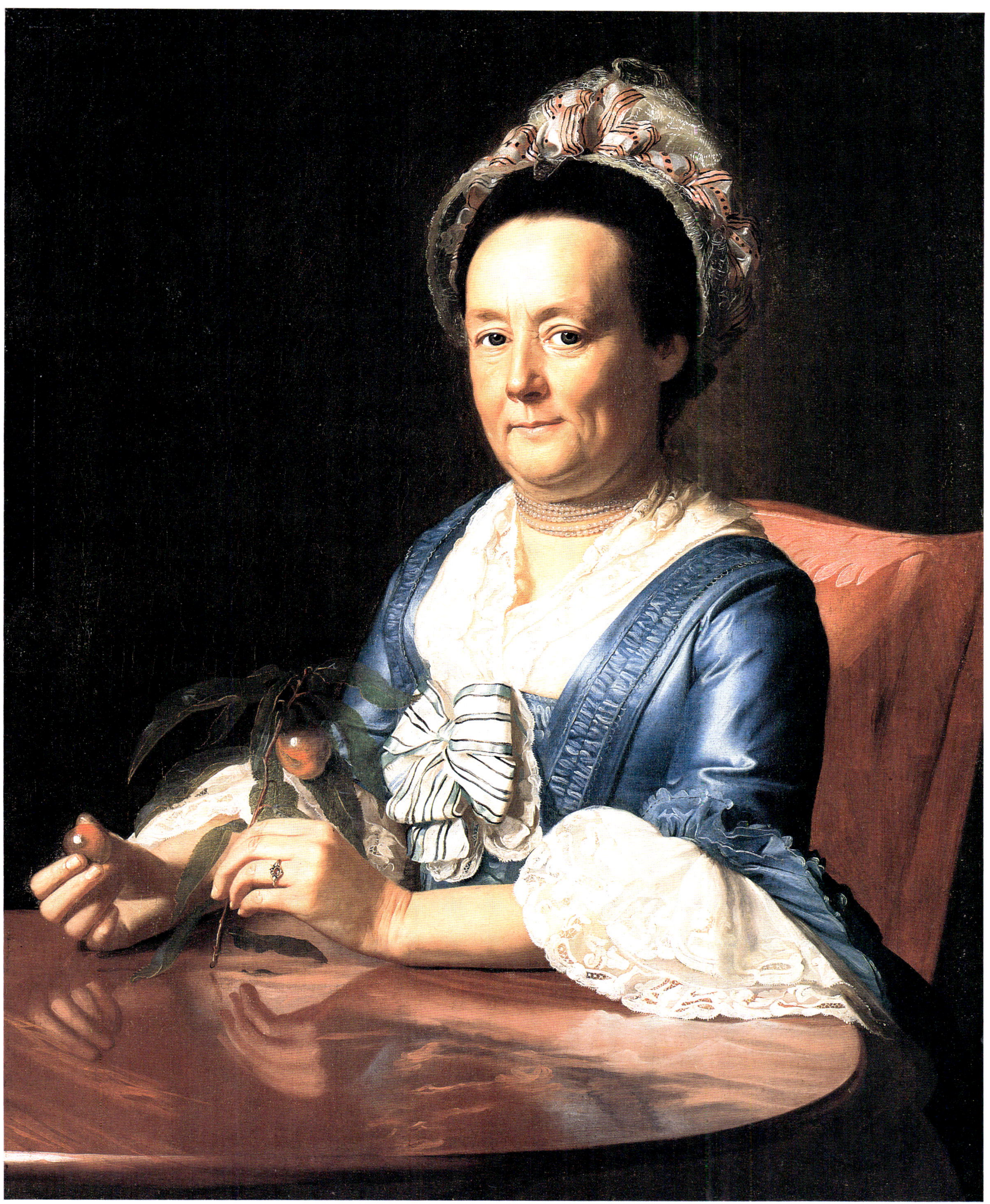

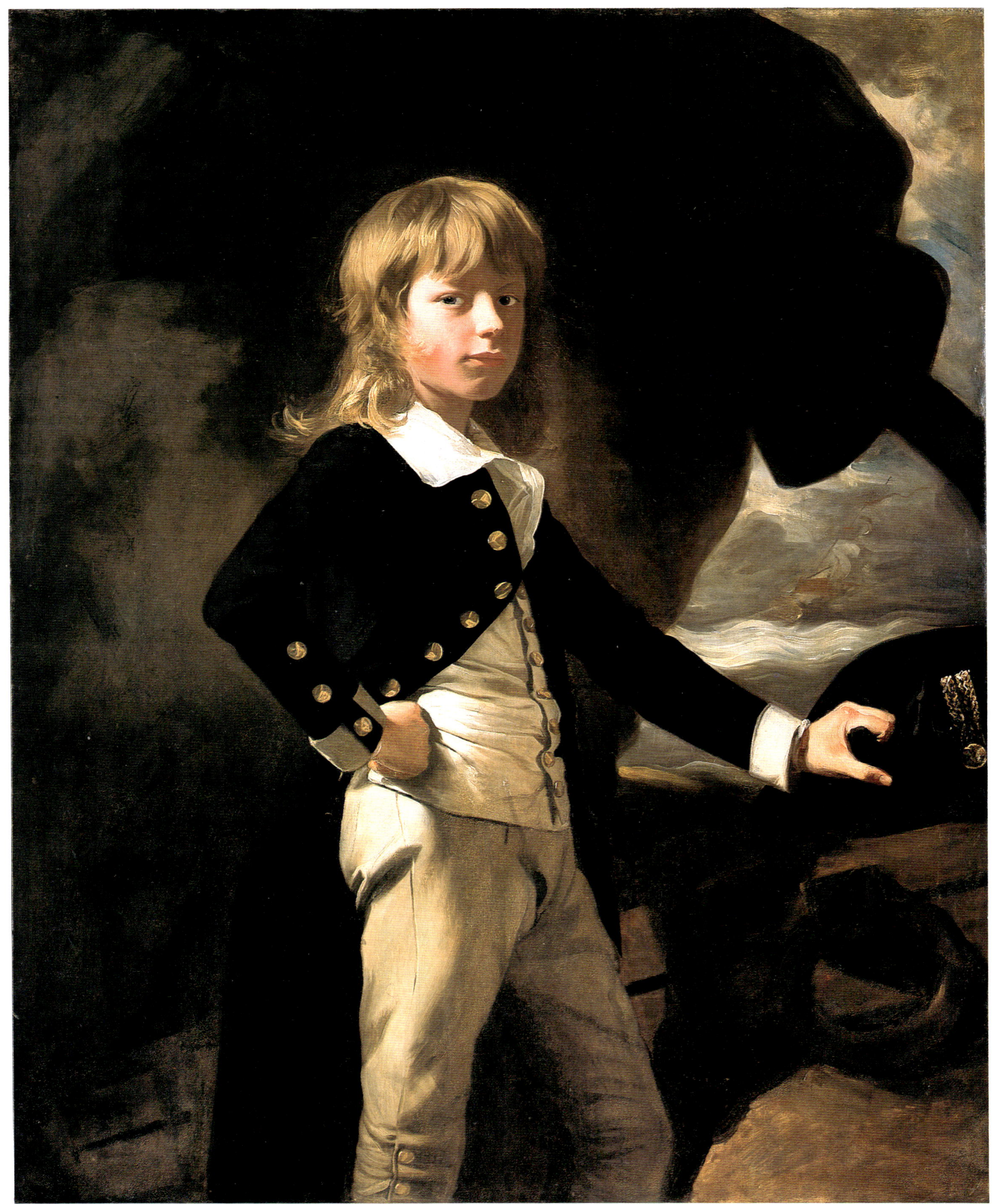

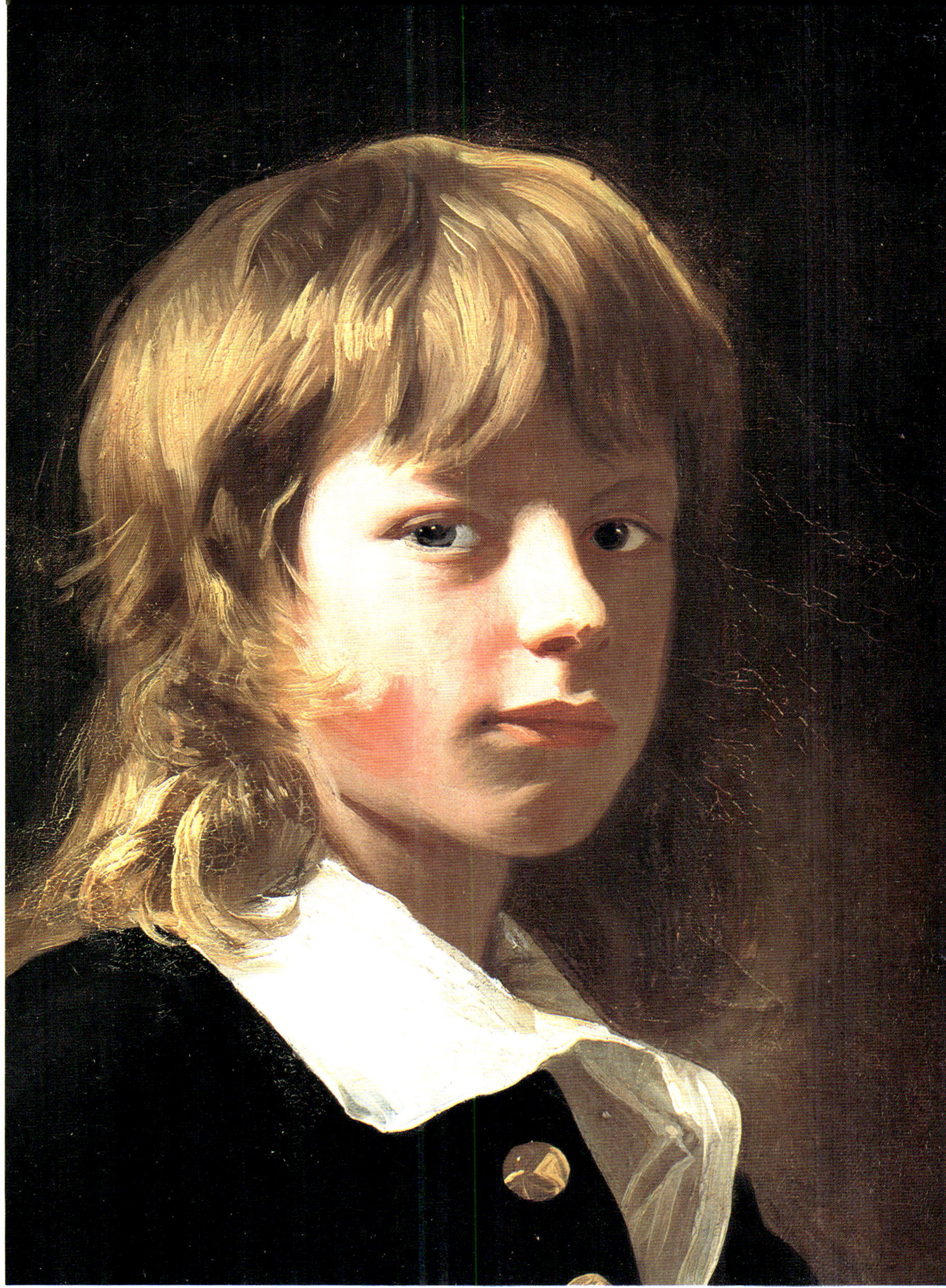

John Singleton Copley
1738–1815

Midshipman Augustus Brine

Oil on canvas
50 x 40 in. (127 x 101.6 cm.)
1782
Signed and dated at left center:
J.S. Copley Pin[xit]/1782
Bequest of Richard De Wolfe Brixey, 1943
(43.86.4)

JOHN SINGLETON COPLEY painted this portrait of the thirteen-year-old seaman in England the year the boy enlisted in the Royal Navy under his father, Admiral James Brine. It is natural to compare the painting with the Museum's other Copley portrait of a child, that of the American Daniel Crommelin Verplanck (pages 28–29). Though younger than Augustus Brine, the Verplanck boy seems already weighted with his ethical obligations. The young midshipman, however, is proud and self-confident. A threatening sea, a towering cliff, and a huge upturned anchor dwarf his slim boy's figure, but nothing perturbs his air of competence. The assured urbanity of Copley's English style, too, here replaces the precision, linearity, and insistent forthrightness of his American portraits with fluent, broadly brushed passages and a dramatic use of light and contrasts.

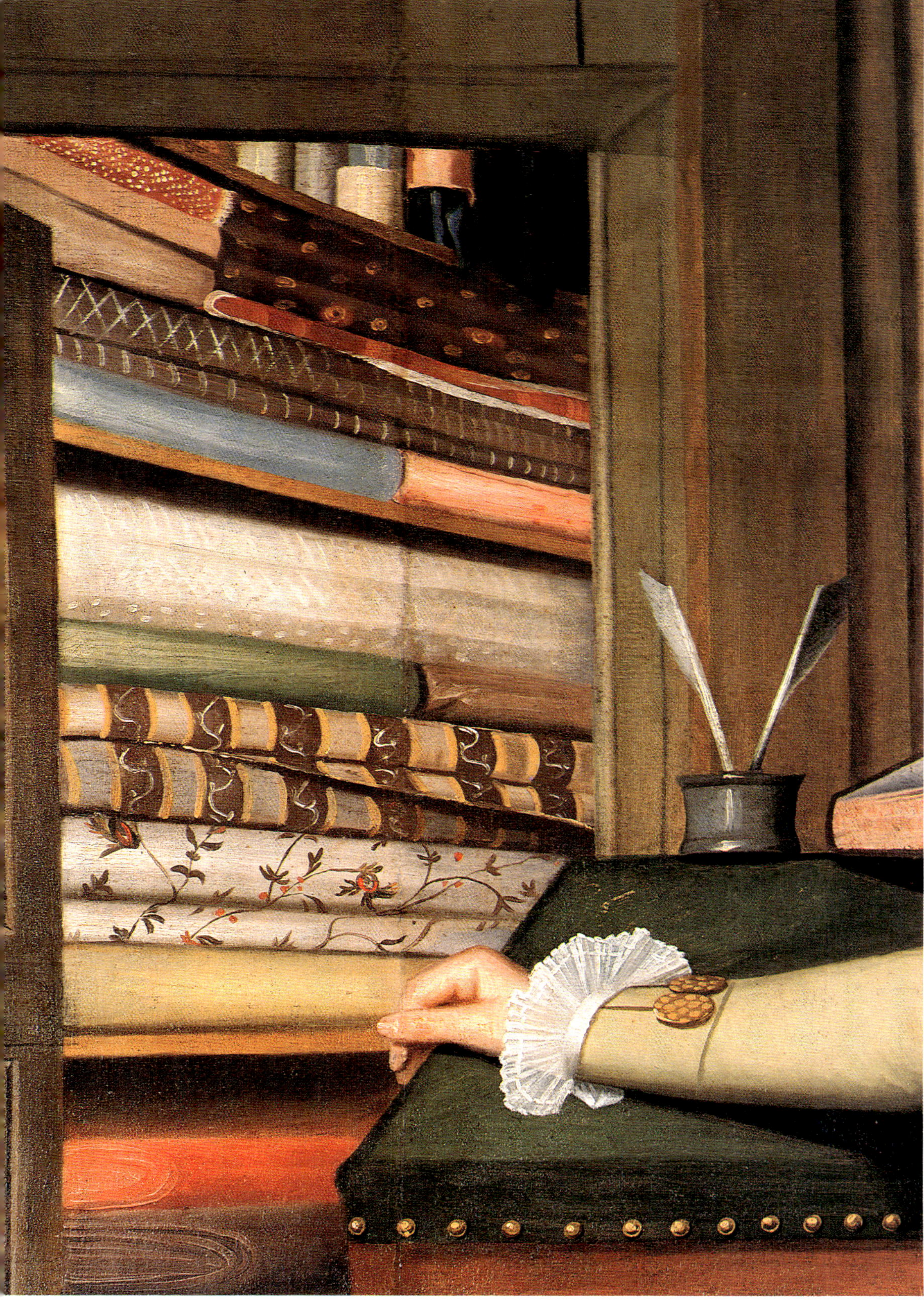

Ralph Earl
1751–1801

Elijah Boardman

Oil on canvas
83 x 51 in. (210.8 x 129.5 cm.)
1789
Signed and dated at lower left:
R. Earl pinxt 1782.
Bequest of Susan W. Tyler, 1979 (1979.395)

THIS EXTREMELY TALL, distinguished young man, Elijah Boardman (1760–1832), conducted a thriving business in dry goods in New Milford, Connecticut, with his brother. Ralph Earl portrays Elijah standing in their store in a room that is probably a business office, but volumes of Shakespeare, Milton, and Dr. Johnson declare a gentleman's acquaintance with literature. In an adjoining room the yard goods, brightly colored and attractive, are stacked on shelves. Although many of the men in his large family were Congregational ministers, Elijah became a merchant. He was apparently very successful, not only in Connecticut, but in Ohio, where he founded a town called Boardman. When the Revolutionary War had broken out, Elijah, at the age of sixteen, had enlisted immediately. Afterward, he became active in politics, serving six times as a state legislator and, at the end of his life, as a United States senator.

When Earl painted this portrait he was back in America after seven years in England, where the influence of the great eighteenth-century portrait painters had shaped and refined his style. Earl also painted nineteen other Boardmans, as well as a view of the town green in New Milford showing Elijah's imposing house standing beside the profitable store.

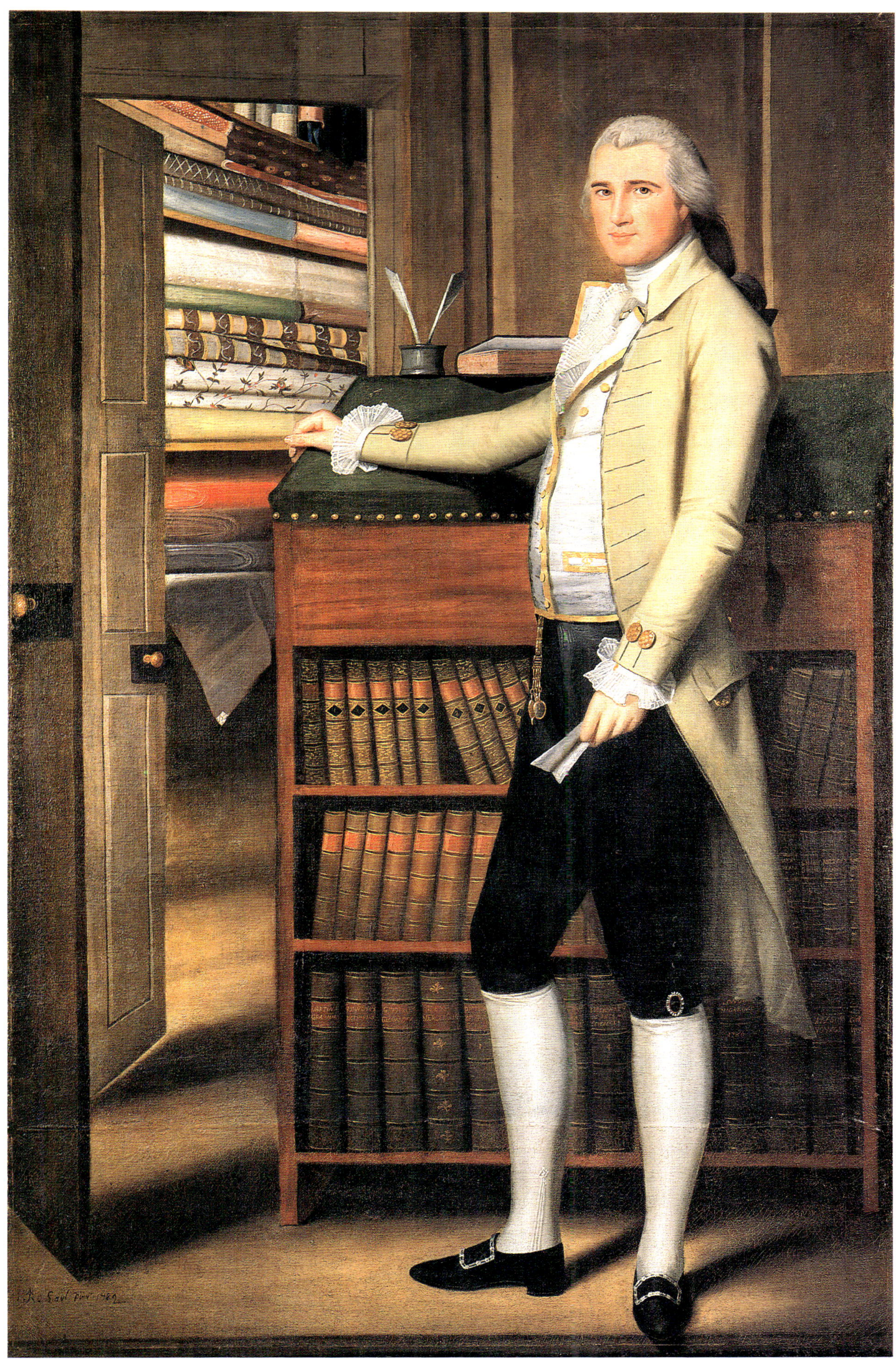

Charles Willson Peale
1741–1827

George Washington

Oil on canvas
95 x 61¾ in. (241.3 x 156.8 cm.)
ca. 1780
Gift of Collis P. Huntington, 1897 (97.33)

CHARLES WILLSON PEALE was the colonial equivalent of the Renaissance man. Immensely versatile in his enthusiasms and abilities, he was a painter of miniatures, portraits, and landscapes; a naturalist; an inventor; and the founder of a picture gallery combined with a museum of natural history in Philadelphia, the first of its kind in North America. Early in his career an appreciative patron arranged for him to go to London, where he studied with Benjamin West. On his return to his native Maryland, and later in Philadelphia, he painted very fine life-sized portraits and made a specialty of family group portraits that showed much originality and skill. In 1779, Peale painted from life a full-length portrait of George Washington (1722–1799) commissioned by the state of Pennsylvania and now in the Pennsylvania Academy of the Fine Arts. The picture was so much admired that orders poured in for replicas, destined for foreign courts and for private patrons. The Museum's painting, which descended through the family of the general, was probably ordered by Martha Washington. The background varies in the different versions; here it represents Trenton, New Jersey, where Washington fought a famous battle. He wears the blue moiré ribbon, abandoned in 1780, that signifies his high rank and a slim, elegant rapier, rather than the battle sword seen in the other replicas. Anyone with a mental image of Washington based on the paintings that Gilbert Stuart made later, a few years before the general's death, will be jolted by the fleshy face and easy nonchalance of Peale's earlier portrayal.

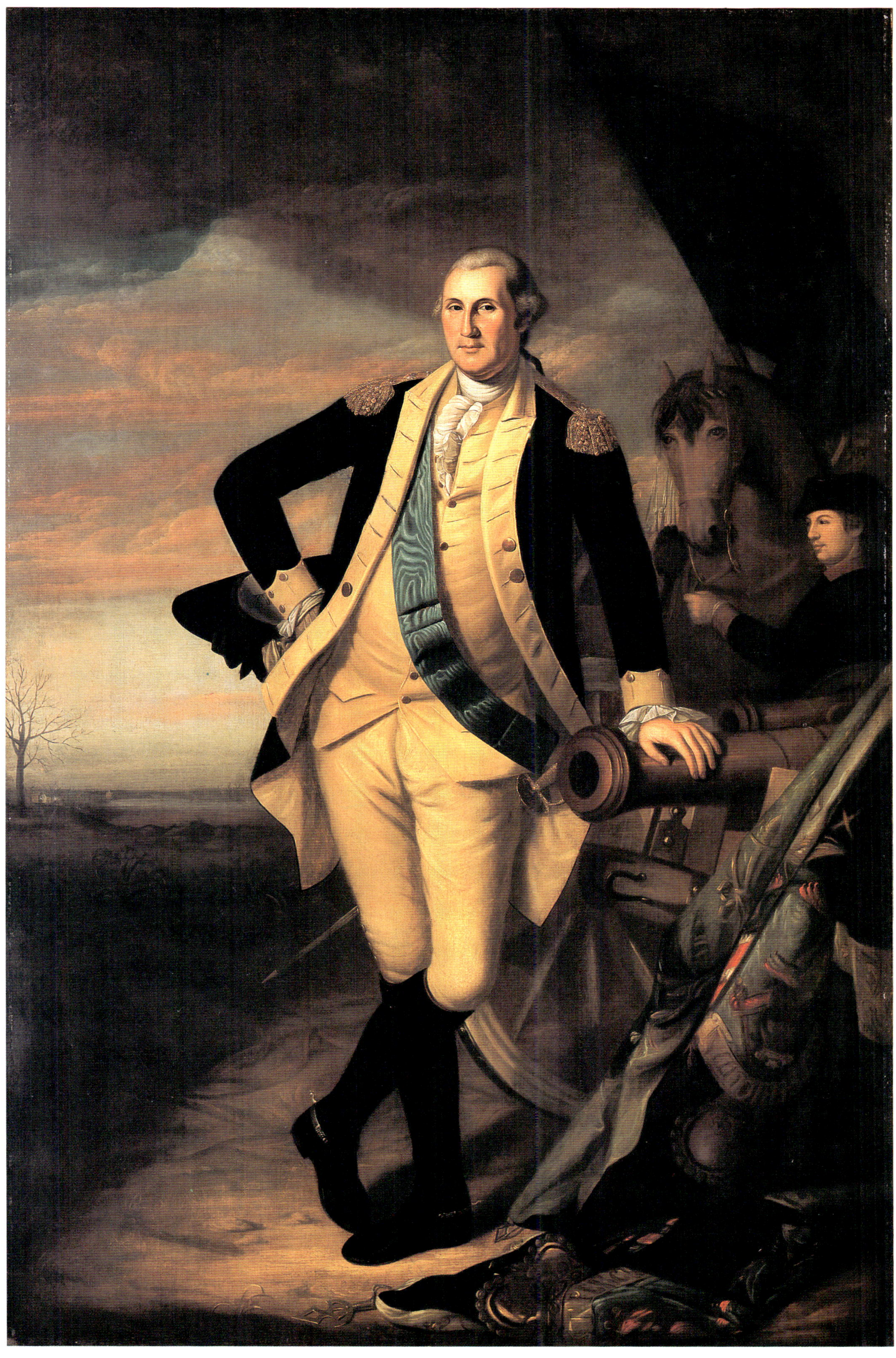

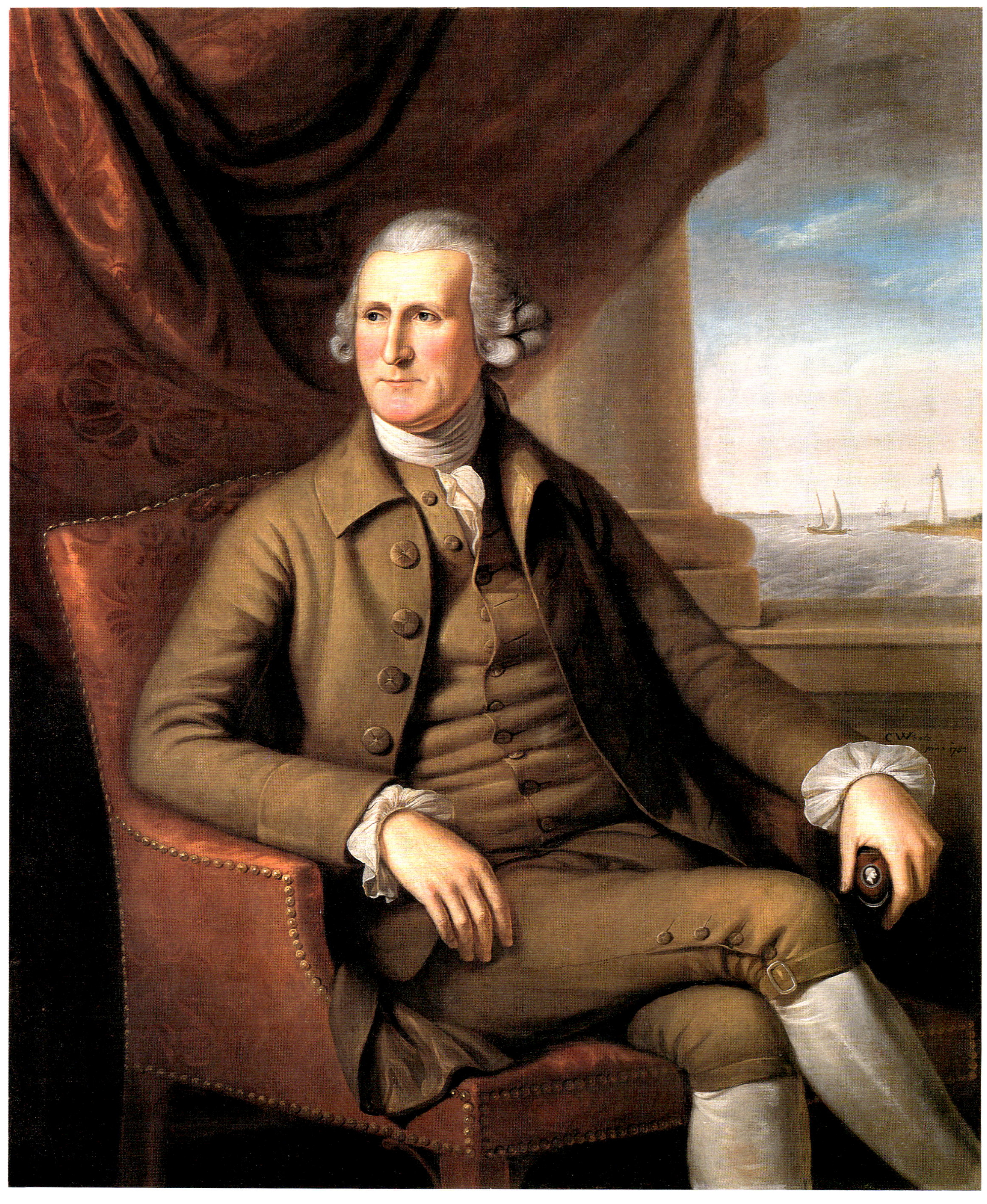
CWPeale
pinx 1782

Charles Willson Peale
1741–1827

Thomas Willing

Oil on canvas
49½ x 39¾ in. (125.7 x 101 cm.)
1782
Signed and dated in black at right, below parapet edge: C W Peale/pinx 1782
Purchase, from the Collection of James Stillman, Gift of Dr. Ernest G. Stillman, by exchange, 1966 (66.46)

THOMAS WILLING (1731–1821), a wealthy and sucessful Philadelphian, seems really to have had the wisdom and charm that Charles Willson Peale has projected in this portrait, which follows the English conventions of composition and setting. Educated in the law in England, Willing held a number of high judicial offices in Philadelphia and was at one time the city's mayor. Though openly against the Stamp Act, which had been inflicted on the colonies, he had reservations about complete severance from England and pursued a reasonable and unimpassioned course, safeguarding the interests of his own mercantile firm. In 1780, when America was at a point of great need, however, he generously contributed to a fund that made possible the reorganization of the Continental army. The snuffbox in Willing's hand, with a Wedgwood medallion of George Washington on its cover, was perhaps bestowed in recognition of this aid. Through Washington, who evidently thought highly of his financial acumen, Willing was made president of the first Bank of the United States.

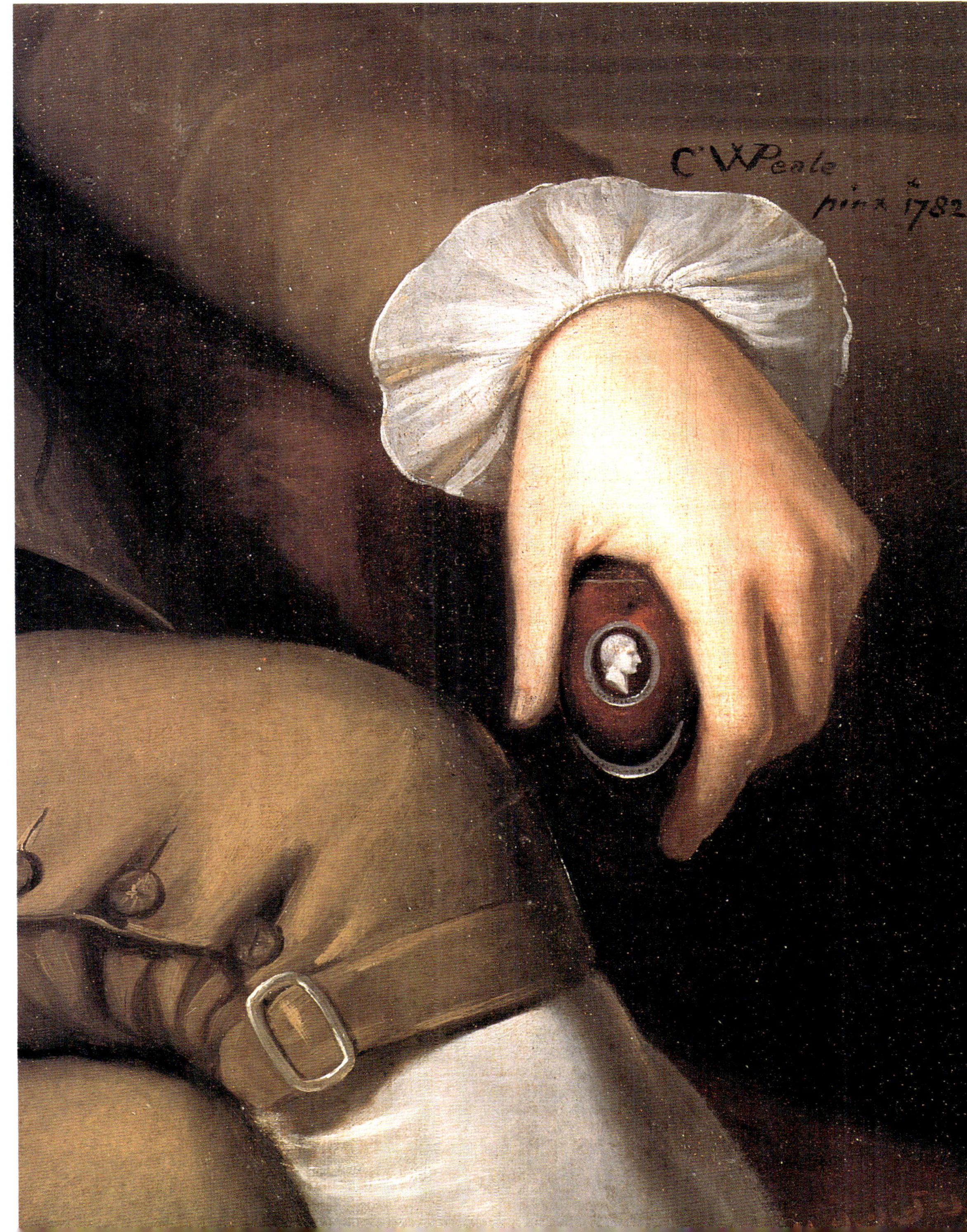

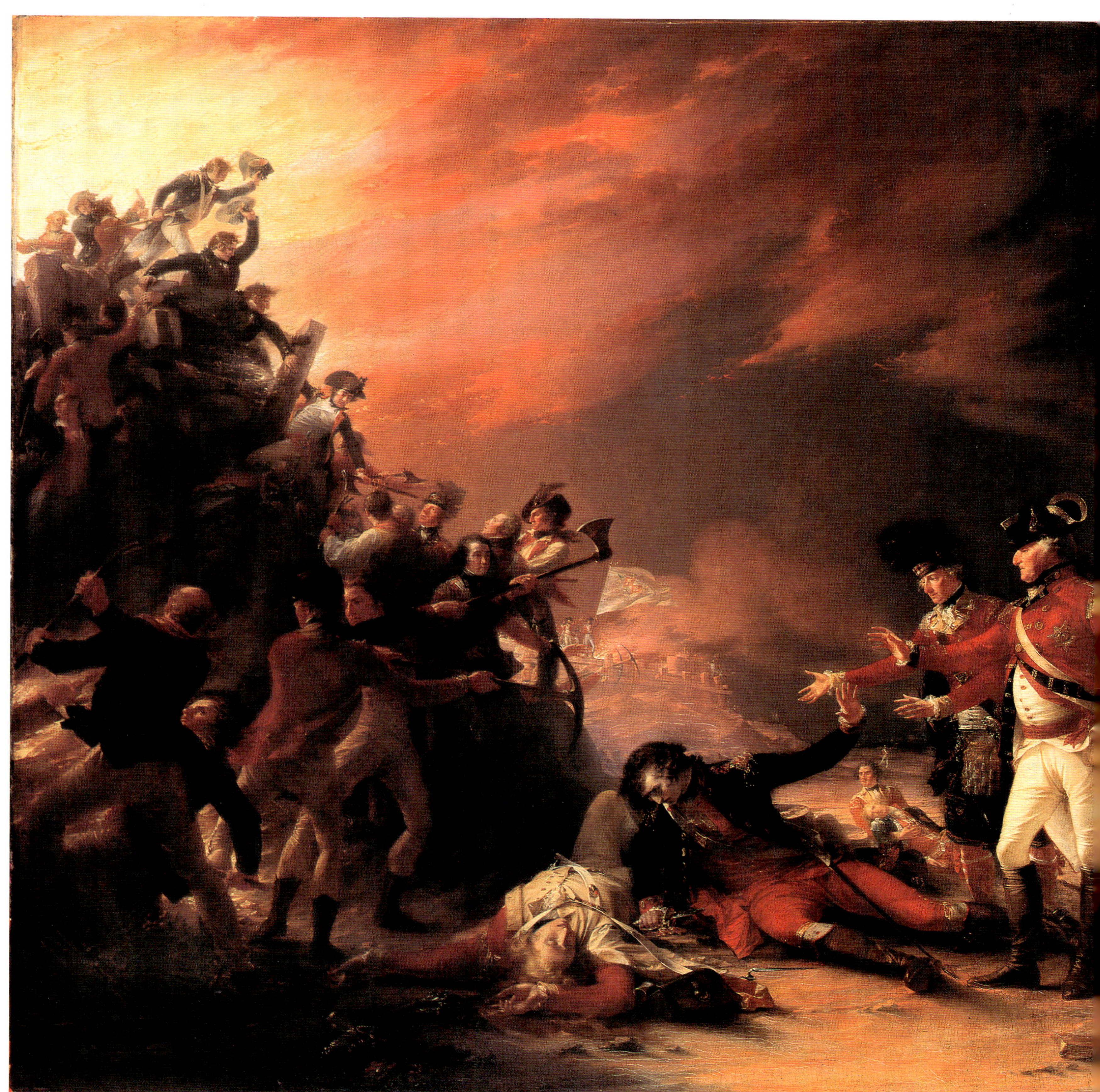

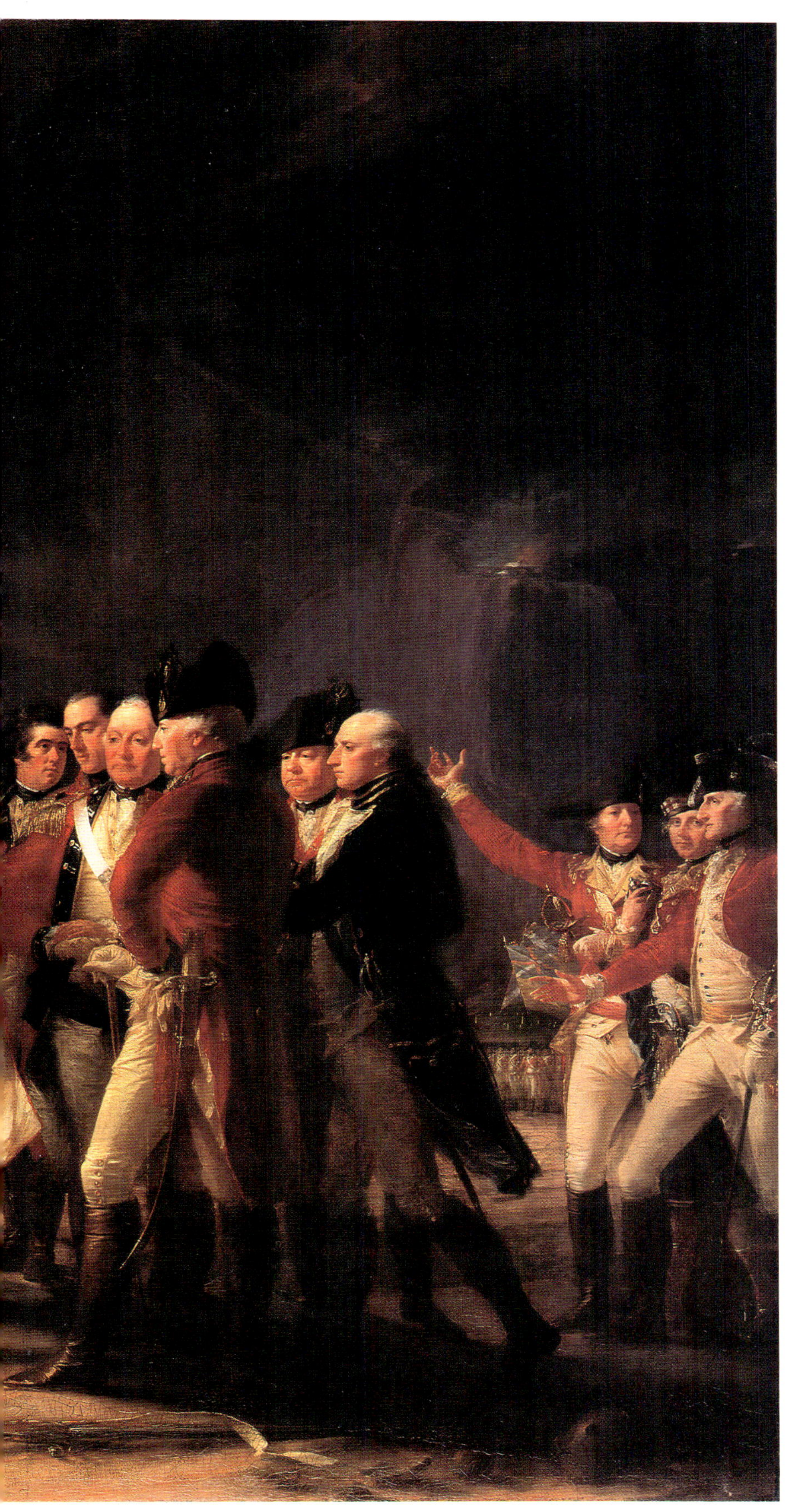

John Trumbull
1756–1843

The Sortie Made by the Garrison of Gibraltar

Oil on canvas
71 x 107 in. (180.3 x 271.8. cm.)
1789
Signed and dated at lower left: John Trumbull/1789
Purchase, Pauline V. Fullerton Bequest, Mr. and Mrs. James Walter Carter Gift, Mr. and Mrs. Raymond J. Horowitz Gift, Erving Wolf Foundation Gift, Vain and Harry Fish Foundation, Inc. Gift, Gift of Hanson K. Corning, by exchange, and Maria DeWitt Jesup and Morris K. Jesup Funds, 1976 (1976.332)

JOHN TRUMBULL, who was from a prominent Connecticut family, was graduated from Harvard in 1773 and two years later joined the Continental army. After the war he studied in London with Benjamin West. His four historical scenes for the rotunda of the Capitol in Washington, D.C., were probably his most important commission.

Trumbull shared with his American contemporaries Benjamin West and John Singleton Copley the ambition to excel at history painting in the grand manner, and to create pictures large in scale and heroic in import. This painting, the last and by far the largest of Trumbull's three treatments of the theme, depicts an important episode in the long siege of Gibraltar, when the British, to secure their garrison, took the rock from the hands of the defending Spaniards. During this engagement, a young and indomitable Spanish officer, mortally wounded, rejected all offers of aid and died at the feet of the British victors. Trumbull has made his death the focal point of a complex composition, giving the young man the posture of the famous Greek sculpture of the *Dying Gaul* and endowing him with the elegant features of the popular English contemporary portrait painter Sir Thomas Lawrence. He has imbued the English officers, especially General Eliot in the foreground, with an air of majesty and compassion.

John Trumbull
1756–1843

George Washington Before the Battle of Trenton

Oil on canvas
26½ x 18½ in. (67.3 x 45 cm.)
ca. 1793
Bequest of Grace Wilkes, 1922 (22.45.9)

THIS PAINTING is a considerably smaller version of the large portrait of George Washington that John Trumbull had painted from life at Philadelphia in 1792 (now in the Yale University Art Gallery). The artist wanted this portrait to show the military character of the general, at the sublime moment when he conceived a successful strategy against the vastly superior approaching enemy. The deep significance of the moment is expressed in the drama of the threatening sky, the excitement of the horse held in check by a soldier-groom, and the tension of restraint evident in the rhetorical pose so much at variance with the concentration of the face. The Museum's picture, commissioned for the city of Charleston, South Carolina, was rejected because of this emotional quality, but Trumbull considered it the best of his portraits of Washington. Its style indeed reveals him at the top of his artistic powers.

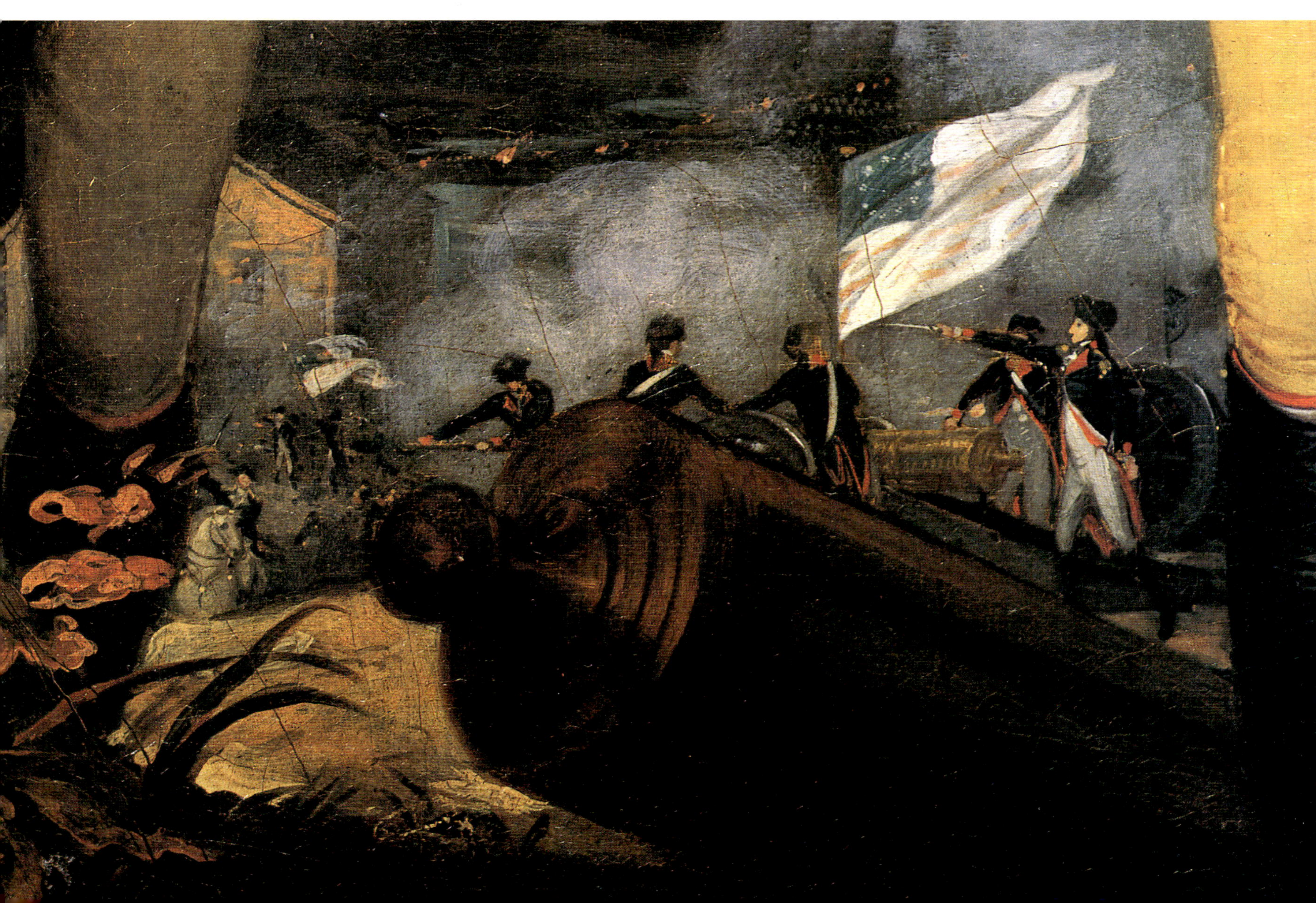

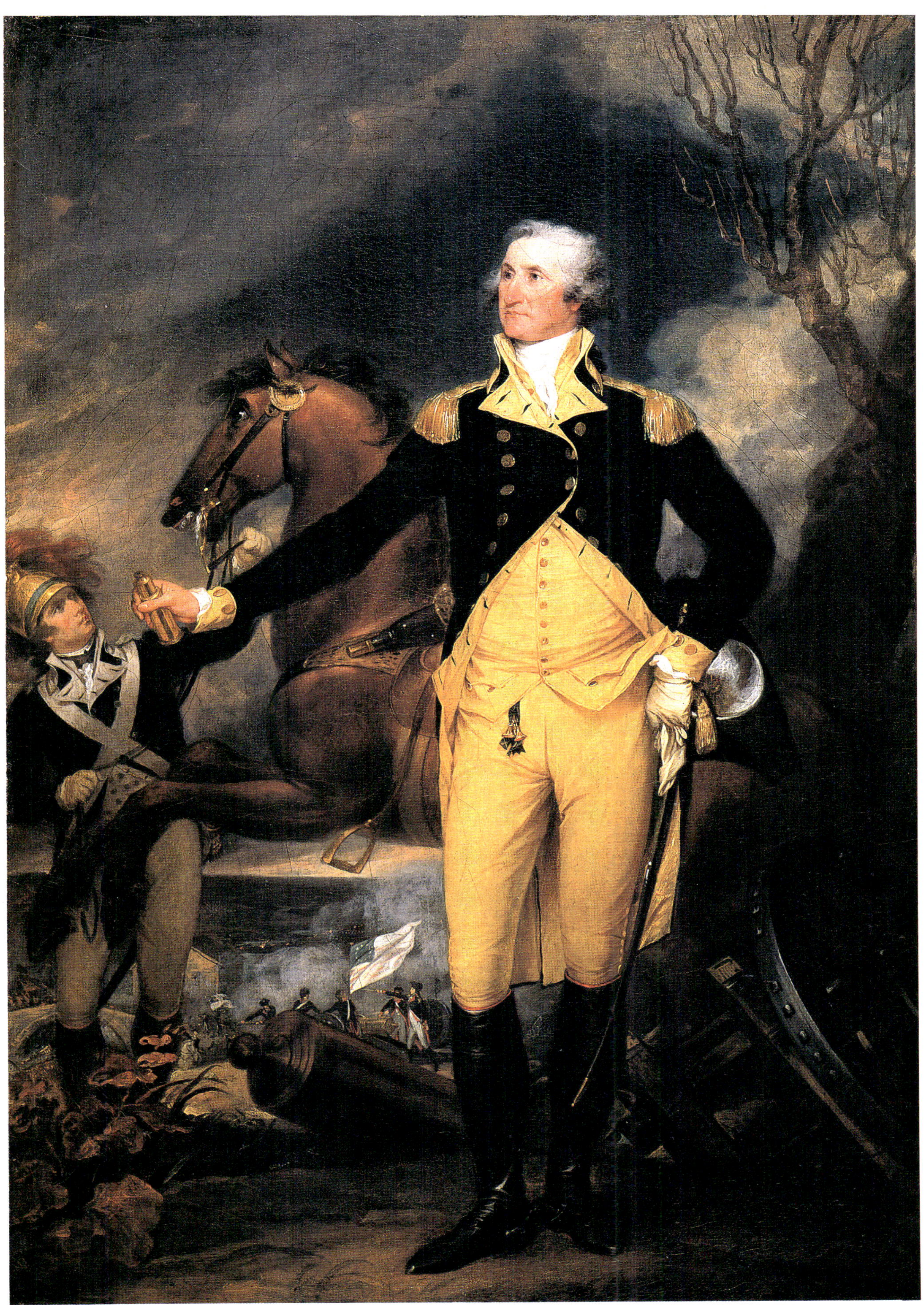

Gilbert Stuart
1755–1828

Horatio Gates

Oil on canvas
44¼ x 35⅞ in. (112.4 x 91.1 cm.)
1793–1794
Gift of Lucille S. Pfeffer, 1977 (1977.243)

GILBERT STUART, the most important American portrait painter of the early period, left the colonies when he was twenty to spend eighteen years painting splendid likenesses in England and Ireland. He returned to America in 1793, and among his many commissions were the four portraits included in this collection.

Horatio Gates (1728–1806), who was born in England, joined the British army early in life and was commissioned captain when he was only twenty-six. He served in various campaigns in America before retiring from the army in 1765. Becoming dissatisfied with life in England, he moved to Virginia, where he lived quietly as a planter until the outbreak of the Revolution. His sympathies lay with the patriots, and, joining the Continental army, he soon rose to the rank of brigadier general. He fought under Washington and had various commands, but it was for his victory at Saratoga in 1777 that he achieved his greatest fame. In 1780, however, before the end of the war, Gates's troops suffered a disastrous defeat at the hands of Cornwallis in the battle of Camden, South Carolina. The last decades of his life were spent in fashionable and prosperous retirement, first in Virginia and then in New York, where Stuart, recently returned from England, painted this portrait of him. Gates is shown in the uniform of an American brigadier general, proudly wearing the badge of the Order of the Cincinnati and the medal Congress had had struck in his honor after Saratoga. Stuart has represented him as a man of commanding presence and given the painting all the distinction of his brilliant London portraits.

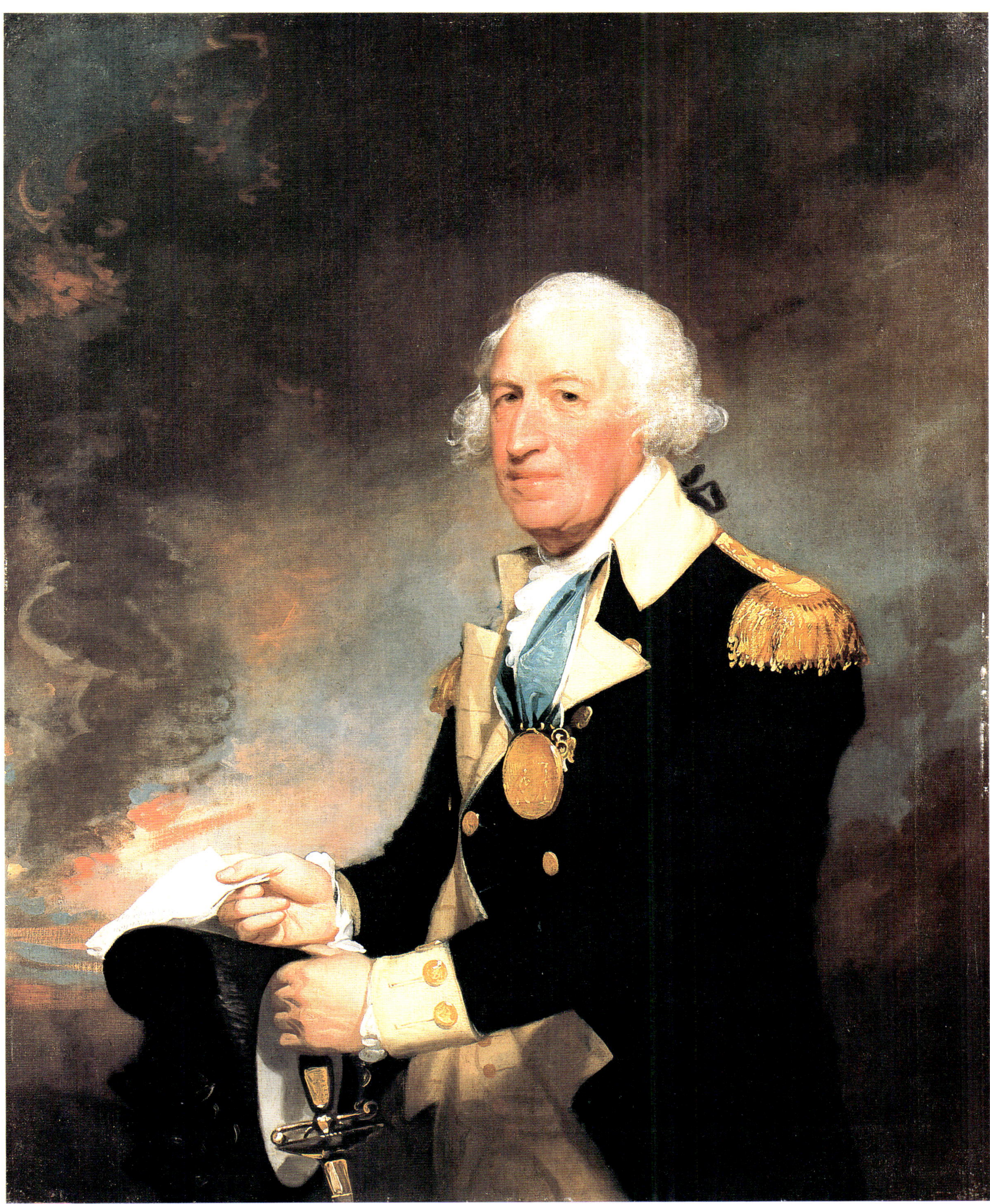

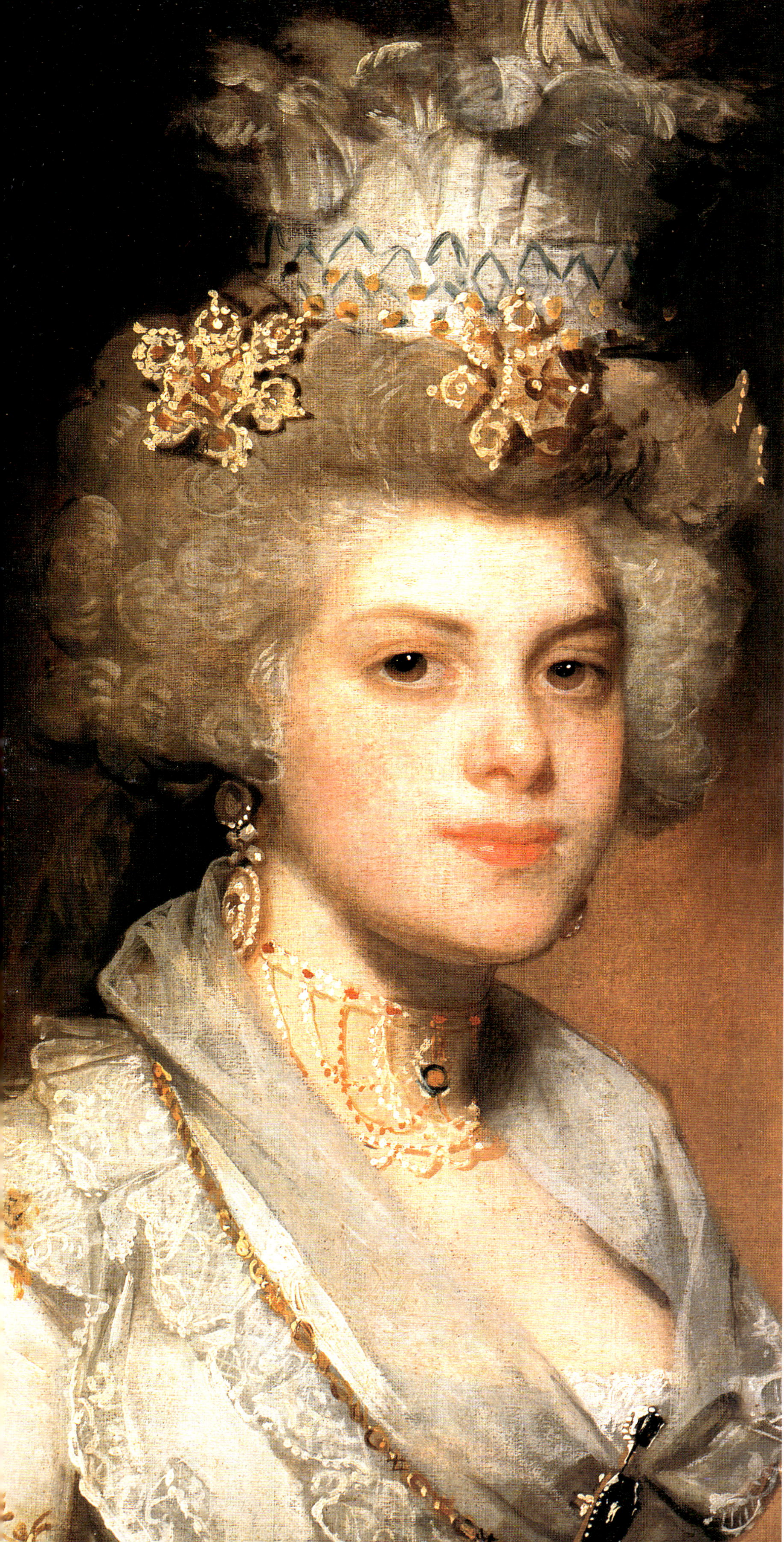

Gilbert Stuart
1755–1828

Matilda Stoughton de Jaúdenes

Oil on canvas
50⅝ x 39½ in. (128.6 x 100.3 cm.)
1794
Signed, inscribed, and dated at lower left:
G. Stuart, R.A., Sept. 8/1794.
Rogers Fund, 1907 (17.76)

THE SIXTEEN-YEAR-OLD BRIDE of Josef de Jaúdenes, Matilda Stoughton de Jaúdenes (1778–after 1822), was born in New York. Her American father served as Spanish consul in Boston for thirty years. Although her rich, resplendent costume and her many jeweled ornaments would have been regarded as excessive and in bad taste for a young Anglo-Saxon, this display, including the fan she holds, was completely appropriate for the wife of a wealthy and ambitious Spanish diplomat. A contemporary diarist acidly compared the couple to little dolls. Matilda's portrait is a harmonious pendant to the one of her husband (also in the Museum's collection), but it has a separate artistic integrity. The painting is a superb example of Stuart's firm, brilliant style just after his return to the United States from England. The coat of arms and the inscription at the upper left are later additions, made in Spain by another hand.

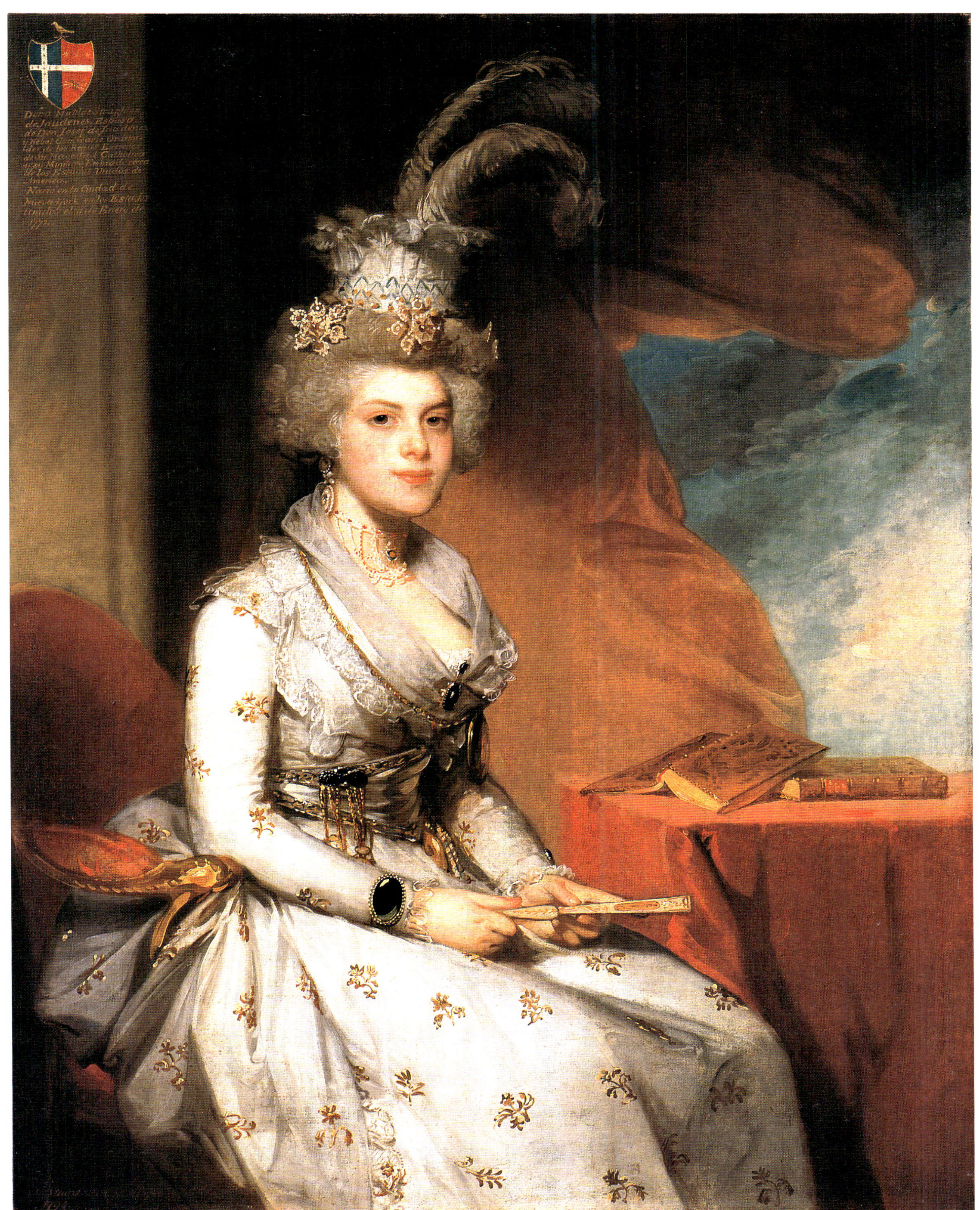

Gilbert Stuart
1755–1828

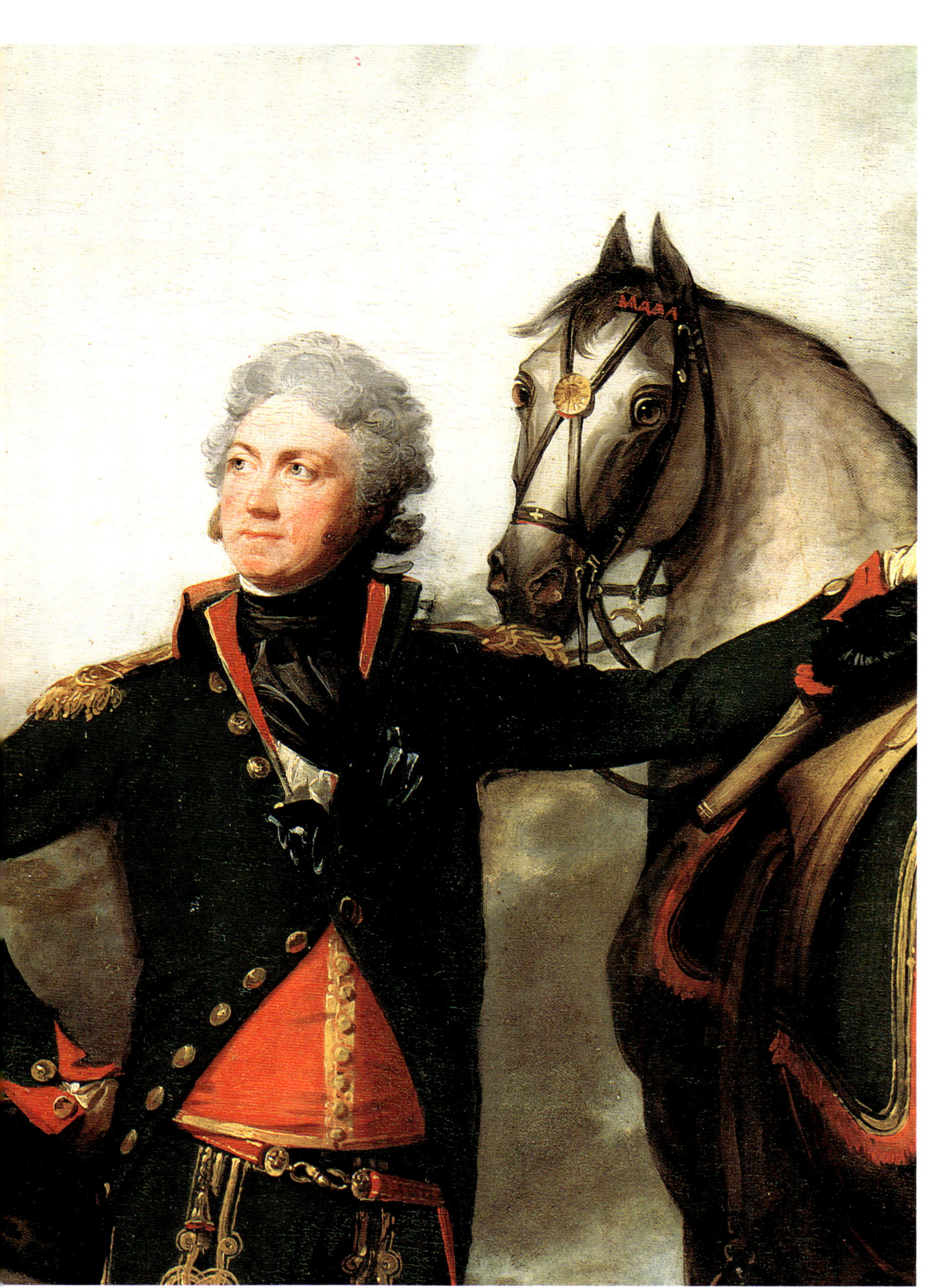

Vicomte de Noailles

Oil on canvas
50 x 40 in. (127 x 101.6 cm.)
Signed and dated lower left:
G. Stuart 1798
Purchase, Henry R. Luce Gift, Elihu Root, Jr., Bequest, Rogers Fund, Maria DeWitt Jesup Fund, Morris K. Jesup Fund, and Charles and Anita Blatt Gift, 1970 (1970.262)

THE VICOMTE DE NOAILLES (1756–1804), who was famed as much for his charm and elegant style as for his courage and skill as a soldier, seemed to have been deeply attracted to the idea of democracy and the revolutionary spirit that championed it. Born into one of France's noble families and the brother-in-law of the Marquis de Lafayette, he sympathized with America's determination to free herself from British rule: he served twice with the French in the Revolutionary War, representing France at the surrender at Yorktown. On his return to France he played an important role in the abolishment of the old regime there, was president of the National Assembly, and held a high rank in the newly formed French national army. Always a supporter of reason and law, however, he fled from the Terror and returned to America in the spring of 1793. In Philadelphia, where he dedicated his considerable talents to banking and the stock exchange, he met Gilbert Stuart, who made this portrait of him in 1798. Noailles is shown imposing and handsome, in full length, though painted on a relatively small canvas. His fine and dashing figure, in the uniform of a colonel in the chasseurs à cheval d'Alsace, dominates the richly varied scene, which is enlivened by a tumultuous sky and by a troop of cavalry charging in strict formation at the base of the cliff on which he stands.

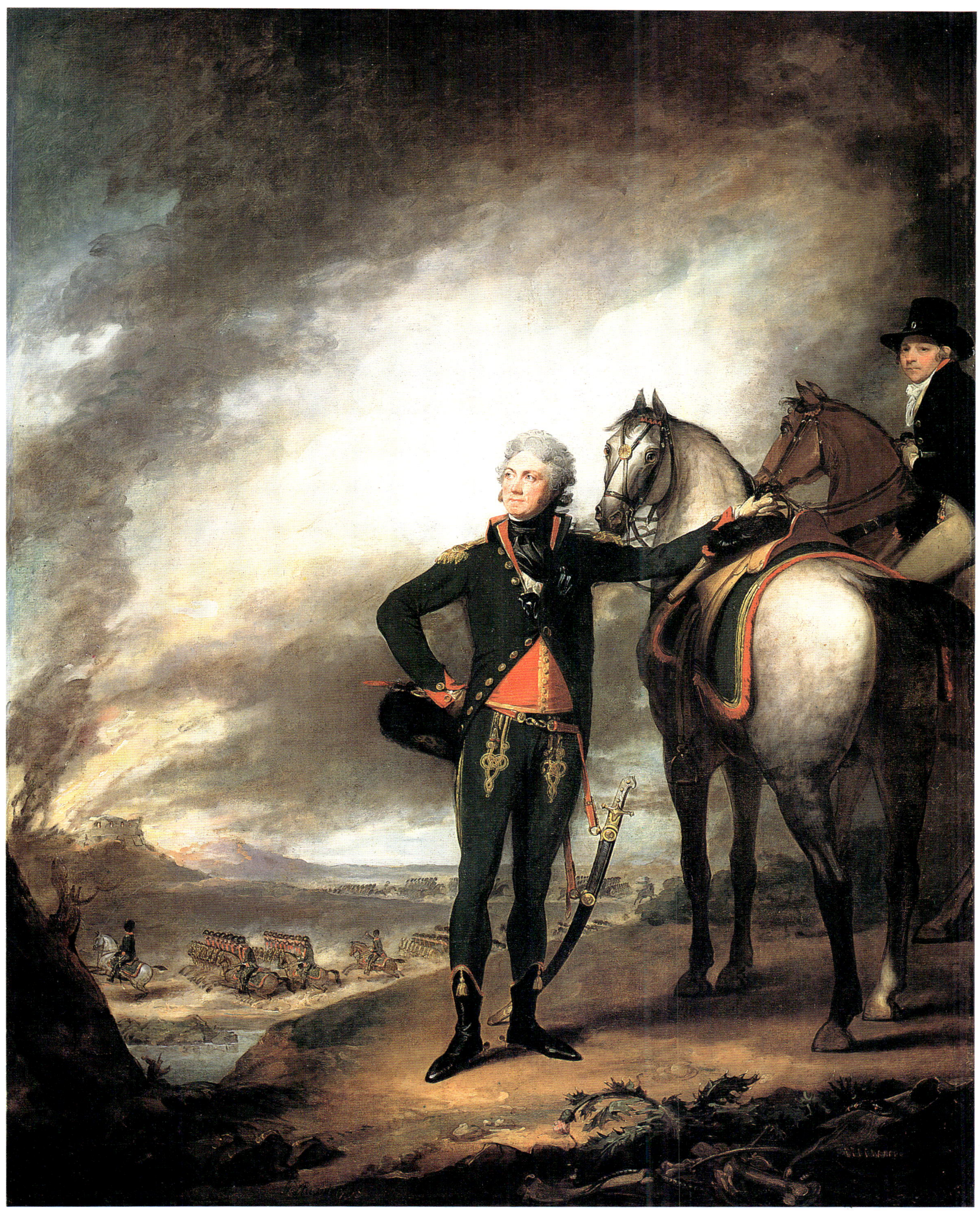

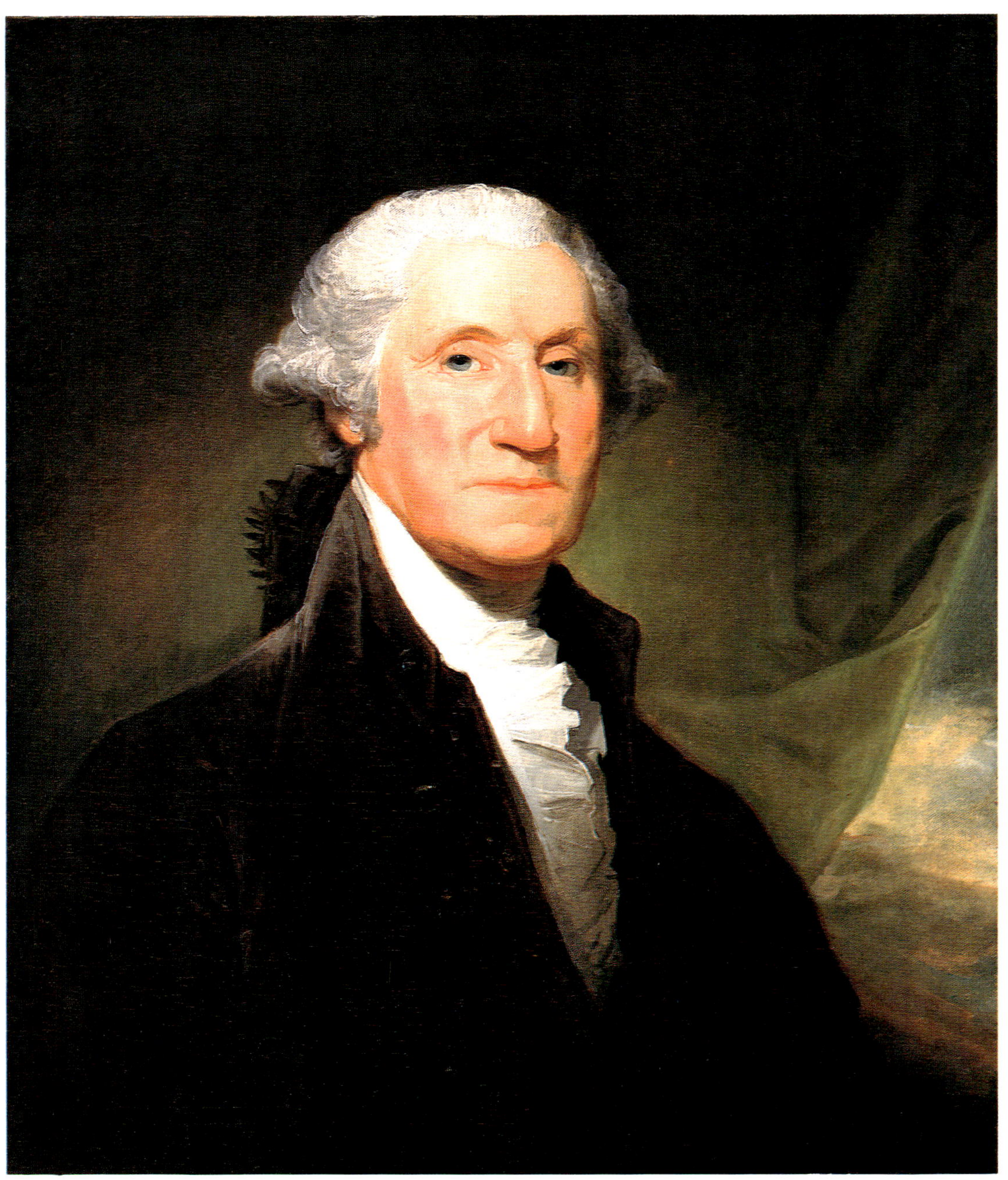

Gilbert Stuart
1755–1828

George Washington

Oil on canvas
30¼ x 25¼ in. (76.8 x 64.1 cm.)
1795 or shortly thereafter
Rogers Fund, 1907 (07.160)

THIS DISTINGUISHED PORTRAIT, one of the three likenesses of George Washington by Gilbert Stuart in the Museum's collection, is known as the Gibbs-Channing-Avery Washington, from the names of the previous owners. The portrait can be securely traced back to the artist himself. It is among the finest and earliest of the many replicas Stuart was called upon to make from his original, now in the National Gallery of Art, Washington, D.C., for which Washington sat in the spring of 1795, four years before his death. He was at that time sixty-three years old and in the middle of his second term in office. In the original, which had been commissioned by a close friend of Washington's, there is much realistic detail and the president looks younger and more vigorous than he does in the Metropolitan's example. Here the lifelike energy of the features has been suppressed in favor of a distant formal expression. Using a curtained background to lend impressiveness, Stuart presents a national hero who, though still living, has already achieved a kind of apotheosis.

Gilbert Stuart
1755–1828

James Monroe

Oil on canvas
40¼ x 32 in. (102.2 x 81.3 cm.)
1820–1822
Bequest of Seth Low, 1916 (29.89)

THE FIFTH PRESIDENT of the United States, James Monroe (1758–1831), was a Virginian who enjoyed the advantages of being the disciple and political protégé of Thomas Jefferson. Before becoming president in 1817, he had held many diplomatic posts, including those of ambassador to France and to England. In 1823, soon after this picture was completed, he issued the famous Monroe Doctrine, a statement against any intervention from foreign governments in the affairs of the Western Hemisphere. This portrait and one of James Madison now at Amherst College are the only survivors of a set Gilbert Stuart was commissioned to paint representing the first five presidents. The three-quarter pose at a desk with books and papers, the billowing drapery, and the liberal use of a strong, pure red are elements of a formula that Stuart employed in portraits of statesmen.

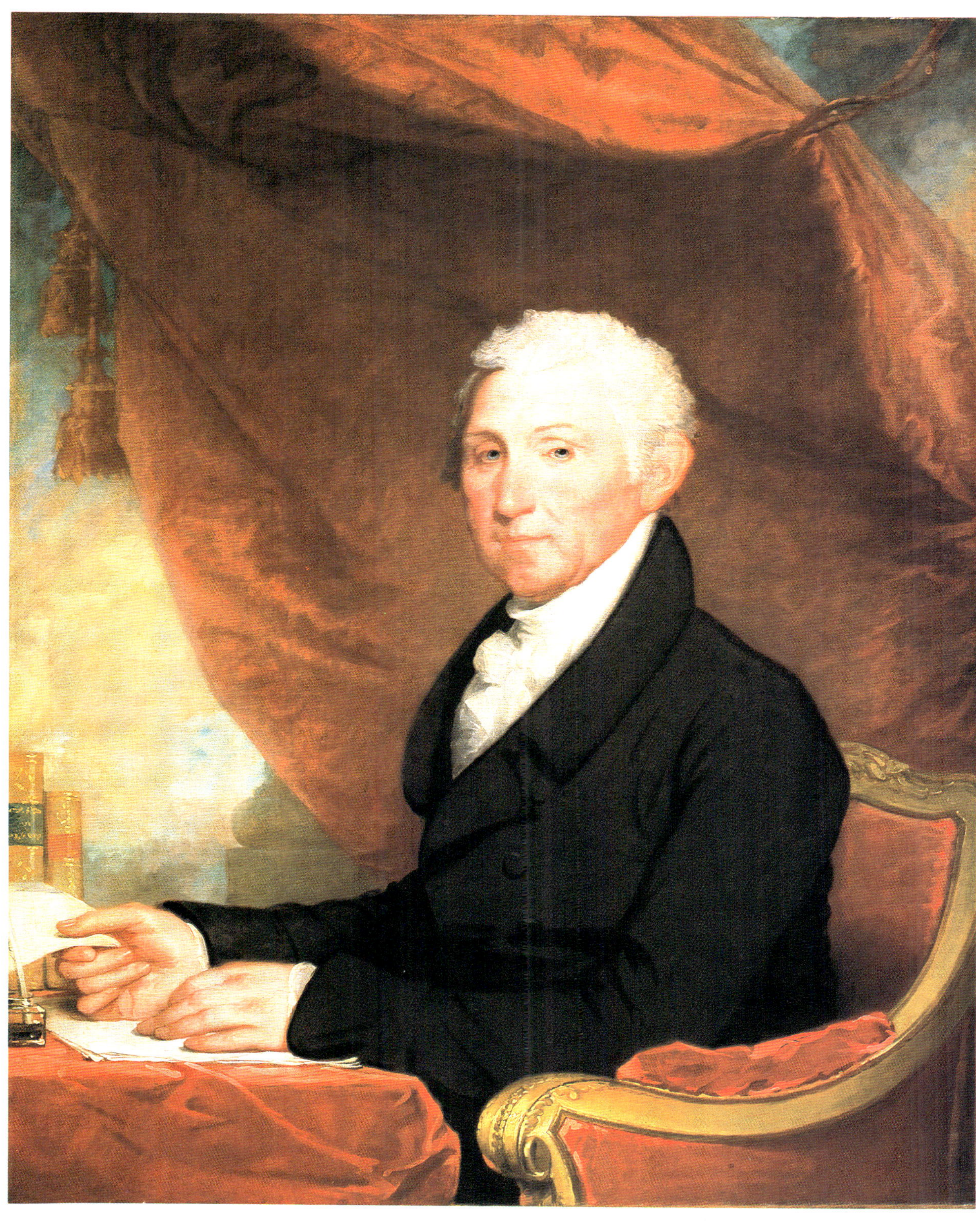

James Peale
1749–1831

Still Life: Balsam Apple and Vegetables

Oil on canvas
20¼ x 26½ in. (51.4 x 67.3 cm.)
1820s
Maria DeWitt Jesup Fund, 1939 (39.52)

JAMES PEALE was the youngest brother of Charles Willson Peale, who taught him how to paint. In the early part of his career he assisted Charles Willson in filling numerous commissions for portraits, especially for the many repetitions of his brother's famous likeness of George Washington (pages 36–37). Later James Peale specialized in painting miniatures, and for more than a decade at the end of his life he concentrated on still lifes. The Museum's picture, probably painted in the 1820s, is a decorative assemblage of vegetables, finely modeled and precisely drawn, in a thoughtfully planned arrangement. The colors of the various cabbages, the glossy eggplant, and the old-fashioned tomatoes are bright and attractive, and the carefully differentiated shapes and textures are interesting. More exuberant than the Dutch still lifes of the seventeenth century, less chaste and selective than Chardin's vegetables and fruit, this picture has a quality of authentic originality that by itself secures for James Peale the status of an American master of still life.

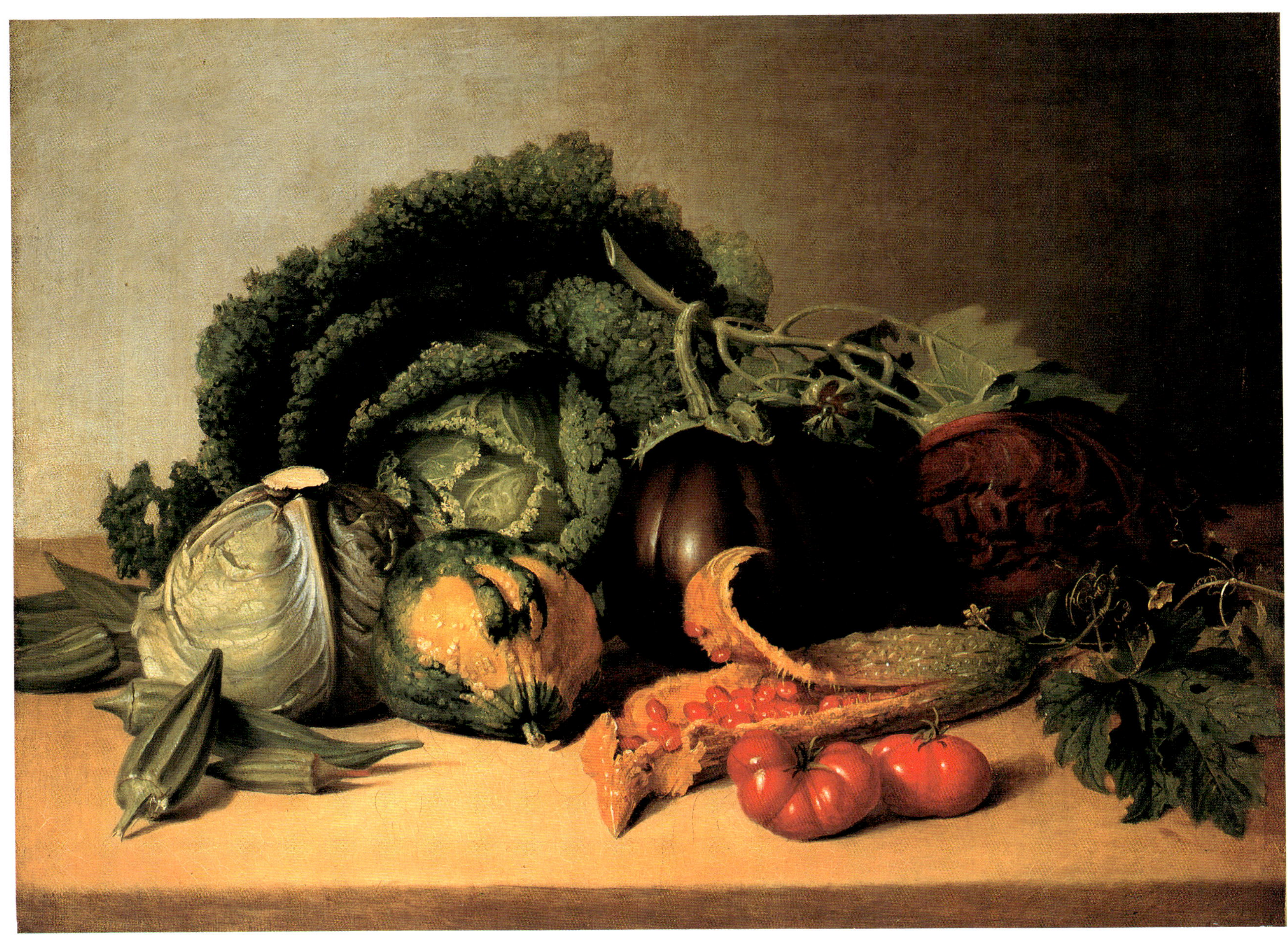

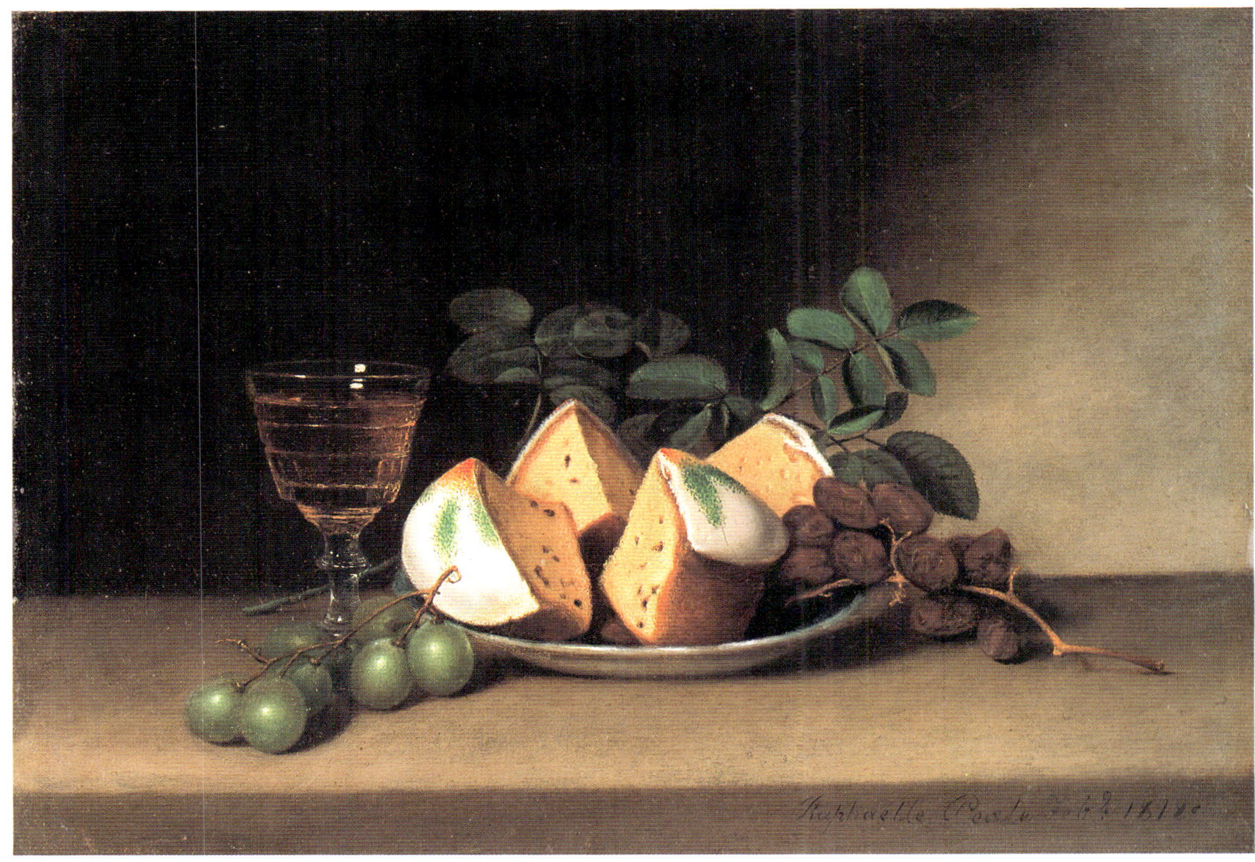

Raphaelle Peale

1774–1825

Still Life With Cake

Oil on wood
10¾ x 15¼ in. (27.3 x 38.7 cm.)
1818
Signed and dated at lower right:
Raphaelle Peale Feb 9: 1818
Maria DeWitt Jesup Fund, 1959 (59.166)

RAPHAELLE PEALE was a son of the painter and versatile craftsman Charles Willson Peale. Like his uncle James Peale, whose still life with a balsam apple is shown on the facing page, Raphaelle began as a portrait painter under his father's tutelage, but later devoted himself largely to still lifes. *Still Life With Cake,* subdued in color and in composition, has an air of propriety, like that of a dining table recently crumbed and arranged for dessert. Yellow, orange, and green are related in a thoughtfully conceived harmony, and the gray tone of the table is a sophisticated inspiration. The fine rings of light on the crystal wine glass and the delicate shading of the background are subtle details that give the painting an air of reticent refinement.

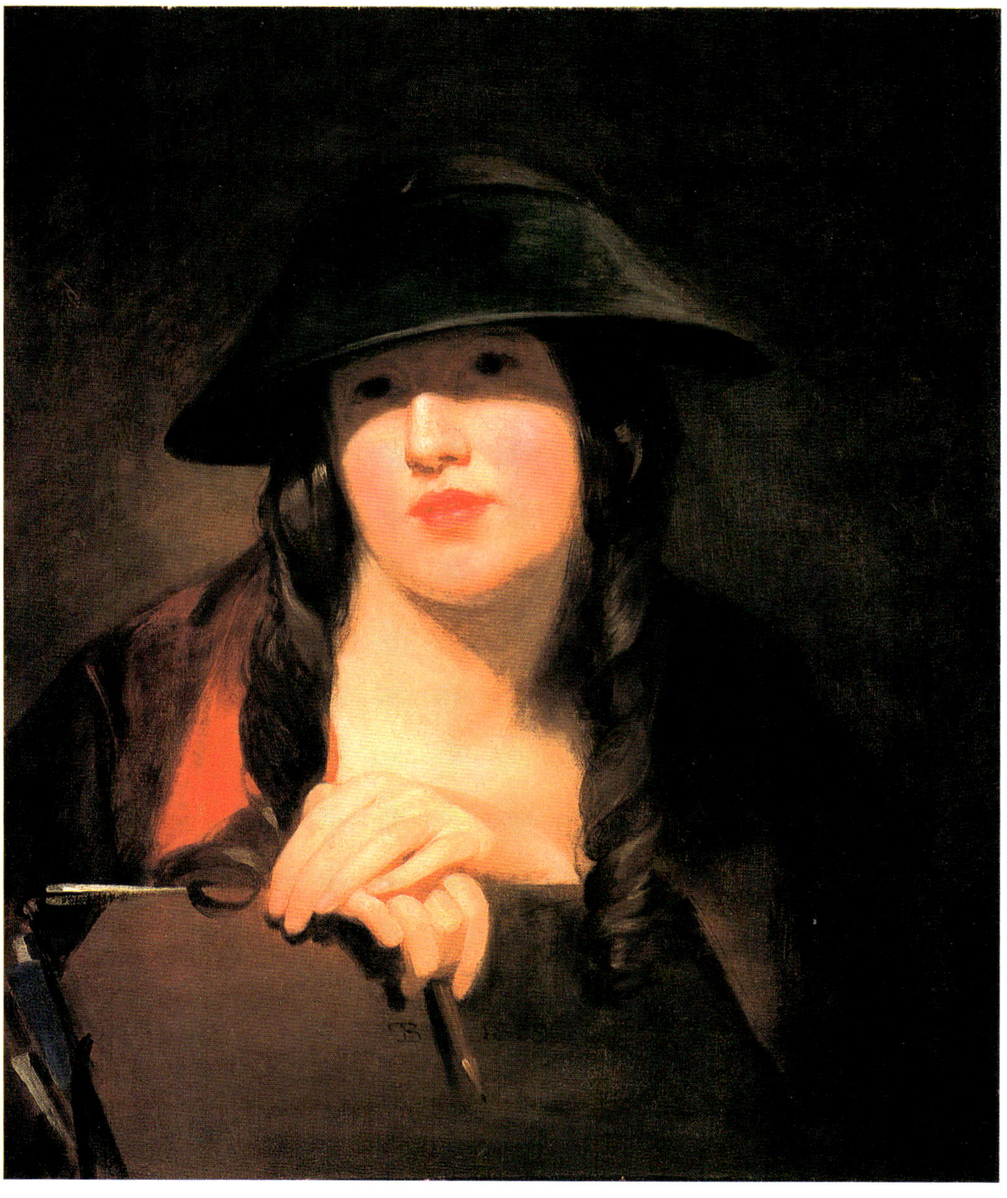

Thomas Sully
1783–1872

The Student

Oil on canvas
23½ x 19½ in. (59.7 x 49.5 cm.)
1839
Signed, dated, and inscribed at lower center: TS (monogram) 1839;
on the back: The Student/TS1839
Bequest of Francis T. Sully Darley, 1914 (14.126.4)

THOMAS SULLY'S DAUGHTER Rosalie (1818–1847) posed for this picture, which remained in the artist's family until it was bequeathed to the Museum by a descendant. Sully inscribed the title on the back of the canvas, and gave the young woman a portfolio to lean on and a drawing pencil to hold in her hand. The crownless wide-brimmed hat she wears has given rise to the legend that it was really a lampshade supplied by her father. What is certain is the artist's interest in the band of deep shadow cast by the hat across half the girl's face and in the strongly contrasted chiaroscuro effect he achieved.

Sully, born in England to a family that settled in the United States when he was eleven, began his career as a miniaturist but went on to become a sought-after and successful portrait painter. At the end of the 1820s he was considered the best portraitist in America. Just two years before painting *The Student,* he had had the distinction of painting Queen Victoria, who granted him sittings to make his preliminary sketches (there is a sketch in the Museum's collection).

Samuel F. B. Morse
1791–1872

The Muse—Susan Walker Morse

Oil on canvas
73¾ x 57⅝ in. (187.3 x 147.4 cm.)
1835–1837
Bequest of Herbert L. Pratt, 1945 (45.62.1)

WHEN SAMUEL F. B. MORSE painted this picture of his eldest daughter, Susan (1819/20–1885), he was deeply involved in his famous invention of the telegraph and at the end of his career as a painter. The representation of the girl, who was about sixteen, is forthright, simple, and convincing, but only to a limited degree is it a portrait. The neoclassical setting, the luxurious draperies and upholstery, and the expensively elegant costume are surely an idealized and fanciful vision. Morse, who had enjoyed deplorably little worldly success as an artist, apparently intended this work to be a personification of the arts of design. His basic importance to the entire realm of communication has almost obscured the fact that he was a strong and at the same time delicately finished artist.

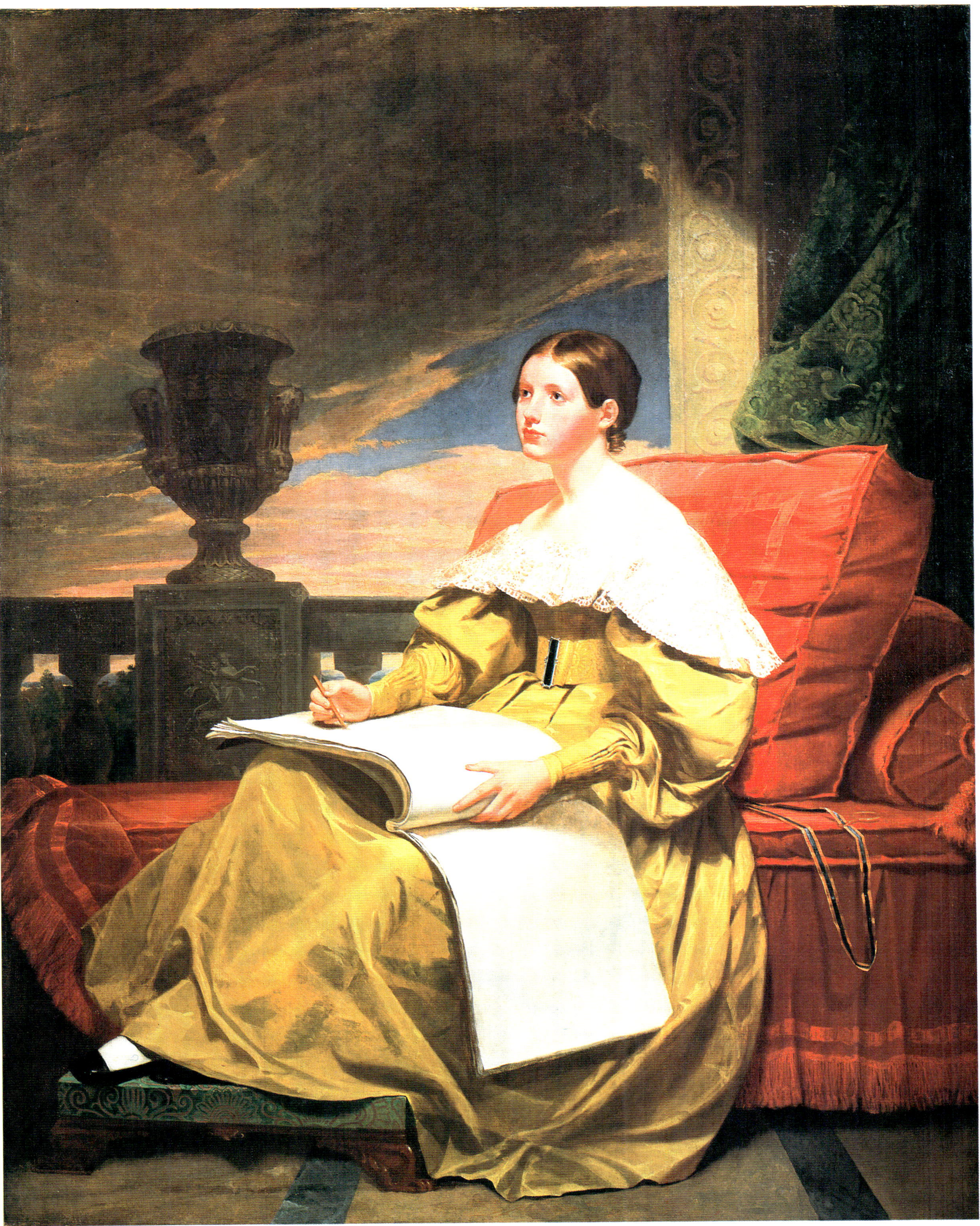

Cephas Giovanni Thompson
1809–1888

Spring

Oil on canvas
36 x 28¾ in. (91.4 x 73 cm.)
1838
Signed and dated at lower right:
C. G. Thompson/Oct. 1838
Gift of Mrs. Madeleine Thompson Edmonds, 1971 (1971.244)

IN SPITE OF A negligible artistic education, Cephas Giovanni Thompson enjoyed success as a portrait painter before he was twenty. He worked at first in various cities of New England and in Philadelphia, where he came to know the paintings of Thomas Sully. From 1837 on, except for some months in Rome, Thompson spent most of his time in New York.

Romanticized portraits of pretty, fashionable women were very popular in the middle of the nineteenth century, and this allegory of Spring is one of the best of its kind, probably Thompson's most able and attractive work. The huge neoclassical urn in the background shows the painter's awareness of the taste of his time. The warm glow on the satin of the dress and on the smoothly modeled flesh is held within the limits set by the large, shadow-casting hat; the sitter's appeal, too, is kept within bounds, stopping short of sentimentality.

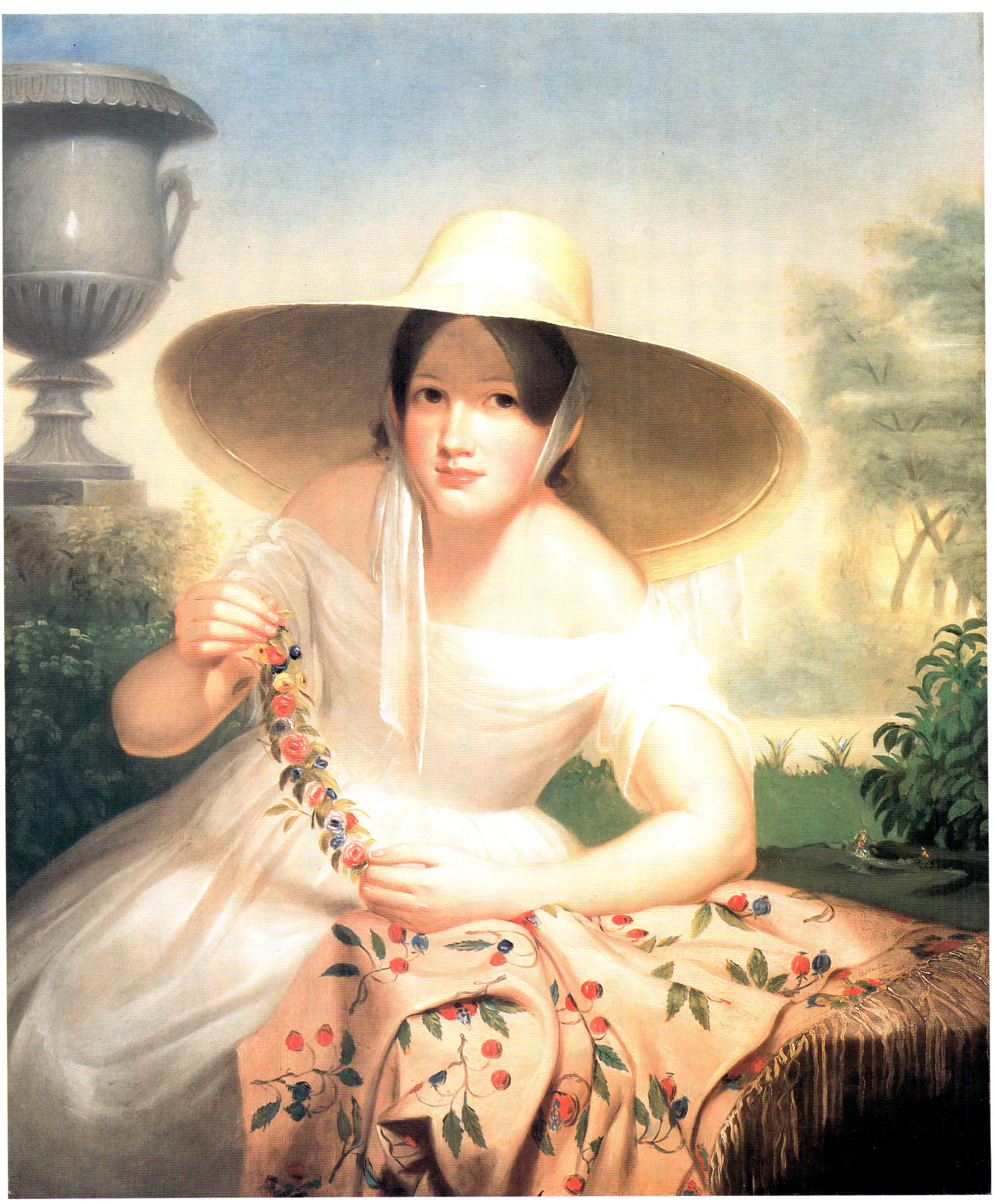

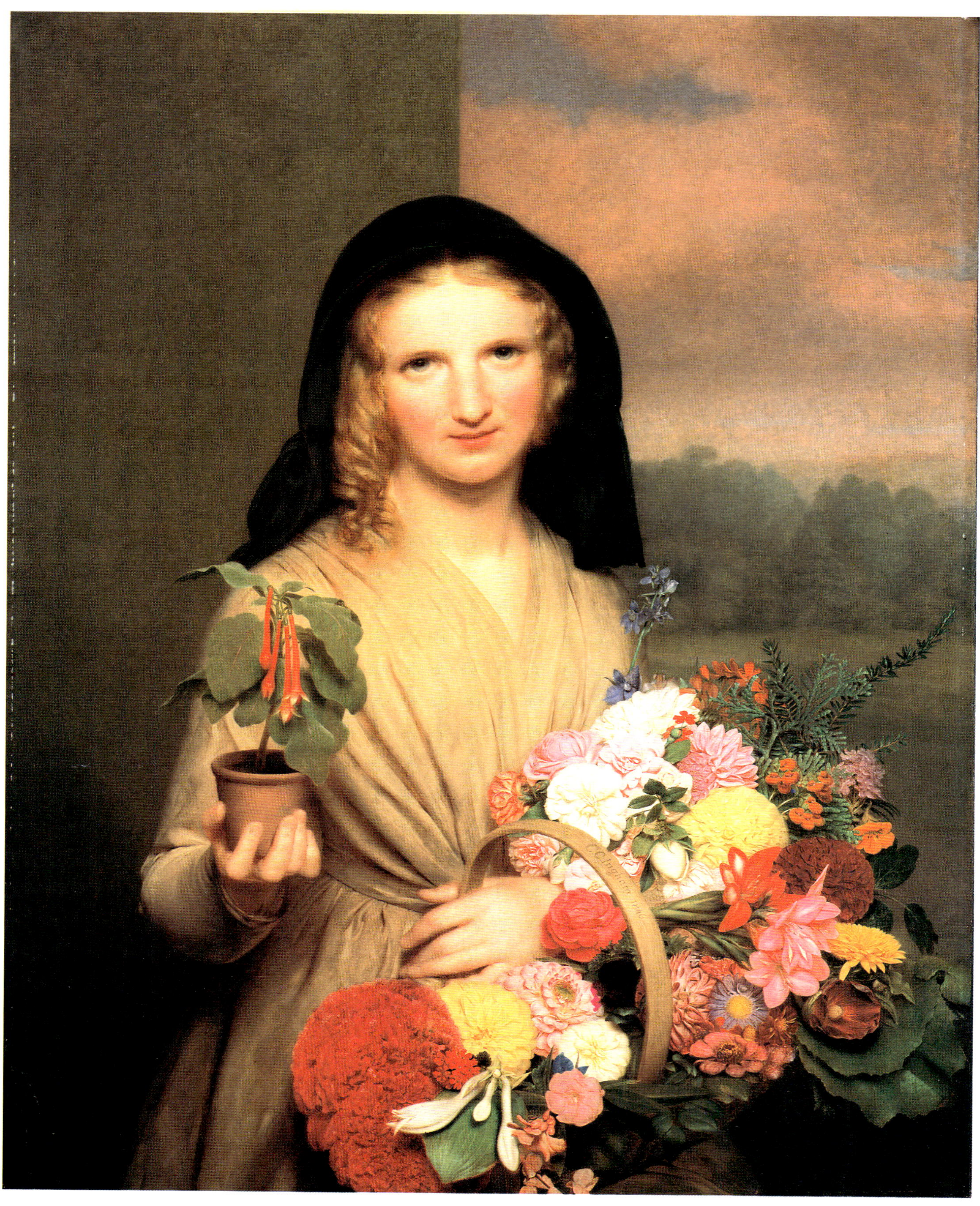

Charles Cromwell Ingham
1796–1863

The Flower Girl

Oil on canvas
36 x 28⅞ in.
(91.4 x 73.3 cm.)
1846
Signed and dated on basket handle:
C.C. Ingham, 1846–
Gift of William Church Osborn, 1902 (02.7.1)

CHARLES CROMWELL INGHAM, born and trained in Dublin, must have known well the old tradition of prints and paintings representing vendors hawking various wares in the streets of London, and it is likely that he knew the popular paintings on similar themes by his American contemporaries. With his passion for painting brilliant, clearly identifiable flowers and his predilection for young women as models, it is not surprising to find Ingham selecting a flower girl rather than a newsboy or a strawberry seller, both favored subjects of the day. The poor young woman's starkly plain dress and her mournful black head covering contrast with the garishly intense colors of the flowers. Appearing slightly weary, the vendor proffers her wares with a mute, expressionless appeal. In one hand she holds a potted fuchsia, a plant that enjoyed great popularity in Victorian England and, somewhat later, in America. In books on flower symbolism it is associated with love, amiability, and enjoyment.

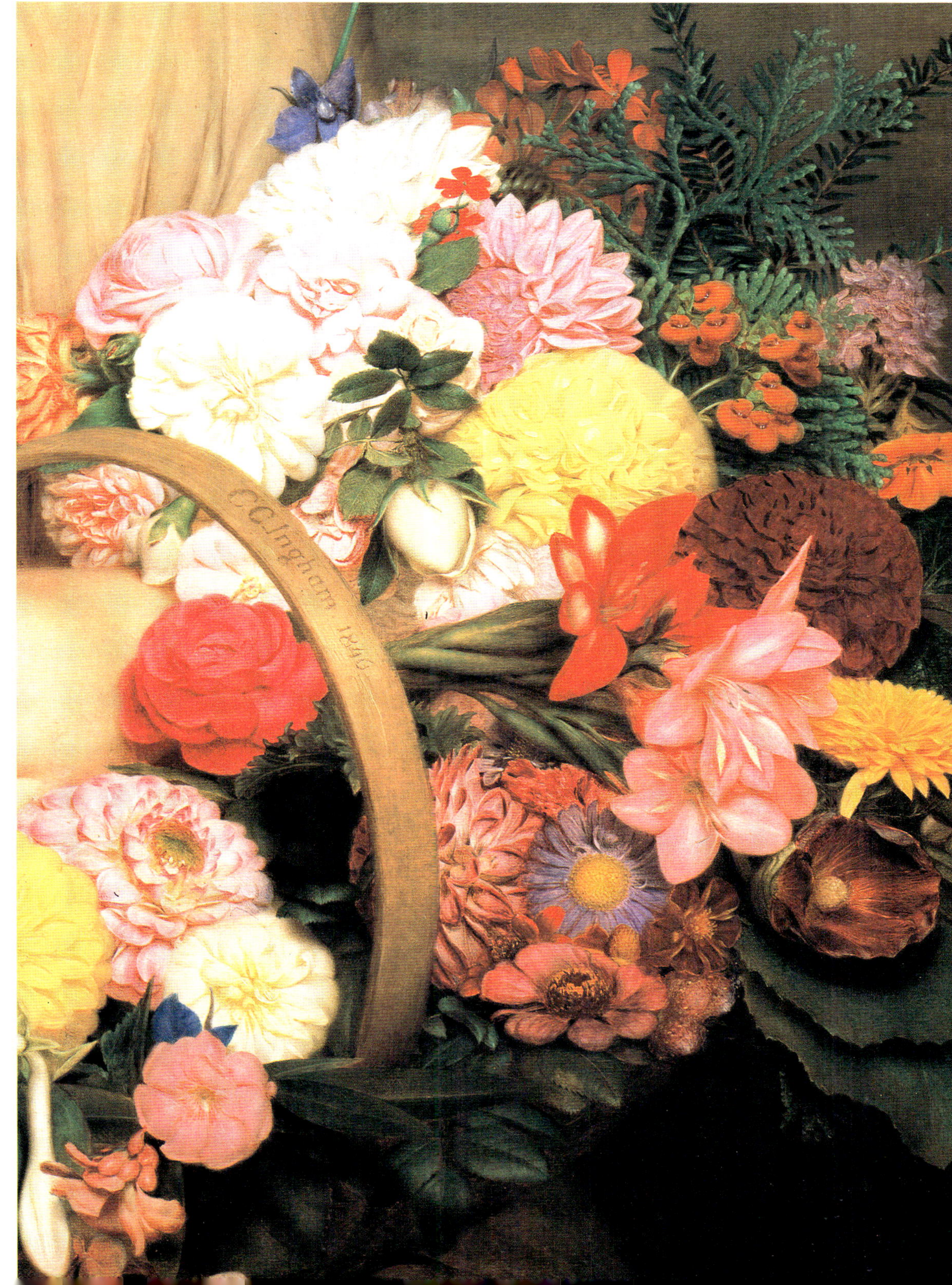

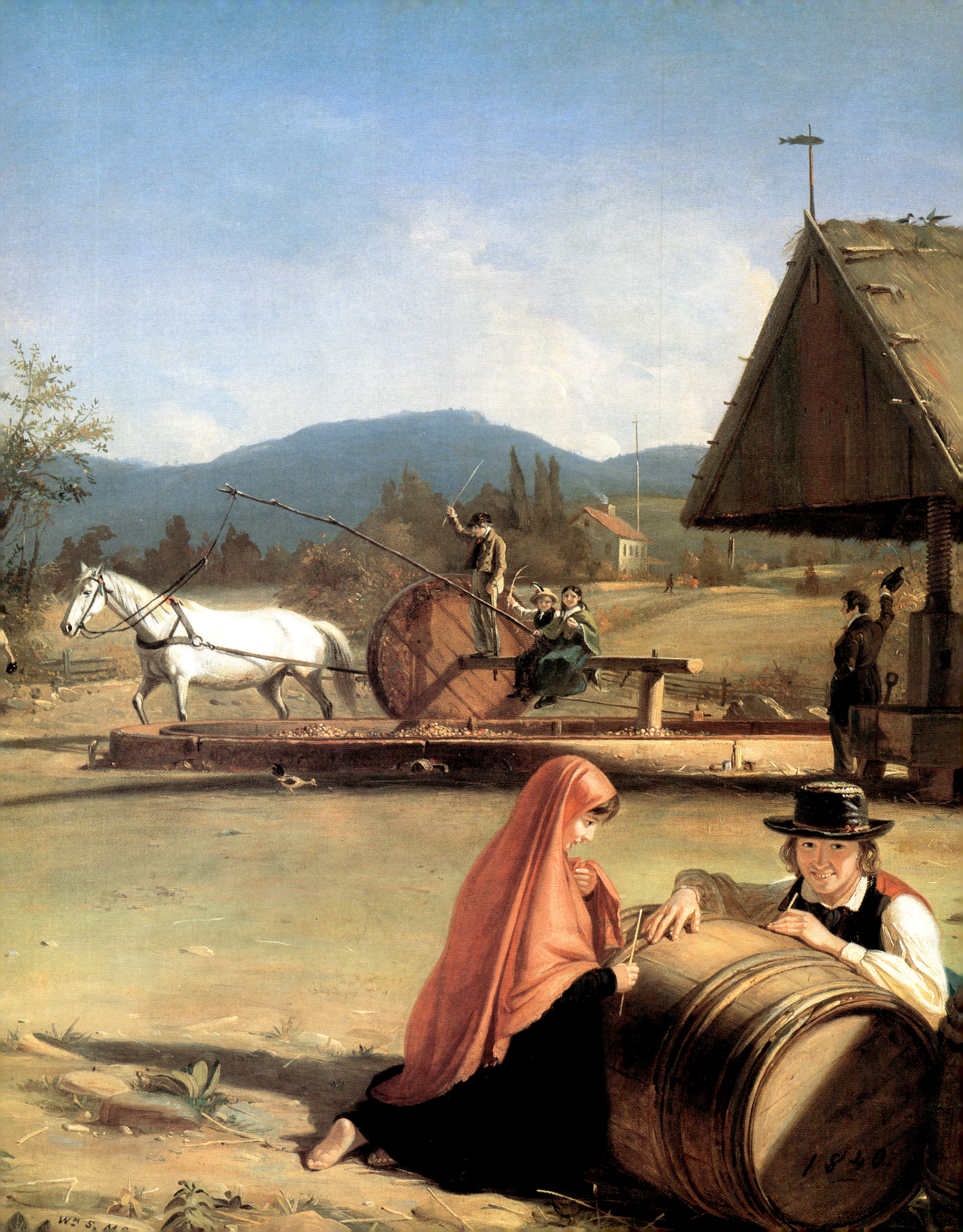
1840

William Sidney Mount
1807–1868

Cider Making

Oil on canvas
27 x 34⅛ in. (68.6 x 86.7 cm.)
1841
Signed and dated at lower left: Wm S. Mount. [in black]/1841 [in red]. Dated on barrel: 1840; inscribed on the back in black paint: CIDER MAKING. Wm S. Mount./1841./Painted for/C. Augt Davis/N. York.
Purchase, Charles Allen Munn Collection, Bequest of Charles Allen Munn, by exchange, 1966 (66.126)

WILLIAM SIDNEY MOUNT, an extraordinarily observant countryman, recorded in this painting with great explicitness the various steps in the making of cider. The presentation of life on a farm is vivid and cheerful. There are countless realistic details, such as the burly man in shirt-sleeves treating himself to a generous swig from the keg. The locale is Setauket, in Suffolk County on Long Island, and this particular mill is said to have survived into the 1940s. *Cider Making*, superficially an everyday country scene, carries a thinly veiled allusion to political events. Cider played a key role in the presidential campaign of 1840, when the Whig candidate, William Henry Harrison, was represented as a "man of the people." In a successful public relations strategy to establish this popular image, cider was distributed free from log cabins built for the purpose.

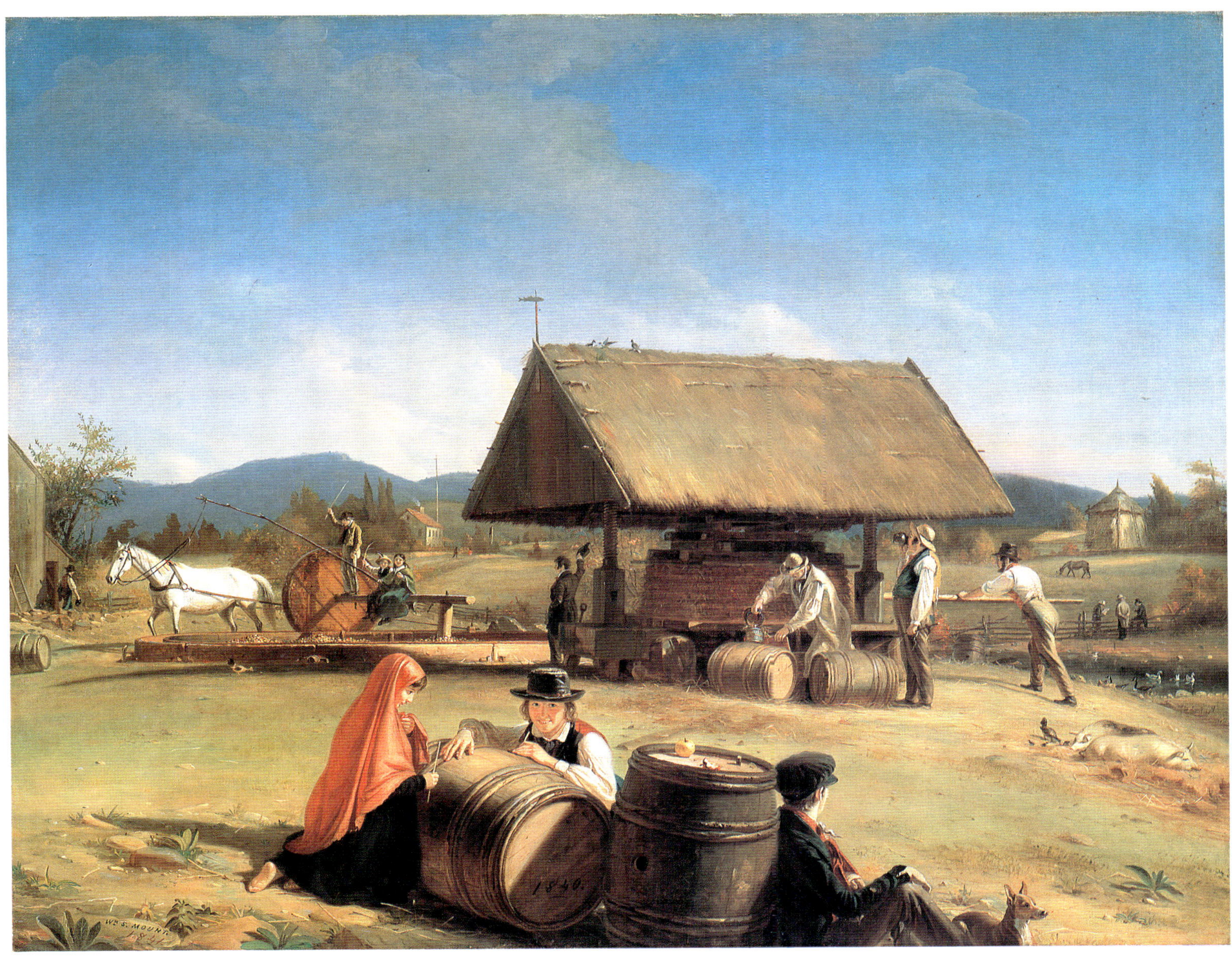

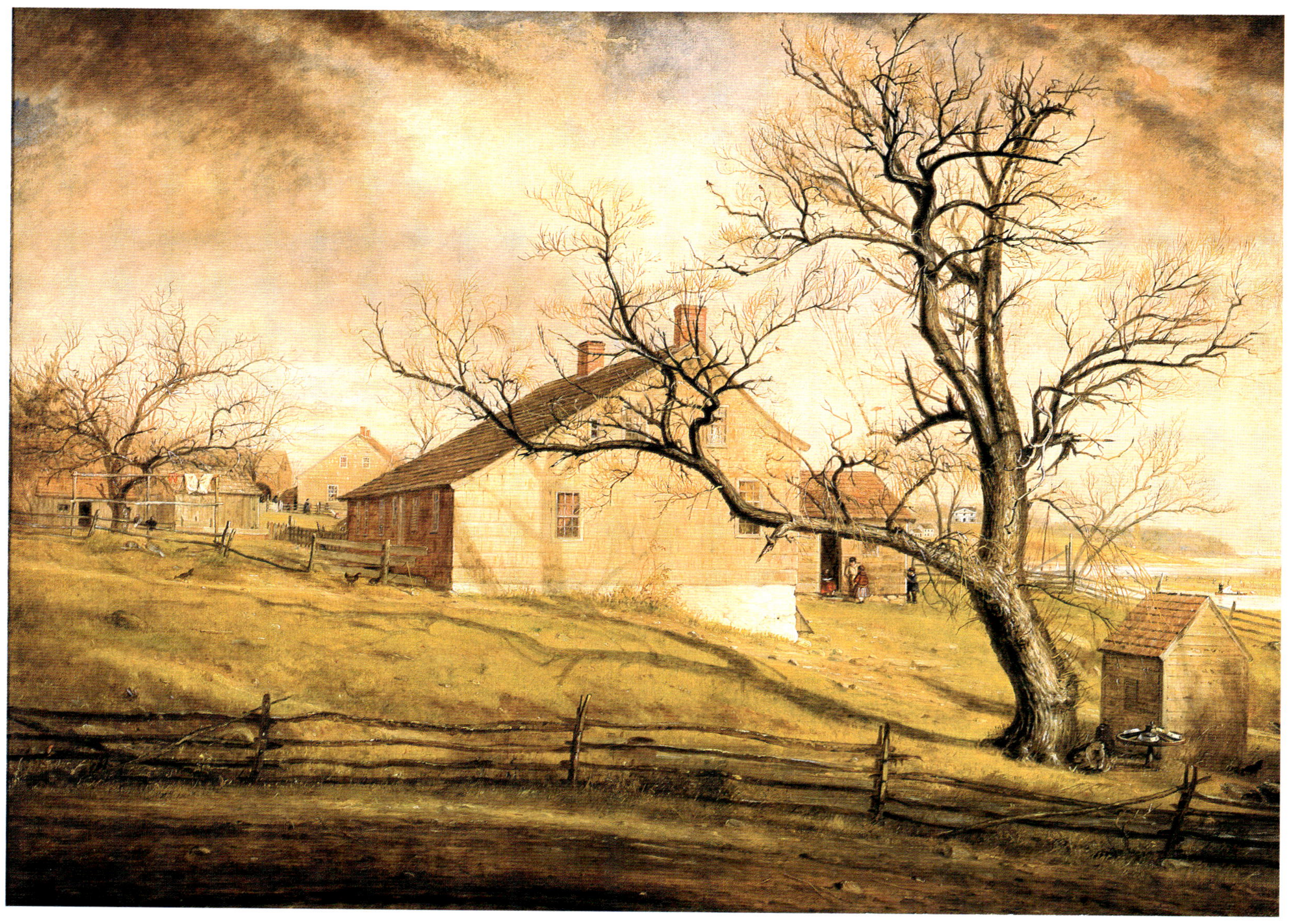

William Sidney Mount
1807–1868

Long Island Farmhouses

Oil on canvas
21 7/8 x 29 7/8 in. (55.6 x 75.9 cm.)
1862–1863
Signed at lower left: W S. Mount.
Gift of Louise Floyd Wickham, in memory of her father, William H. Wickham, 1928 (28.104)

IN HIS DIARY for November, 1862, William Sidney Mount records beginning a painting—almost certainly this one—showing a view from his studio window of the houses of his brother Robert and of John Davis, who lived at Setauket, Long Island. Though Mount began the picture in November, he must have done most of his work on it in the first months of 1863—the willow tree has sprouted and robins are perched on its branches, melting snow has left puddles, and the children no longer wear winter clothing. The sky unmistakably declares the wakening of nature. In the spring of 1863, an entry in Mount's diary and a letter from him to Abraham Lincoln reveal that he was swept by a great wave of patriotic feeling at this time and trusted in a happy outcome for the Union forces.

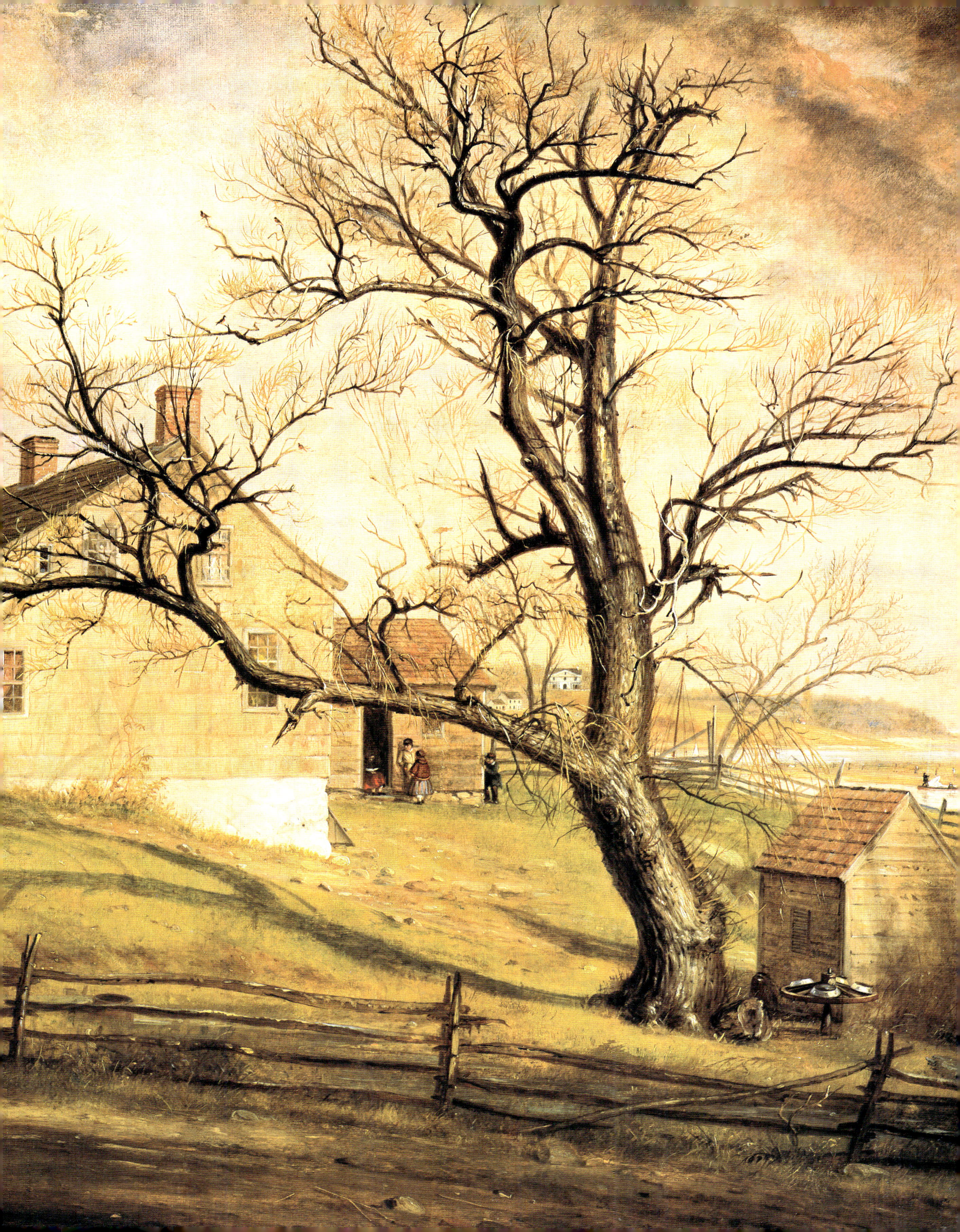

George Caleb Bingham
1811–1879

Fur Traders Descending the Missouri

Oil on canvas
29 x 36½ in. (73.7 x 92.7 cm.)
ca. 1845
Morris K. Jesup Fund, 1933 (33.61)

THIS IS ONE of the Museum's most popular pictures, partly because its subject and setting are purely indigenous, but surely also because of its magic. George Caleb Bingham had grown up in Missouri and knew firsthand the life on the great river that rises near the Canadian border and joins the Mississippi at Saint Louis. There must have been haggling and brutality when the pelts were procured from the Indians in the northern wilderness, and noisy deals would mark the sales at the southern end. The transit, however, in the gliding dugout, guided by the staring old French trader and guarded with a rifle by his resting son, is marked by mists and silence, impenetrable and bewitched.

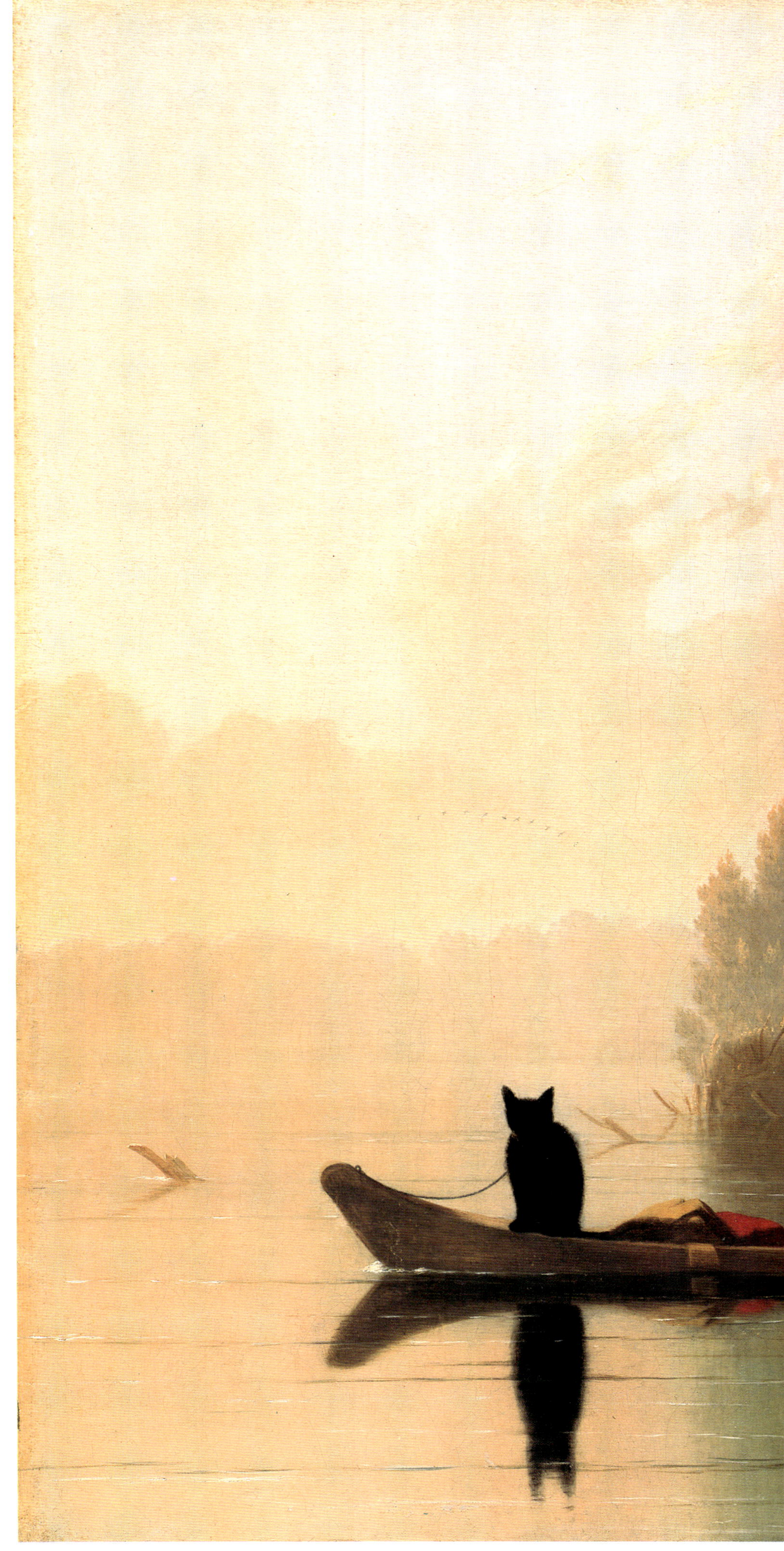

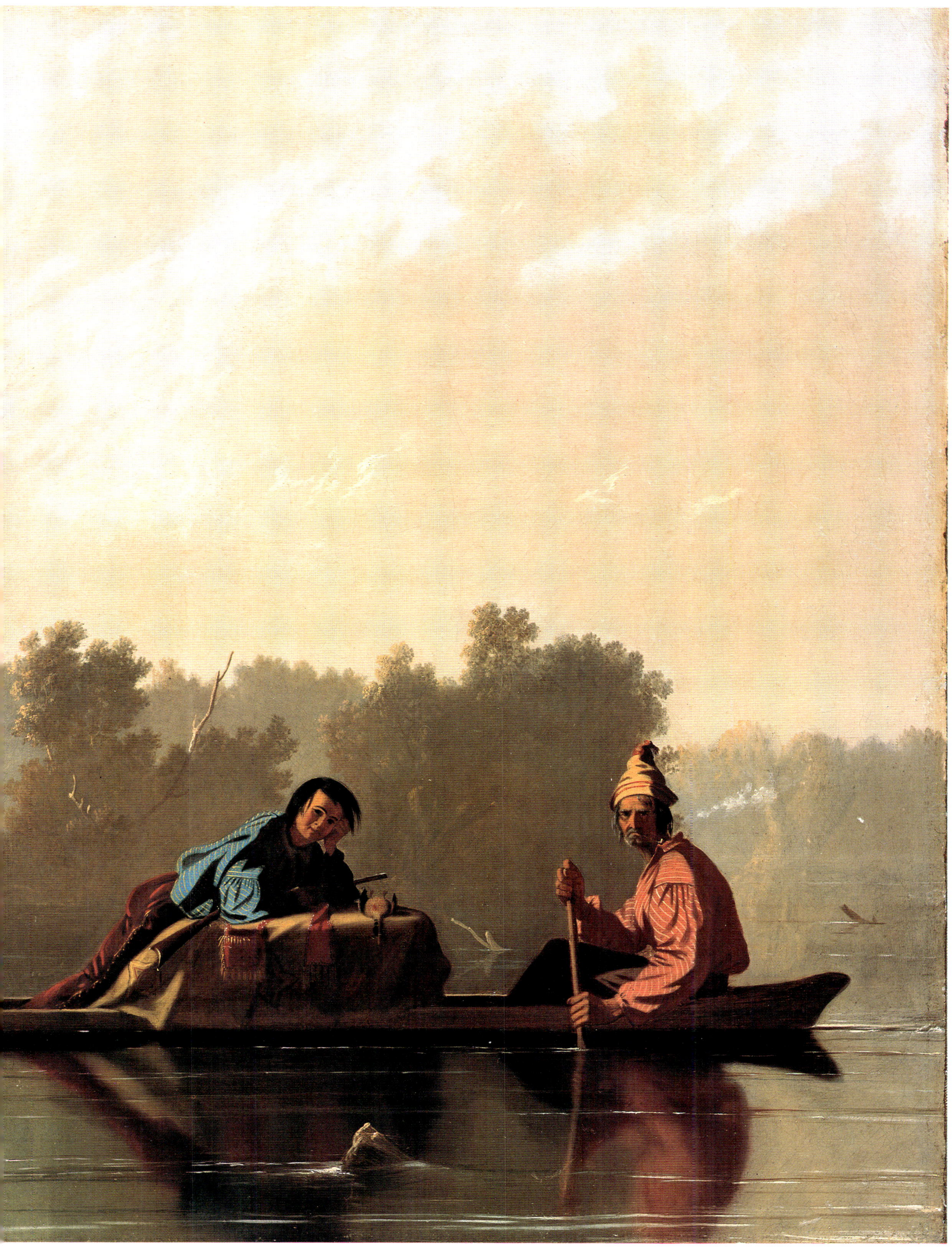

Thomas Cole
1801–1848

A View Near Tivoli (Morning)

Oil on canvas
14¾ x 23⅛ in. (37.5 x 58.7 cm.)
1832
Signed, dated, and inscribed on the back:
T. Cole/Florence/1832/Presented to W. A. Adams/by T. Cole/Sep. 1834.
Rogers Fund, 1903 (03.27)

THOMAS COLE came to this country from England when he was about seventeen. He specialized in romantic landscape, ultimately becoming the acknowledged leader of the group of painters known as the Hudson River School. A three-year stay abroad, first in England, then in France and Italy, gave Cole an opportunity to study great paintings, especially the landscapes of Turner, Claude, and Poussin; it also afforded him a store of riches in picturesque and sublime natural scenery, which he preserved in innumerable drawings and paintings. He lived in Florence and later in Rome, where he was especially impressed by the ruins of antiquity. Among his many sketches is one showing a fragment of the Claudian aqueduct at Tivoli, a classical structure with a watchtower grafted on in medieval times—it was from this sketch that Cole painted this picture. In the center of the painting is a bridge, constructed upon the ruins of another aqueduct, and far off, partly veiled in clouds and mist, are the famous and poetic Sabine Hills. The colors are rich in tonal values, with sophisticated and subtle delicacy and variation.

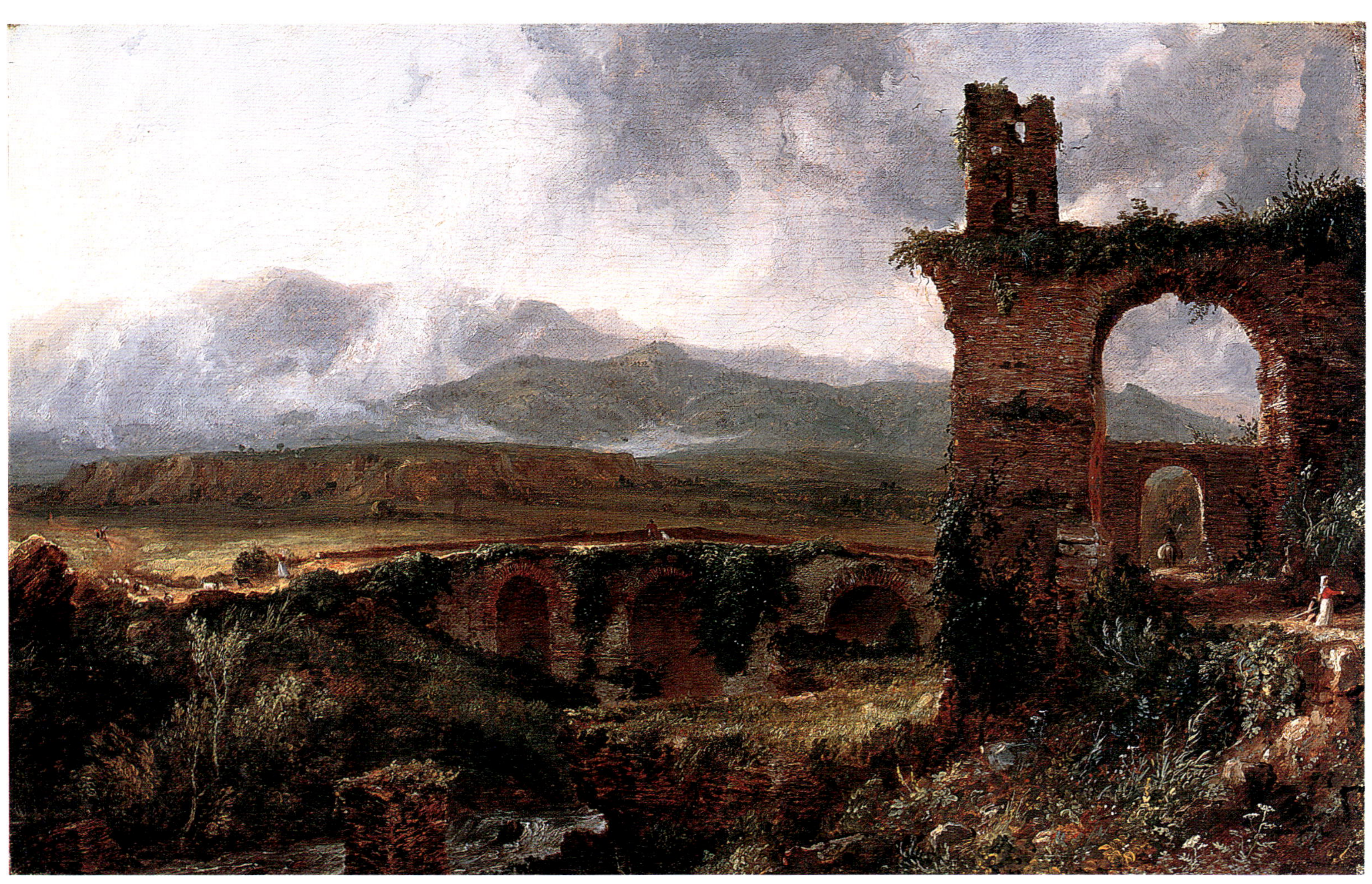

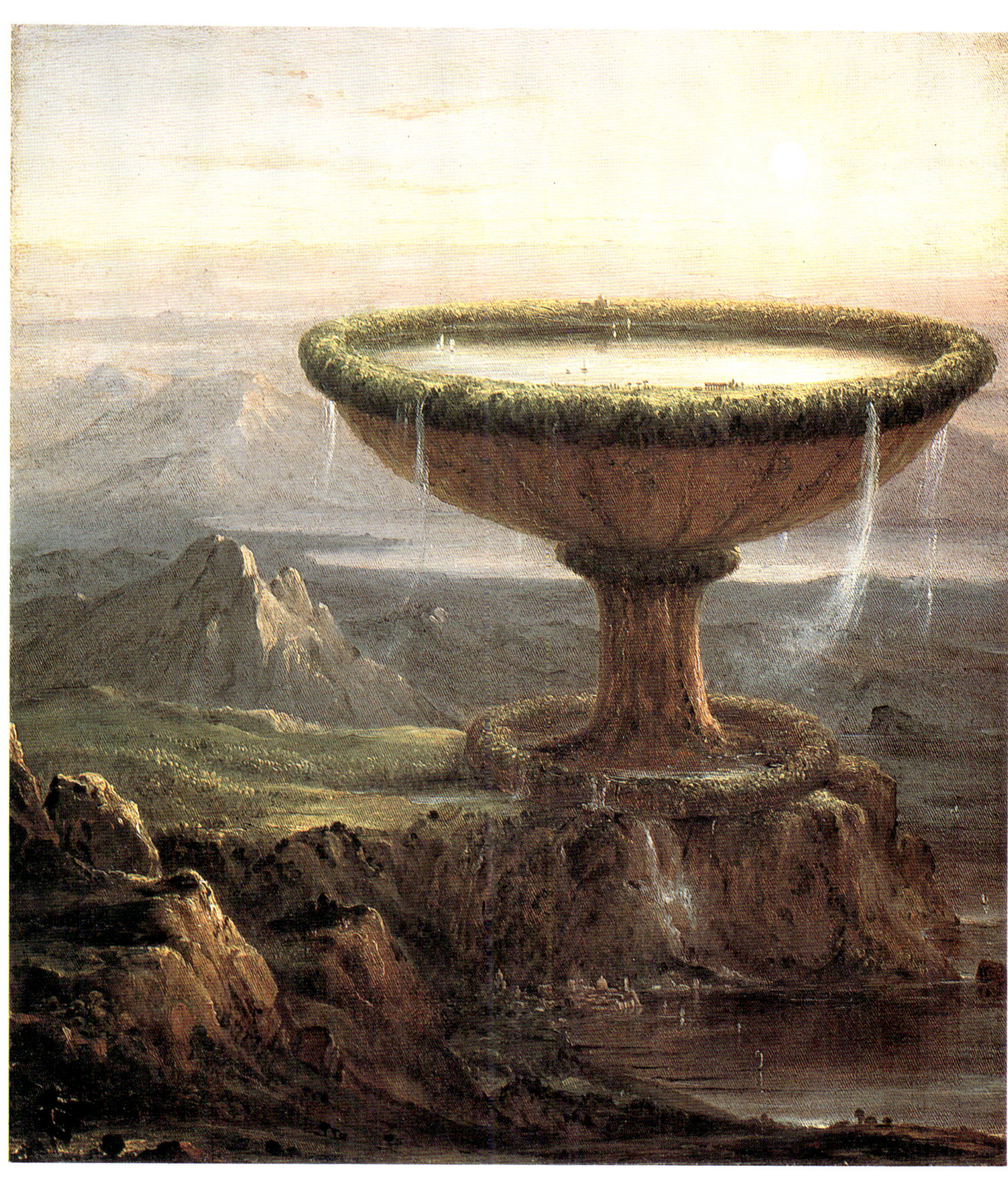

Thomas Cole
1801–1848

The Titan's Goblet

Oil on canvas
19⅜ x 16⅛ in. (49.2 x 41 cm.)
1833
Signed, dated, and inscribed at lower right: T. Cole 1833; on paper on the back, recording inscription on the back before lining: The Titan's Goblet/ T. Cole/1833.
Gift of Samuel P. Avery, Jr., 1904 (04.29.2)

IN MANY OF HIS PICTURES Thomas Cole included elements that are clearly symbols and he often provided explanations of their meaning. Unfortunately, he did not supply any help for unraveling this difficult subject, and the absence of any clue to the meaning of the giant goblet in its vast, universal landscape setting has prompted many interpretations. The key must lie in the brilliant representation of the sun in the upper part of the painting. Ancient writings identify the sun with one of the original Titans, those giants of Nature who presided before Olympus came into being, but who were finally brought into subjection under Zeus. As the sun made his night's journey from the West back to the East at dawn, he was thought to have rested in a giant goblet. Cole, traveled and well read, must have known this myth, but in the painting he goes beyond it, suggesting in the huge goblet, overgrown with foliage, an age that has passed, and in the landscape below, realistic and convincing, the present time as it is perceived by poets and artists.

Thomas Cole
1801–1848

The Oxbow (The Connecticut River Near Northampton)

Oil on canvas
51½ x 76 in. (130.8 x 193 cm.)
1836
Signed and dated at lower left:
T. Cole/1836; on the artist's portfolio:
T. Cole
Gift of Mrs. Russell Sage, 1908 (08.228)

FOR A NUMBER OF YEARS before he painted this picture, Thomas Cole had been fascinated by the curious winding of the Connecticut River below Mount Holyoke in Massachusetts. He had studied the site in a travel book and had made a drawing on the spot as well as an oil sketch. When he determined to make it the subject of a large and, he hoped, salable picture to be sent to the annual exhibition at the National Academy of Design, he imbued the scene with drama by lighting it with the eerie theatrical glow that follows immediately after a thunderstorm. The left half of the painting is still shadowed with lingering dark clouds and the right half, below the wooded hill, especially the expanse of curving water, shimmers with brightness. In the center foreground Cole has posed himself as the small figure of an artist hard at work, and he signed his name farther to the right on the artist's portfolio lying on the ground near the projecting umbrella. This is one of Cole's pictures in which a real locale has been transfigured by his artistic vision and imagination.

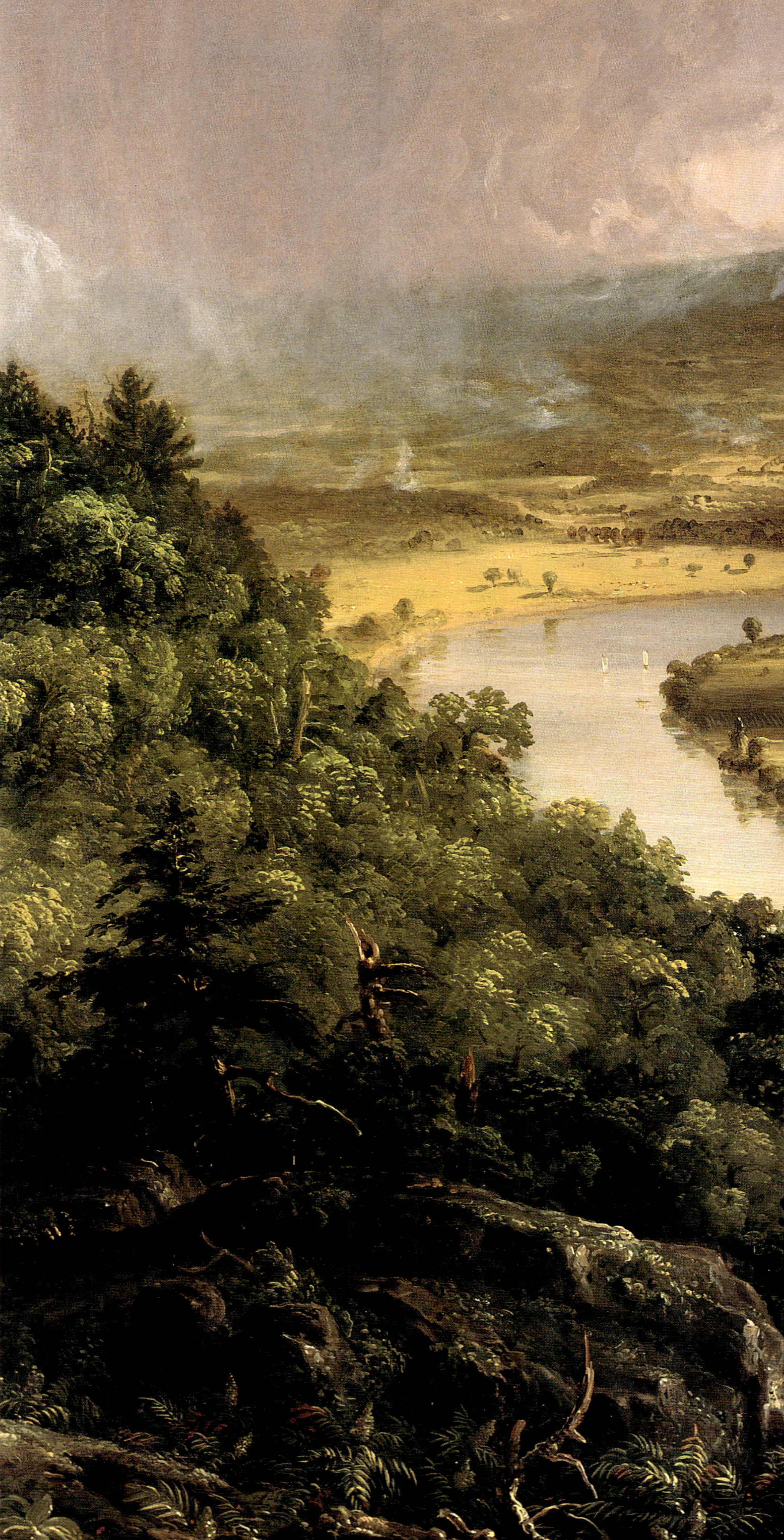

The Oxbow (detail)

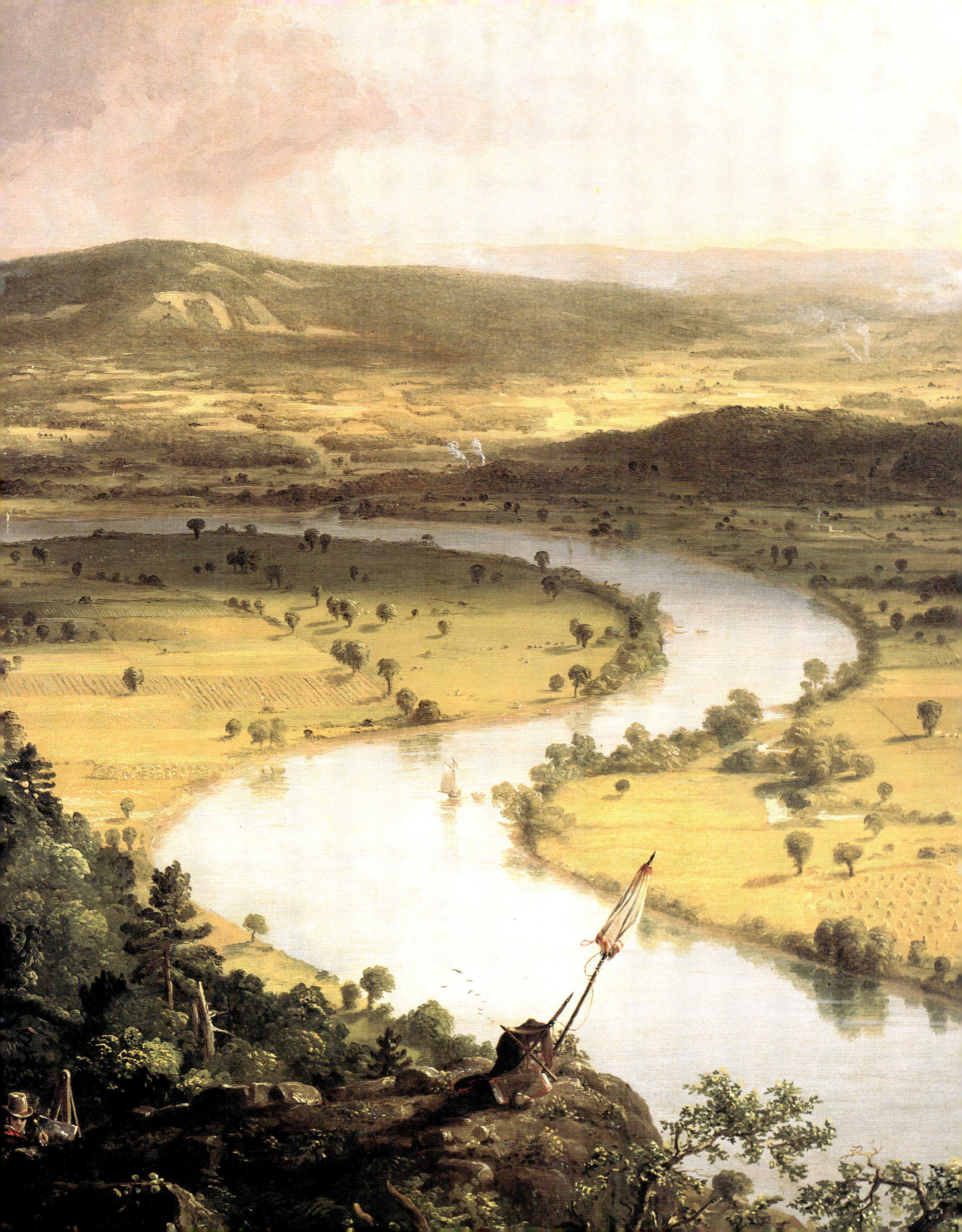

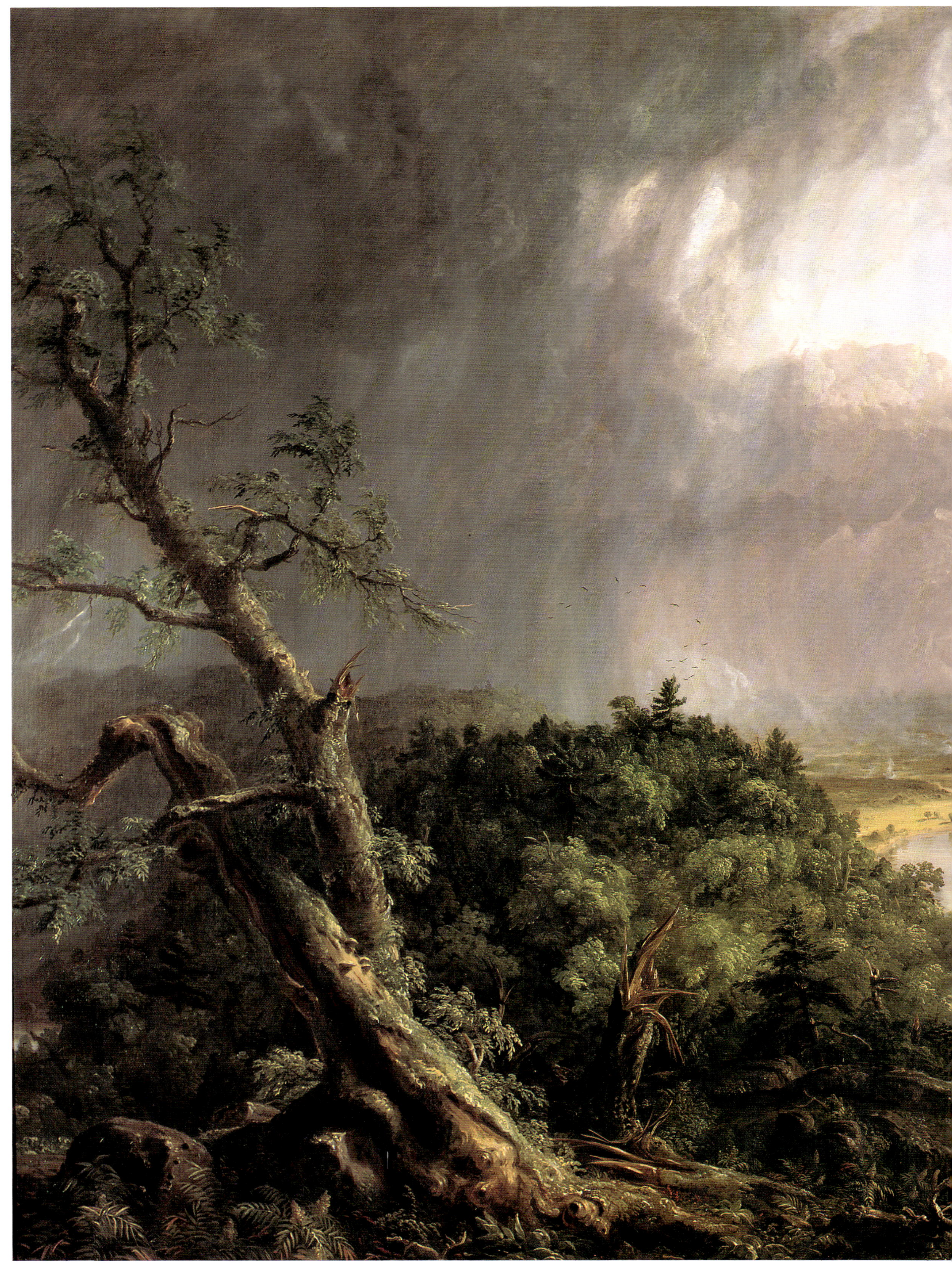

Thomas Cole: *The Oxbow*

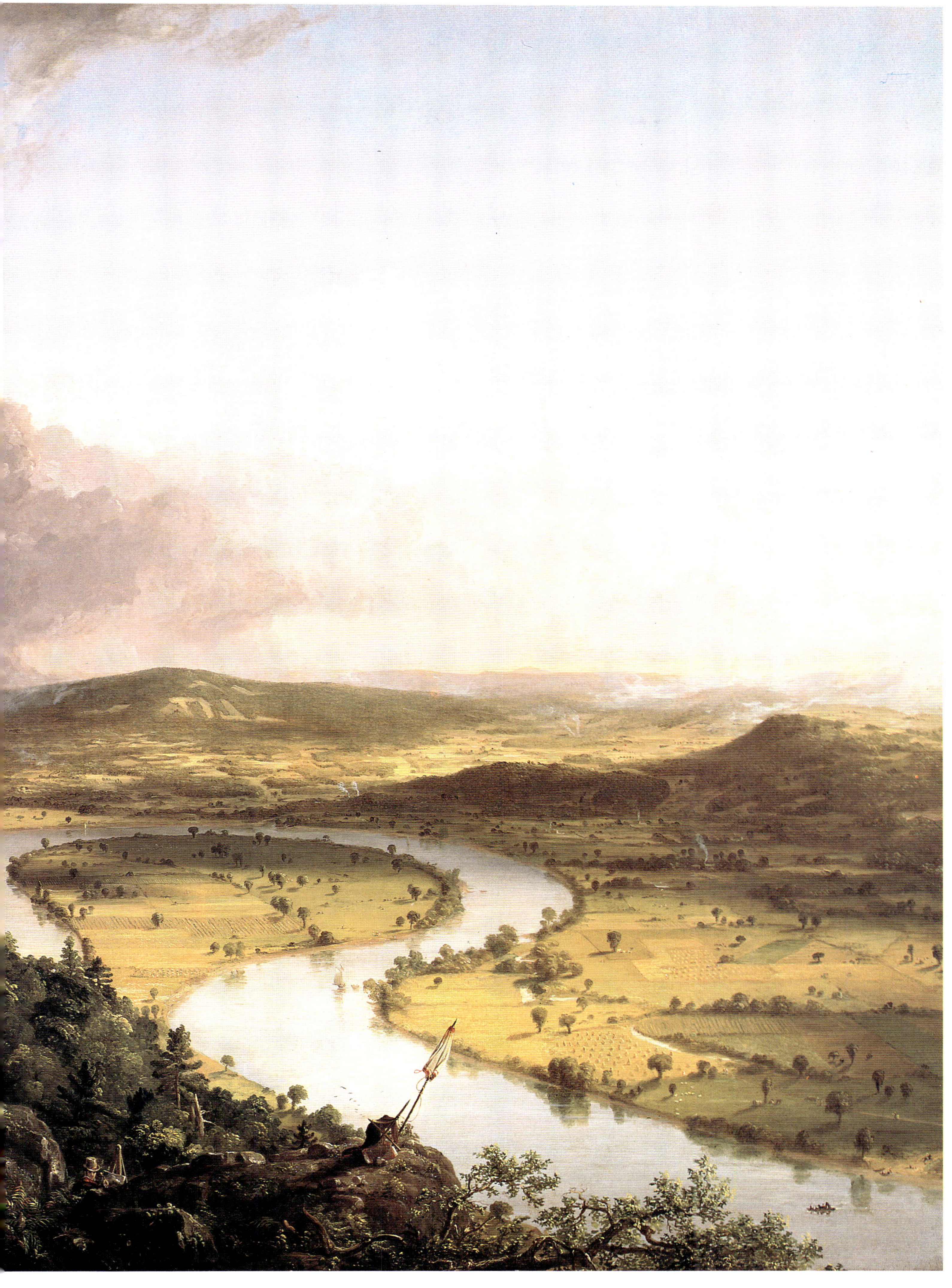

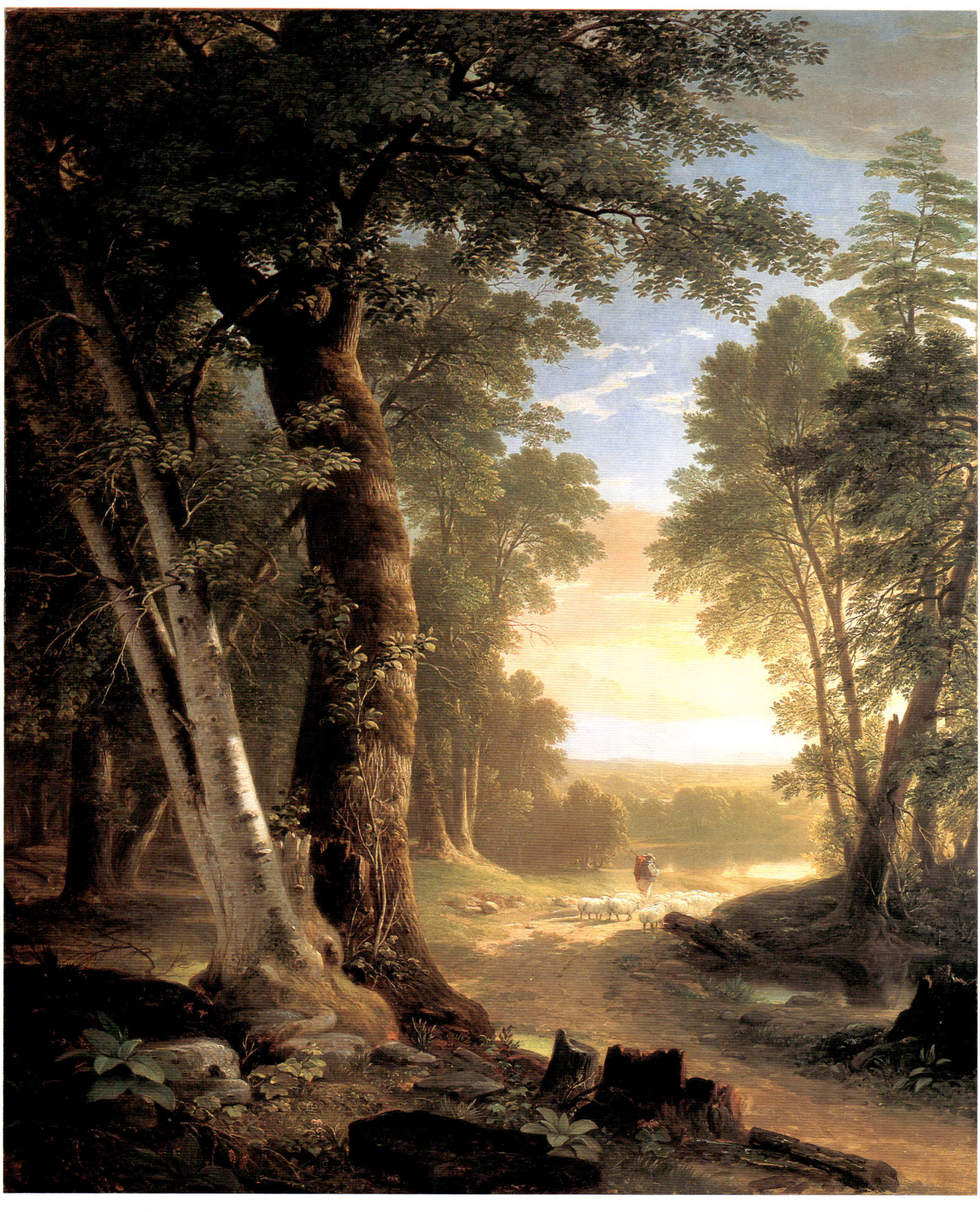

Asher B. Durand
1796–1886

The Beeches

Oil on canvas, 60⅜ x 48⅛ in. (153.4 x 122.2 cm.)
1845
Signed and dated at lower left: A. B. DURAND/1845
Bequest of Maria DeWitt Jesup, from the collection of her husband, Morris K. Jesup, 1914 (15.30.59)

IN ITS VERTICAL FORMAT, this painting by Asher B. Durand differs from the majority of landscapes by his American contemporaries. Thomas Cole and other members of the Hudson River School usually preferred wide horizontal canvases, better suited to conveying the effect of infinitude that they sought. Before he painted *The Beeches,* Durand had traveled in Europe, especially in England. He was so impressed by Constable that he adopted that painter's method of composing landscapes from studies made on the spot. In *The Beeches,* Durand seems to have taken over one of Constable's compositions, *The Cornfield* of 1826, with a clear similarity of design and effect.

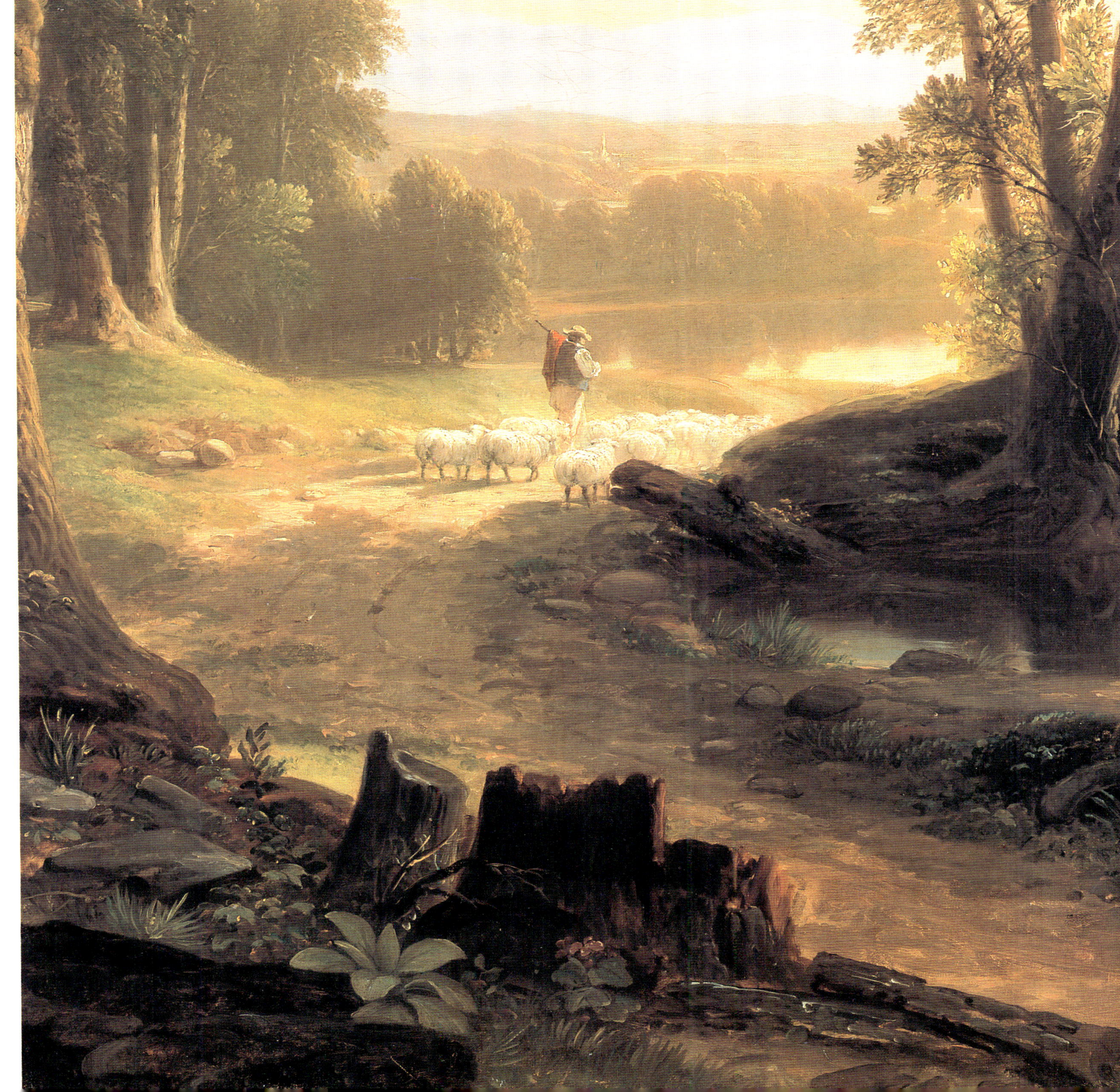

Asher B. Durand
1796–1886

Thanatopsis

Oil on canvas, 39½ x 61 in.
(11.3 x 154.9 cm.)
1850
Signed and dated at lower left:
A. B. Durand, 1850
Gift of J. Pierpont Morgan, 1911 (11.156)

THIS VAST LANDSCAPE was expressly associated by the artist with William Cullen Bryant's famous poem of meditation on death. It is perhaps Asher B. Durand's clearest tribute to the landscape style of Cole, who had died two years before this picture was painted. Although the Bryant poem is stoical and melancholy, Durand's scenery is not at all depressing. It is true that the animals look lost and alone, and that in the dark and somber section of the painting there is a funeral procession with tiny obscure figures, but the bright shining waters of the meandering river suggest, optimistically, that they will eventually join the sea, and the skies that bathe the majestic mountains with light are rose and gold.

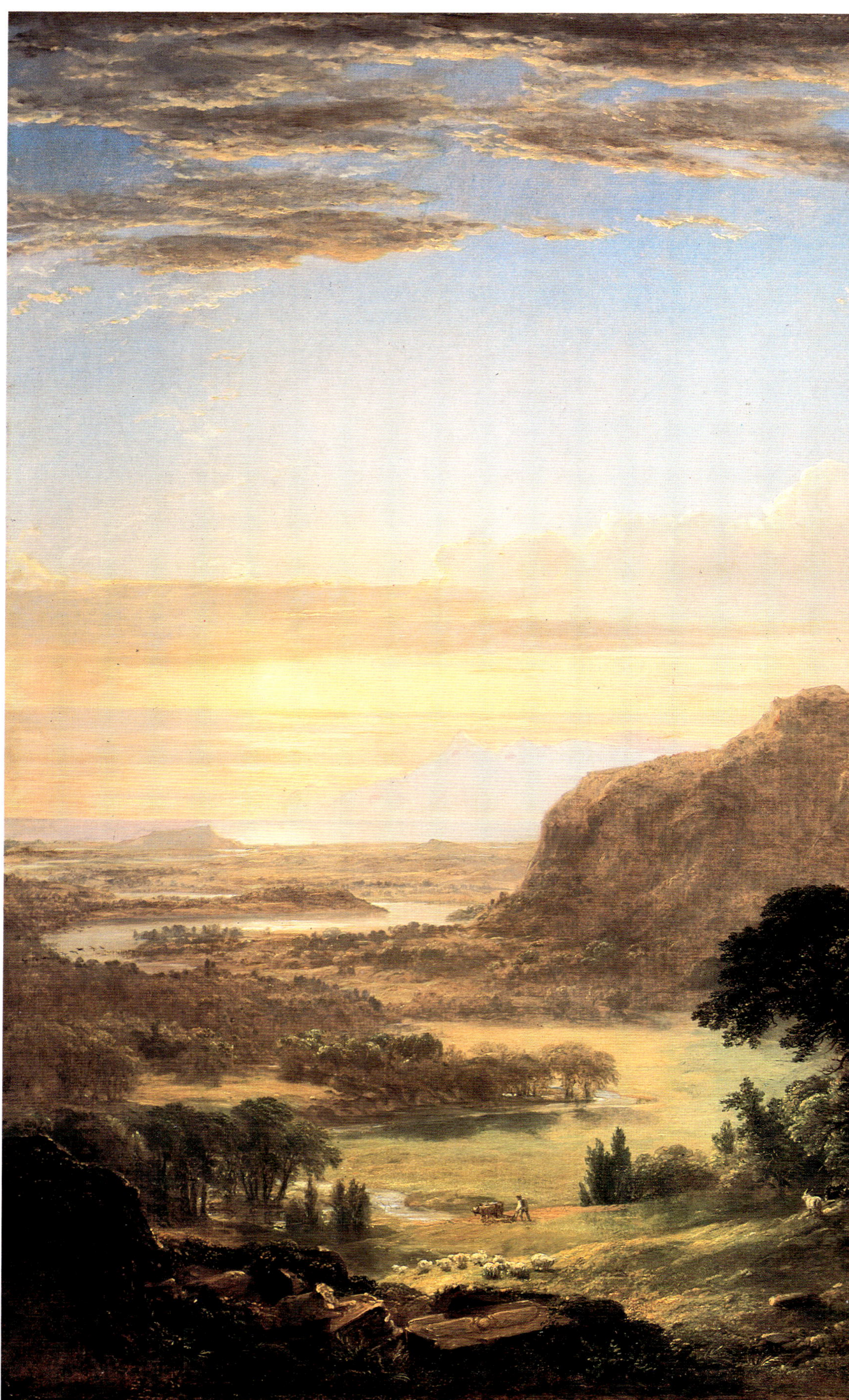

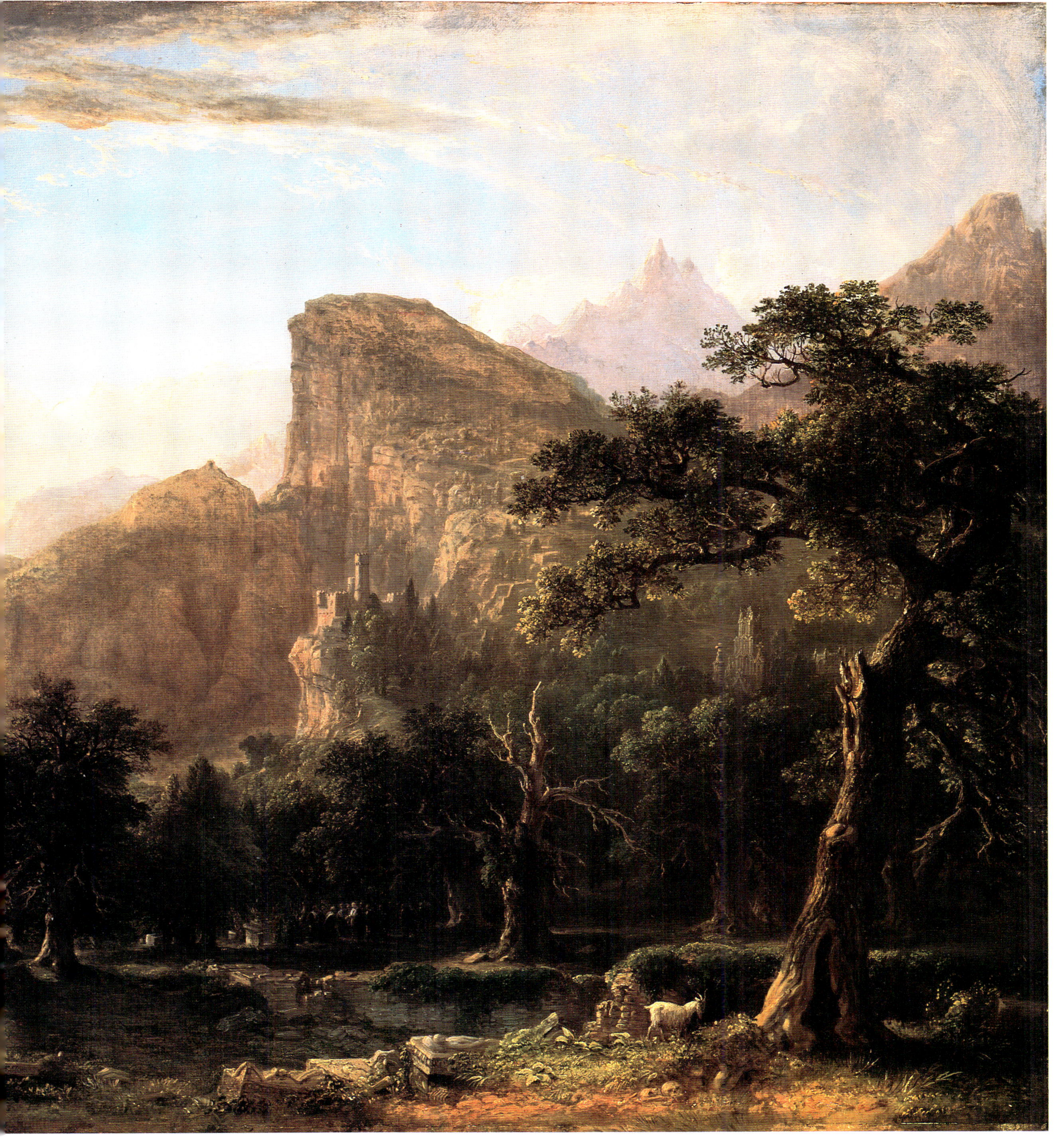

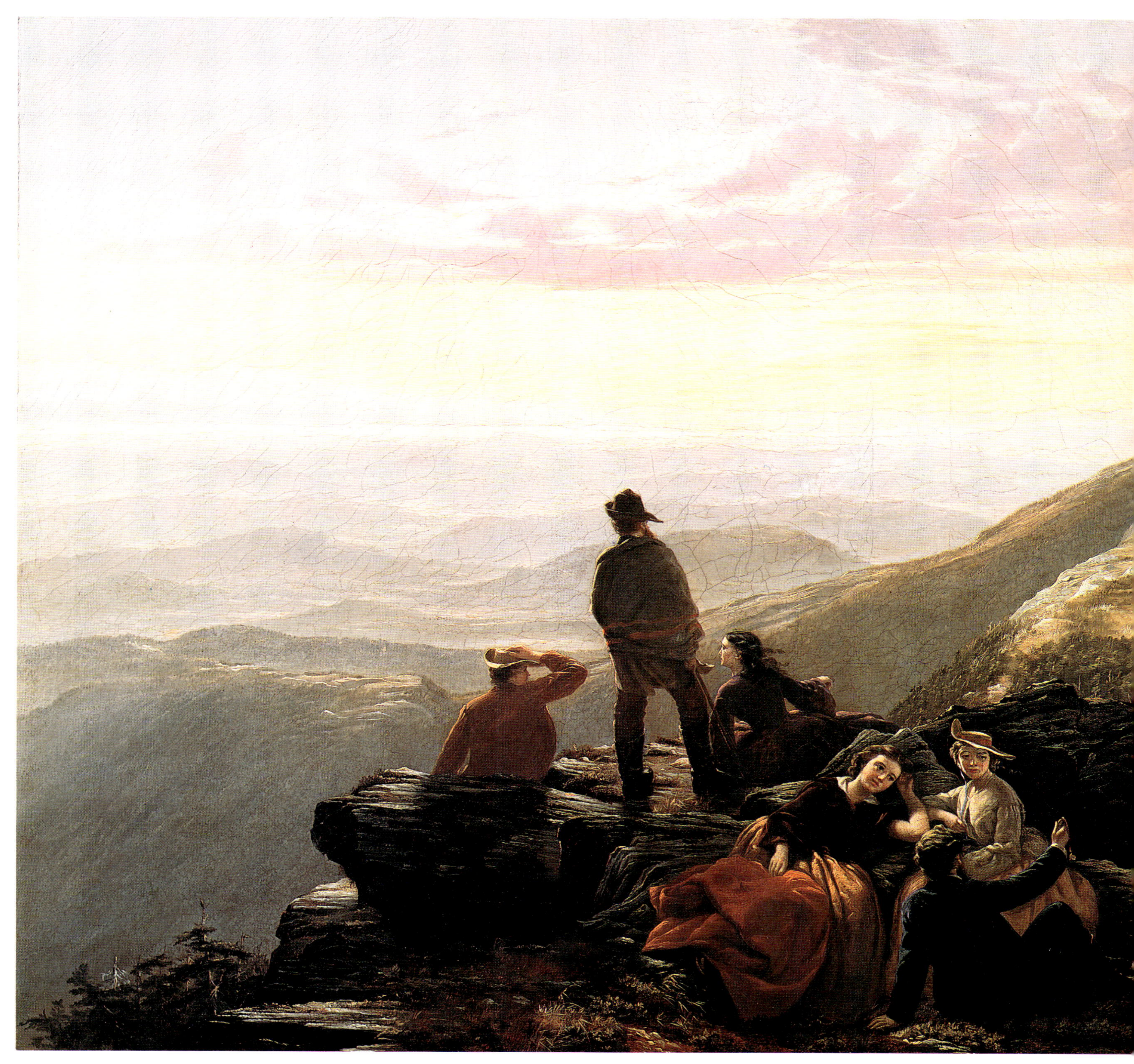

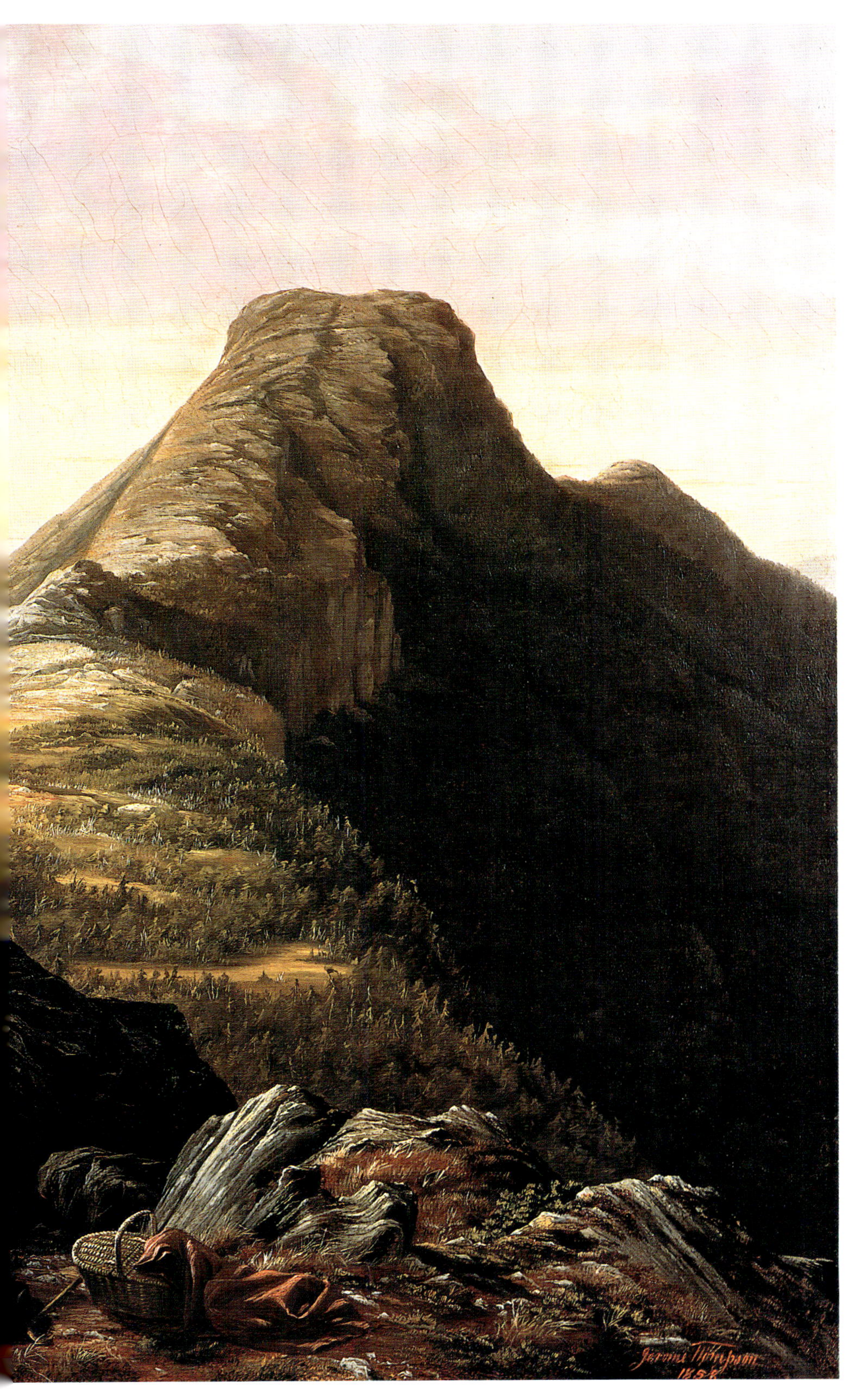

Jerome B. Thompson
1814–1886

The Belated Party on Mansfield Mountain

Oil on canvas, 38 x $63\frac{1}{8}$ in. (96.5 x 160.3 cm.)
1858
Signed and dated at lower right, in red: Jerome Thompson/1858
Rogers Fund, 1969 (69.182)

JEROME THOMPSON, the younger brother of Cephas Giovanni Thompson, started his career as a portrait painter, but about 1850 began to concentrate on combinations of landscapes with figures, creating a kind of genre at which he excelled. He usually worked from studies made on the spot. The theme of several of his outdoor scenes was the picnic, which provided a reason for assembling people in a natural setting. In *The Belated Party* the human element exceeds the setting in importance. Four members of a picnic party seem inclined to linger on the mountain peak, but the man in the foreground holds up his watch, and a young woman stares at it with concern. The have a long descent to make, and darkness has already shrouded the near side of the mountain. Mount Mansfield—Vermont's highest point—and the vast stretch of the Champlain Valley lying to the west of it, are awesome and impersonal in the setting sun.

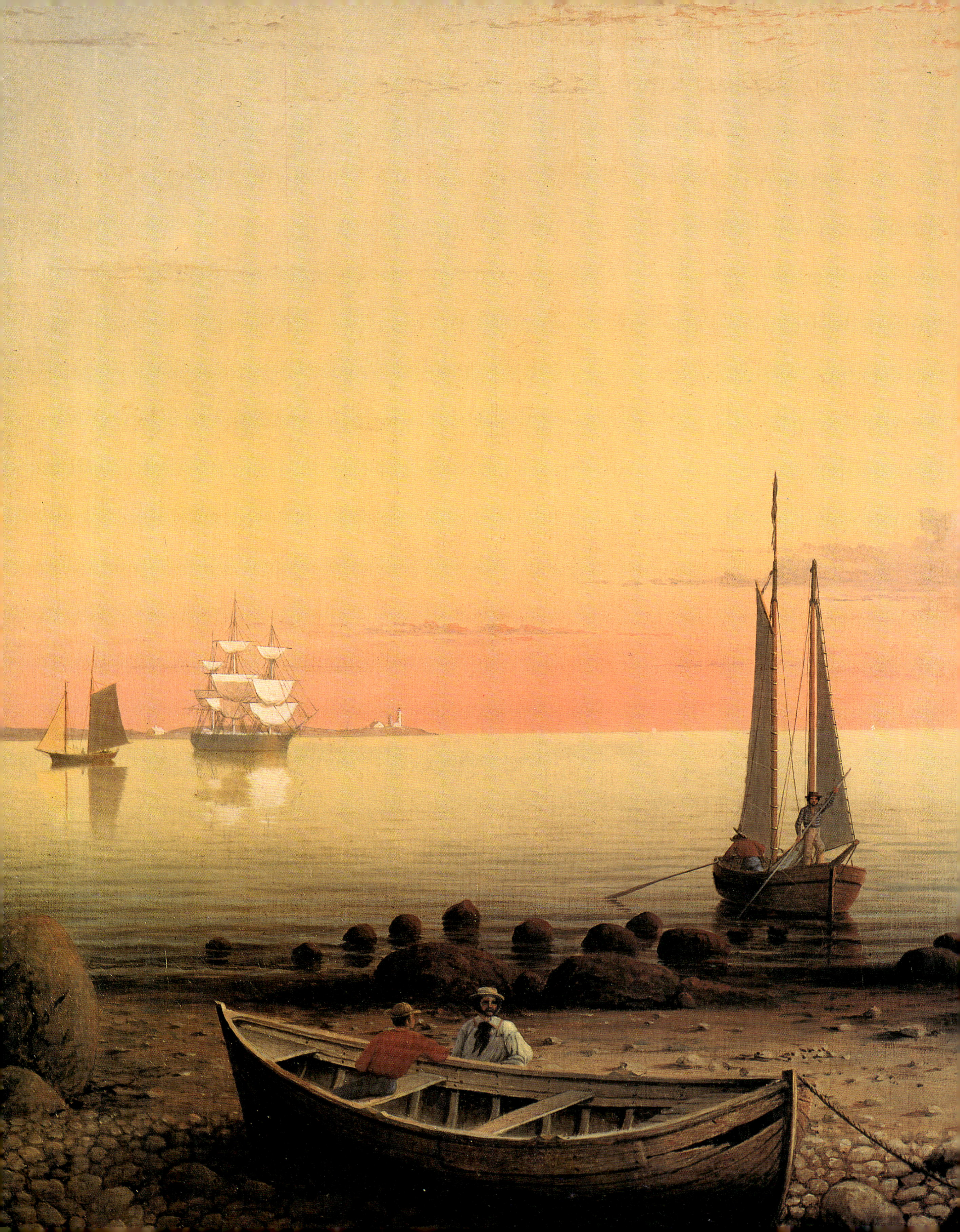

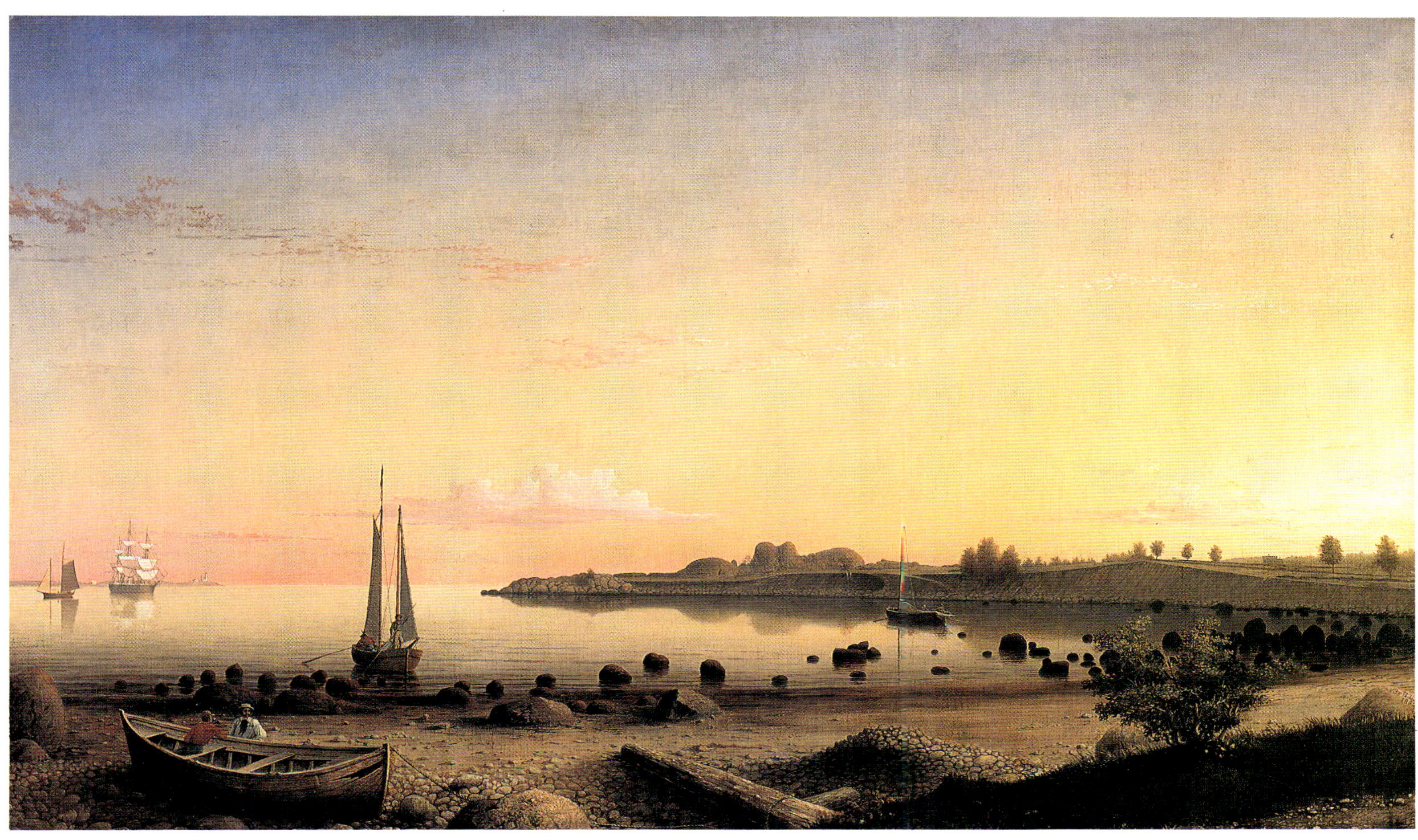

Fitz Hugh Lane
1804–1865

Stage Fort Across Gloucester Harbor

Oil on canvas, 38 x 60 in.
(96.5 x 152.4 cm.)
1862
Signed and dated at lower right:
Fitz H. Lane/1862
Purchase, Rogers and Fletcher Funds, Erving and Joyce Wolf Fund, Raymond J. Horowitz Gift, Bequest of Richard De Wolfe Brixey, by exchange, and John Osgood and Elizabeth Amis Cameron Blanchard Memorial Fund, 1978 (1978.203)

THIS LANDSCAPE, like all of Fitz Hugh Lane's best works, endows the truthful rendering of a specific site with a mood so magically compelling that the picture seems the product of pure imagination. His means are unearthly light and the hush that sometimes lies on water and seashore. The sails are slack, and the sharp clarity of the reflections proclaims the utter stillness of the air. This view was painted three years before the artist's death. Lane was a shy and lonely paralytic, but it was only in the fine works of his last years that he allowed his earlier triumphant optimism to give way to an expression of gentle sorrow.

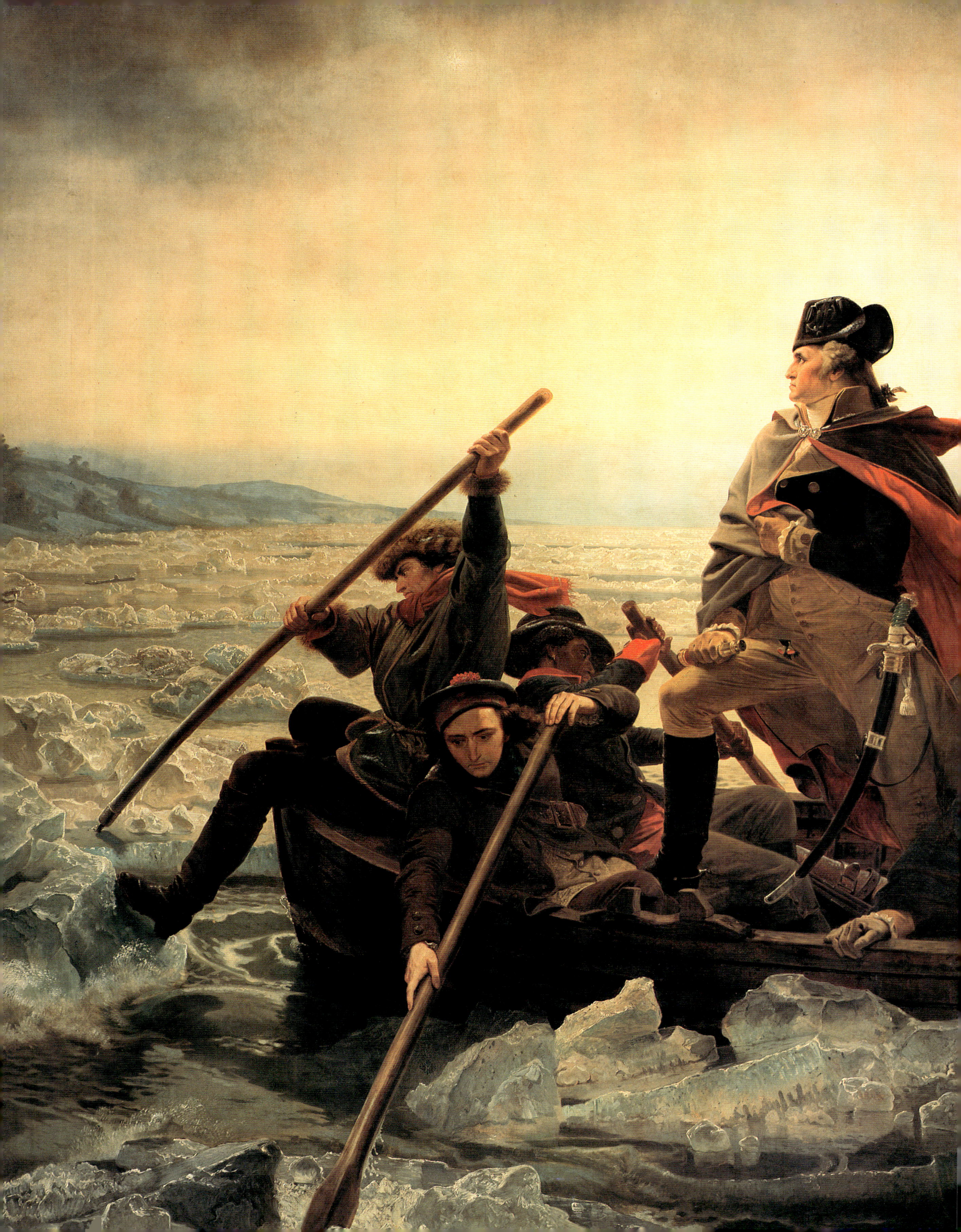

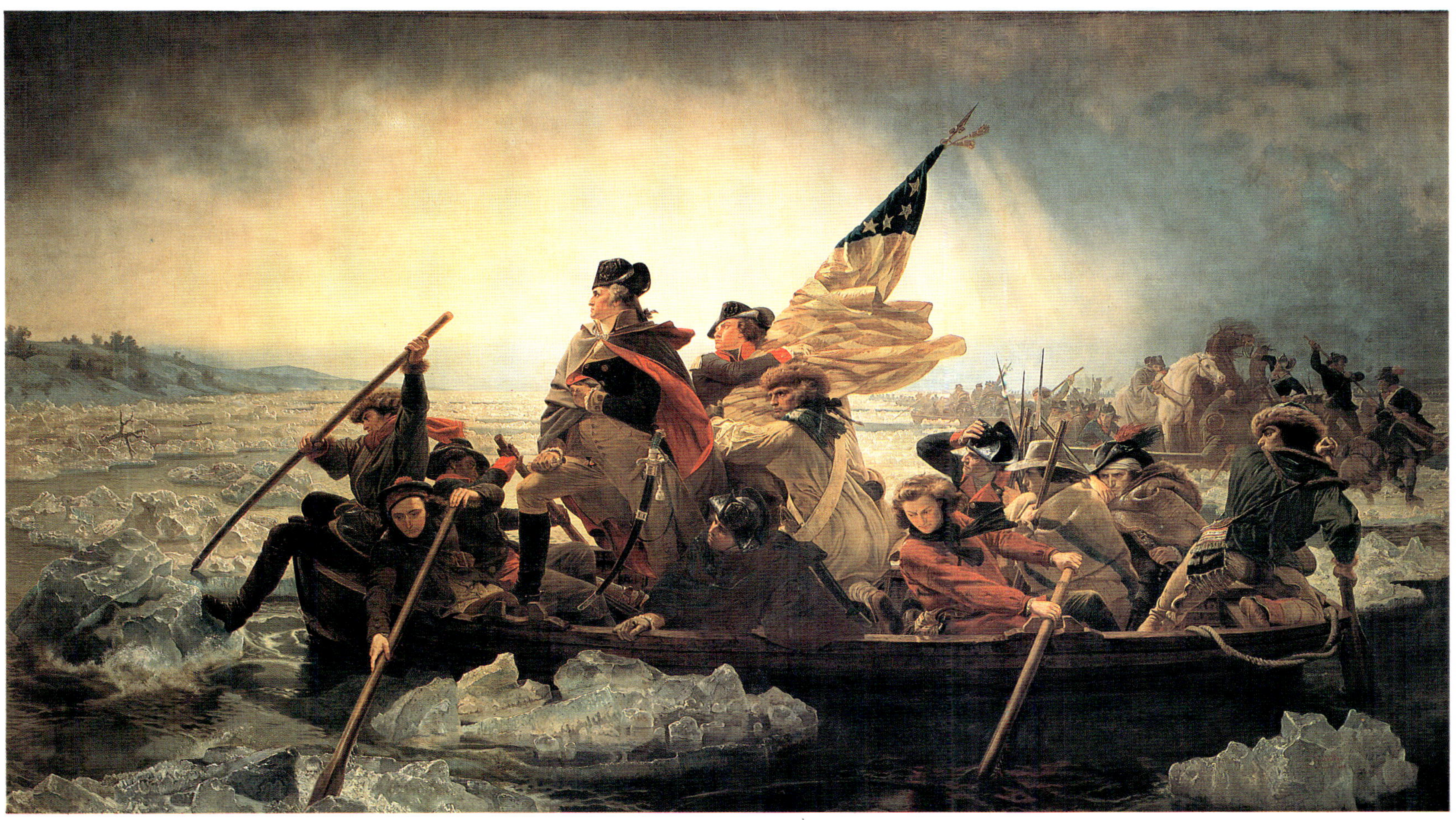

Emanuel Leutze
1816–1868

Washington Crossing the Delaware

Oil on canvas
149 x 255 in. (378.5 x 647.7 cm.)
1851
Signed, inscribed, and dated at lower right: E. Leutze/Düsseldorf 1851; dated at lower left: 16.4.51.
Gift of John S. Kennedy, 1897 (97.34)

GEORGE WASHINGTON's crossing of the Delaware on Christmas night in 1776 to make a surprise attack on the recuperating Hessian revelers is one of the best-known and loved events of American history. Many people are surprised to learn that this most American of pictures was painted in Düsseldorf by an artist who was born in Germany and spent half his life in Europe. Brought to this country at the age of nine, Emanuel Leutze studied art in Philadelphia, where his early portraits were so successful that he was provided with funds and encouraged to study abroad. His first trip lasted ten years, including wide travel and the establishment of his own studio in Düsseldorf. The Museum's picture, completed and brought to America by the painter in 1851, is the second, slightly larger version of one that was seriously damaged by a fire in his studio and that was ultimately destroyed in a bombing raid in 1942. Full of historical inaccuracies, but infused with patriotic fervor and nobility, especially in the lofty calm of Washington's profile, the Metropolitan's picture has become a national monument.

Martin Johnson Heade
1819–1904

The Coming Storm

Oil on canvas
28 x 44 in. (71.1 x 111 cm.)
1859
Signed and dated at lower left:
M. J. Heade/1859
Gift of Erving Wolf Foundation and Mr. and Mrs. Erving Wolfe, 1975 (1975.160)

HIGHLY APPRECIATED by modern critics, in his own time Martin Johnson Heade was not a popular painter. His startling originality gave his still lifes and landscapes a quality of strangeness that shocked the conventional eye. In his early twenties he made his first trip to Europe, the beginning of a lifetime of restless travel. His numerous journeys took him three times to Brazil, which provided him with rich, exotic material. He made careful studies of hummingbirds and combined these with orchids in pictures of unusual intensity. In Florida, during the last decades of his life, he painted striking representations of single flowers—roses and magnolia blossoms—enlarged, with the clear outlines of fine botanical illustrations and pure, singing color. The Museum's view of land and sea hushed before an ominous approaching storm is the first of a group of similar scenes that suggest the influence of Fitz Hugh Lane. Both Lane and Heade are painters whose eerie views of water and sky work their moody spells with an exciting suffusion of enveloping light.

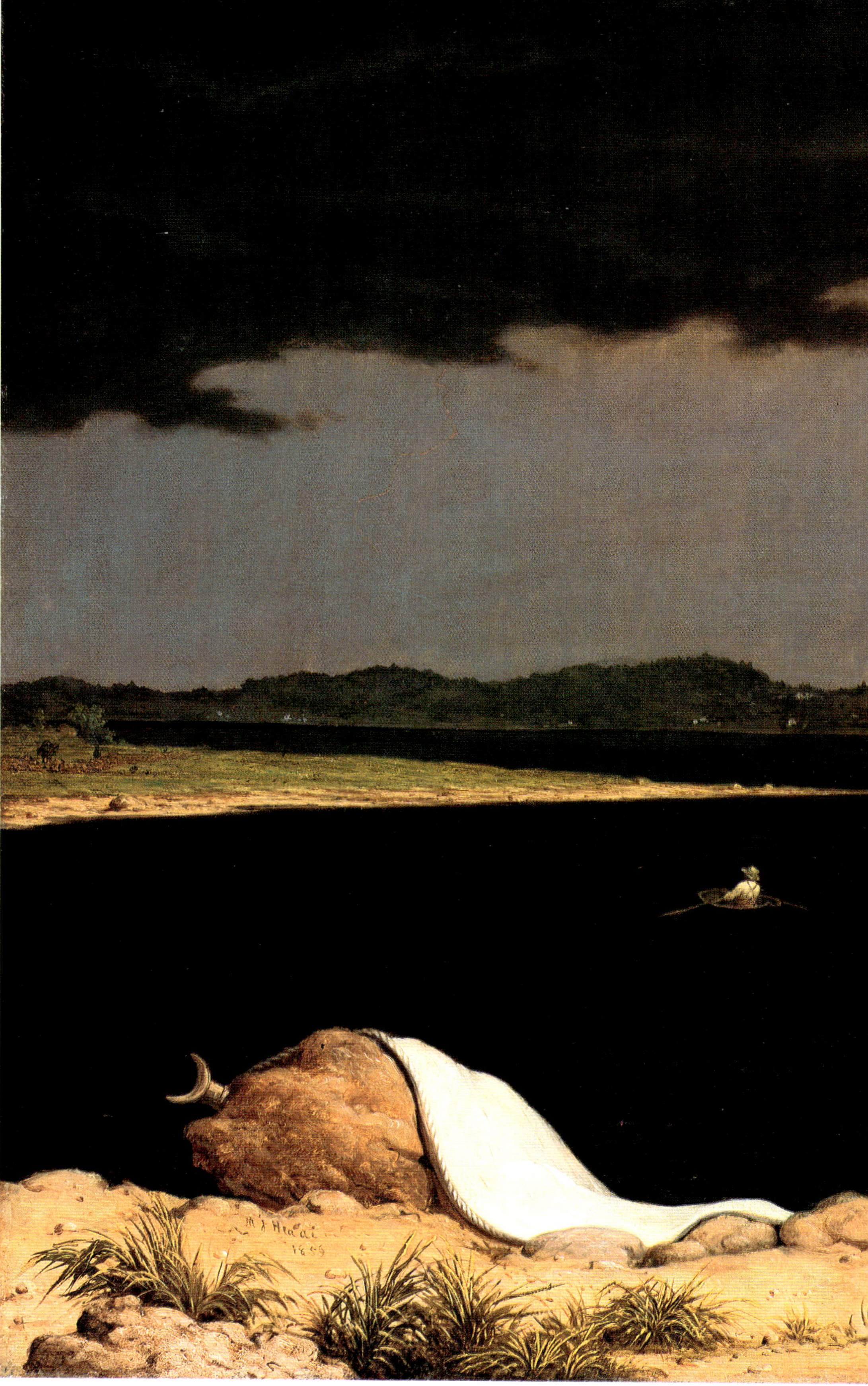

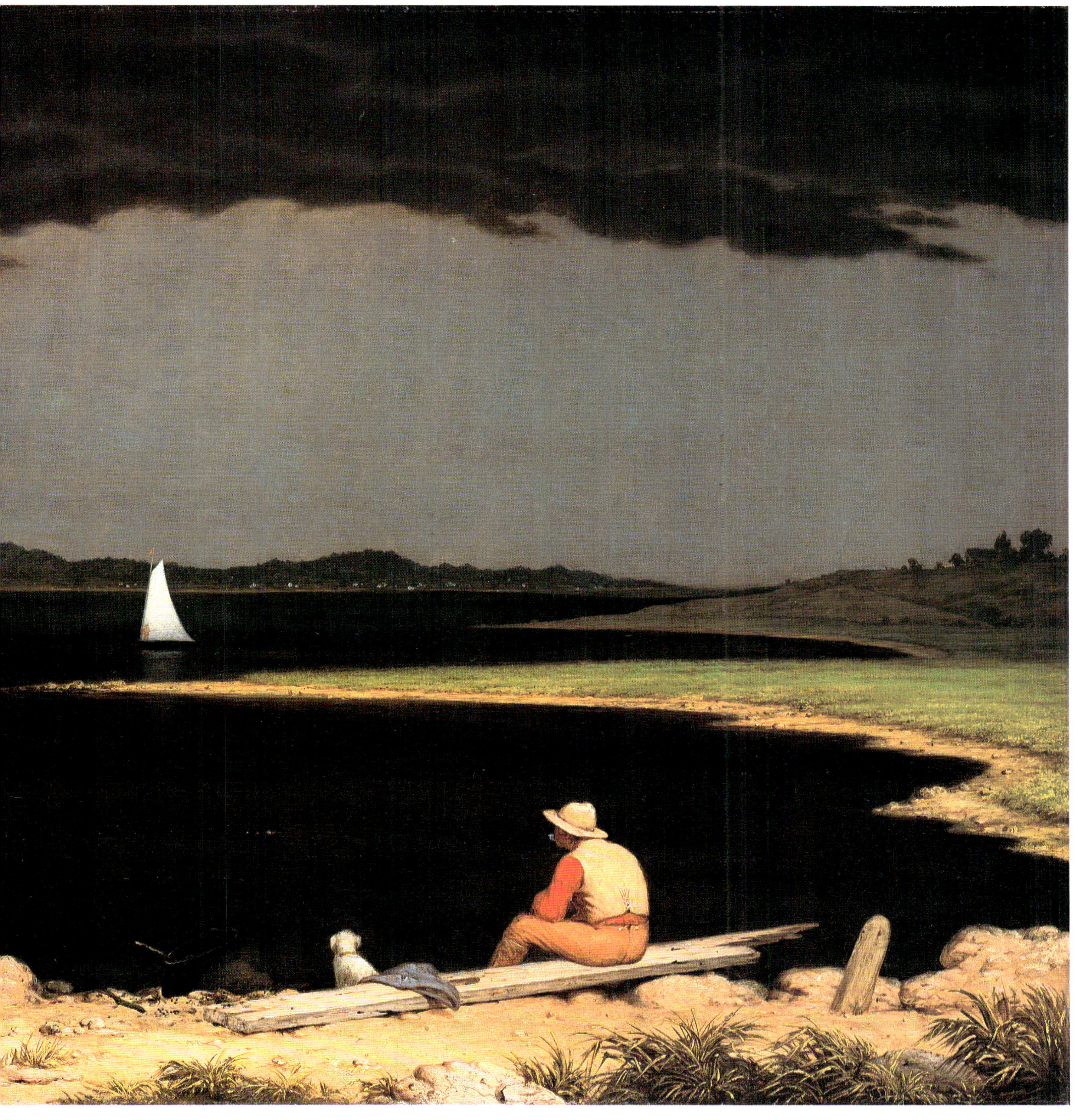

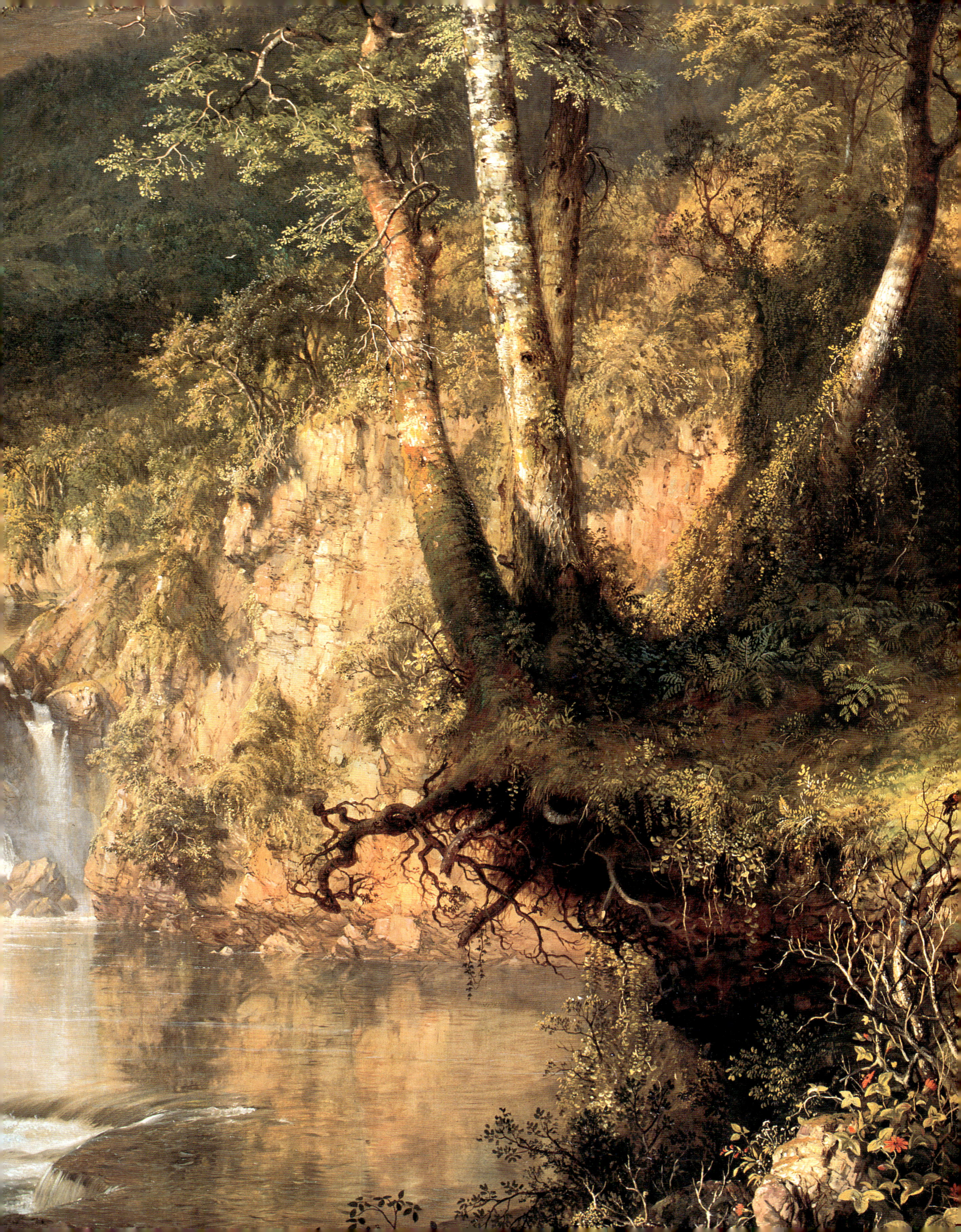

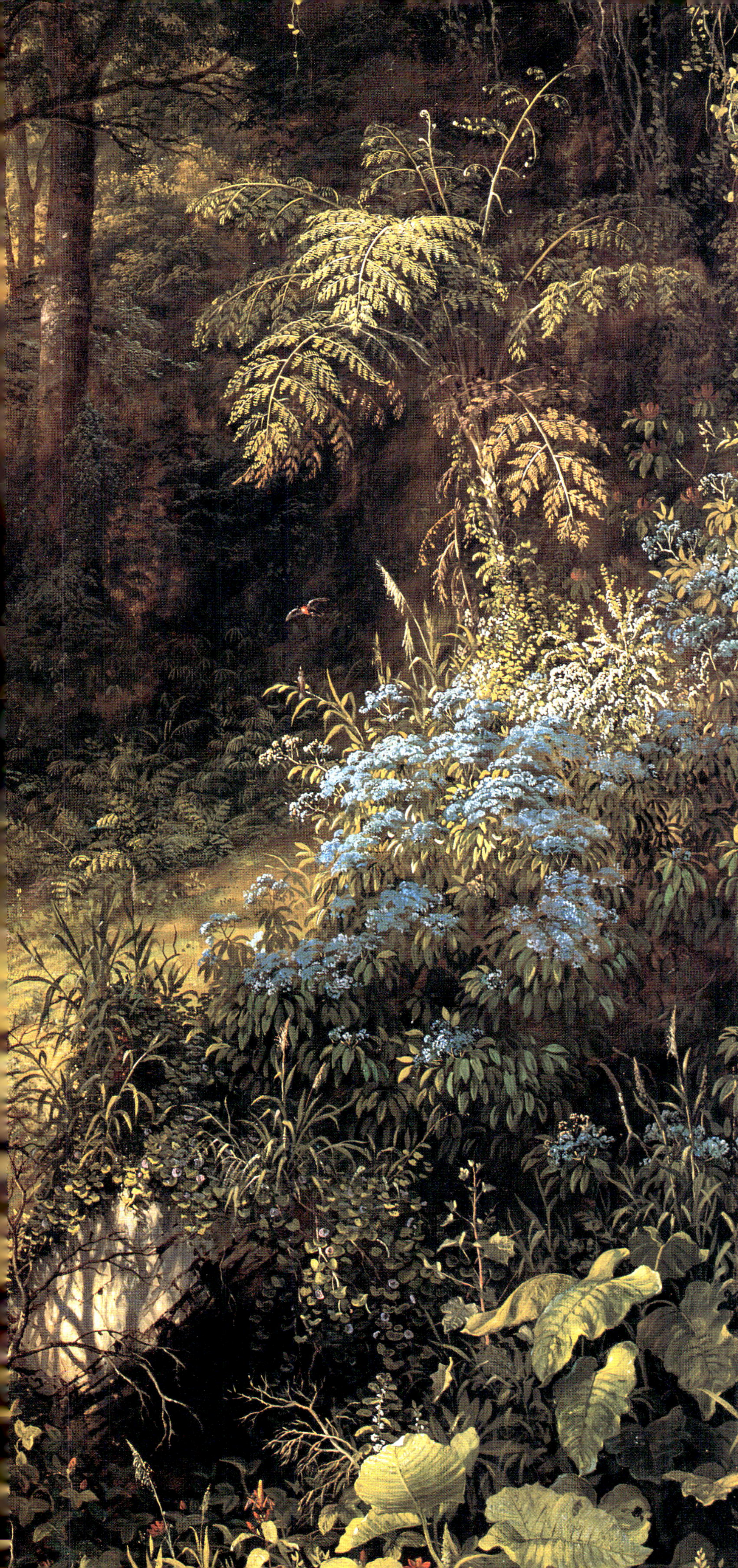

Frederic Edwin Church
1826–1900

Heart of the Andes

Oil on canvas
66⅛ x 119¼ in. (168 x 302.9 cm.)
1859
Signed and dated on tree at lower left:
1859/ F. E. Church
Bequest of Margaret E. Dows, 1909 (09.95)

Frederic Edwin Church studied for two years with Thomas Cole, and at the beginning of his career painted large romantic landscapes of the Hudson River and New England scenery rather like Cole's. In 1853, however, inspired by the writings of the German naturalist Alexander von Humboldt, who had explored South America, he went on a trip to Colombia and Ecuador; he went again in 1857 to make a more extensive study of the mountains of Ecuador, especially in the region around Mount Chimborazo. Church's diary reveals that even while he was tirelessly sketching details with the conscientious fervor and exactitude enjoined by Ruskin, the final composition of *Heart of the Andes* was taking form in his mind. Two years later this picture was put on public exhibition in a dramatically lit studio in New York, where it drew thousands of people who paid twenty-five cents apiece to view the canvas and examine its separate areas through a magnifying glass. The roots and vines of the immediate foreground are painted in explicit detail, but the far terrain, rendered with sweeping breadth, enforces an effect of grandeur and sublimity.

Heart of the Andes (detail)

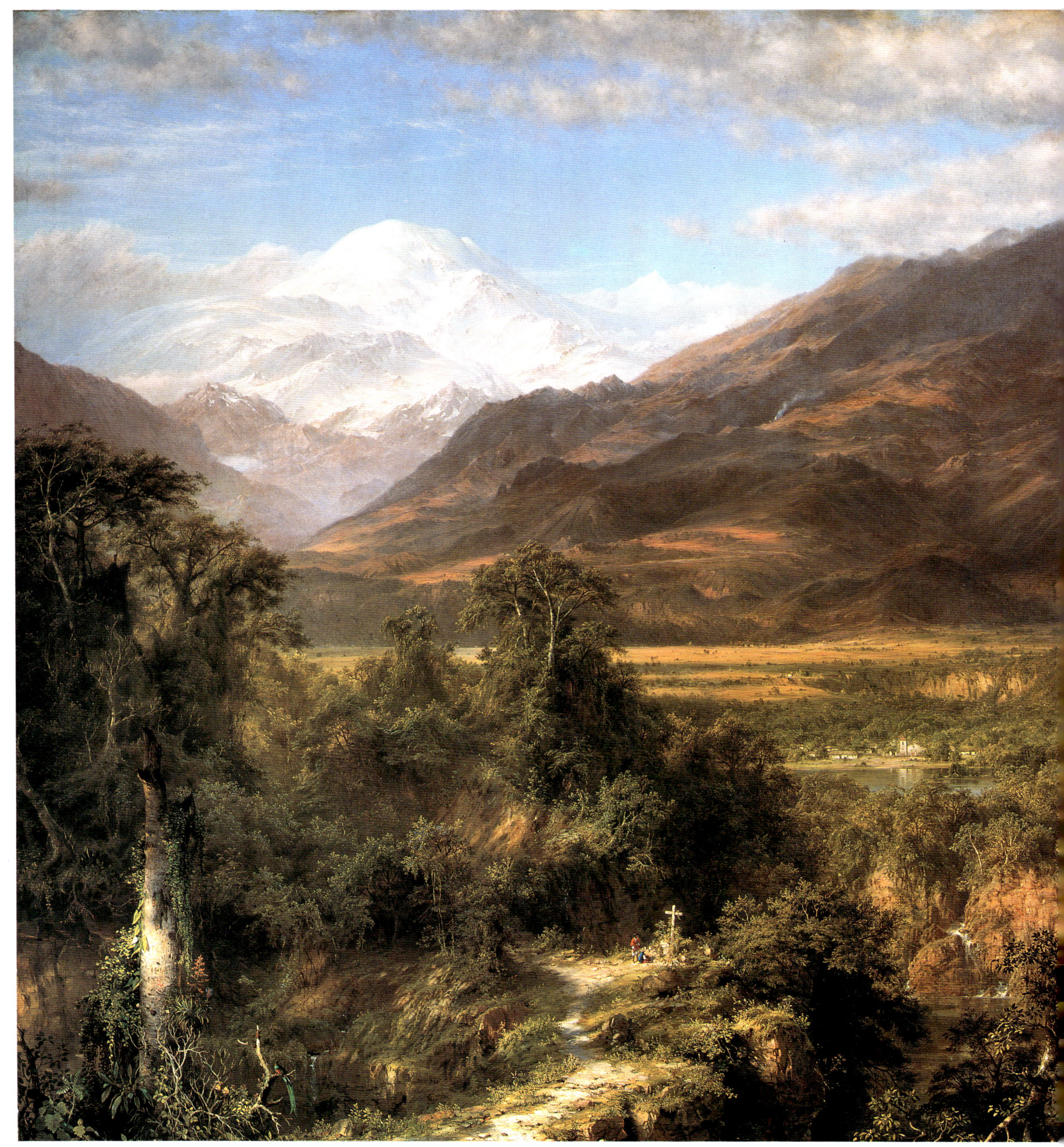

Frederic Edwin Church: *Heart of the Andes*

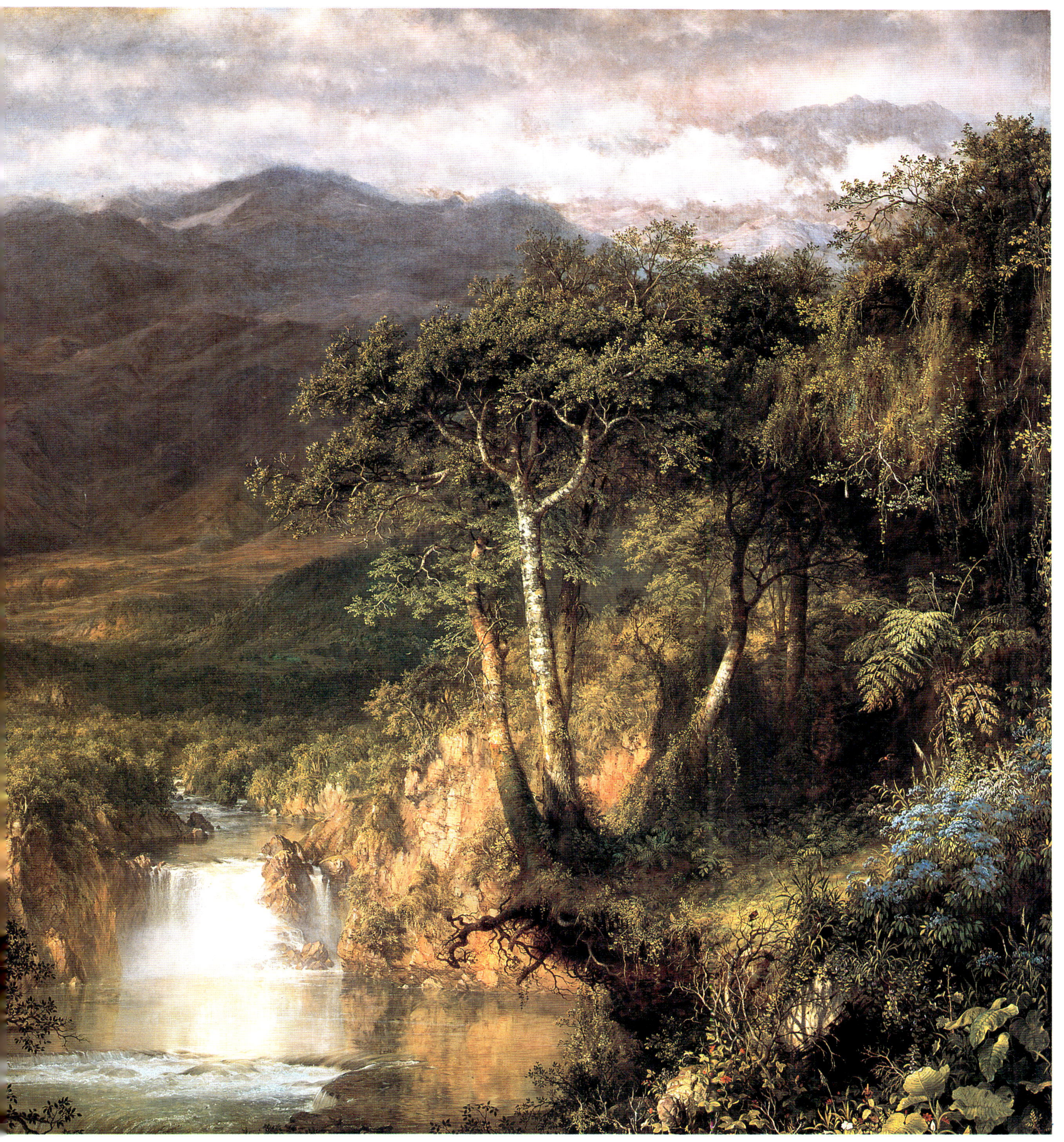

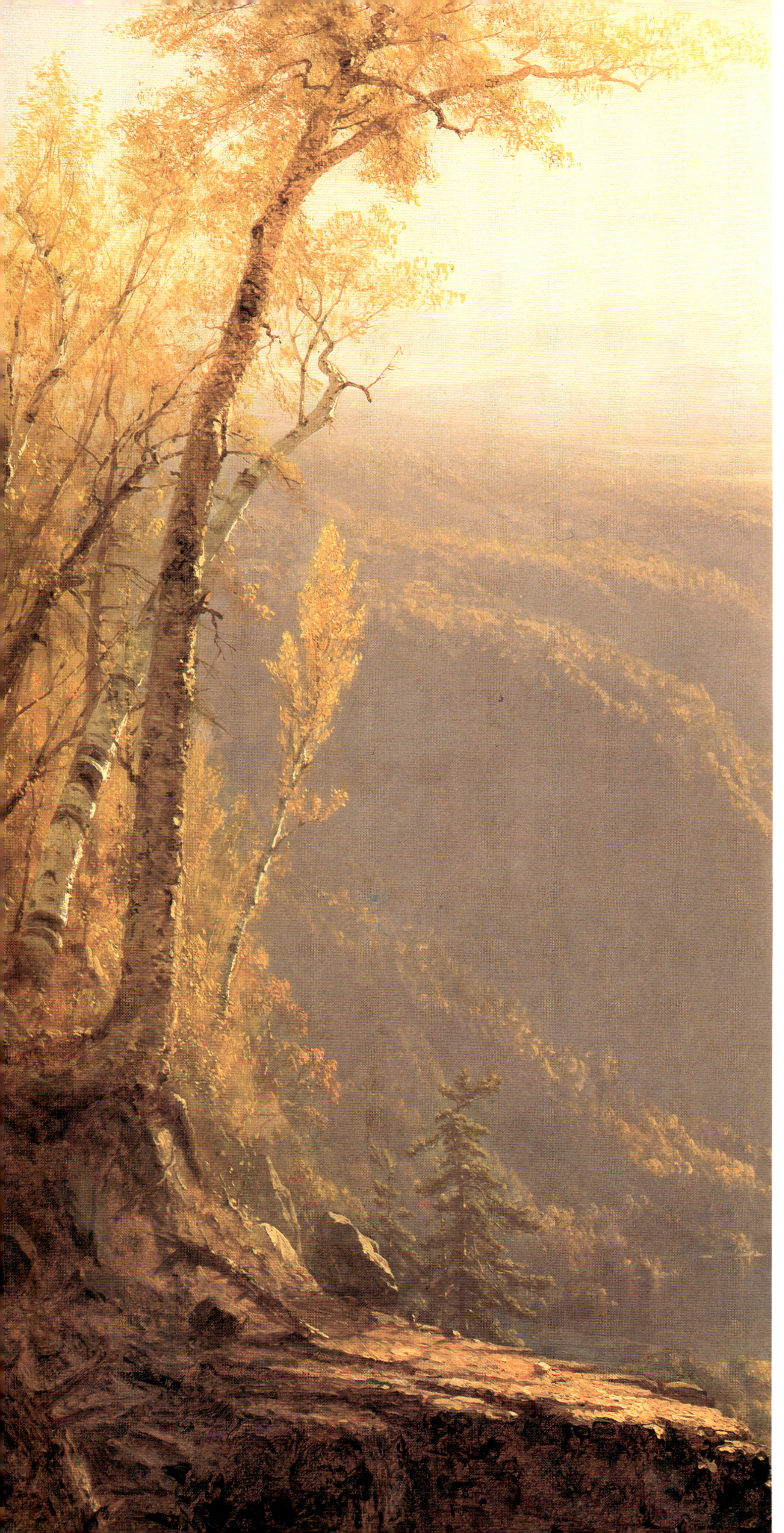

Sanford Robinson Gifford
1823–1880

Kauterskill Clove

Oil on canvas
48 x 39⅞ in. (121.9 x 101.3 cm.)
1862
Signed and dated at lower left:
S. R. Gifford/1862
Bequest of Maria DeWitt Jesup, from the collection of her husband, Morris K. Jesup, 1914 (15.30.62)

THE CATSKILL MOUNTAINS, especially the area around the deep ravine known as the Kauterskill Clove, about twelve miles west of the village of Catskill, were a favorite haunt of Sanford Gifford during most of his career. He knew the region intimately and over the years amassed quantities of sketches. From these he constructed, probably in the studio, this poetic, moody landscape. It is a view looking west to Haines Falls, about two miles away. The picture does not, however, completely record any particular spot, but is a composite of elements arranged at will to give a special effect of light and atmosphere.

Gifford was immensely popular in his day. After his death he was honored by the Museum with a large memorial exhibition that included 160 of his paintings.

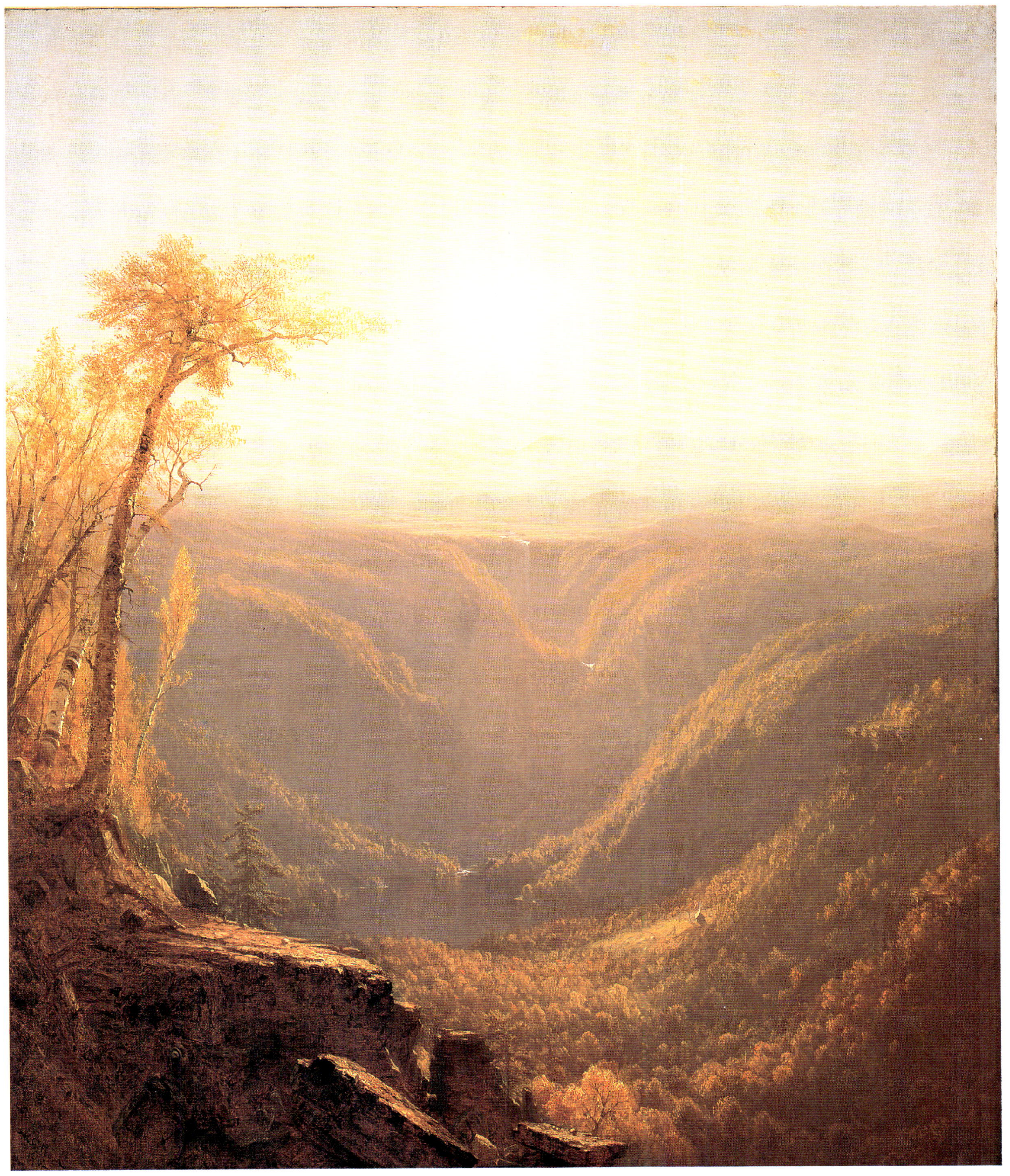

Albert Bierstadt
1830–1902

The Rocky Mountains, Lander's Peak

Oil on canvas
73½ x 120¾ in. (186.7 x 306.7 cm.)
1863
Signed and dated at lower right:
ABierstadt/1863
Rogers Fund, 1907 (07.123)

In his early twenties, Albert Bierstadt, who had been brought to America from Germany as an infant, went to Düsseldorf, a city near his birthplace, to study painting. There he admired the works of German landscape painters and traveled through the countryside of Europe, making numerous studies on the spot that he later developed into huge finished pictures in the studio. Returning to America in 1857, he made the first of three important trips to the American West, where the breathtaking majesty of the highest peaks reminded him of the Bernese Alps. He also felt a keen interest in the American Indian, sketching individuals and encampments and collecting various objects relating to Indian culture. In this picture, Bierstadt shows a camp of the Shoshone tribe beside the Green River, which flows at the base of the Wind River Mountains in Wyoming. The Lander's Peak of the title is now called Fremont Peak. The artist has combined here a very detailed foreground with small figures, a transitional middle ground with a waterfall, and a distant background view of the cold, shimmering snow-covered Rockies.

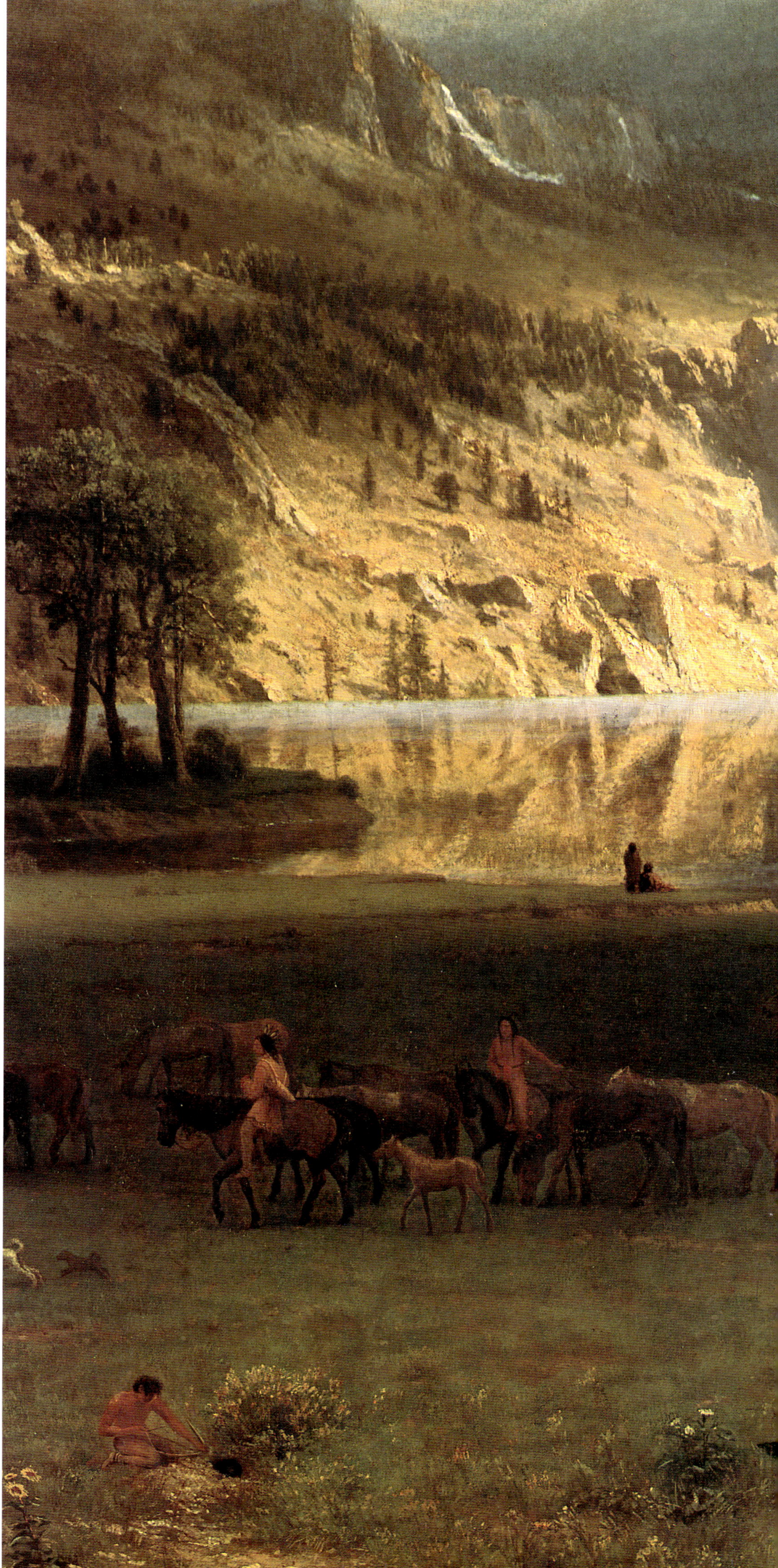

The Rocky Mountains, Lander's Peak (detail)

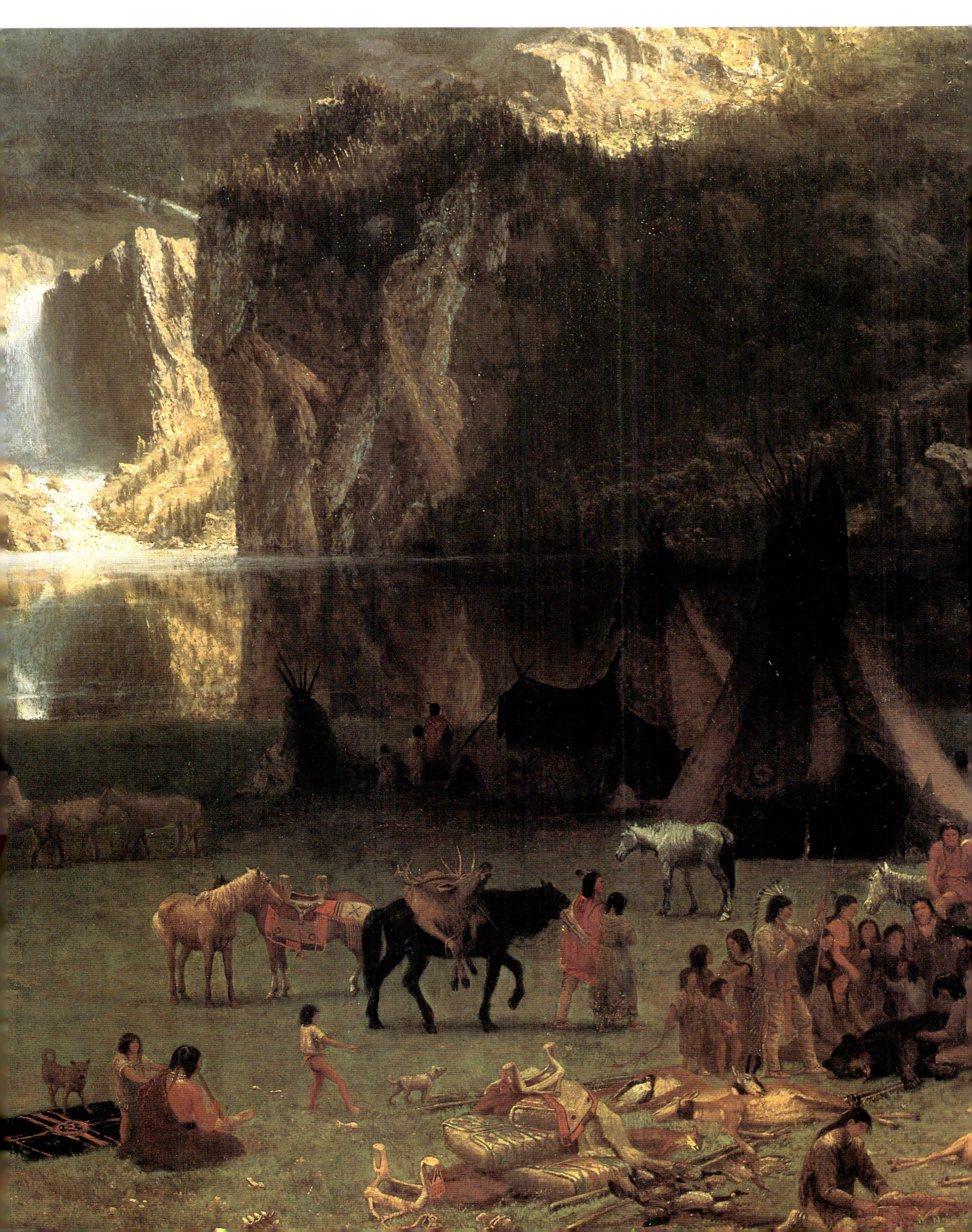

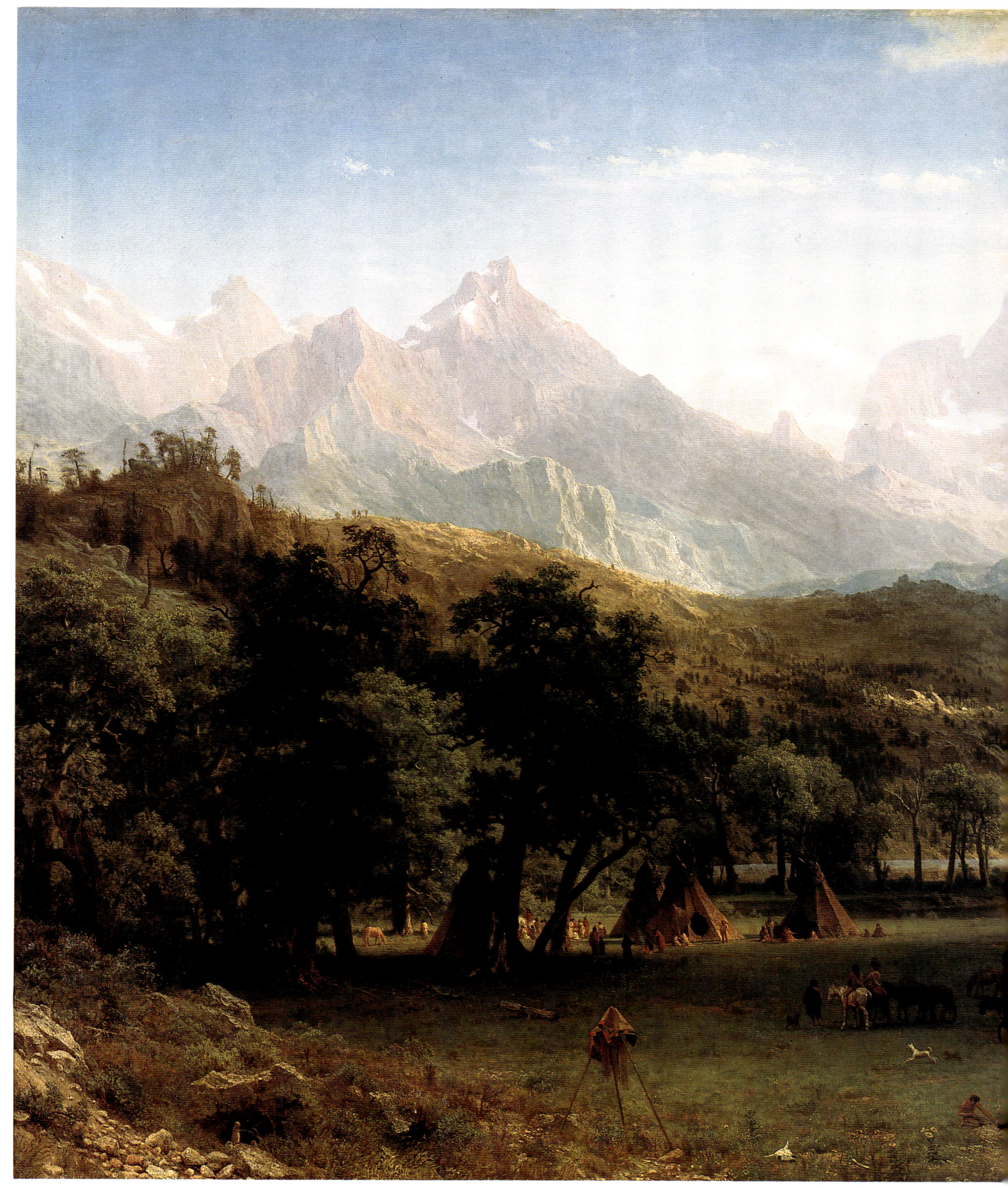

Albert Bierstadt: *The Rocky Mountains, Lander's Peak*

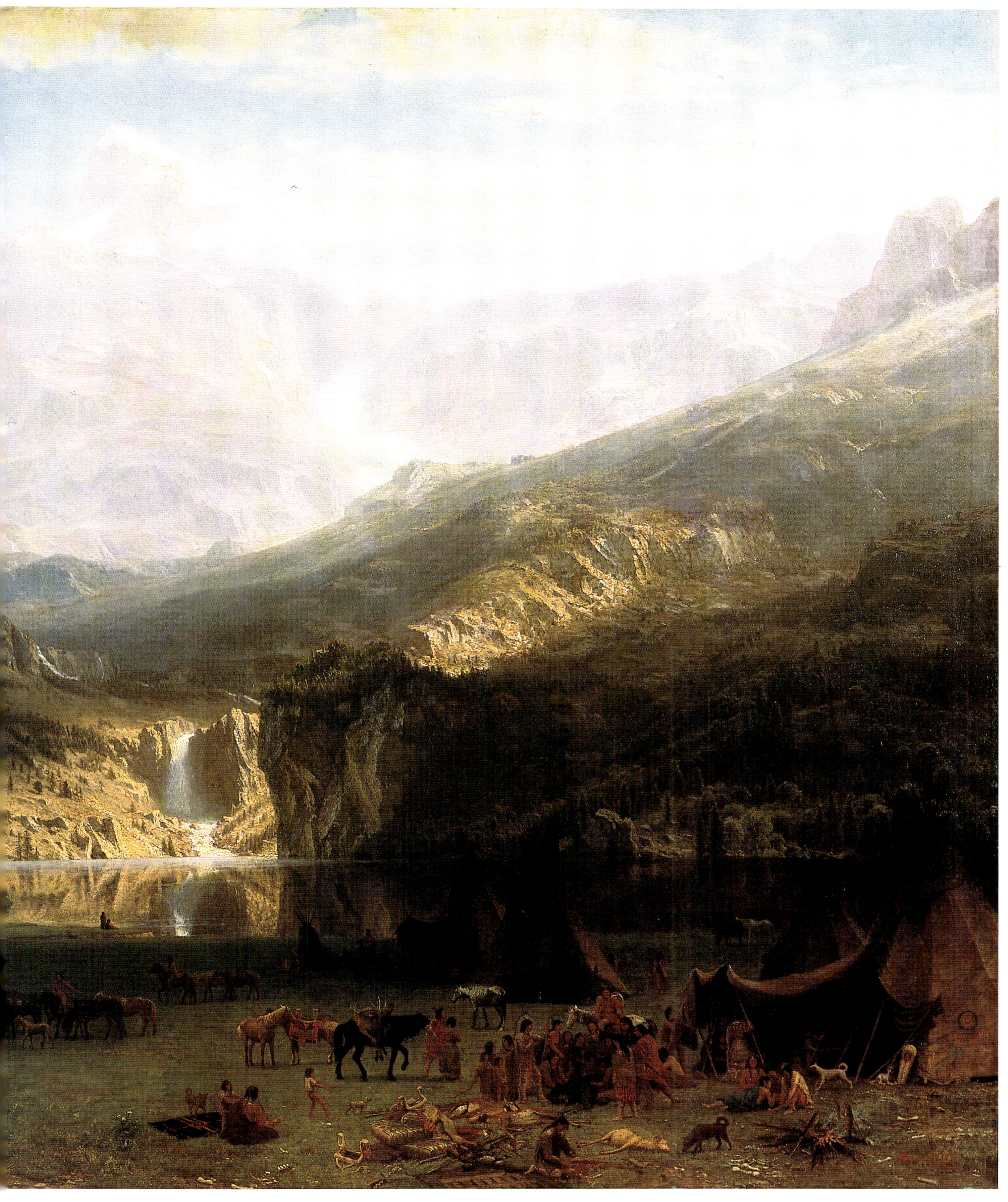

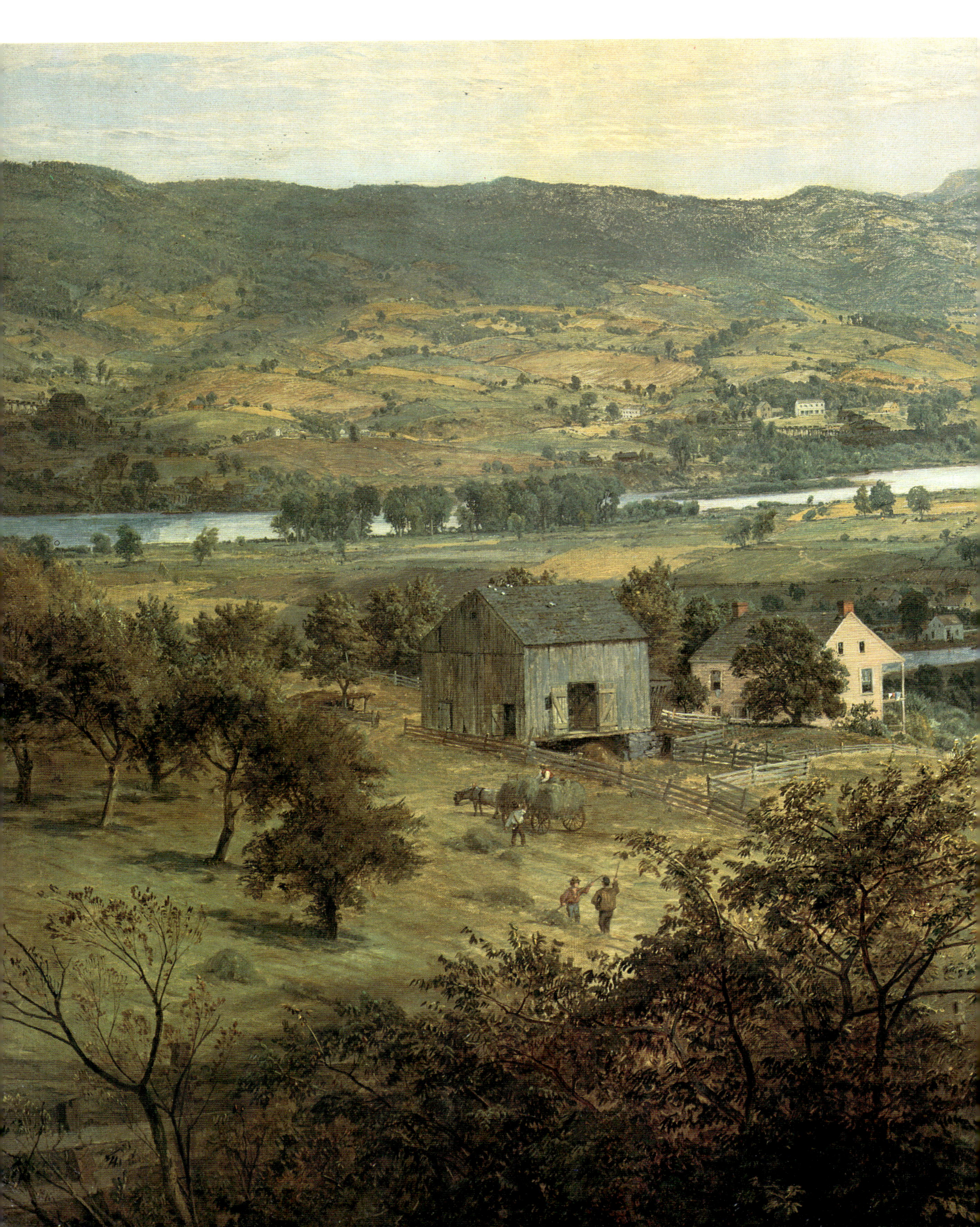

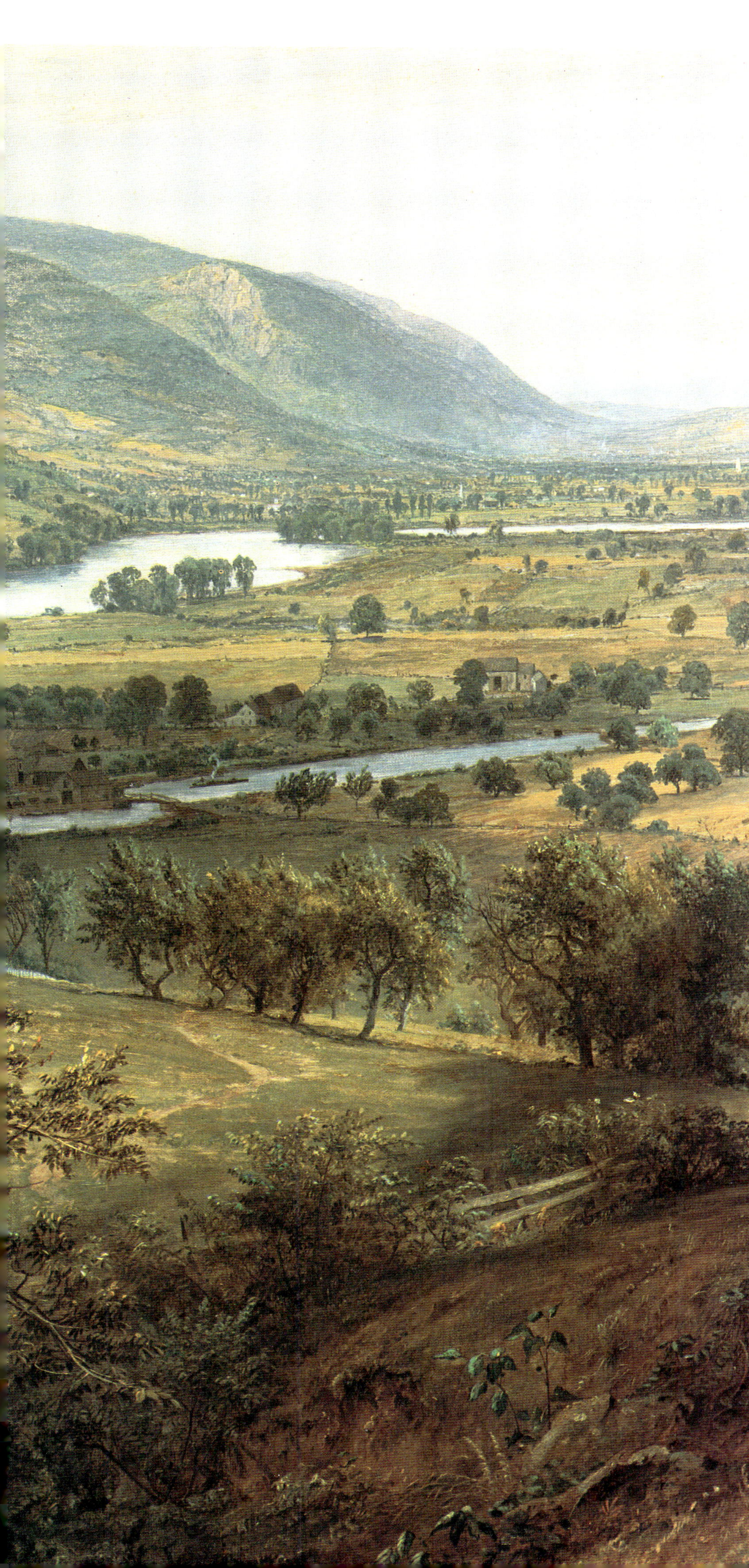

Jasper Francis Cropsey
1823–1900

The Valley of Wyoming

Oil on canvas
48½ x 84 in. (123.2 x 213.4 cm.)
1865
Signed and dated at lower right:
J. F. Cropsey/1865–
Gift of Mrs. John C. Newington, 1966 (66.113)

THE NAME WYOMING is a corruption of an Indian word meaning "on the great plains," and the Wyoming Valley—a picturesquely varied stretch along the banks of the Susquehanna River in Pennsylvania —was given this name long before the state of Wyoming in the American West came into being. Jasper Francis Cropsey was commissioned to paint this picture in 1864 by a wealthy patron who had been born and raised in the area. The valley, celebrated for its history and for its associations in literature and art, was devastated by Indians in the eighteenth century. The English poet Thomas Campbell wrote a long poem about its beauties, lines from which are inscribed on the frame. Cropsey's great panorama is replete with minute detail. His preparatory oil sketch is also in the Museum's collection.

The Valley of Wyoming (detail)

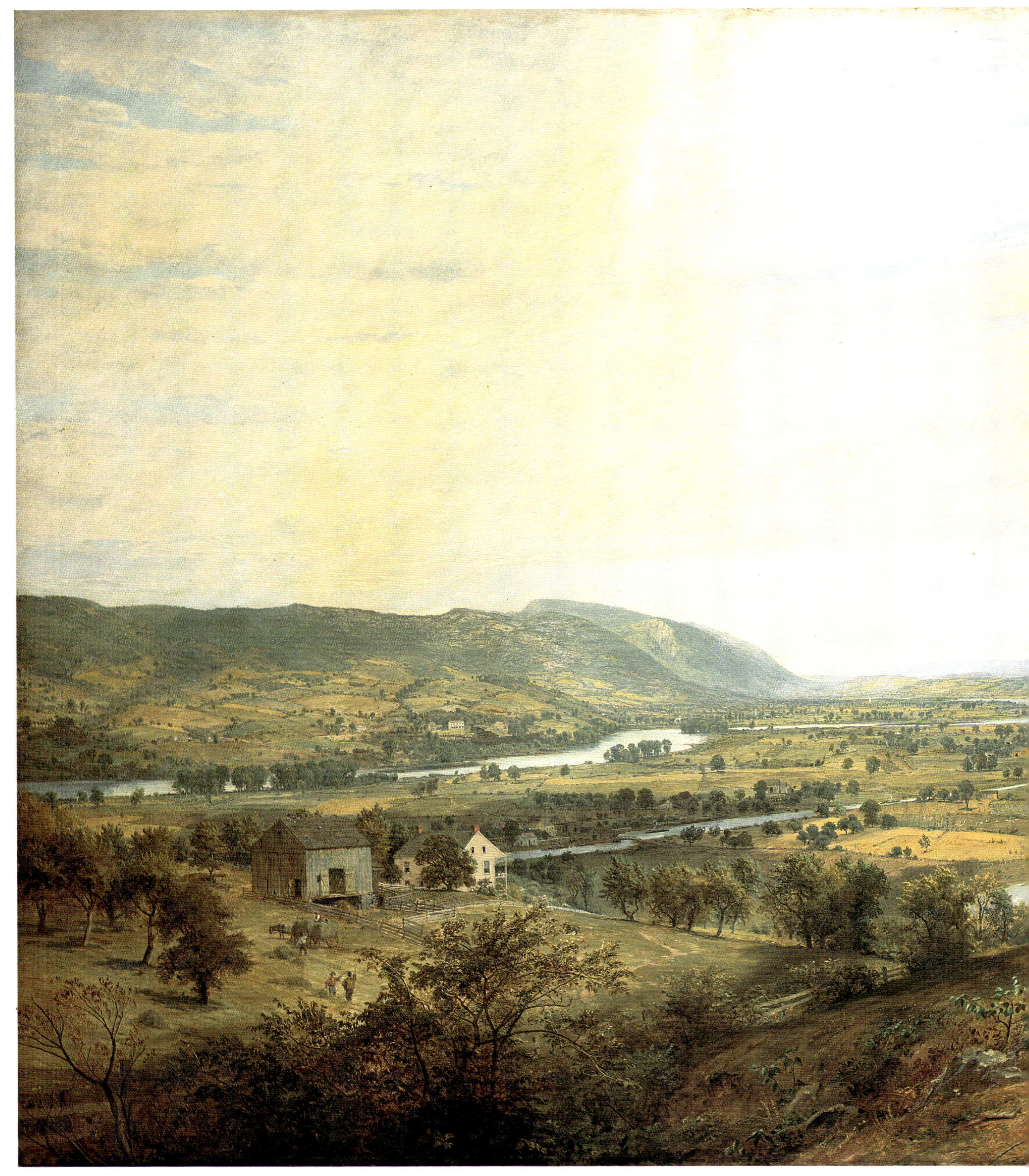

Jasper Francis Cropsey: *The Valley of Wyoming*

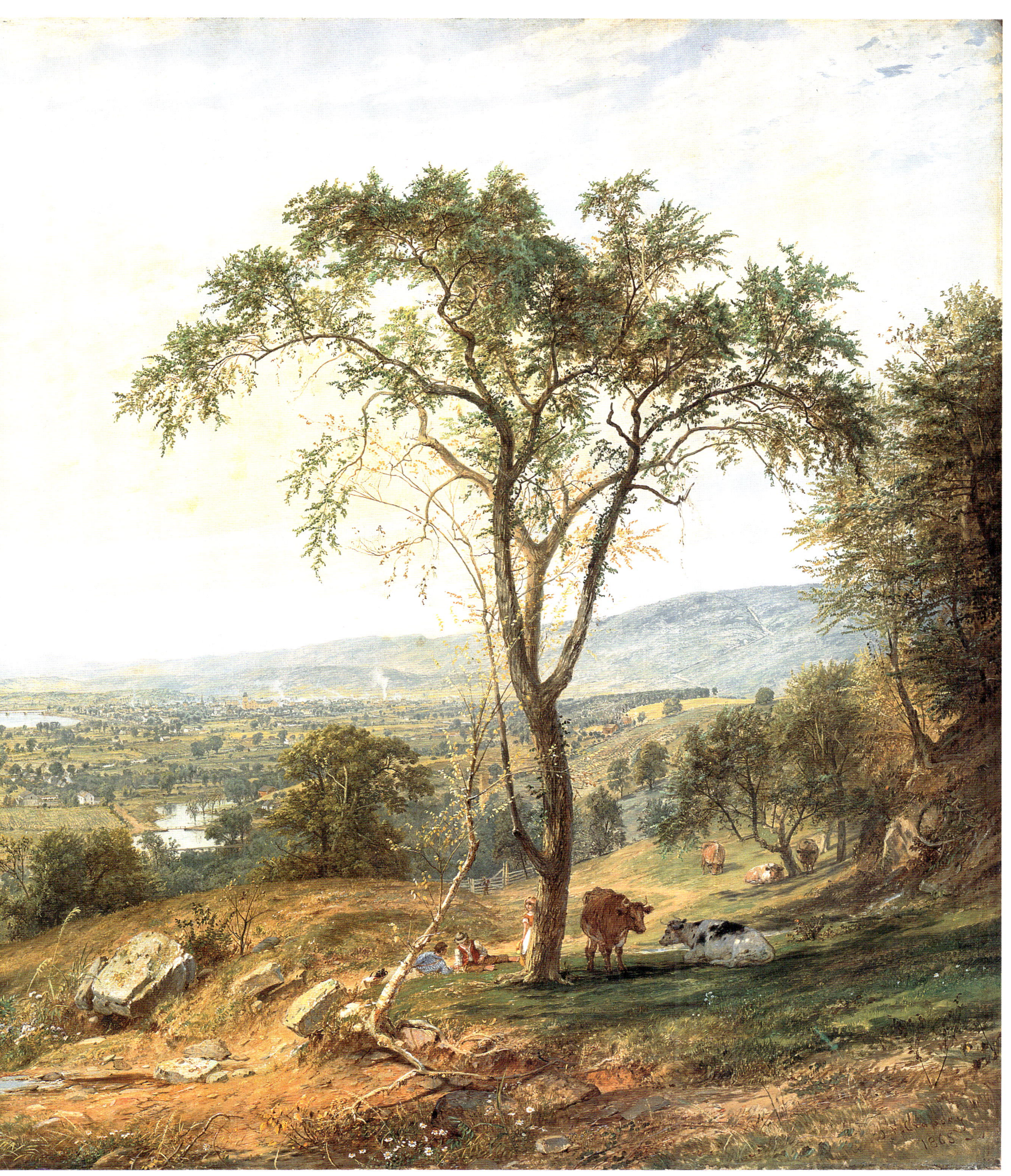

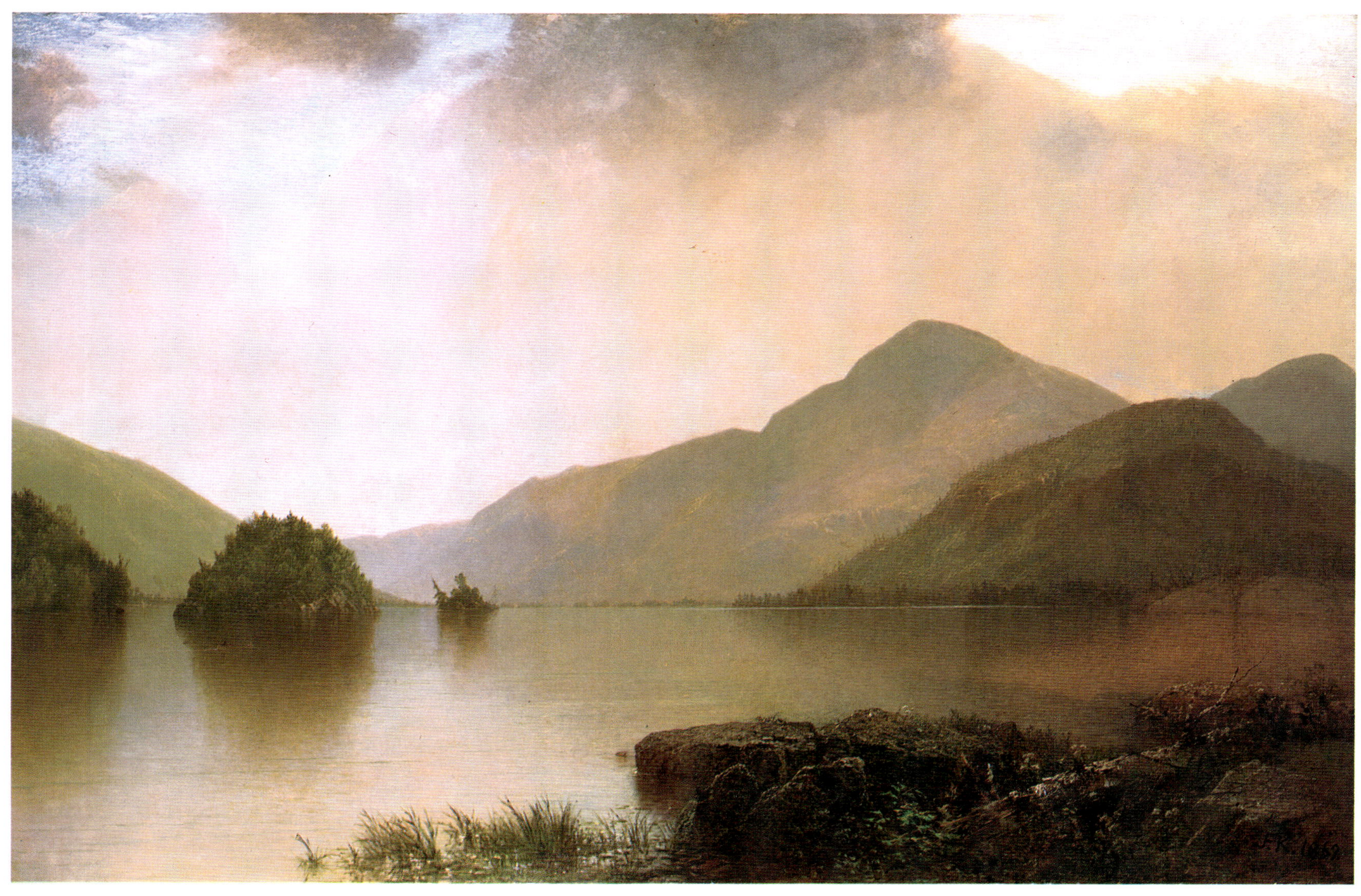

John Frederick Kensett
1816–1872

Lake George

Oil on canvas
44⅛ x 66⅜ in. (112.1 x 168.6 cm.)
1869
Signed and dated at lower right:
JF. (monogram) K. 1869.
Bequest of Maria DeWitt Jesup, from the collection of her husband, Morris K. Jesup, 1914 (15.30.61)

TO JOHN FREDERICK KENSETT, in his early years, painting was a diversion from his regular work as an engraver. On his first trip to Europe, which lasted seven years, he traveled widely on the Continent but made a special study of the English countryside and English landscape painting. The pictures he sent home from his travels established his reputation in the United States, and on his return he was soon a success. In the summers he spent many days in a boat on Lake George, making sketches from nature that he worked up into finished paintings in his studio. In this mature work, detail, like the foreground plants and grasses, is kept to a minimum; attention is focused on the larger forms of water, mountains, and sky, unified and related in subtly different atmospheric tones.

George Inness
1824–1894

Autumn Meadows

Oil on canvas
30 x 45½ (76.2 x 115.6 cm.)
1869
Signed at lower right: G. Inness 1869
Gift of Walter Knight Sturges, 1974 (1974.75)

GEORGE INNESS, one of America's most important landscapists, had little formal training in painting, receiving some instruction during his youth from an itinerant artist and a brief series of lessons subsequently from a little-known French painter in New York. He had a sensitive, searching mind, however, and during several stays in Europe he took the opportunity to study the great masters, including, surely, the Dutch landscapists of the seventeenth century and the French artists Poussin and Claude of the same period. In France, he also became familiar with the landscapes of the contemporary Barbizon School and must have seen the startling earliest work of the Impressionists. During a stay in Rome in the early 1870s, he acquired a first-hand knowledge of the Italian masters and of the natural scenery on which they drew.

Unlike most American landscape painters of his time, who followed the formulas of the Hudson River School, Inness imparted a more emotional and personal tone to his work. The peaceful, lazy river and the slow-moving cattle of *Autumn Meadows* recall Barbizon landscapes, but Inness's mood is more openly poetic.

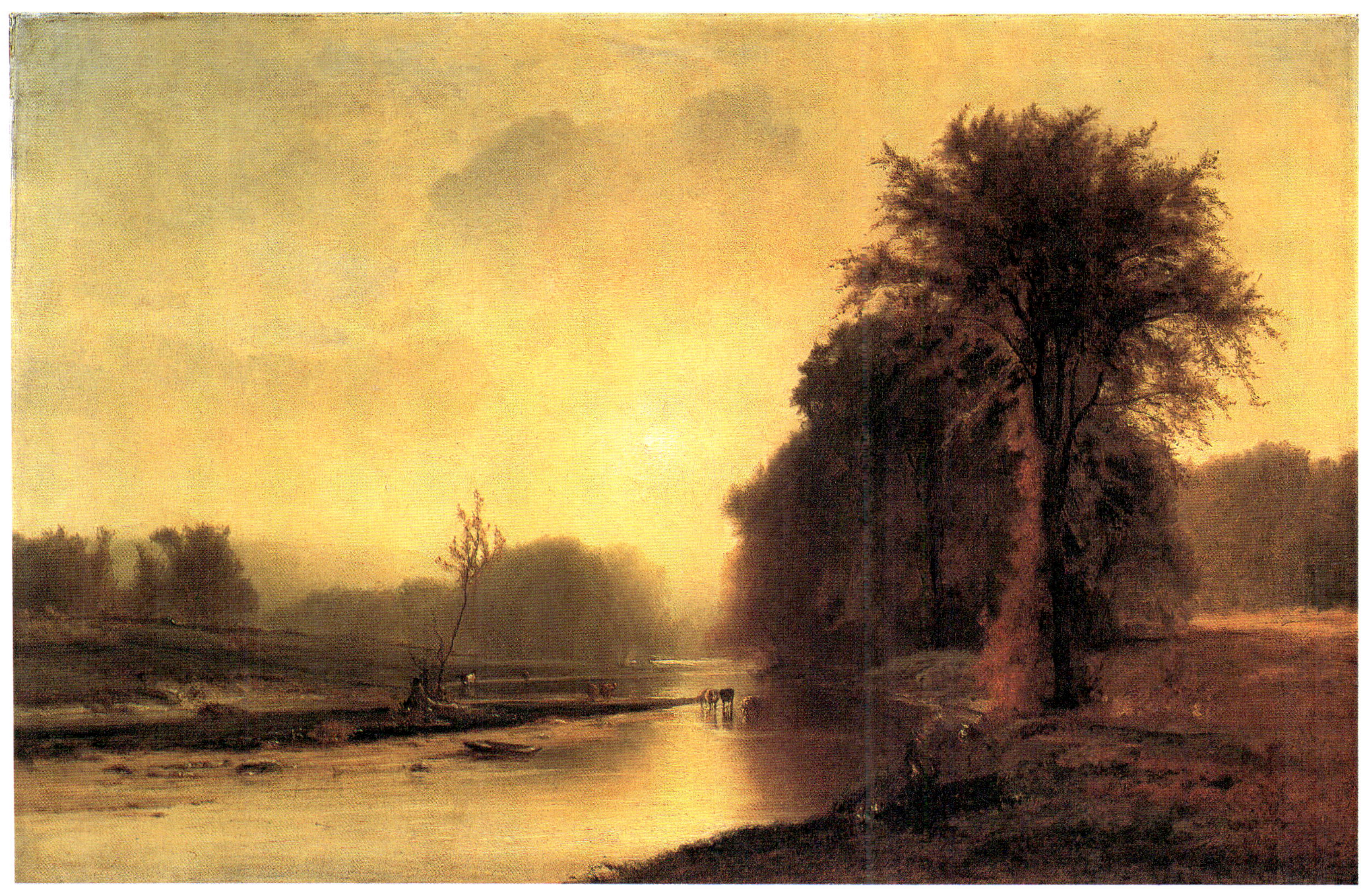

George Inness
1824–1894

Autumn Oaks

Oil on canvas
20⅜ x 30⅛ in. (54.3 x 76.5 cm.)
ca. 1878
Signed at lower right: G. Inness
Gift of George I. Seney, 1887 (87.8.8)

The resounding autumn colors of the great clump of sunlit trees in this painting by George Inness make the trees dominate the entire landscape; the richness of their colors is intensified by the deep foreground shadow and the blue-violet tones of the lowering sky. Inness's composition is splendidly orchestrated, with a unity and emphasis that did not exist in his works of a decade earlier. He apparently did this one about 1878, a few years after his return from a four-year trip to Europe. Here he shies away from naturalistic effects and disparate detail, tending toward coherent arrangements in which everything is subordinate to a single motif. This extremely beautiful landscape, so direct in its aspects of smiling nature masterfully handled, illustrates Inness's conscious objectives: the rendering of the solidity of objects and the transparency of shadows in a breathable atmosphere.

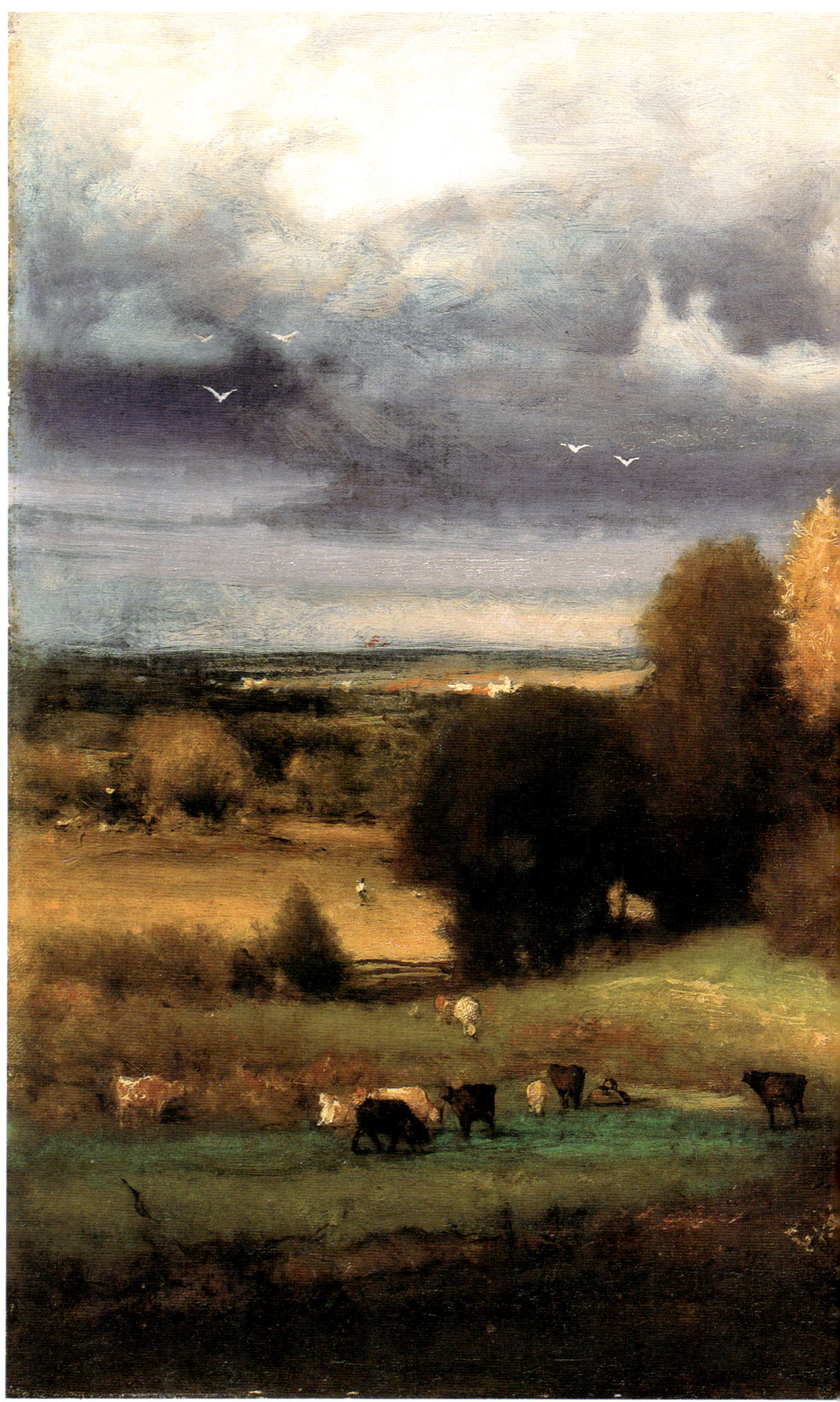

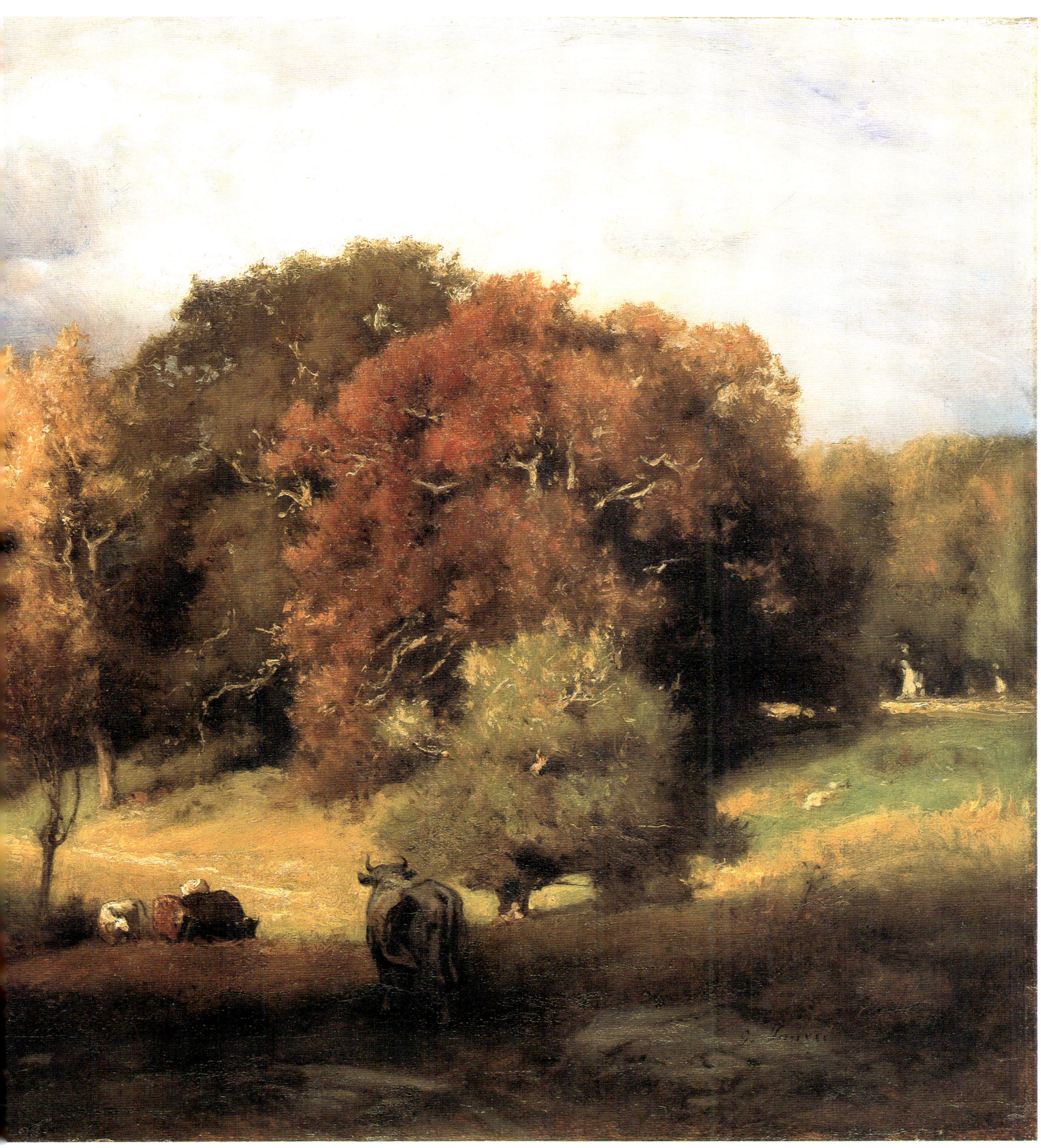

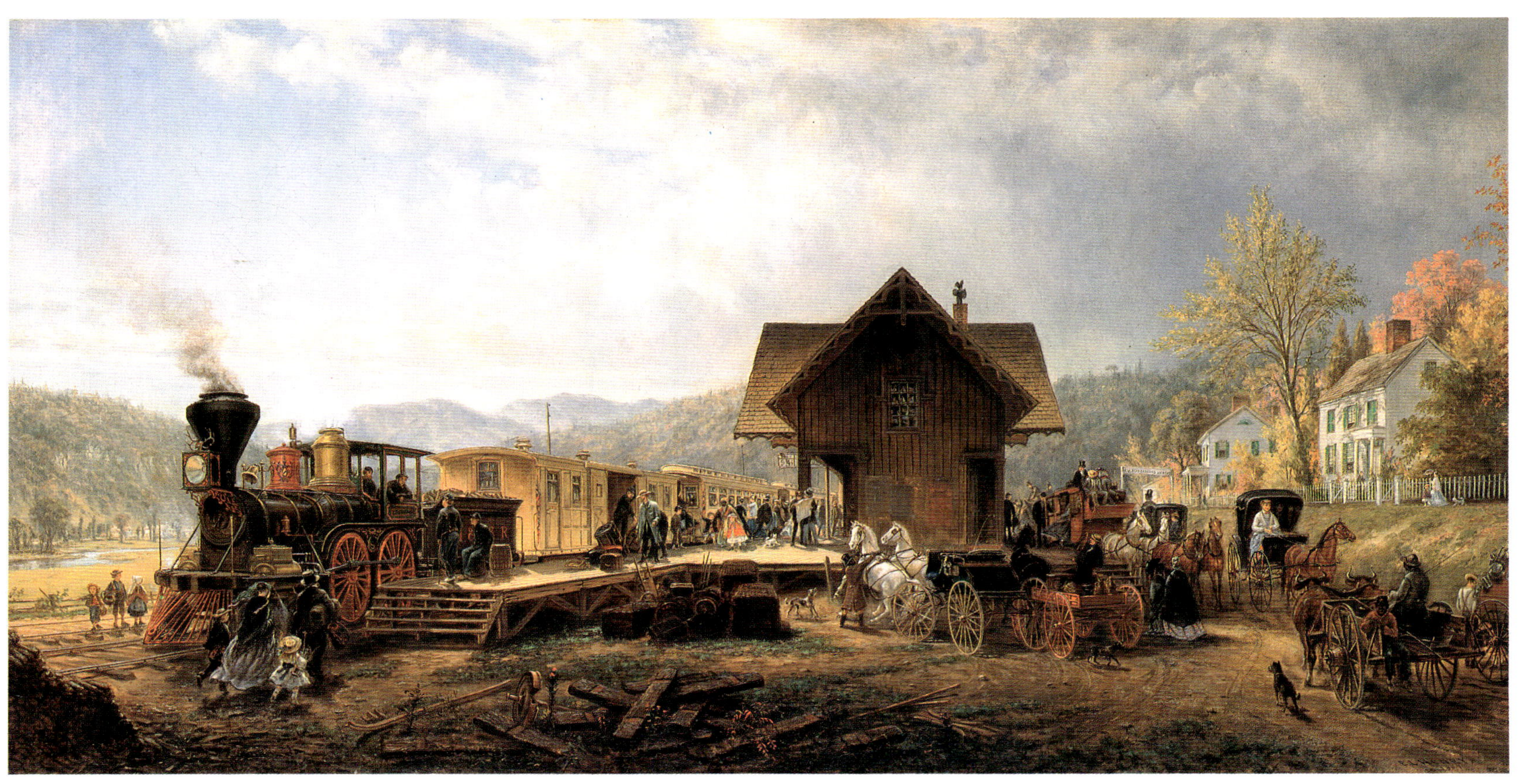

Edward Lamson Henry
1841–1919

The 9:45 Accommodation

Oil on canvas
16 x 30⅝ in. (40.6 x 77.8 cm.)
1867
Signed and dated at lower right:
E. L. Henry, / P.1867
Bequest of Moses Tanenbaum, 1937 (39.37.1)

PHOTOGRAPHY was a hobby with Edward Lamson Henry, and the appearance of exact truthfulness in this painting is probably due to reliance on photographs. In an effort to document the past, this artist collected antique furniture and costumes, and, alert to the differing modes of transportation, he also brought together a large group of coaches and carriages. This picture comes early in a series of railroad paintings Henry began in 1864 and continued to paint for at least three decades. It was commissioned by the first president of the Metropolitan Museum, John Taylor Johnston, who was at that time also president of the New Jersey Central Railroad. Many old wooden stations of this type still exist in the Northeast and elsewhere. The scene, just before the departure of a train, has many lively details, including those of hurrying passengers and the conveyances that brought them to the station, horses—some patient and some restive—and frisky dogs.

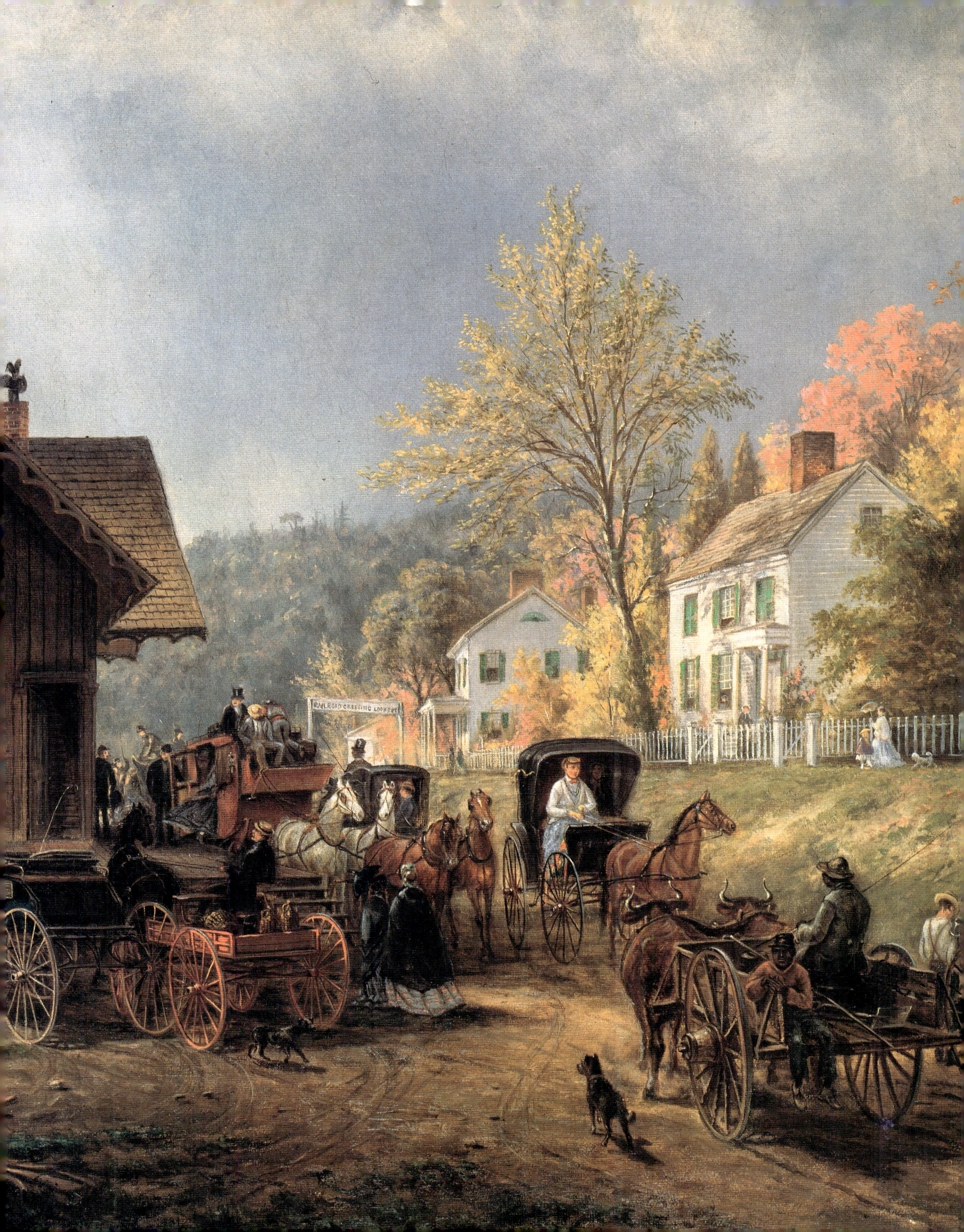
RAILROAD CROSSING

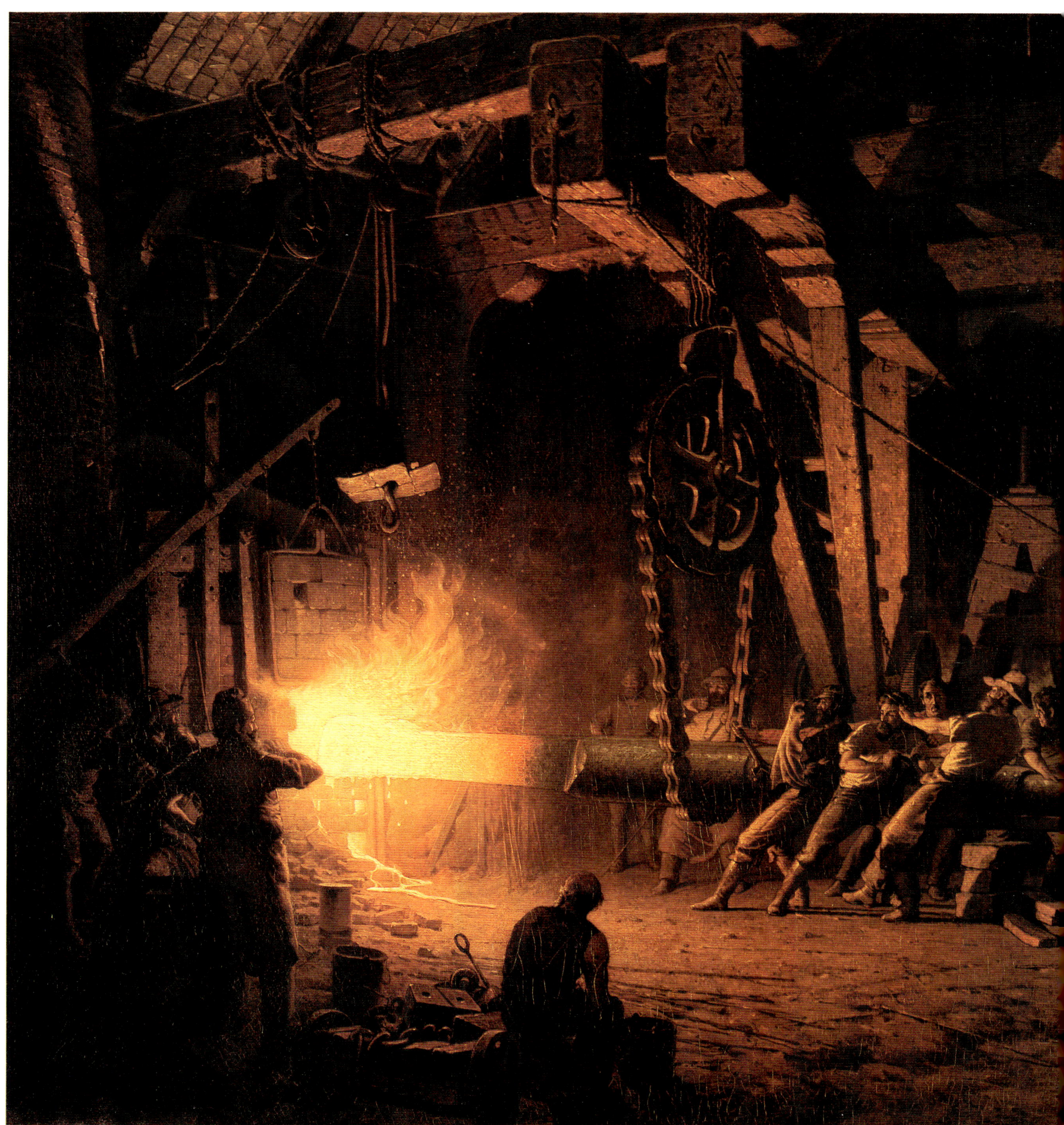

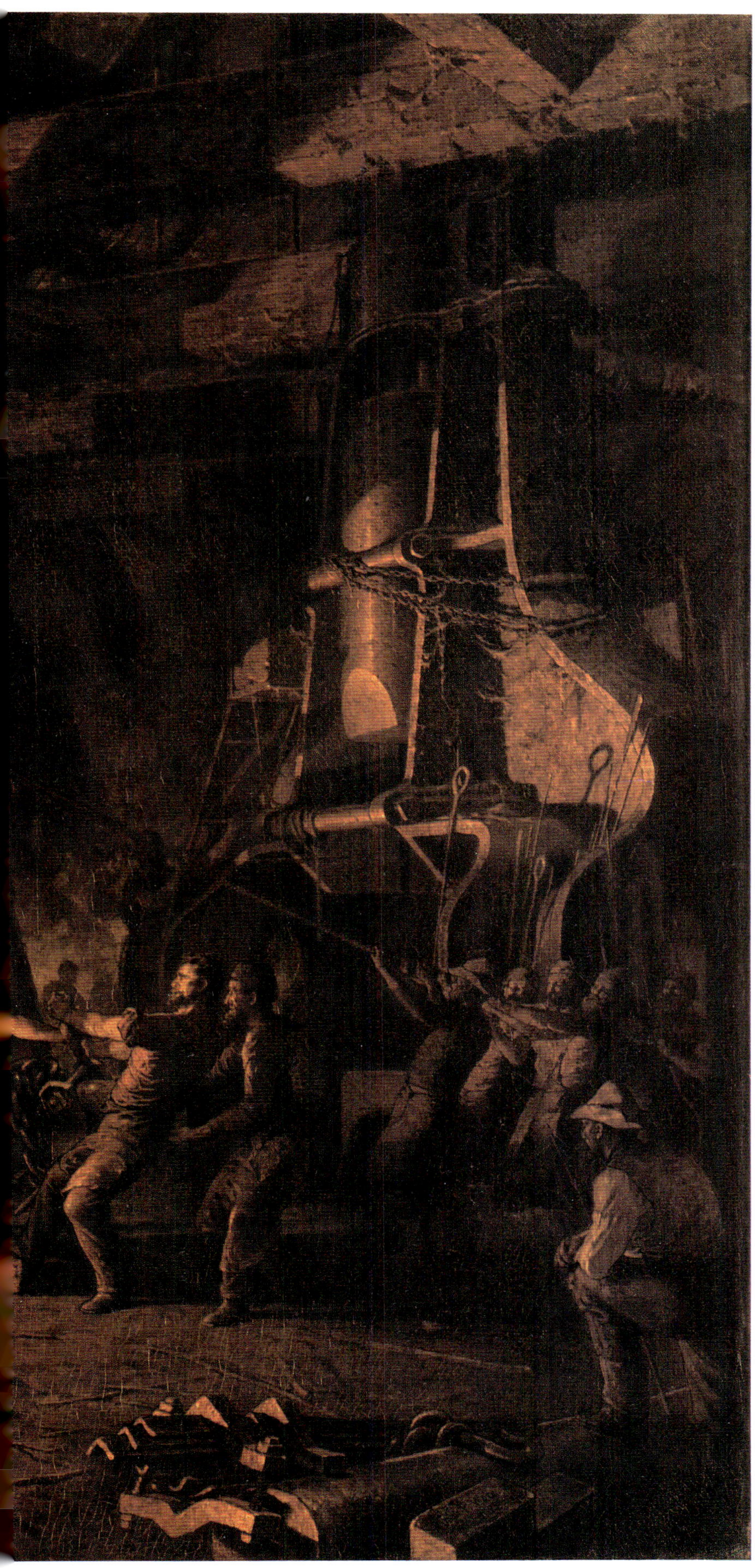

John Ferguson Weir
1841–1926

Forging the Shaft

Oil on canvas
52 x 73¼ in. (132.1 x 186.1 cm.)
1874–1877
Signed at lower left: John F. Weir
Purchase, Lyman G. Bloomingdale Gift, 1901 (01.7.1)

JOHN FERGUSON WEIR, half-brother of the painter J. Alden Weir, directed the Yale School of Fine Arts for more than forty years. He was trained by his father, who taught drawing and painting at the United States Military Academy at West Point on the Hudson River. Young Weir's chief patron was Robert Parrott, who owned the foundry and ironworks on the opposite side of the river at Cold Spring. The interior of this forge and the strenuous activities of the workmen form the subject of this painting and of another important early work by Weir, *The Gun Foundry.* The white-hot, hissing cylinder being pulled from the furnace by a team of cautious, brawny men is destined to become the shaft for a side-wheel steamer. The lofty interior, with its mysterious beams and pulleys, recalls prints by the eighteenth-century Italian engraver Piranesi. In the Museum's painting, all the light is concentrated in a brilliant area of blazing heat at the open mouth of the furnace.

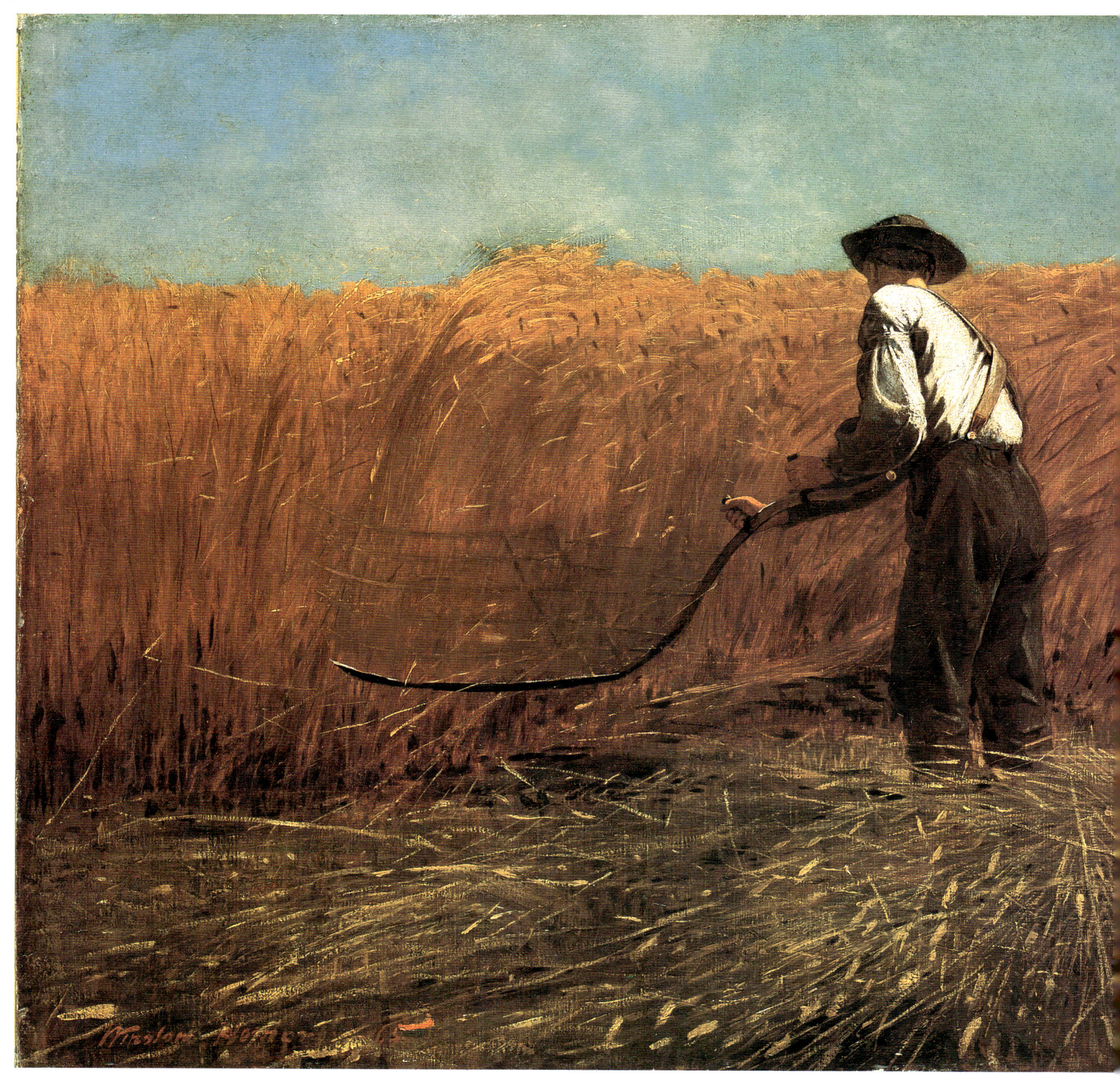

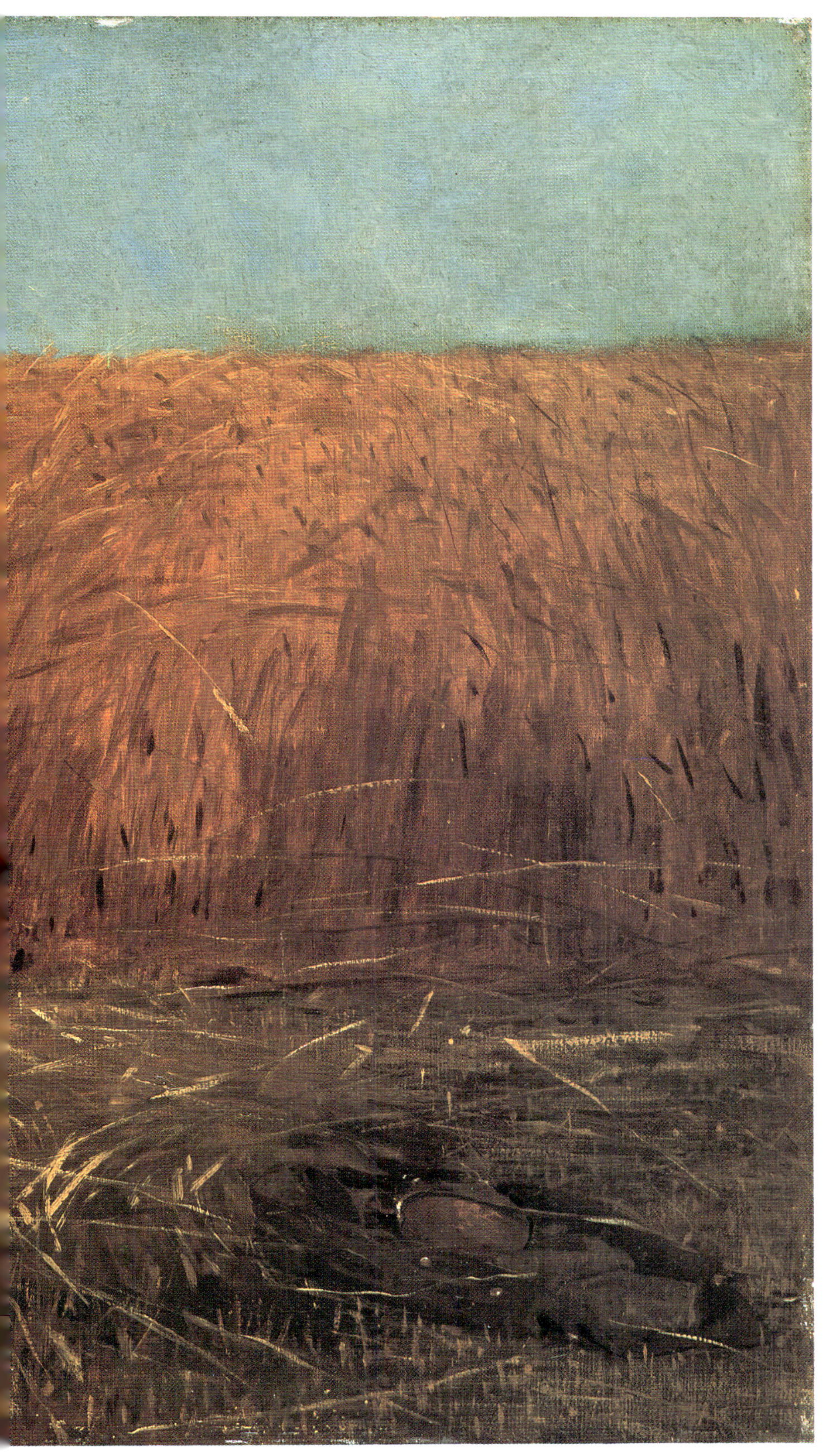

Winslow Homer
1836–1910

The Veteran in a New Field

Oil on canvas
24⅛ x 38⅛ in. (61.3 x 96.8 cm.)
1865
Signed and dated at lower left:
Winslow Homer 65; on canteen at lower right: W.H.
Bequest of Miss Adelaide Milton de Groot (1876–1967), 1967 (67.187.131)

THE BITTER CIVIL WAR ended, soldiers returned not to rest but to "bind up the nation's wounds" and to restore the farms. This lonely figure, in the high sun of midday, scythes down the ripe grain. Lest he be taken for any regular farm worker, Winslow Homer has shown the ex-soldier's jacket lying on the ground with a canteen, on which he has painted, as a distinguishing mark, the red cloverleaf insignia of the division with which Homer had traveled as artist-correspondent. During the 1860s in Europe and America, there was a growing awareness of the farm laborer and his relation to the world of nature, which he was engaged in conquering. The bands of color formed by the sky, the standing grain, and the foreground of fallen grain and chaff stir ideas of immense space and endless hours of work.

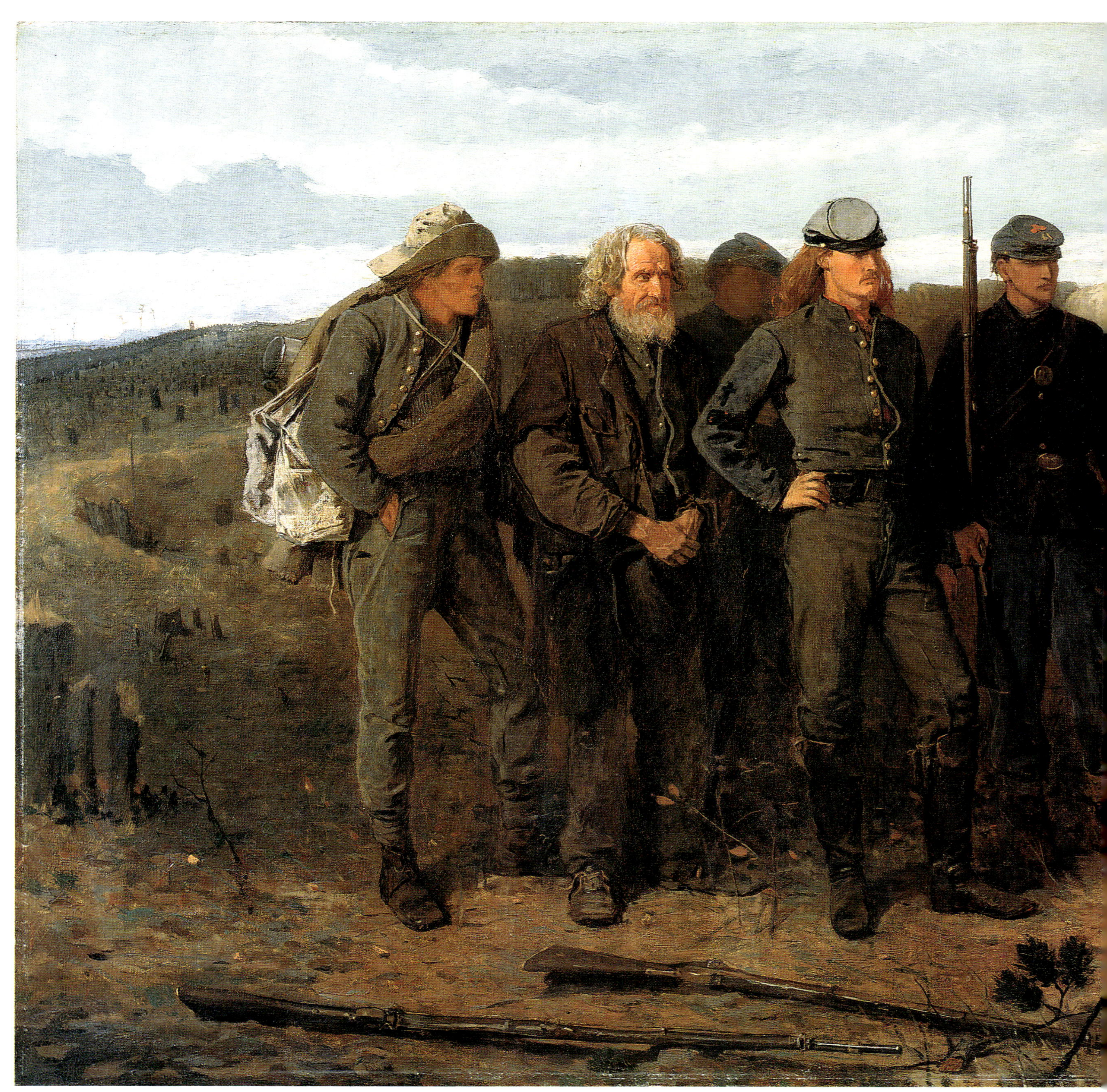

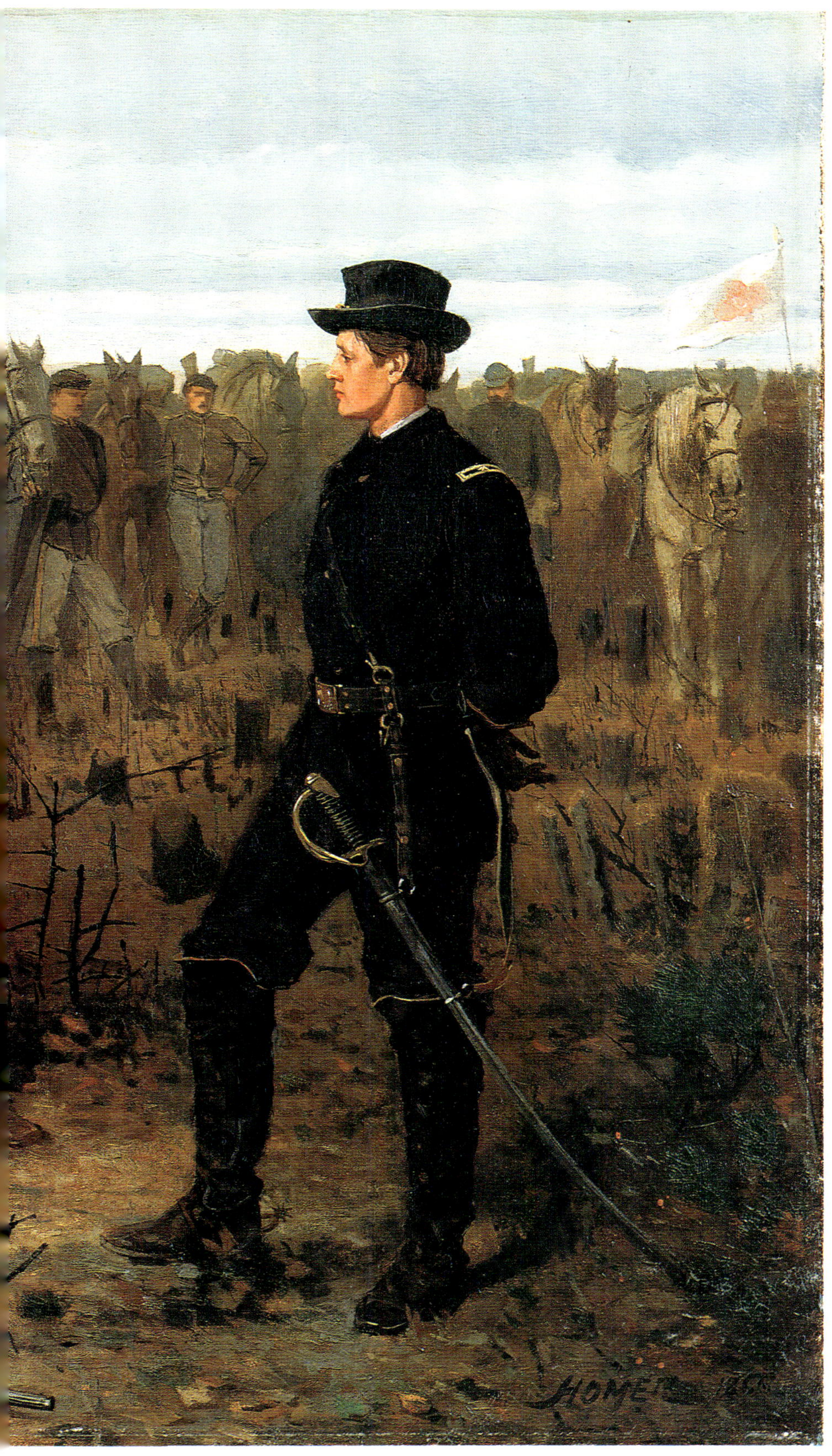

Winslow Homer
1836–1910

Prisoners from the Front

Oil on canvas
24 x 38 in. (61 x 96.5 cm.)
1866
Signed and dated at lower right: HOMER 1866
Gift of Mrs. Frank B. Porter, 1922 (22.207)

THIS PICTURE was painted the year after the Civil War ended. During the war, Winslow Homer had been an artist-correspondent for the magazine *Harper's Weekly*, contributing illustrations based on his observations of camp life in the Army of the Potomac and other divisions. Exhibited at the National Academy of Design in New York in 1866, and the following year in Paris, this painting firmly established the painter's reputation at home and abroad. The foreground has become a stage, on which a Union officer, Brigadier General Francis C. Barlow, examines three Confederates brought in by a pair of Union soldiers. The fine, lithe figure of the general was modeled from another officer, lower in rank but more notable than Barlow in bearing and appearance, and to this figure the portrait head of the general was subsequently affixed. The differentiations in types and attitudes are conscientiously depicted with Homer's unfailing sharpness of vision and passionate veracity.

Winslow Homer
1836–1910

Eagle Head, Manchester, Massachusetts (High Tide)

Oil on canvas
26 x 38 in. (66 x 96.5 cm.)
1870
Signed and dated at lower left:
WINSLOW HOMER 1870
Gift of Mrs. William F. Milton, 1923 (23.77.2)

A CONTEMPORARY CRITIC found this bathing scene of Winslow Homer's "not quite refined"; another reviewer, using some unfathomable standard, judged the legs of the young women not well drawn. These writers were probably responding less to the subject and the facts than to the shock they felt at the painter's frank and direct way of seeing. It is to Homer's credit that even to our bikini-jaded eyes these bathing dresses do not look ridiculous; they somehow manage to reveal the human body in all its beauty of motion and lithe strength. Stark dunes and headlands, bare of vegetation, cast a spell of calm melancholy, and the surf's endless alternation of sound and silence beats an elemental natural rhythm. Homer has responded deeply to his source in nature and presents it to us through the three human participants.

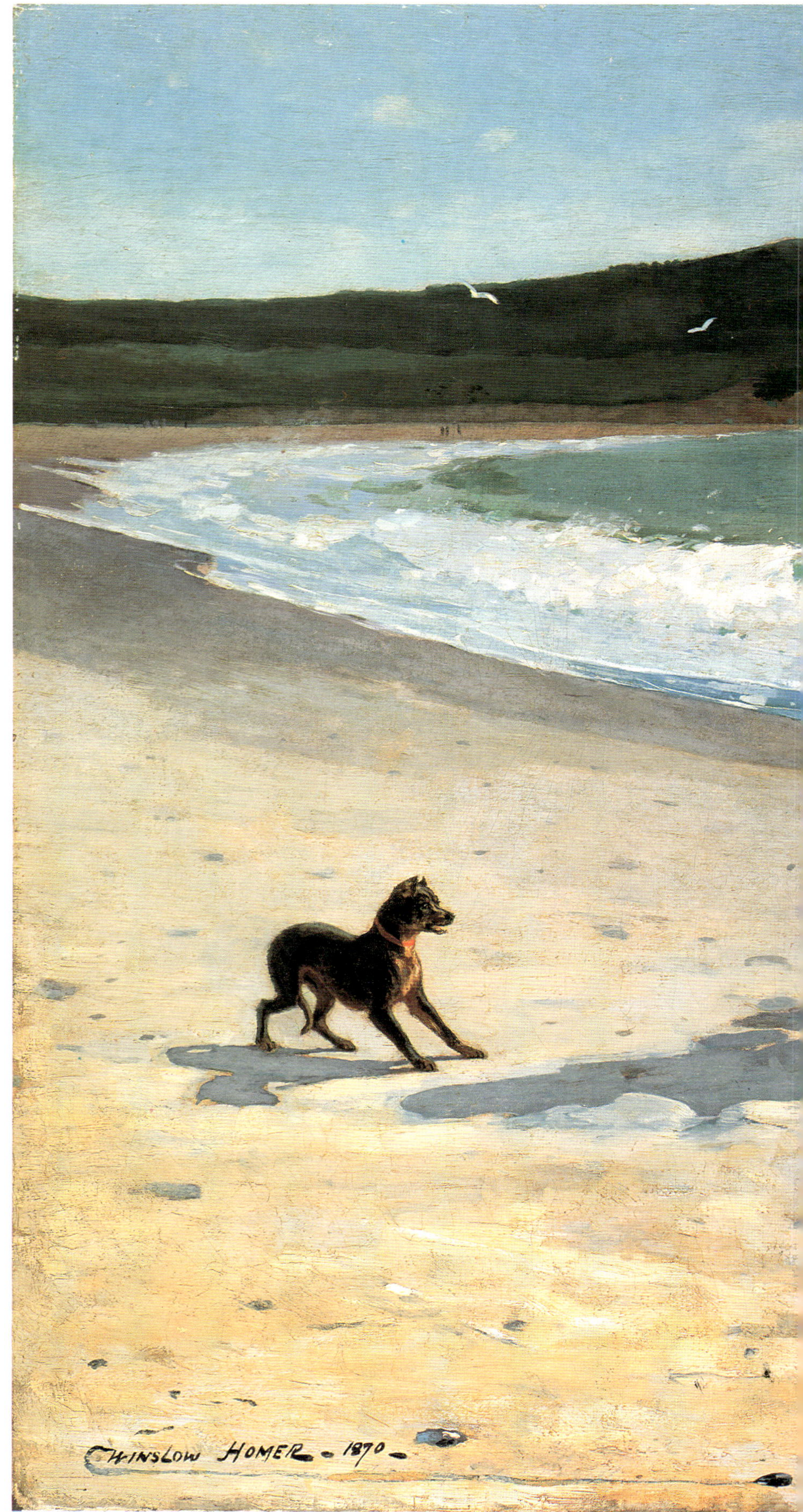

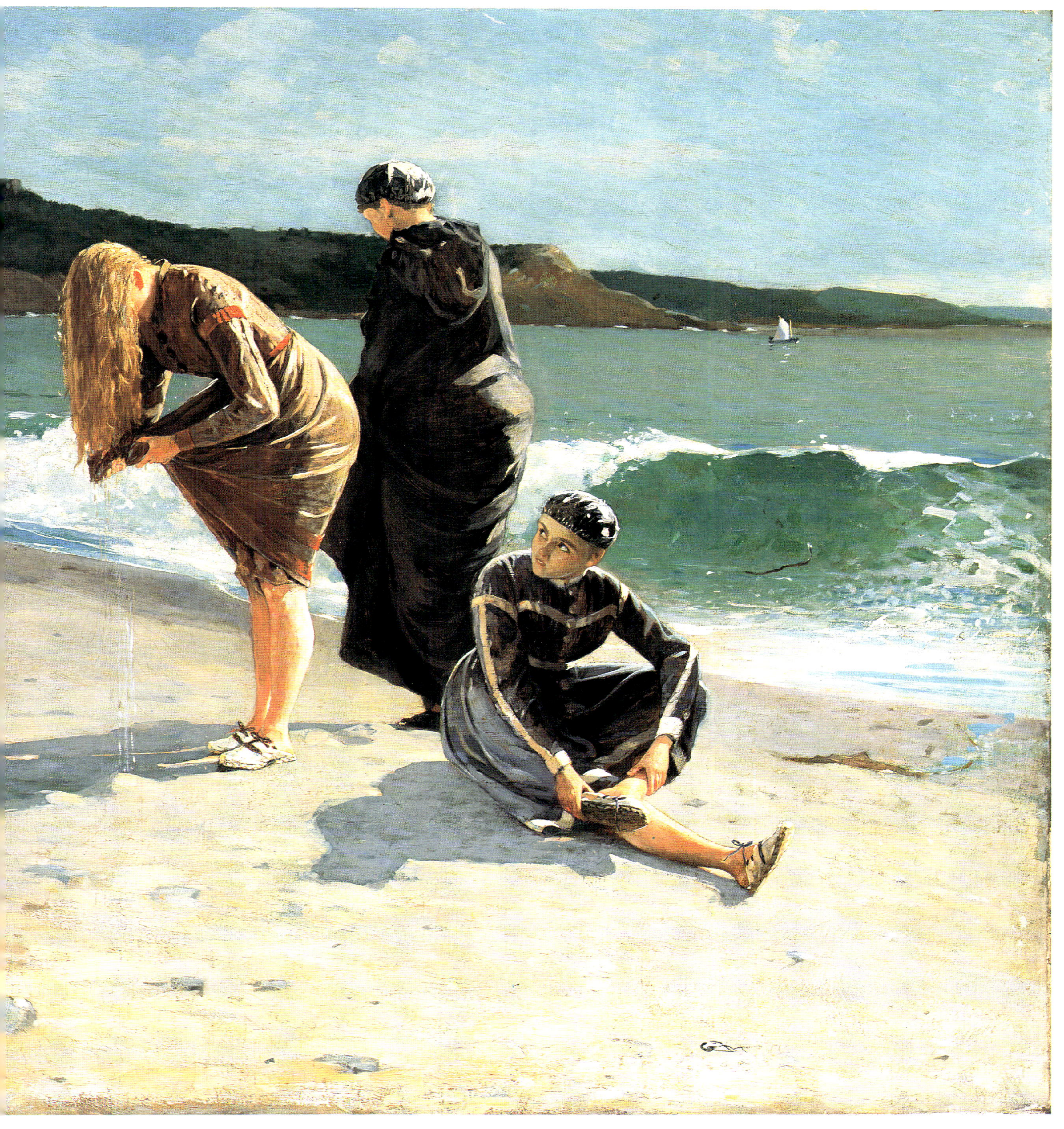

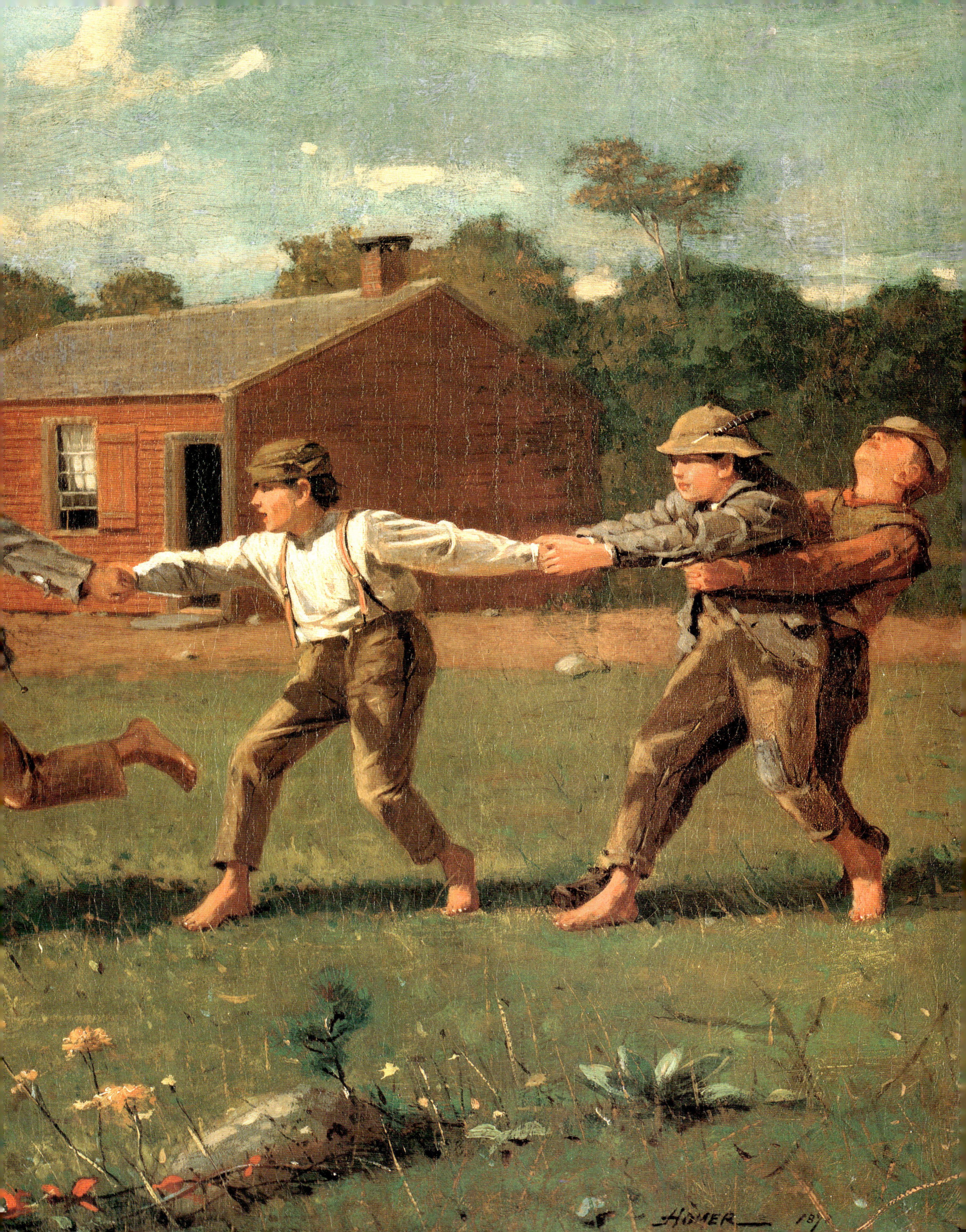
HOMER 187

Winslow Homer
1836–1910

Snap the Whip

Oil on canvas
12 x 20 in. (30.5 x 50.8 cm.)
1872
Signed and dated at lower right:
HOMER 1872
Gift of Christian A. Zabriskie, 1950 (50.41)

IN THE WHOLE RANGE of nineteenth-century American painting, from folk and naive pictures all the way to the fashionable family group portraits of Eastman Johnson and John Singer Sargent, children occupy an important place, and their games and pastimes were favorite subjects with the painters of genre. In the first half of the 1870s, when Winslow Homer painted this picture and several others with schoolboy subjects, he had a studio in New York but showed no interest in city life, concentrating instead on rustic scenes and country amusements. These boys are playing a rough-and-tumble game, as traditional as tag, that had as its object the breaking of the chain; the boy on all fours on the ground at the left has already been whirled off the line. Views of the little red, one-room schoolhouse in the background—its interior as well as its exterior—appear in other pictures of this period in Homer's work. Here, as always, he is candidly and sharply observant.

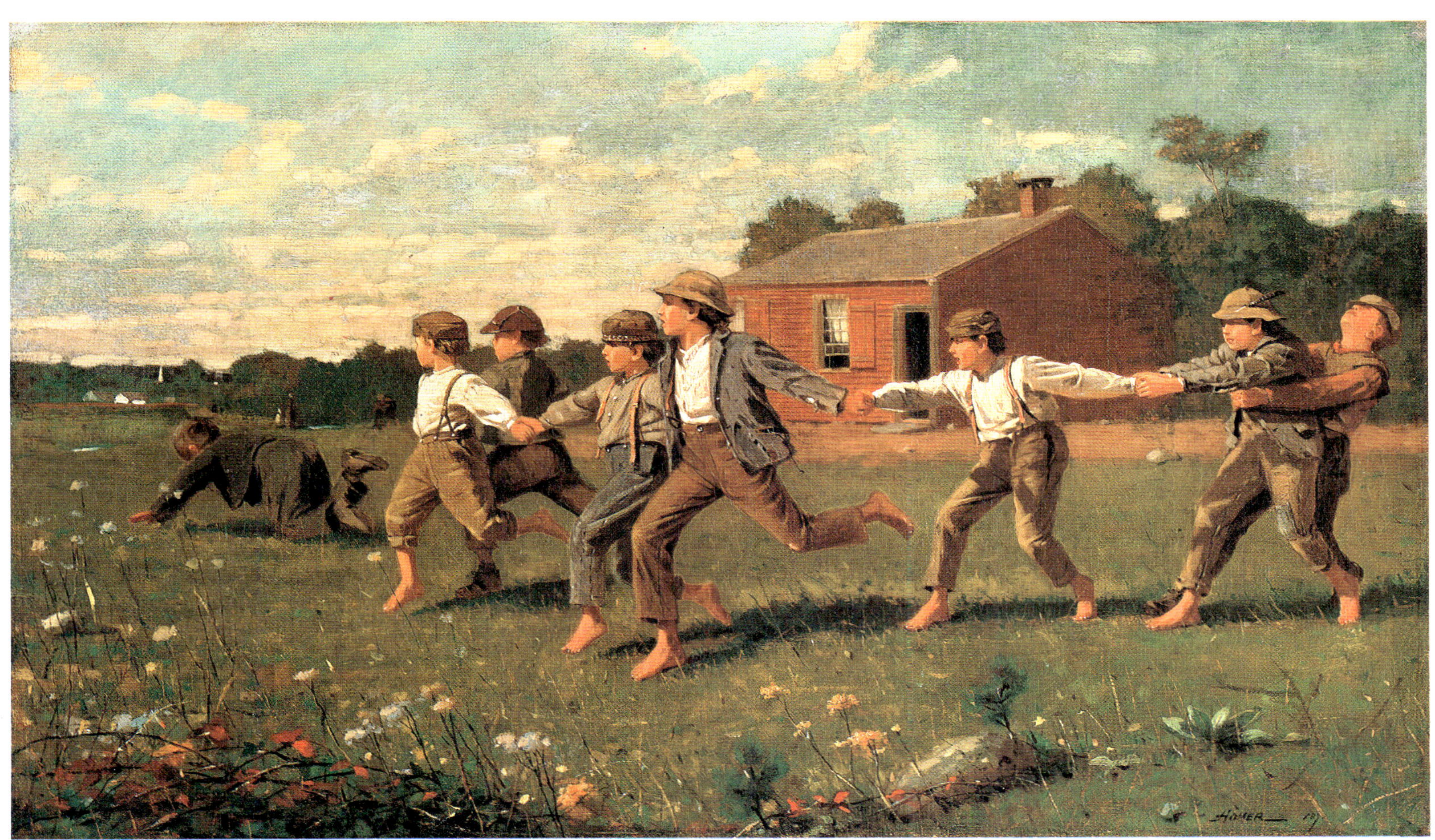

Winslow Homer
1836–1910

Moonlight, Wood Island Light

Oil on canvas
30¾ x 40¼ in. (78.1 x 102.2 cm.)
1894
Signed and dated at lower left:
WH 1894; inscribed on original stretcher (now replaced): Wood Island Light, Winslow Homer
Gift of George A. Hearn, in memory of Arthur Hoppock Hearn, 1911 (11.116.2)

AT PROUTS NECK, Maine, where he settled about 1884, Winslow Homer must have spent countless solitary evenings gazing at the magic of moonlight on water. An unusually beautiful effect once sent him on impulse to the water's edge to work by the light of the moon for four or five hours. Moonlight usually engenders sentimentality, which Homer loathed; he evaded it here by leaving out the moon itself, implying it only by an area of brightness in the clouds and by the silver glamour of its path across the water. Far off on the right horizon is the red dot of the lighthouse on Wood Island, rousing melancholy ideas of watchfulness and danger. Again avoiding excessive lyricism, Homer has painted the realistic splash from the breaking waves in the rocky foreground with huge strokes of white pigment, boldly applied, perhaps with a palette knife.

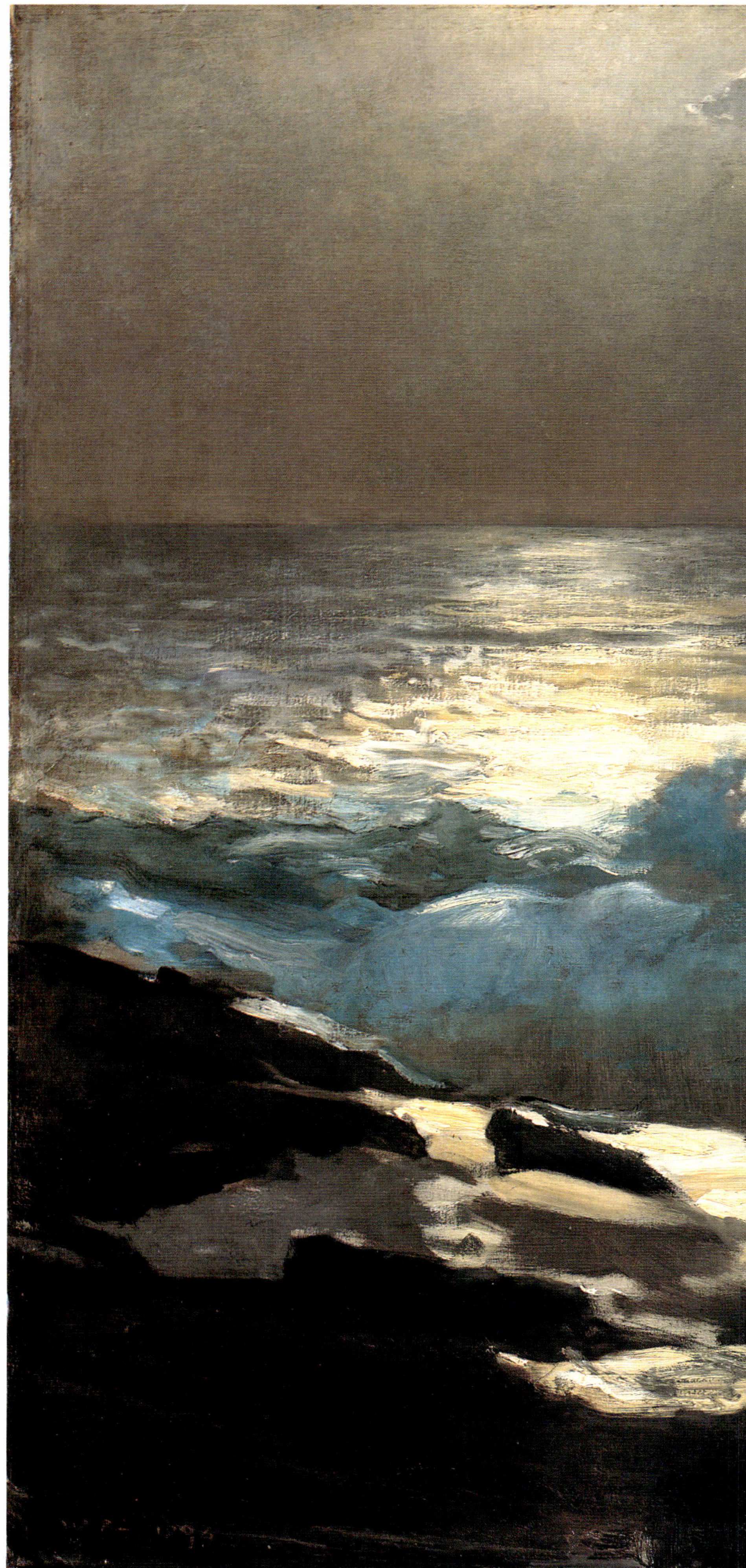

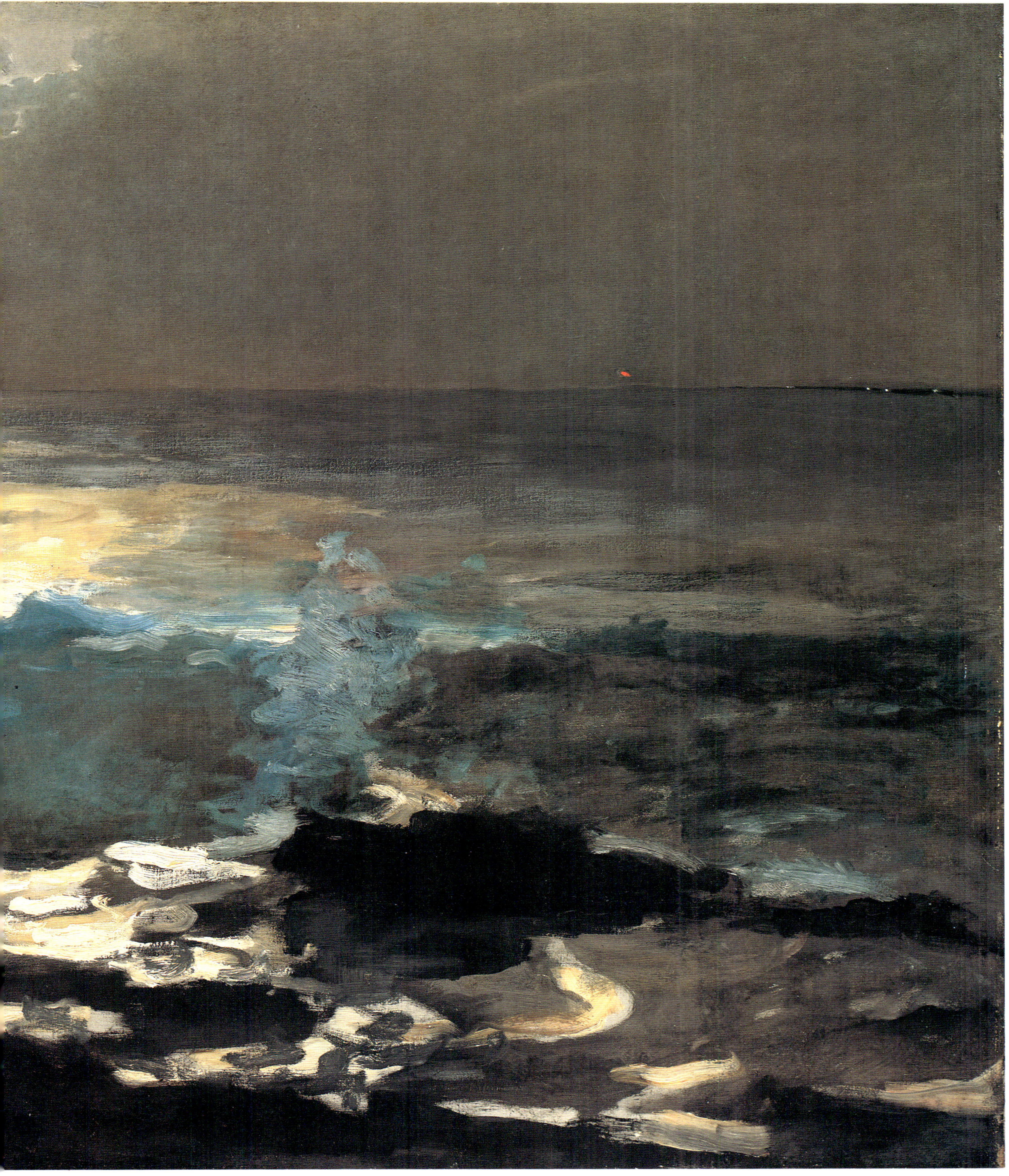

Winslow Homer
1836–1910

Northeaster

Oil on canvas
34½ x 50 in. (87.6 x 127 cm.)
1895
Signed and dated at lower center:
HOMER/1895
Gift of George A. Hearn, 1910 (10.64.5)

EVEN SUMMER VISITORS to the Maine coast have learned that "northeaster" means a vacation-spoiling storm of exceptional violence and duration. In this painting, which Winslow Homer considered better than his great *Cannon Rock* (also in the Museum's collection), he concentrated all the thrust of the storm in a single heaving wave and simplified his composition to one sweeping diagonal, utilizing two of the resources underlying the mightiest expressions of Baroque art. He also created two areas of sharp contrast between light and dark—contrasts that heighten the excitement and drama of the scene. Not the least of the emotions this painting evokes is fear, generated by the ominous pull of undertow in the lower right-hand corner. All these effects are made possible by Homer's extraordinarily broad and free brushstroke, typical of his late works.

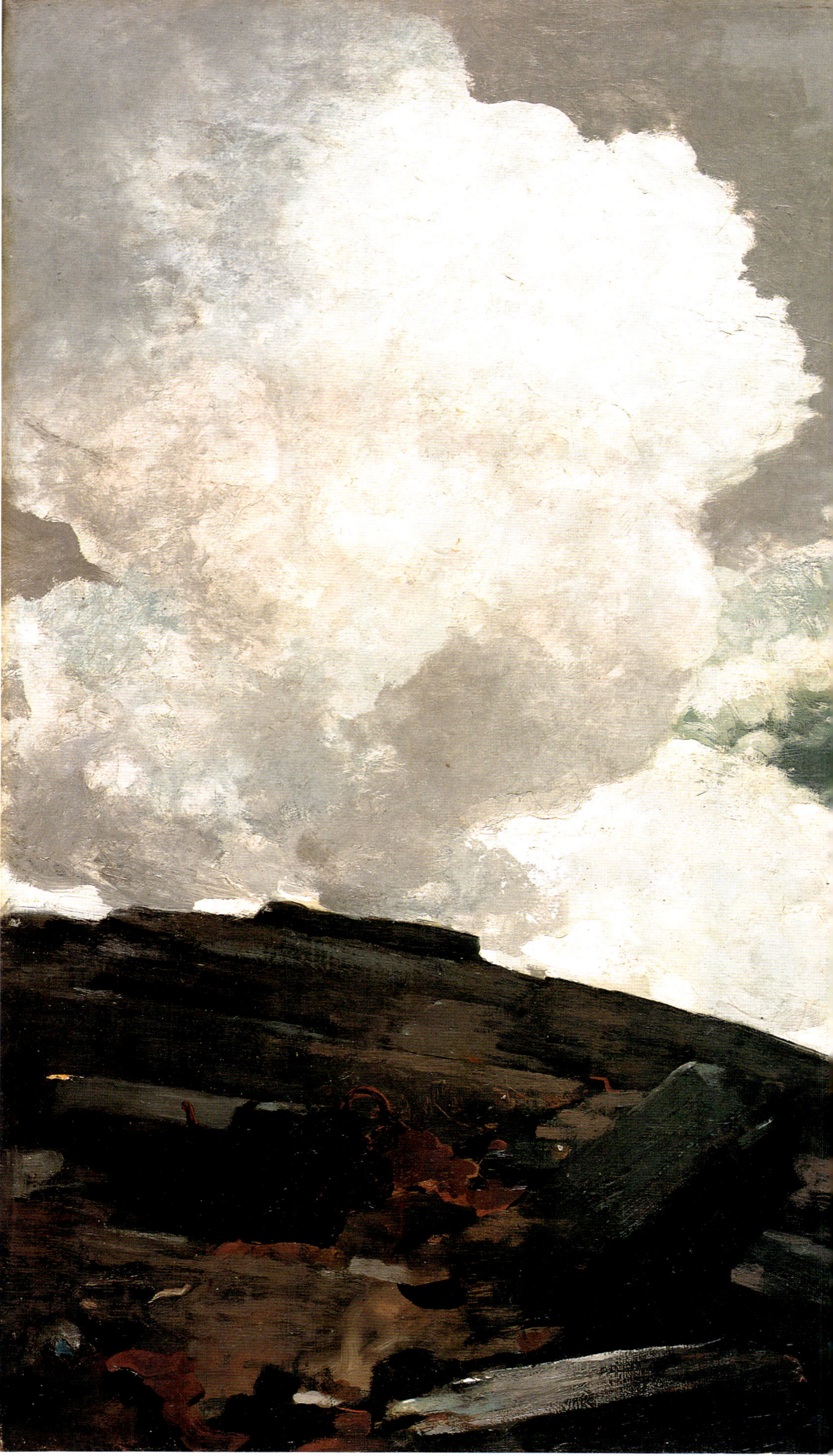

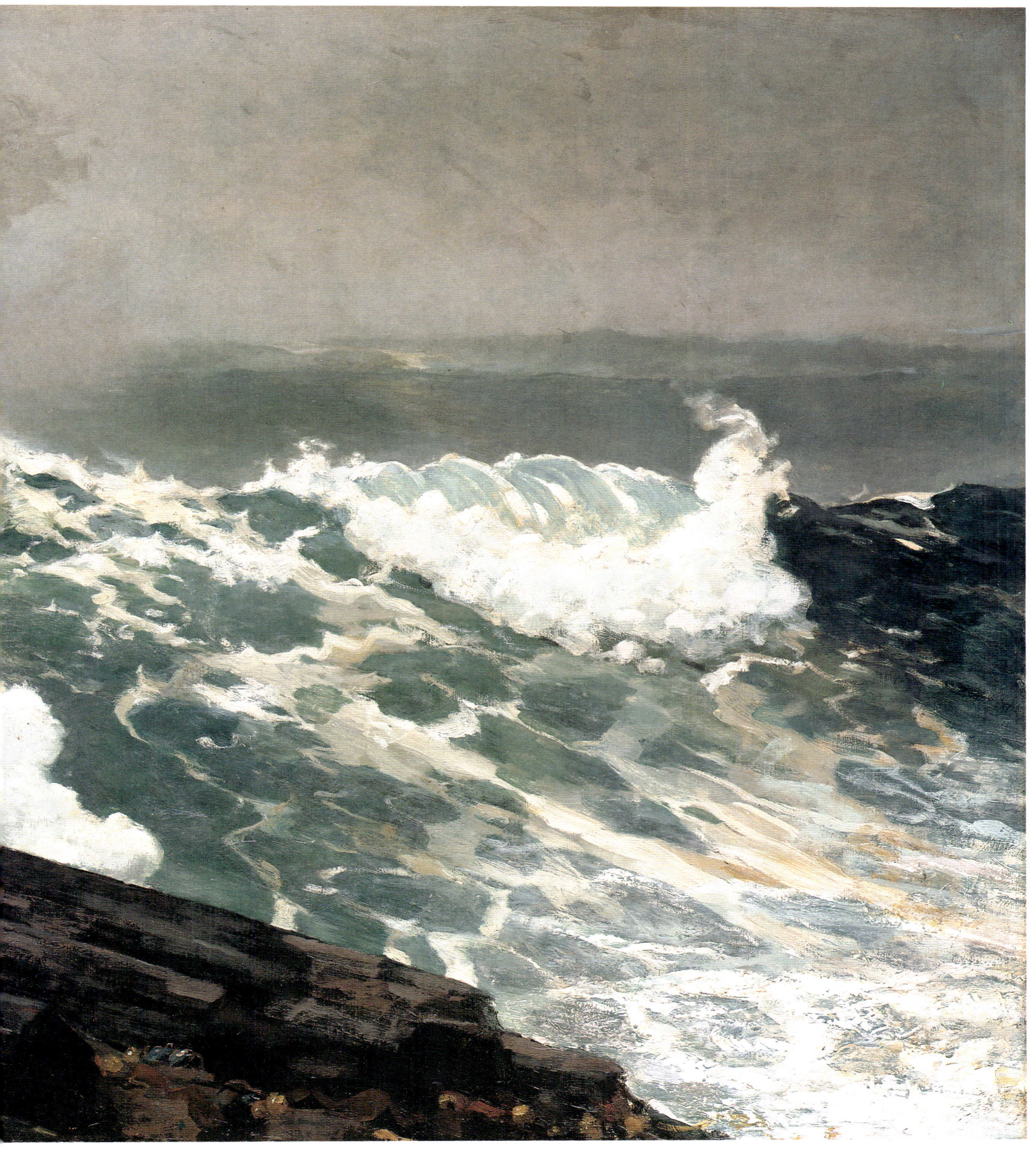

Winslow Homer
1836–1910

The Gulf Stream

Oil on canvas
28⅛ x 49⅛ in. (71.4 x 124.8 cm.)
1899
Signed and dated at lower left: HOMER/1899; inscribed at lower left (partly painted over): At 12 feet from this picture you can see it.
Wolfe Fund, Catharine Lorillard Wolfe Collection, 1906 (06.1234)

WINSLOW HOMER visited Nassau and other islands of the Caribbean during the 1880s and made another trip to Nassau, much later, in the winter of 1898/99. Both stays yielded numerous sketches and studies in watercolor, destined to be worked up later into oil paintings. This picture, begun in September of 1899, had at least two early predecessors in scenes of disaster on the water. Homer very probably had seen one of the versions of Copley's *Watson and the Shark,* and he almost certainly knew *The Raft of the Medusa* by the French Romantic painter Géricault in the Louvre. The black man in Homer's picture, sprawled with surprising nonchalance on the deck of a sloop that has lost its mast, must know that he is facing imminent death, either from the sharks surrounding his helpless, tossing boat or from the approaching waterspout at the right that will certainly overturn it. The full-rigged ship on the distant horizon at the left is so far away that it underlines the certainty nothing will save the wretched survivor. Homer's unlimited respect for nature as a force and his fiercely accurate observation endow this painting with the power to evoke overwhelming terror.

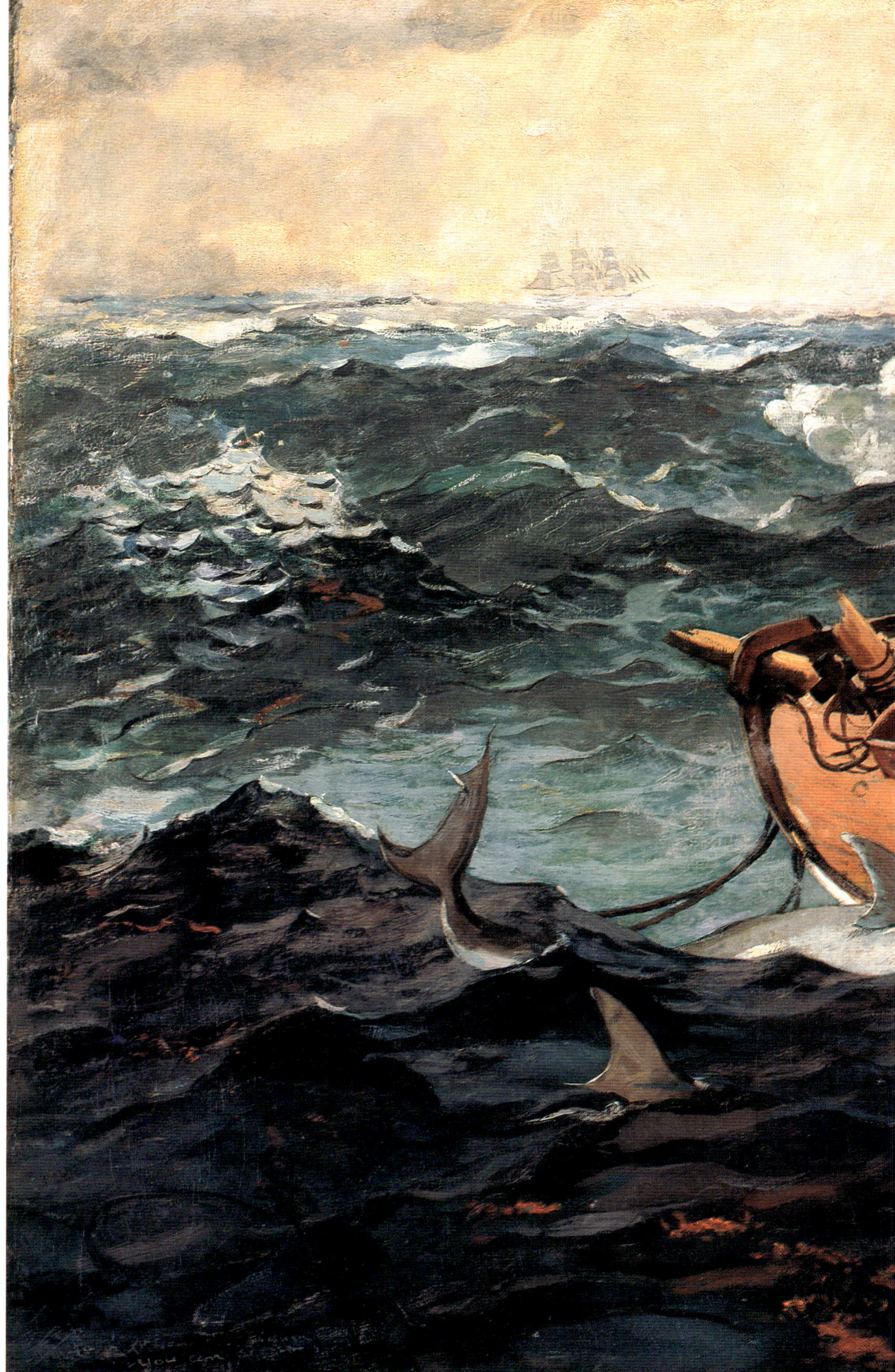

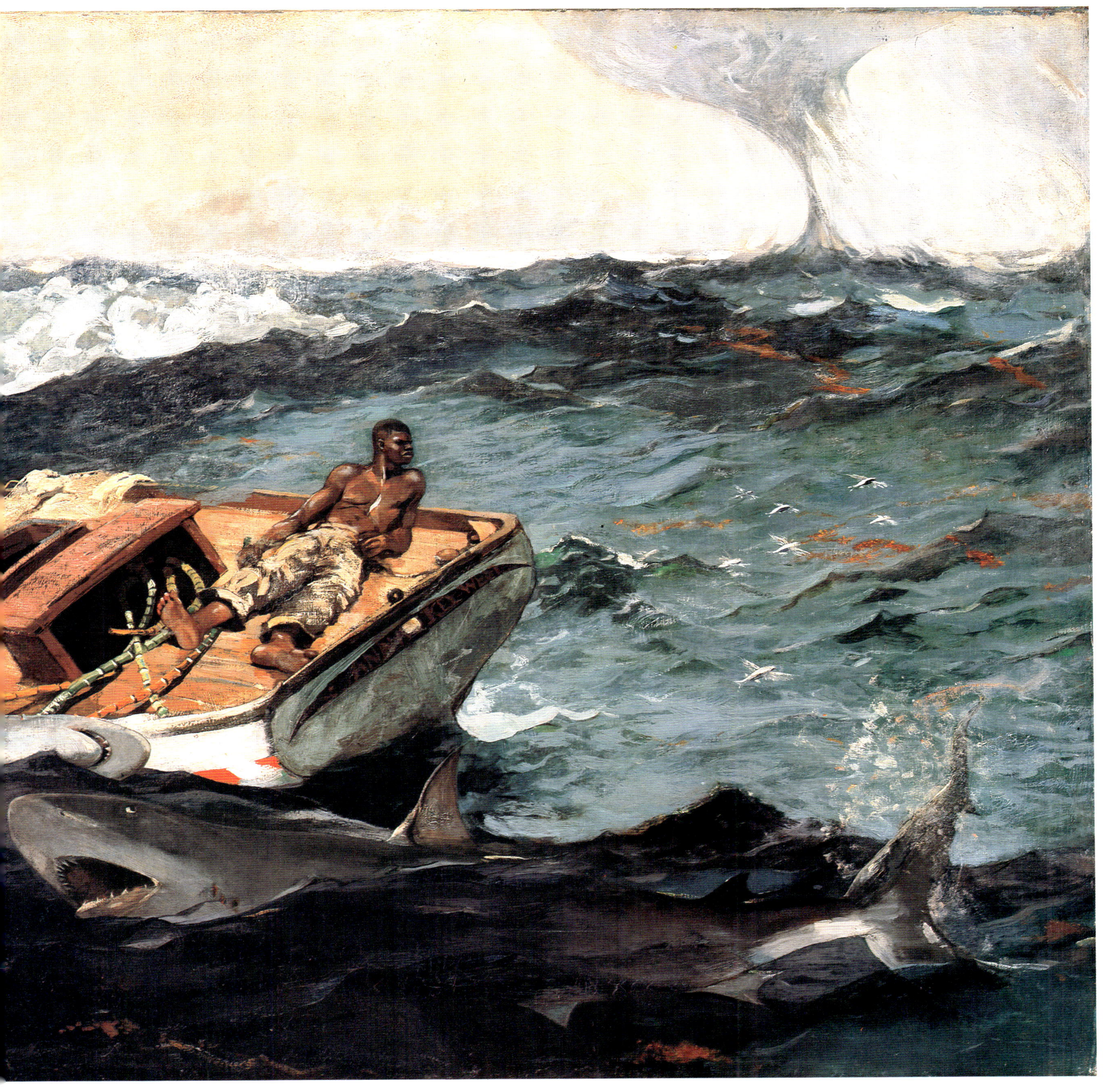

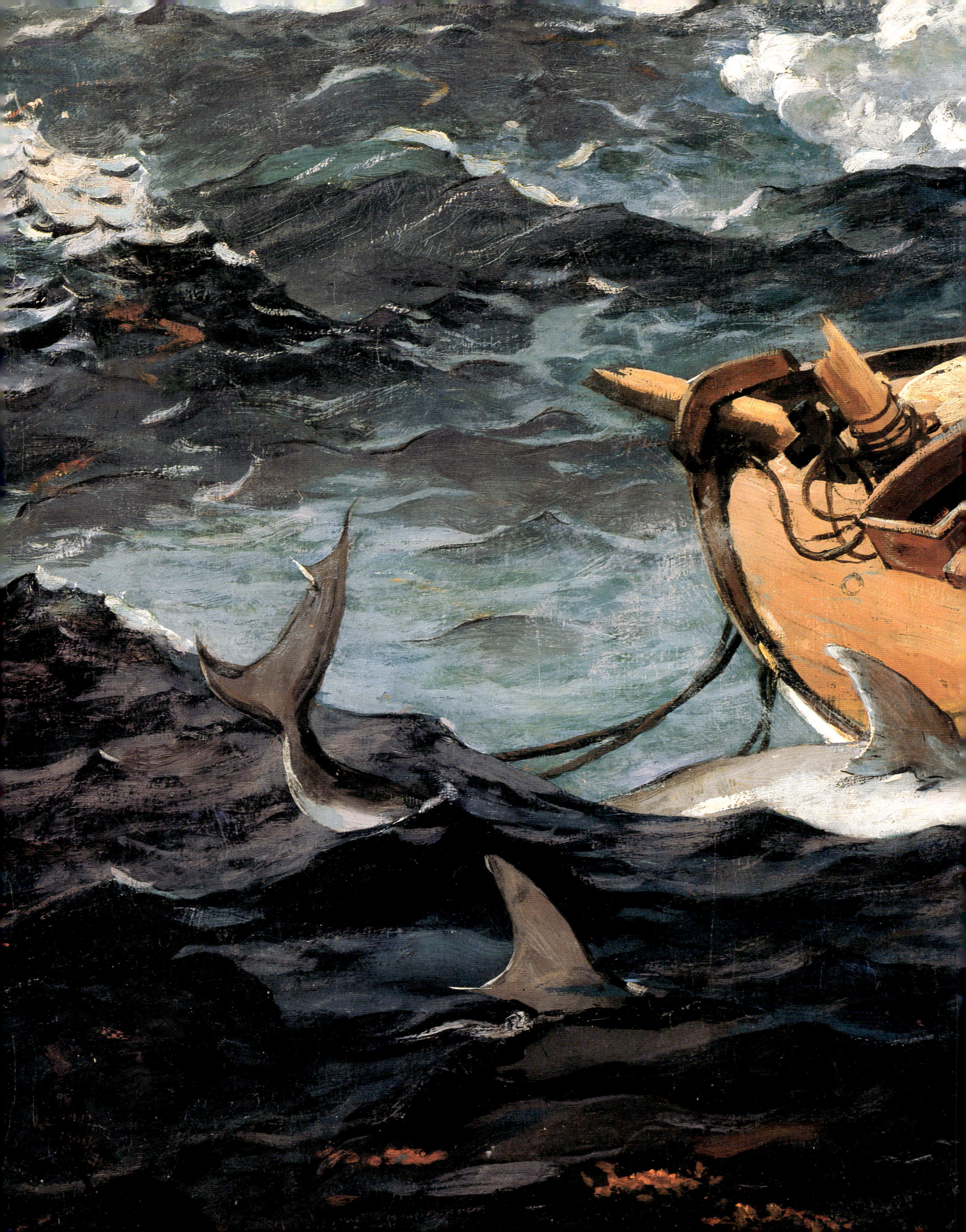

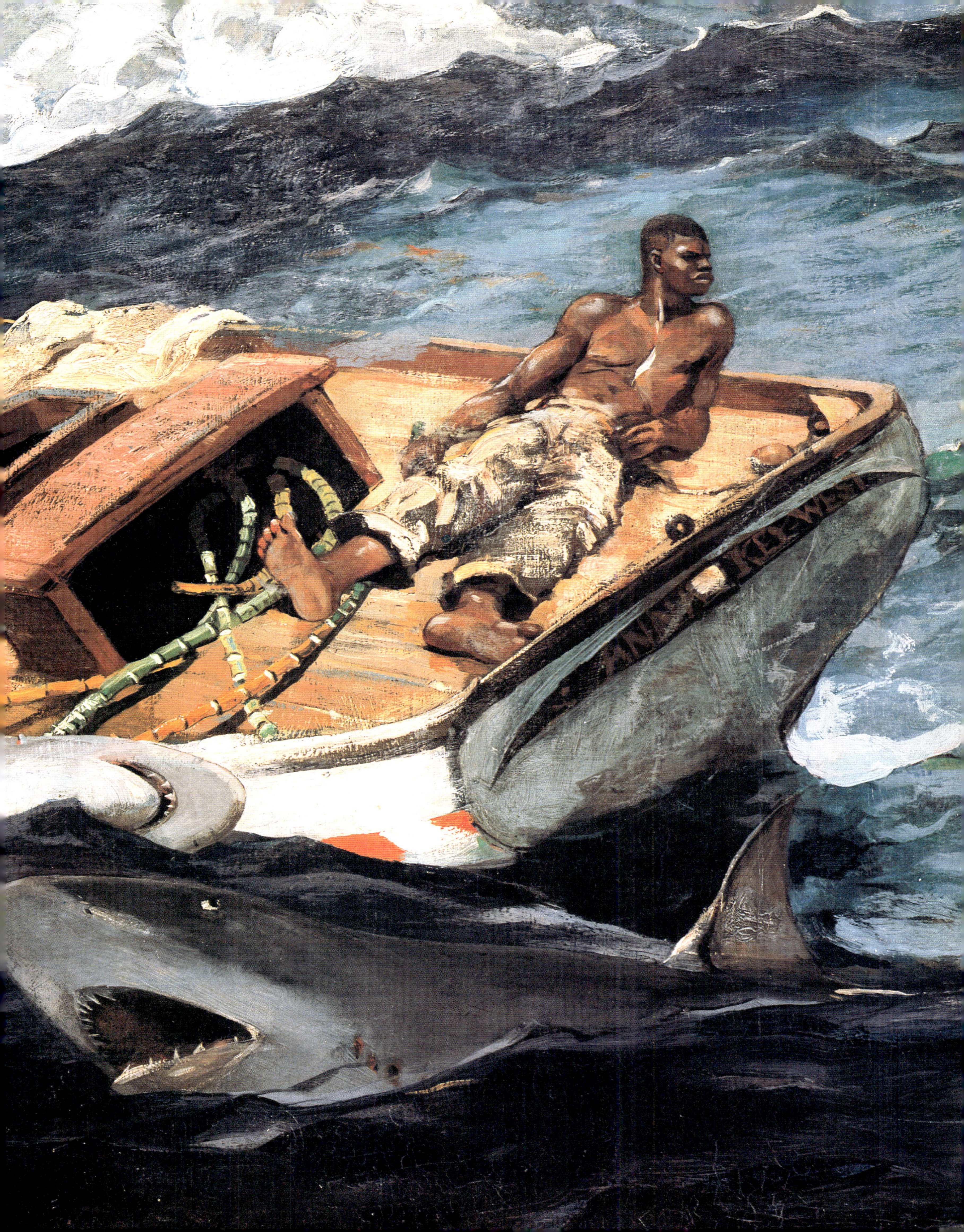
KEY-WEST

Eastman Johnson
1824–1906

The Hatch Family

Oil on canvas
48 x 73⅜ in. (121.9 x 186.4 cm.)
1871
Signed and dated at lower left: E. Johnson 1871
Gift of Frederic H. Hatch, 1926 (26.97)

EASTMAN JOHNSON established himself early in his life as a painter of portraits, at first in his native Maine and later in Boston and Washington. From 1858 on he worked in New York. Probably the most impressive and vividly convincing of his group portraits, and, according to the painter, his best, is this tableau of the family of Alfrederick Hatch (1829–1904), who commissioned it in 1871. Hatch, a broker who later became president of the New York Stock Exchange, enjoyed and collected both European and American paintings. The large family, gathered in the library of their house on the corner of Park Avenue and Thirty-seventh Street, includes, besides Alfrederick Hatch and his wife, his own father, his mother-in-law, and his eleven children, ranging in age from the sixteen-year-old John Ruggles, standing at the left, to the infant Emily Nichols, still in long baby clothes, on the lap of one of her sisters.

Johnson's *Hatch Family* is a matchless evocation of Victorian virtue and security in American society. The wreath in the one unshuttered window declares the moment to be holiday time, and with its heavy draperies the room is a protected enclave of family life. The presence of the grandparents suggests the cheerful indulgence and affection with which his numerous progeny were being raised.

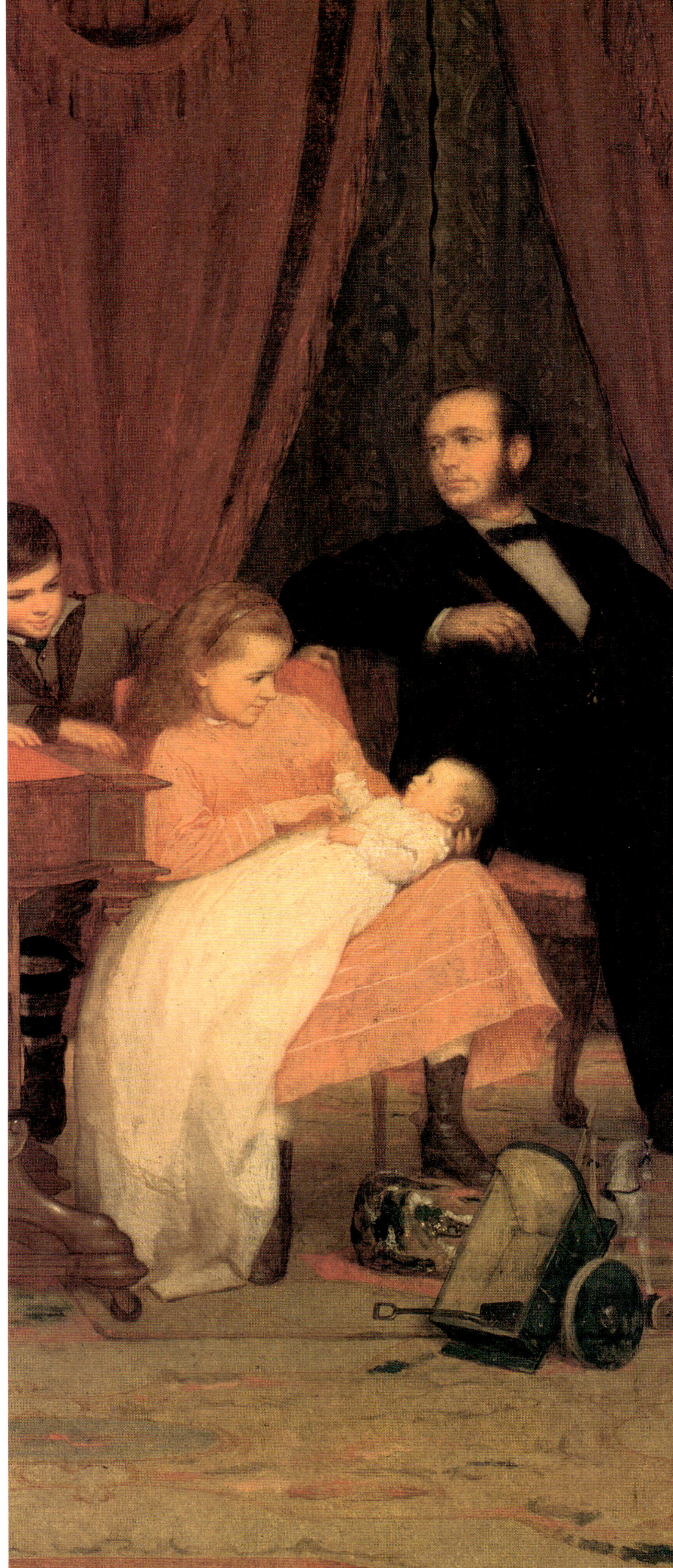

The Hatch Family (detail)

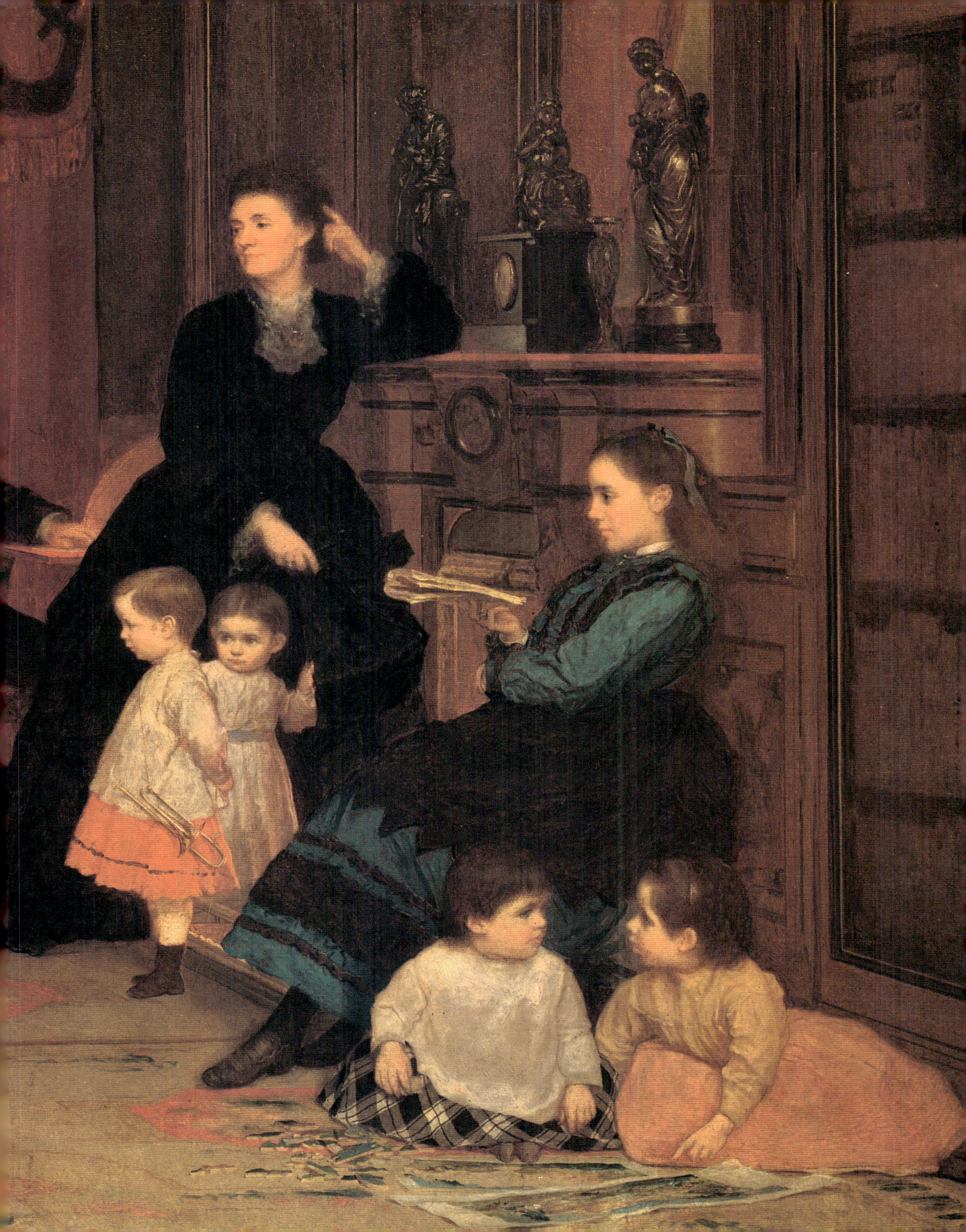

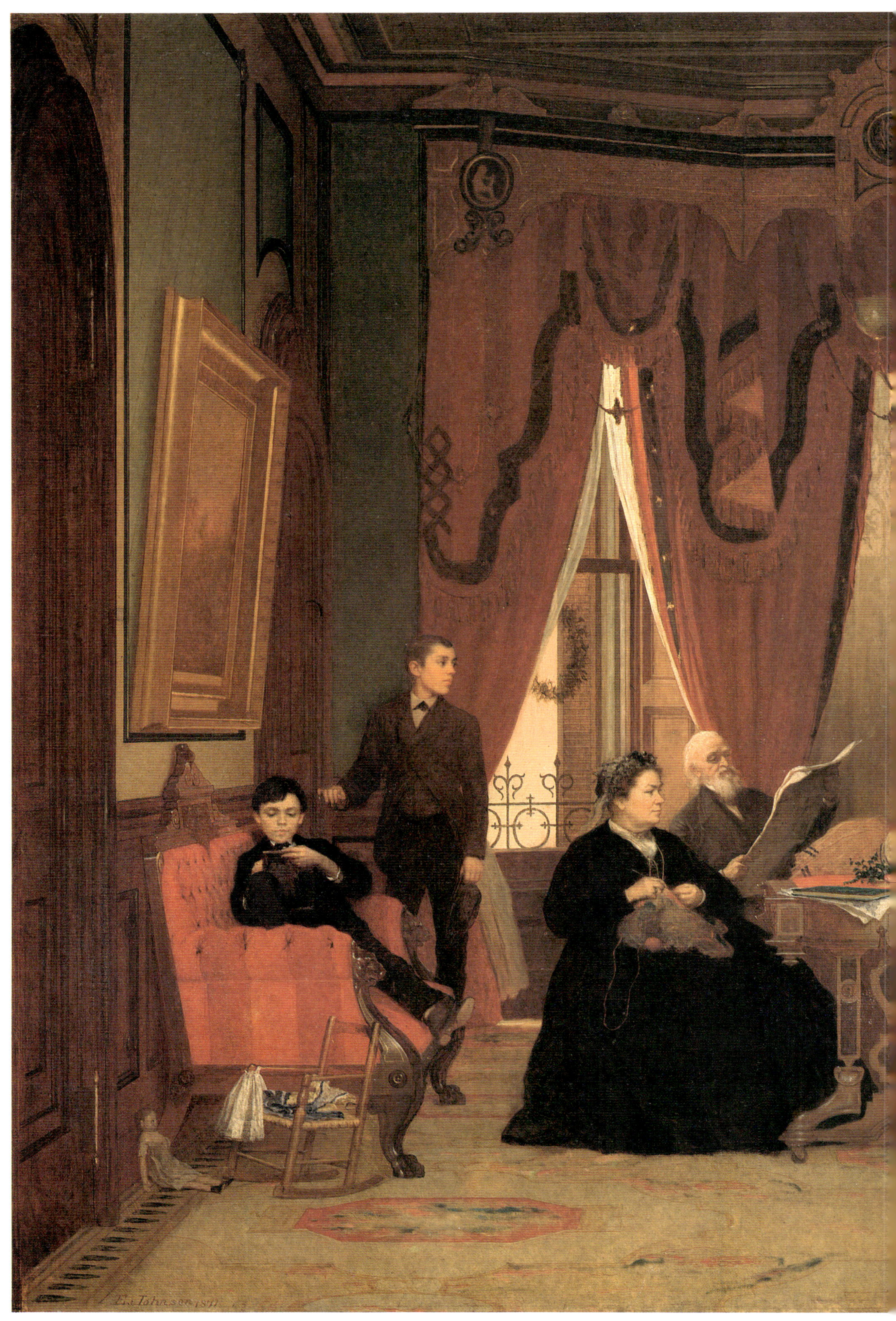

Eastman Johnson:
The Hatch Family

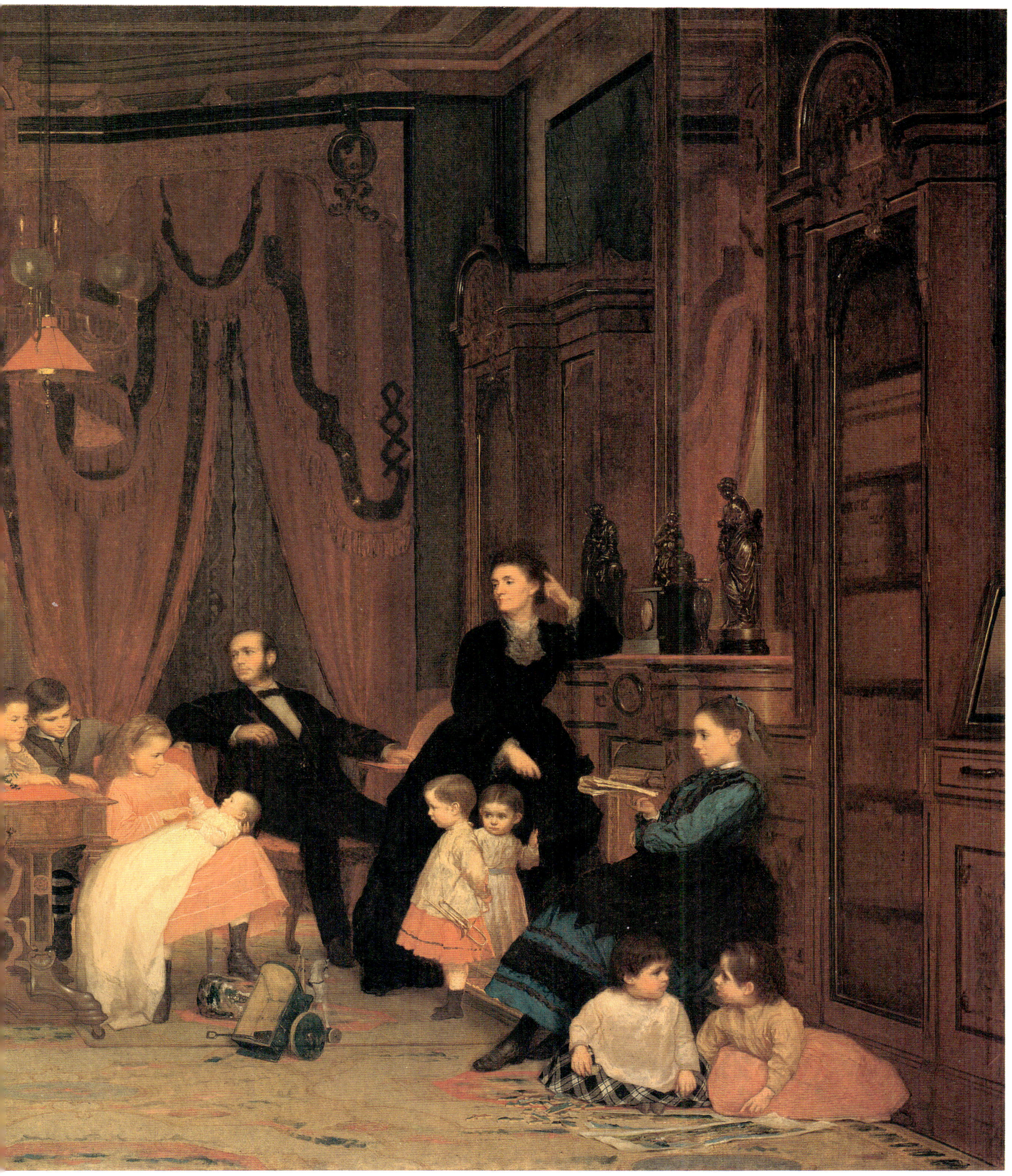

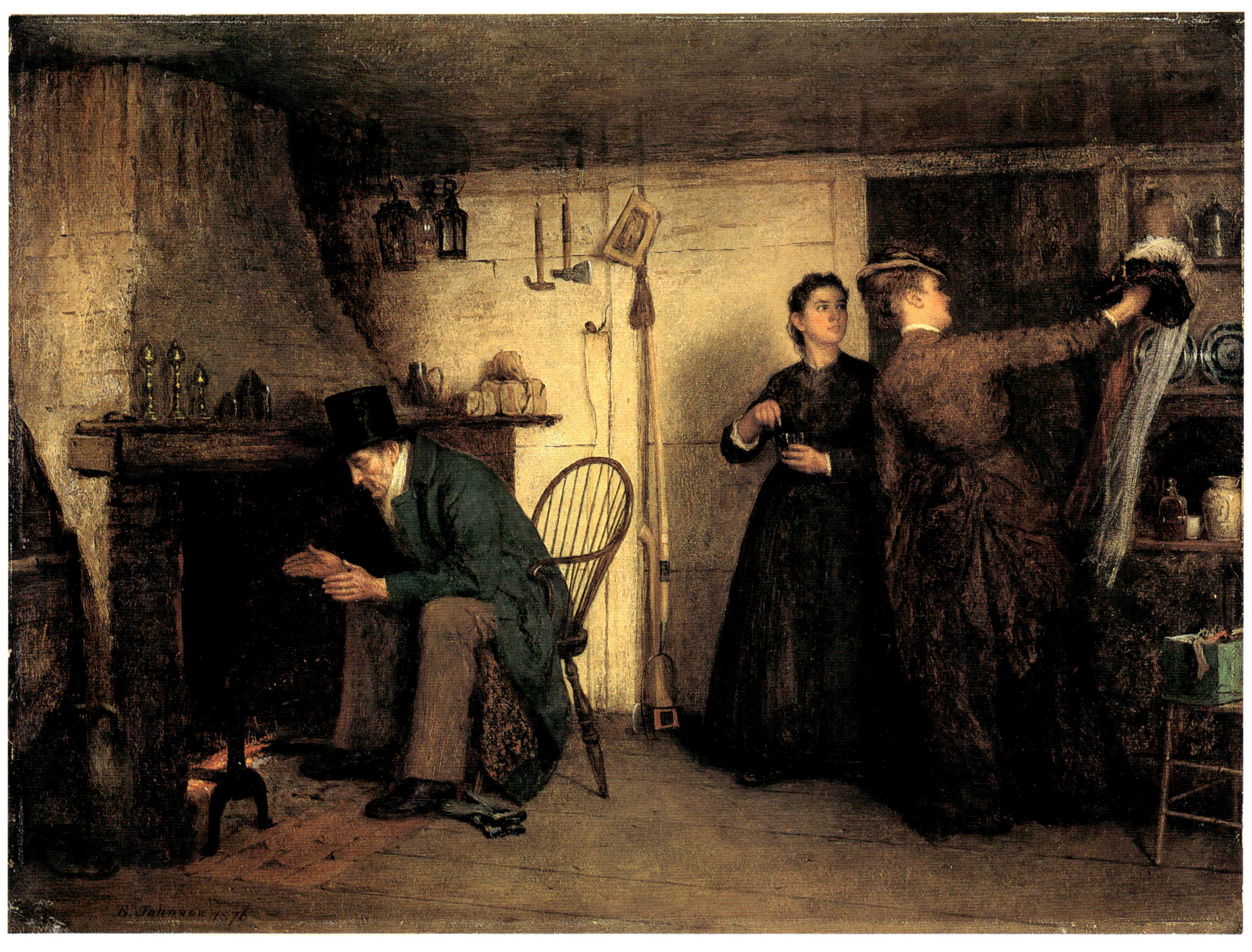

Eastman Johnson
1824–1906

The New Bonnet

Oil on academy board
20¾ x 27 in. (52.7 x 68.6 cm.)
1876
Signed and dated at lower left:
E. Johnson 1876
Bequest of Collis P. Huntington, 1900
(25.110.11)

IN 1871 EASTMAN JOHNSON bought and remodeled two old houses on the island of Nantucket, turning one of them into a studio where he produced some of his best works, inspired by the people of the island and their customs and activities. The low-ceilinged room in a farmhouse, the setting for this picture, contains many of the elements—fireplace, brass candlesticks, and oil lanterns—that appear frequently in his Nantucket interiors. As in so many paintings by Degas, the figures, who tell only part of a story, are related to each other spatially in a subtly planned composition. Has the woman at the right, who holds up the new, fashionable hat, just come in from shopping in the company of the seated man in the top hat? Warming his hands at the hearth, still wearing his overcoat, he turns his back on the other occupants of the room. The more plainly dressed woman seems to be moving toward the man to offer him the drink she is stirring, but turns her head to appraise the new confection, clearly not according it her full approval.

John G. Brown
1831–1913

The Music Lesson

Oil on canvas
24 x 20 in. (61 x 50.8 cm.)
1870
Signed and dated at lower left:
J. G. Brown/N.Y. 1870
Gift of Colonel Charles A. Fowler, 1921 (21.115.3)

THIS DETAILED DEPICTION of a comfortable Victorian parlor, where the "finer things of life," such as art and music, were appreciated, gives the impression of a conscientious reporting of the year 1870. The theme, however, of a cavalier and a pretty young lady sharing an interest in music, as well as an absorbing interest in each other, is an old one that was a favorite with the seventeenth-century painters in Holland. John G. Brown, an Englishman, had studied art in Edinburgh and probably had seen William Holman Hunt's treatment of a similar subject. Once established in New York, Brown rapidly developed a reputation as a painter of children and of working-class genre scenes that were very popular and successful. Pictures such as *The Music Lesson* are characterized by a remarkable degree of realism and accuracy.

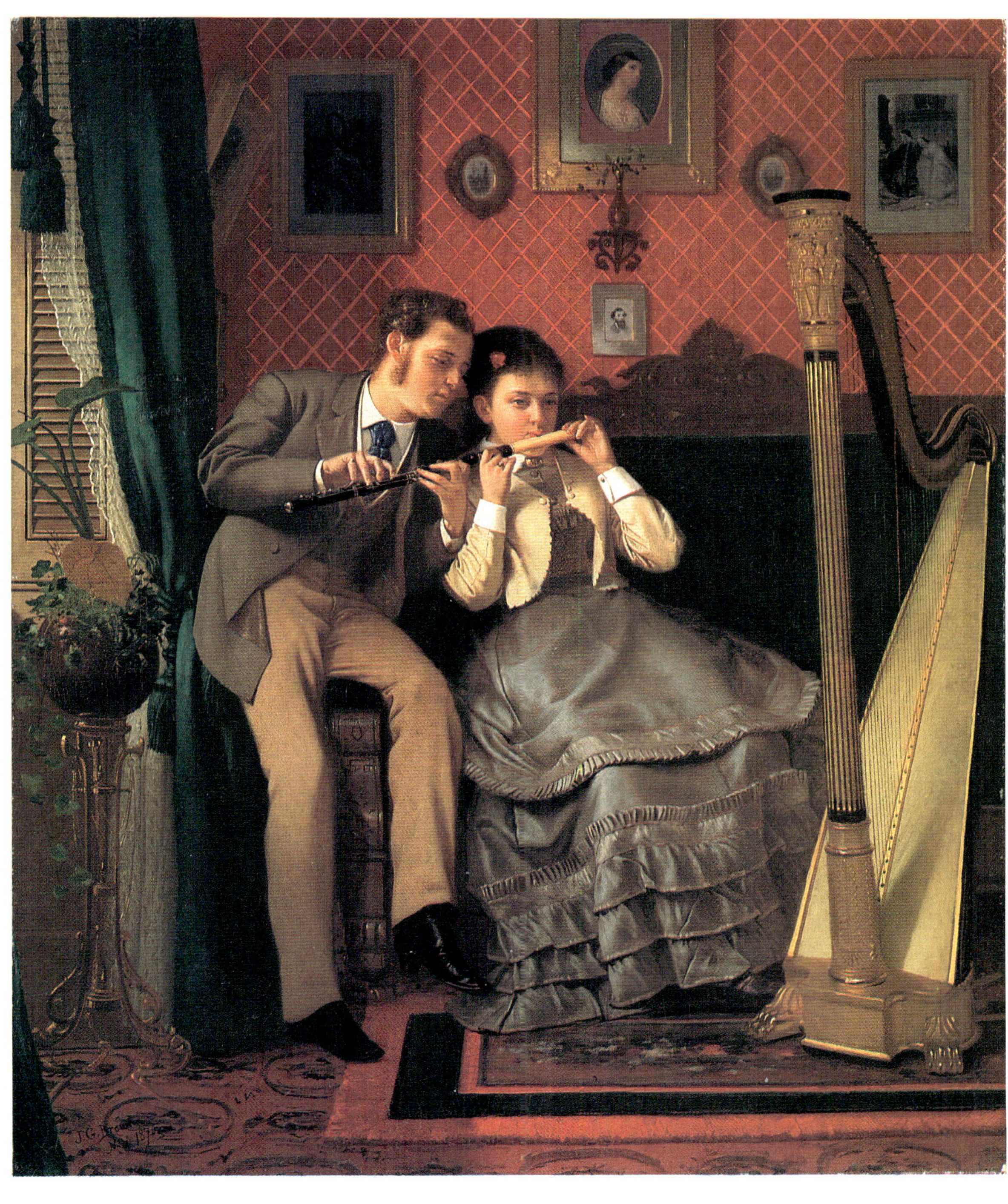

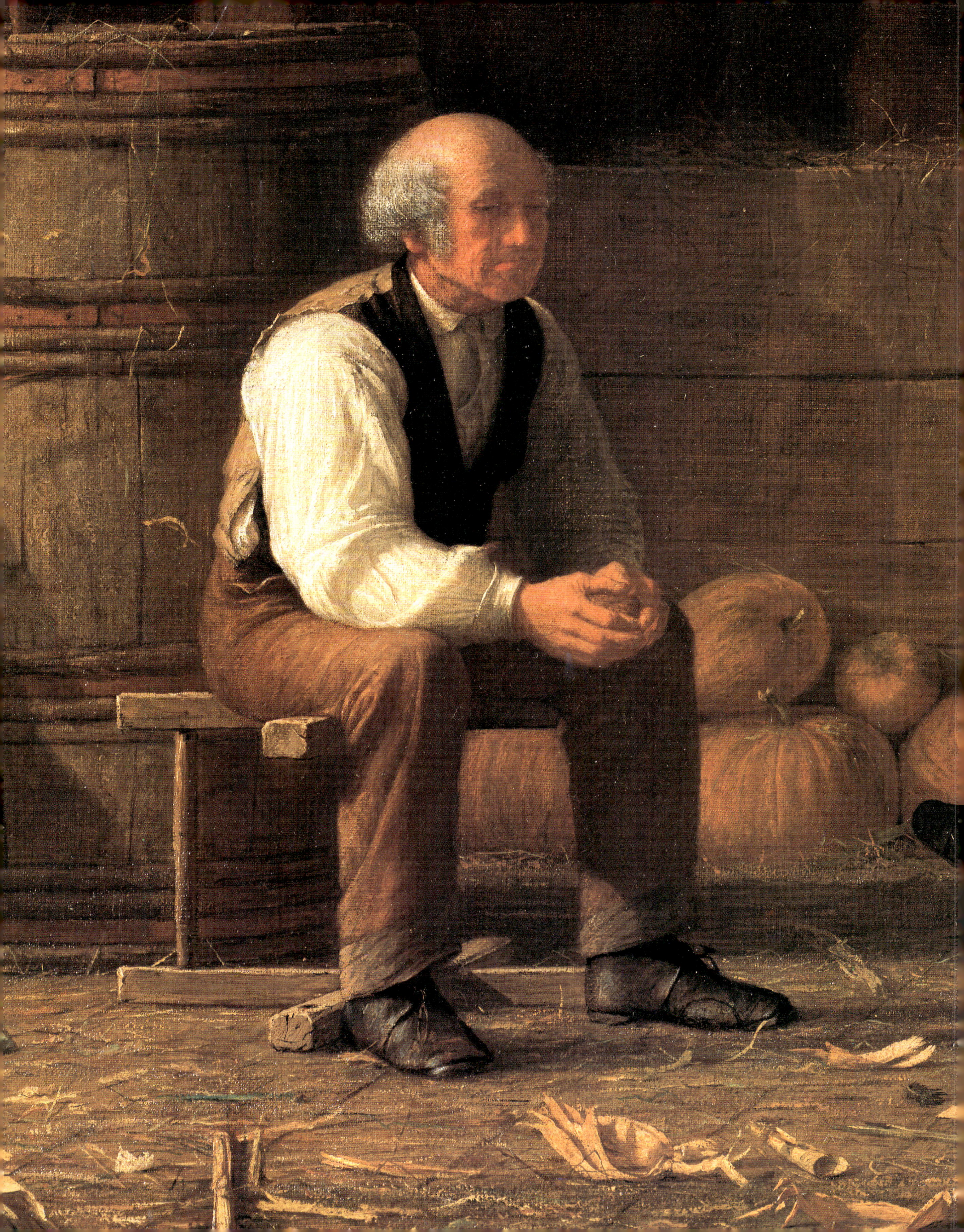

Enoch Wood Perry
1831–1915

Talking It Over

Oil on canvas
22¼ x 29¼ in. (56.5 x 74.3 cm.)
1872
Signed and dated at lower left:
E. W. Perry/[NA]/'72
Gift of Erving and Joyce Wolf, 1980 (1980.361)

THE SKILLFUL RENDERING of this rural subject and the simple clarity of its presentation reflect the excellent training Enoch Perry Wood had received as a young student in Europe. In Düsseldorf he had worked under Emanuel Leutze, and in Paris he had studied with Thomas Couture, one of the best teachers of his time. For about nine years, at the beginning of his career, Perry moved about a good deal, serving as American consul in Venice and then, on his return to the United States, painting portraits in Philadelphia, New Orleans, San Francisco, Honolulu, and Salt Lake City. By the time he settled in New York, he had developed a kind of genre picture that became immensely popular. These paintings had gentle, everyday subjects, enhanced by able drawing and color. In this portrayal of two countrymen, the dignity and uncomplicated matter-of-factness of the scene cast a spell of quiet harmony that is deeply appealing. The literal representation of common farm objects signifies a true familiarity with this kind of setting and first-hand acquaintance with the easy companionship of the two men. Two horses, one seen at the center in his stall and another implied by his cast shadow on the hogshead, seem to be participants in the friendly scene.

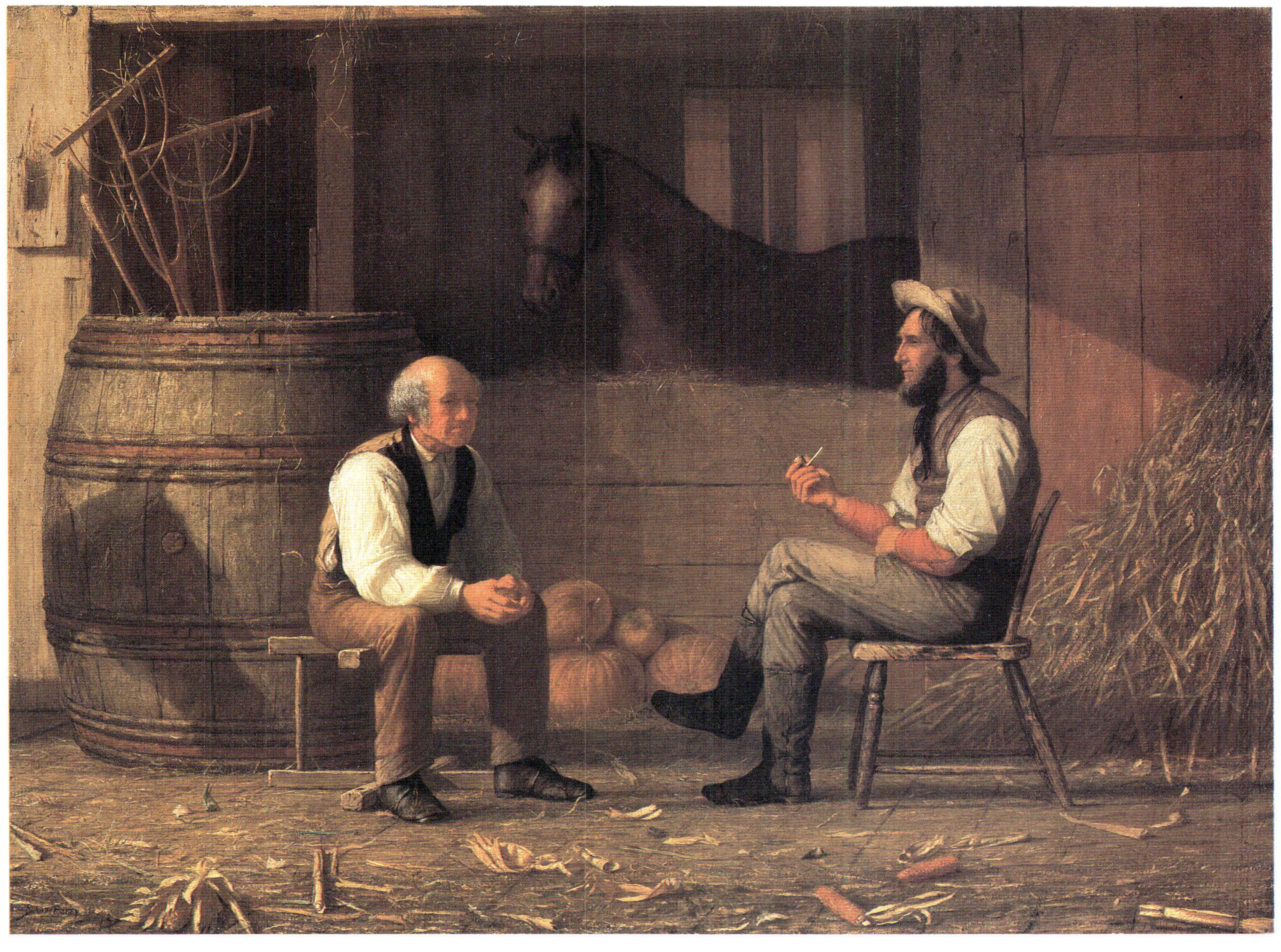

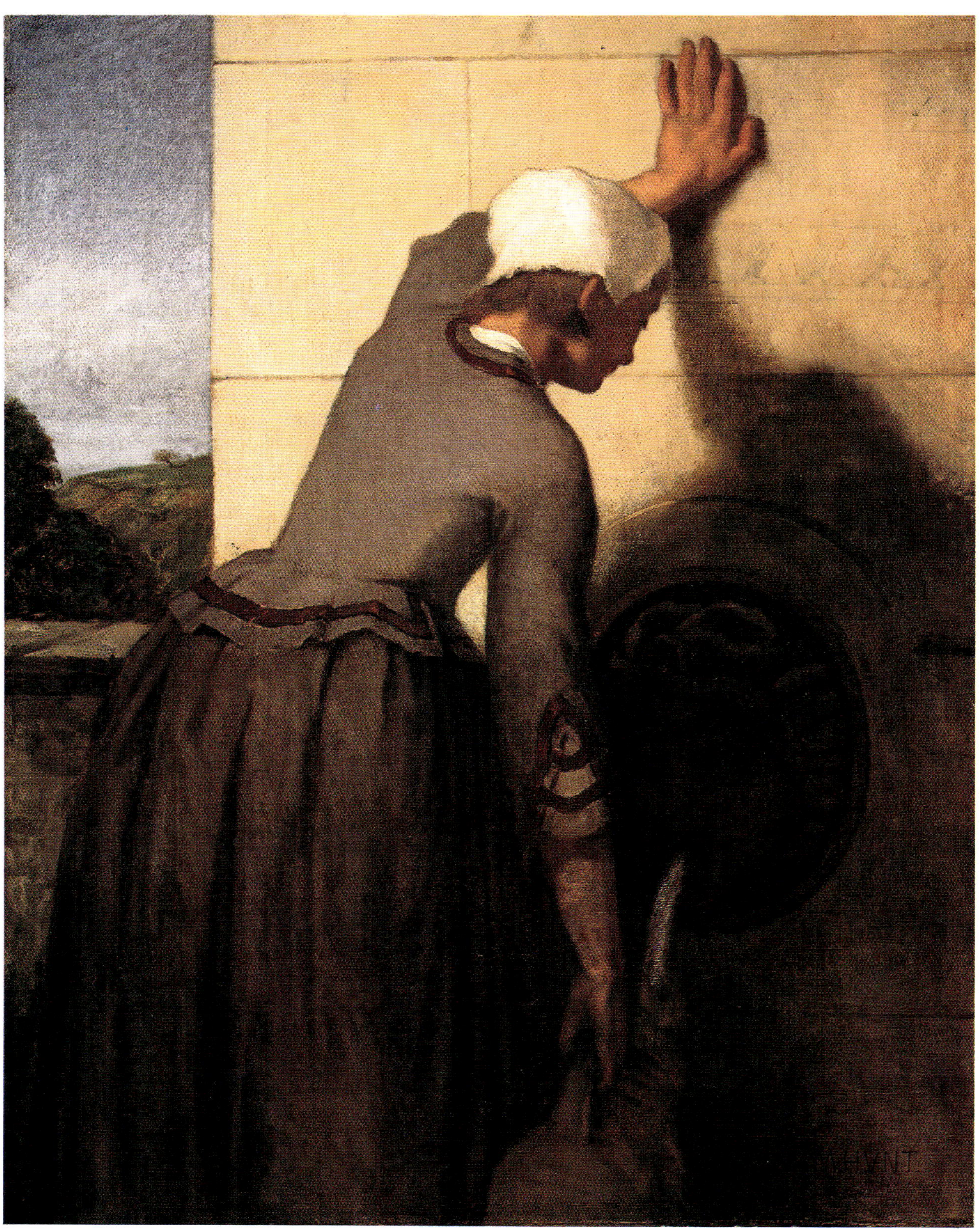

William Morris Hunt
1824–1879

Girl at the Fountain

Oil on canvas
46 x 35½ in. (116.8 x 90.2 cm.)
ca. 1852–1854
Signed at lower right: W. M. HUNT
Bequest of Jane Hunt, 1907 (08.88)

WILLIAM MORRIS HUNT is said to have seen a coachman supporting himself against a wall in the posture of the girl seen here, while drawing water for his horses at a fountain. He conceived the idea that if a shapely young woman were substituted for the coachman, this simple pose would make a good picture. Hunt probably began the painting about 1852 when he was working at Barbizon with Jean-François Millet, the French painter of peasants, whose influence is evident in the sturdy, unaffected gestures of the plainly dressed model. She lays one large, well-formed hand against the wall and, with the other, grasps the handle of a heavy pitcher. Her shadow and the Medusa-head sculpture on the wall give interest to the plain blocks of stone, and a glimpse of trees and hillside opens the composition at the left to air and space.

John La Farge
1835–1910

Bishop Berkeley's Rock, Newport

Oil on canvas
30¼ x 25¼ in. (76.9 x 64.2 cm.)
1868
Signed, inscribed, and dated at lower left: J. La Farge/Newport 1868
Gift of Dr. Frank Jewett Mather, Jr., 1949 (49.76)

THIS MASSIVE barren promontory on the coast of Rhode Island is named for George Berkeley, the Irish bishop who formulated a completely nonmaterialistic philosophy of idealism. The churchman, who spent some time in Newport, is popularly reported to have found this isolated spot on the seashore congenial for thinking and writing. When John La Farge painted this landscape, he had worked in Newport for several years, studying with William Morris Hunt. A devotee and collector of Barbizon paintings, Hunt had fanned La Farge's own enthusiasm for the Barbizon painters and had encouraged him to follow their practice of working directly from nature. By the late 1860s, however, naturalism had given way in La Farge's paintings to simplification of design and subtlety of color. The smooth planes with which he has built this rock and the broadly sweeping continuous strokes delineating the background relate this picture to abstract works of the mid-twentieth century, revealing La Farge as an innovator whose originality and imagination were to exert a widespread influence.

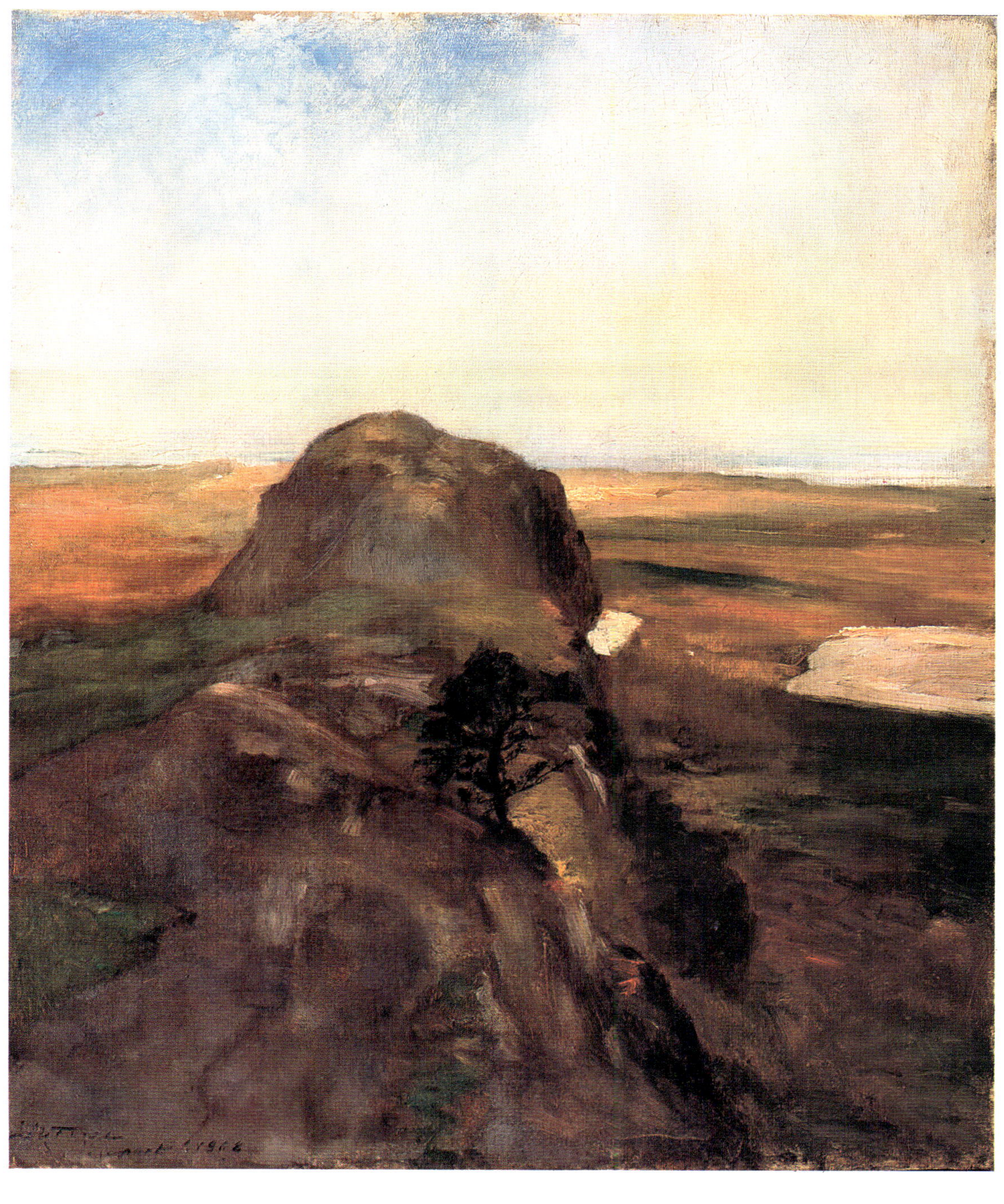

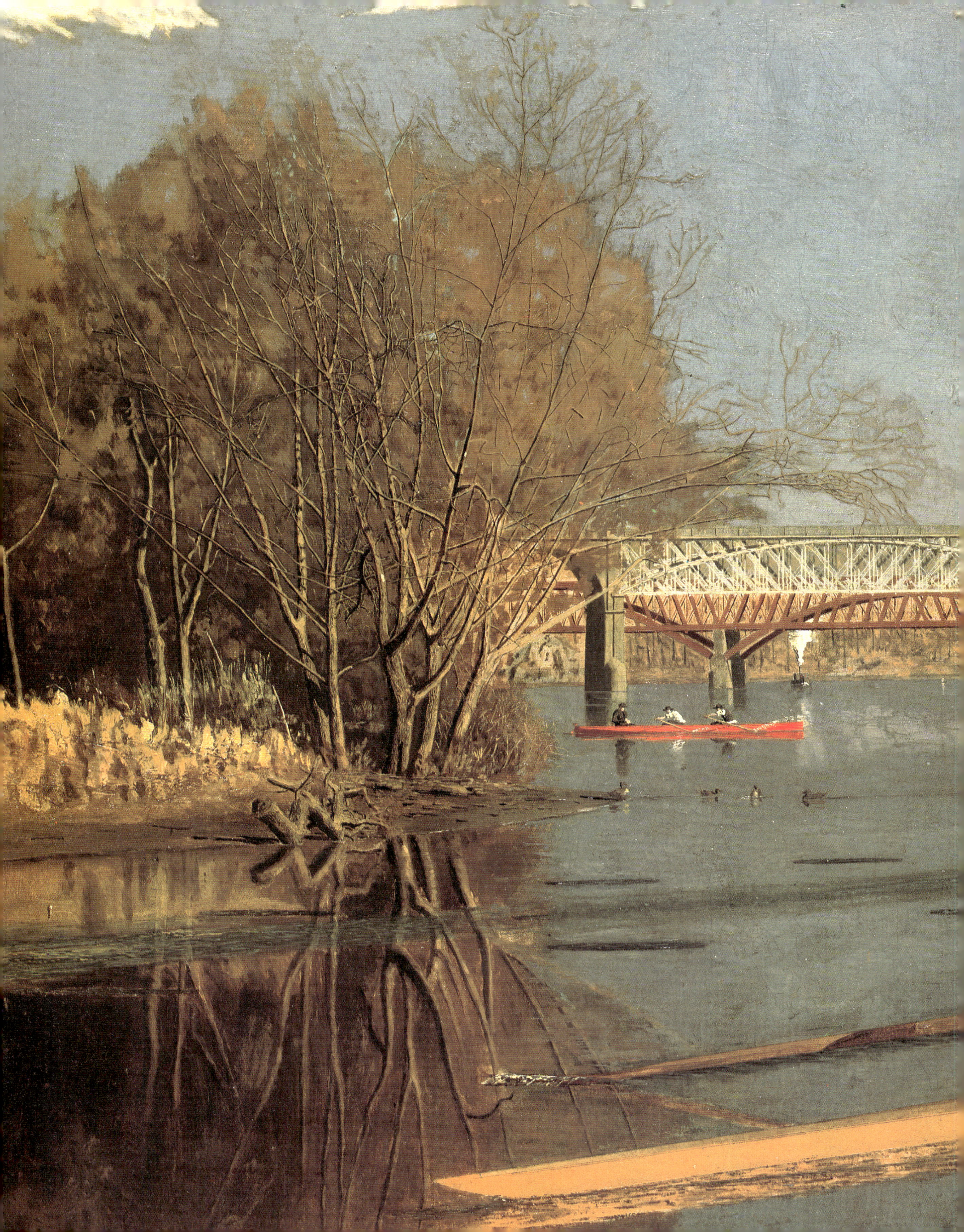

Thomas Eakins
1844–1916

Max Schmitt in a Single Scull, or The Champion Single Sculls

Oil on canvas
32¼ x 46¼ in. (81.9 x 117.5 cm.)
1871
Signed and dated on scull in background: EAKINS/1871; inscribed on scull in foreground the name of Schmitt's sister: JOSIE
Purchase, The Alfred N. Punnett Endowment Fund and George D. Pratt Gift, 1934 (34.92)

ROWING WAS one of many sports Thomas Eakins enjoyed, and early in the 1870s he painted several rowing pictures that show his mastery of mathematical drawing and his close scientific observation of the problems of reflection and refraction. In this extremely accomplished perspective view of a river landscape, Eakins portrays, in the foreground, his boyhood friend Max Schmitt at a moment of rest in a shell; in the middle distance, himself in a second scull; and, still farther back, four oarsmen in a larger craft. Far off, a steamboat plies its way beneath the two bridges spanning this section of the Schuylkill River at Philadelphia—the Girard Avenue and the Connecting Railroad bridges. The mechanical exactitude of the vertical piers and their crossing metal trusses contrasts with the natural forms of clouds, trees, and foliage, to which Eakins was always so aesthetically sensitive.

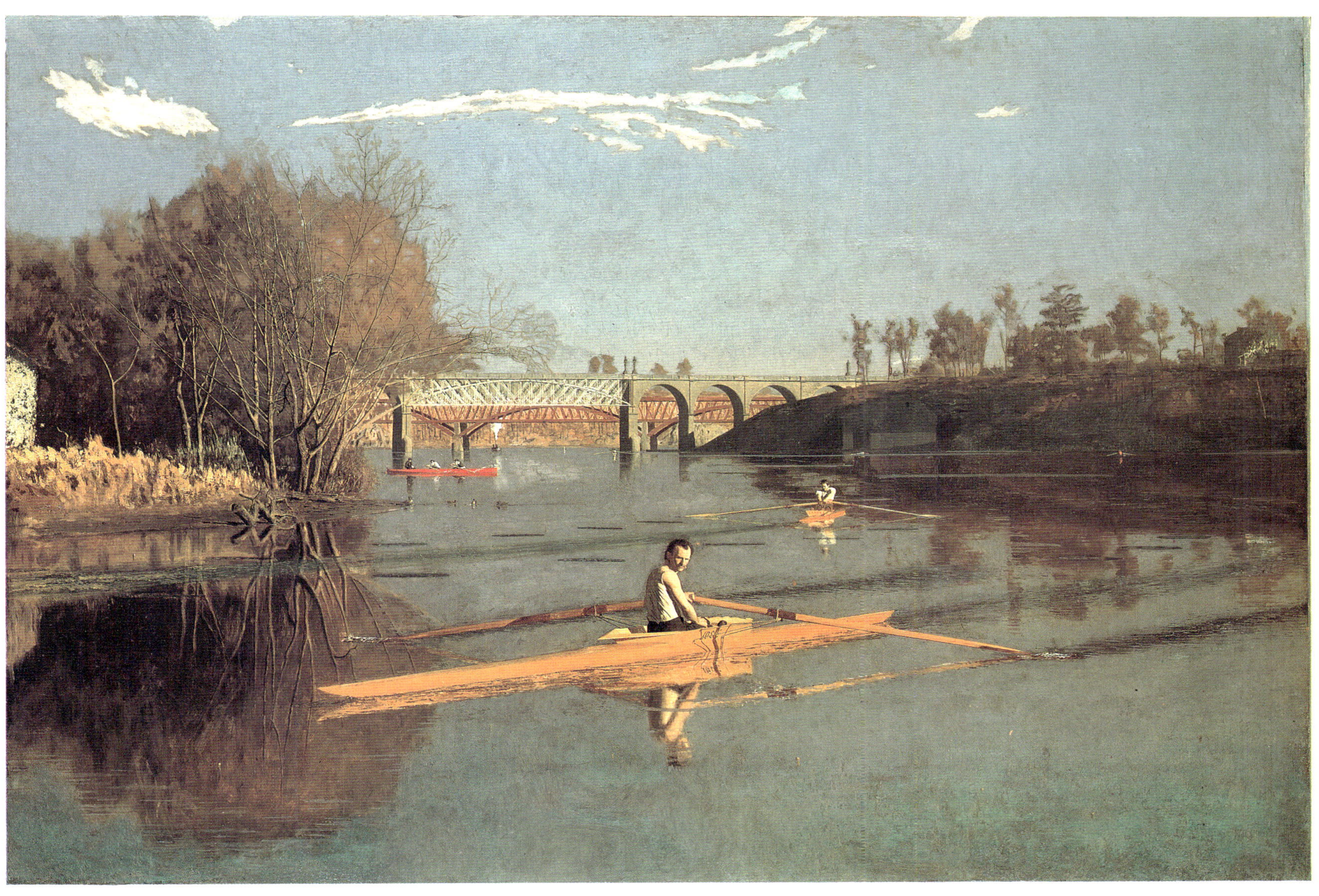

Thomas Eakins
1844–1916

Pushing for Rail

Oil on canvas
13 x 30 1/16 in. (33 x 76.2 cm.)
1874
Signed and dated at lower right: EAKINS 74
Arthur Hoppock Hearn Fund, 1916 (16.65)

THE HUNT FOR RAIL, a game bird that frequents marshes, is only possible at high tide, when the "pusher" can propel a flat-bottomed boat through the thick green reeds. The pusher navigates the boat with an eleven-foot pole, but also stirs up the birds from their deep hiding places in the vegetation, holds the boat fast while the shooter aims, and reclaims the bag with a net. Here, in the Philadelphia area, three pairs of hunters show the varied motions necessary at successive moments of the hunt. The precisely drawn ground is deliberately hazy. Heavy emphasis on horizontals suggests the slow, carefully controlled motion of the boats. Thomas Eakins sent the picture for criticism to Paris to his former teacher Jean-Léon Gérôme, who expressed pride in Eakins as his pupil and commended his progress.

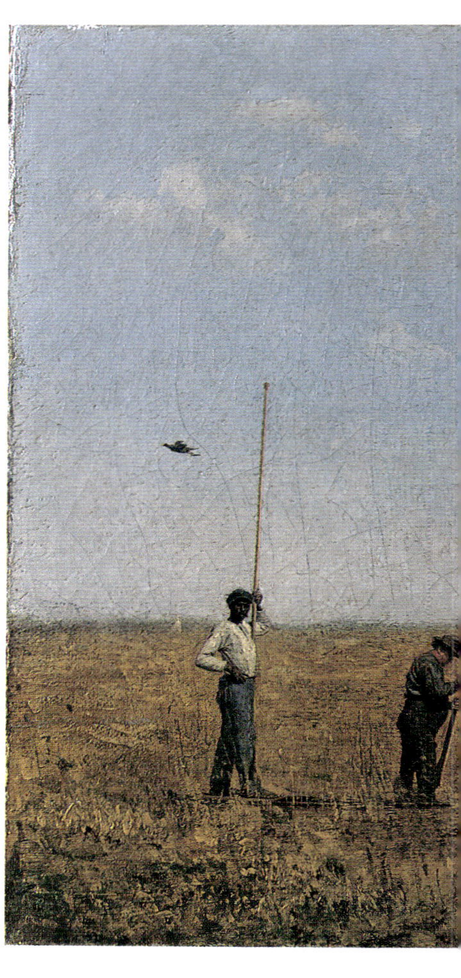

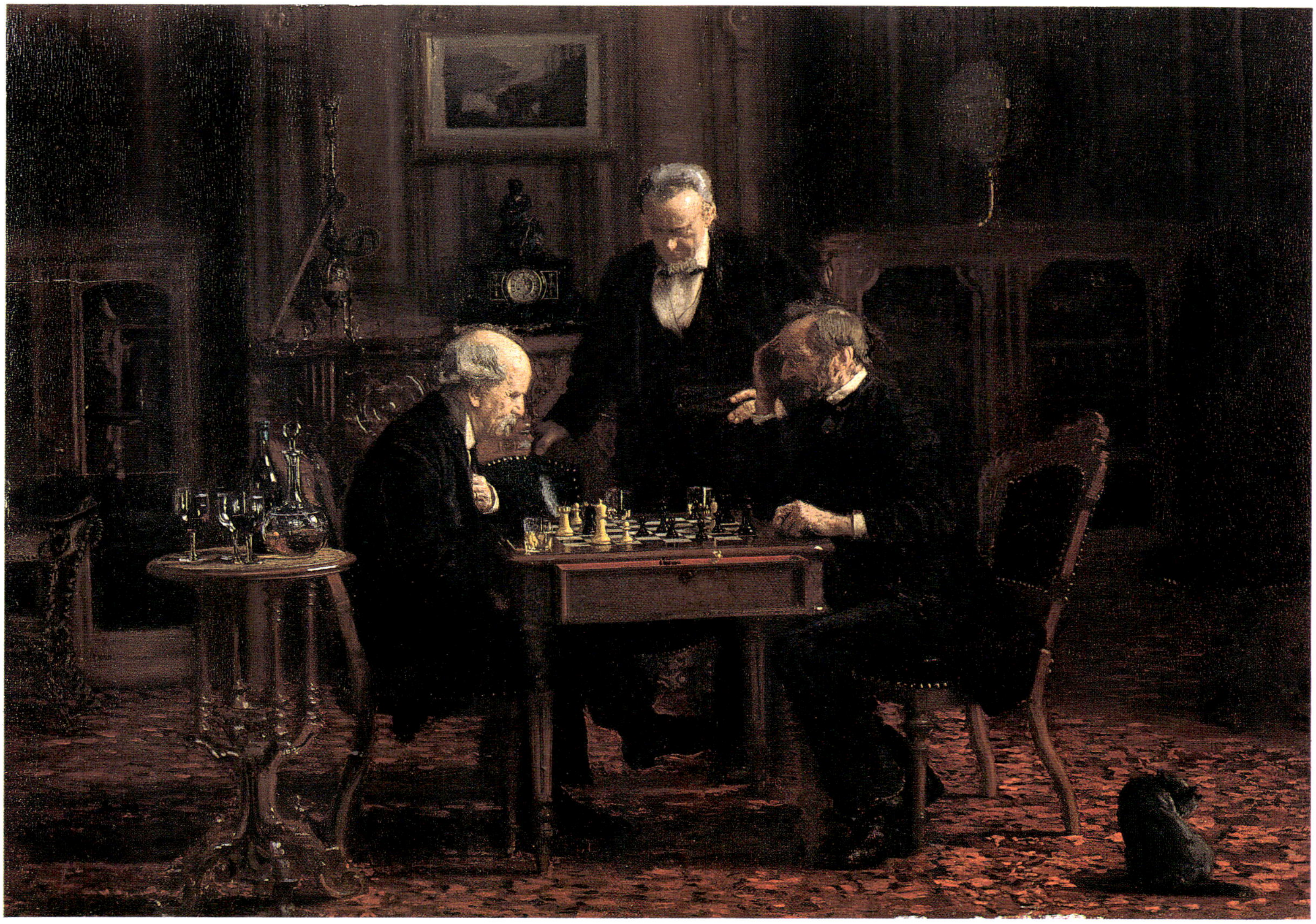

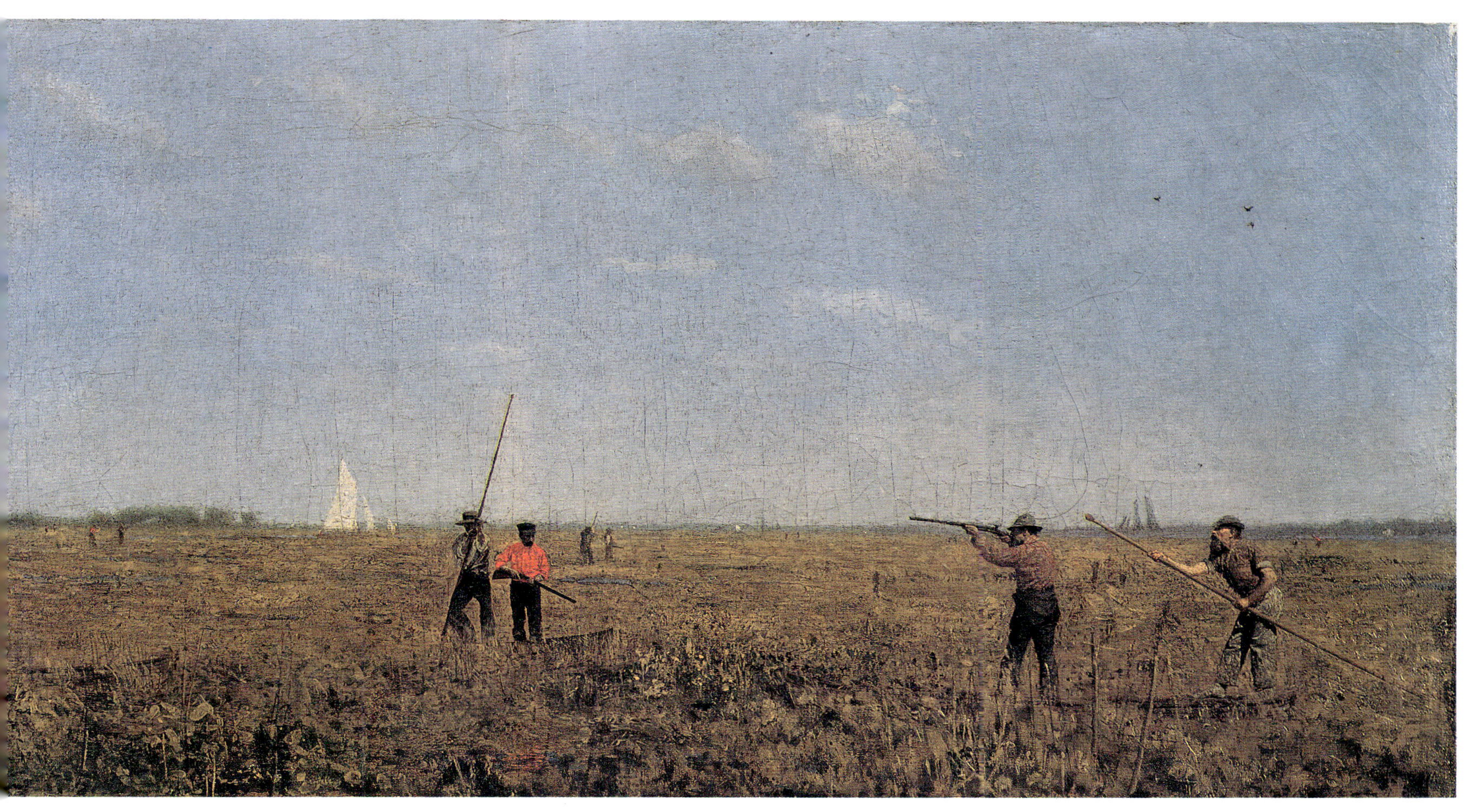

Thomas Eakins
1844–1916

The Chess Players

Oil on wood
11¾ x 16¾ in. (29.8 x 42.6 cm.)
1876
Signed, inscribed, and dated on drawer of central table: Benjamini. Eakins. Filius. Pinxit. 76.
Gift of the artist, 1881 (81.14)

PERHAPS THOMAS EAKINS was remembering pictures by Meissonier and other academic French painters when he filled the background of this little scene with details of the furniture and ornaments in the sitting room of his family's house in Philadelphia. In the foreground, a teacher of French, Bertrand Gardel, and a painter, George W. Holmes, concentrate on a game of chess. The artist's father, Benjamin Eakins, stands behind them, as deeply absorbed as they in their strategies. He gazes downward at the board, and the three intensely thoughtful heads form a compositional triangle that dominates the design, the three lines of vision converging at the center of the picture. One of the two known preparations for this work is in the Museum's collection—an elaborate perspective drawing in ink and pencil that shows how earnestly Eakins studied the structure of his paintings.

Thomas Eakins
1844–1916

The Artist's Wife and His Setter Dog

Oil on canvas
30 x 23 in. (76.2 x 58.4 cm.)
ca. 1884–1885
Fletcher Fund, 1923 (23.139)

THE WOMAN IS the artist's wife, Susan MacDowell Eakins (1851–1938), posing with their dog Harry in a corner of the studio. The painting was probably begun soon after their marriage in 1884, when she was thirty-three and no doubt looked younger and less careworn—X-rays show that the picture was heavily reworked at a later date. Such extensive overpainting accounts for the dense surface. Susan Eakins, who was also a painter, had studied for six years at the Pennsylvania Academy of the Fine Arts, where she was the pupil of Thomas Eakins. In her lap an open picture book, perhaps by Hiroshige, reflects the strong contemporary interest in Japanese art. The relief at the upper right is *Arcadia*, a sculpture by Eakins; there is also a painting by him with this theme in the Museum's collection.

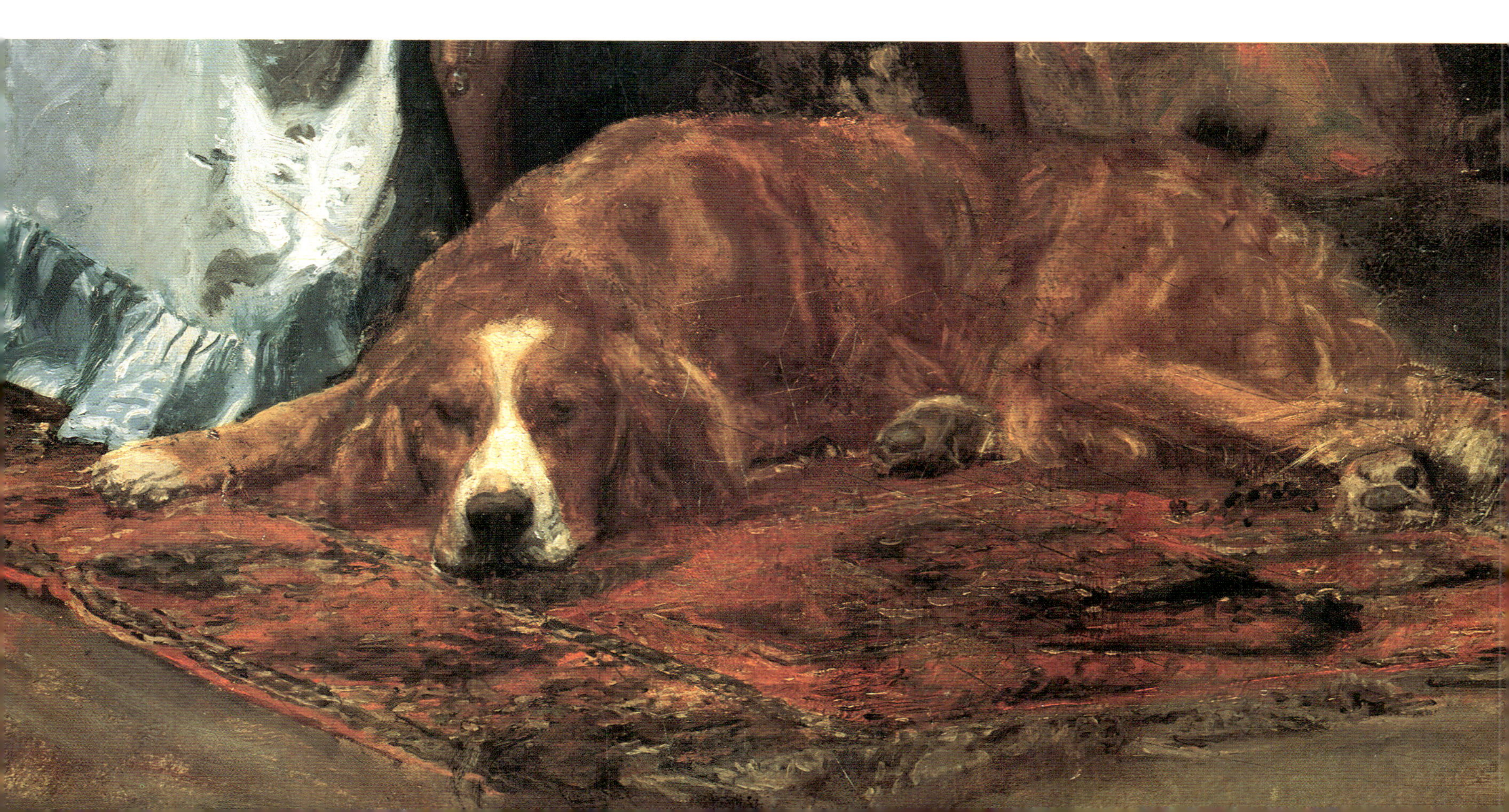

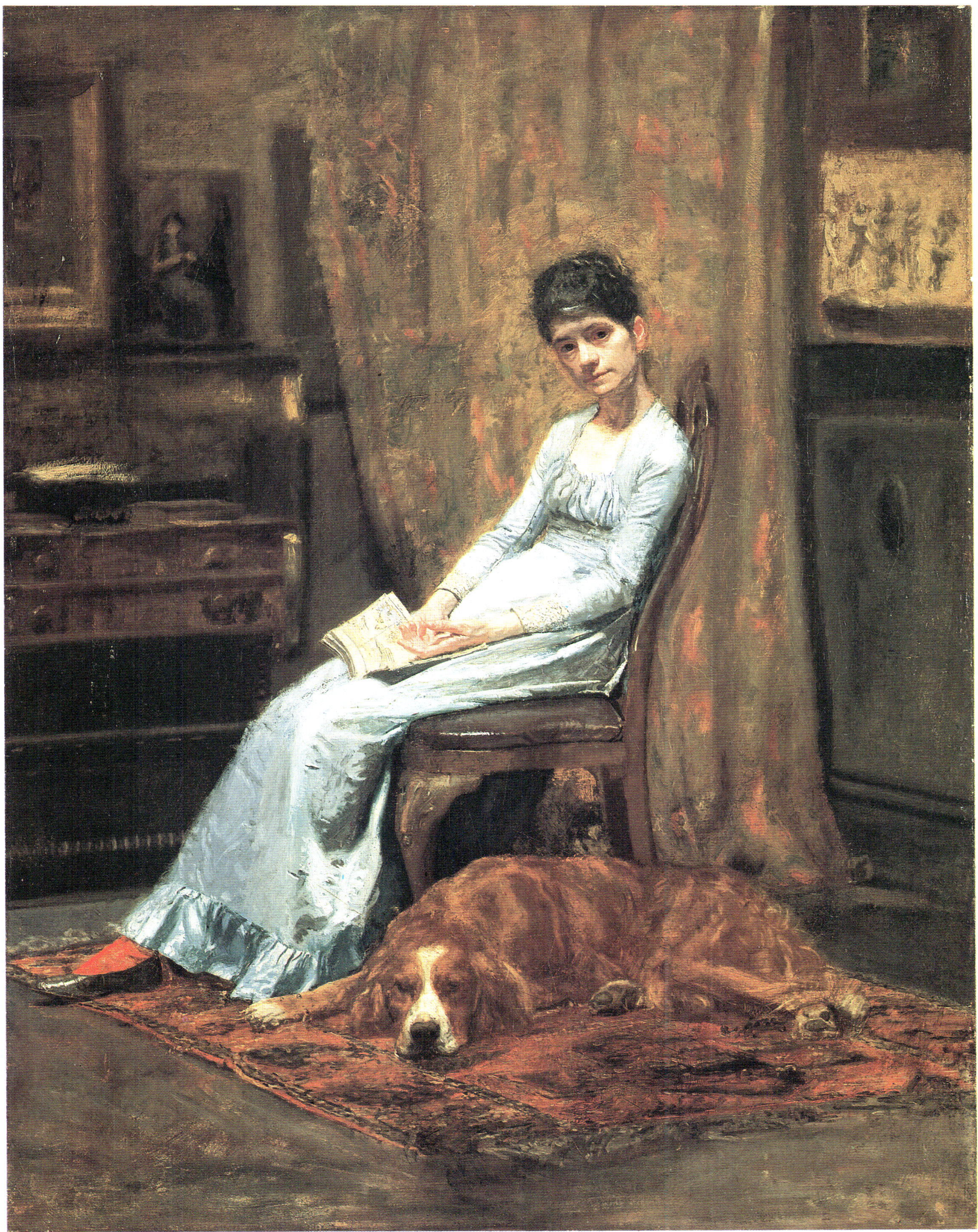

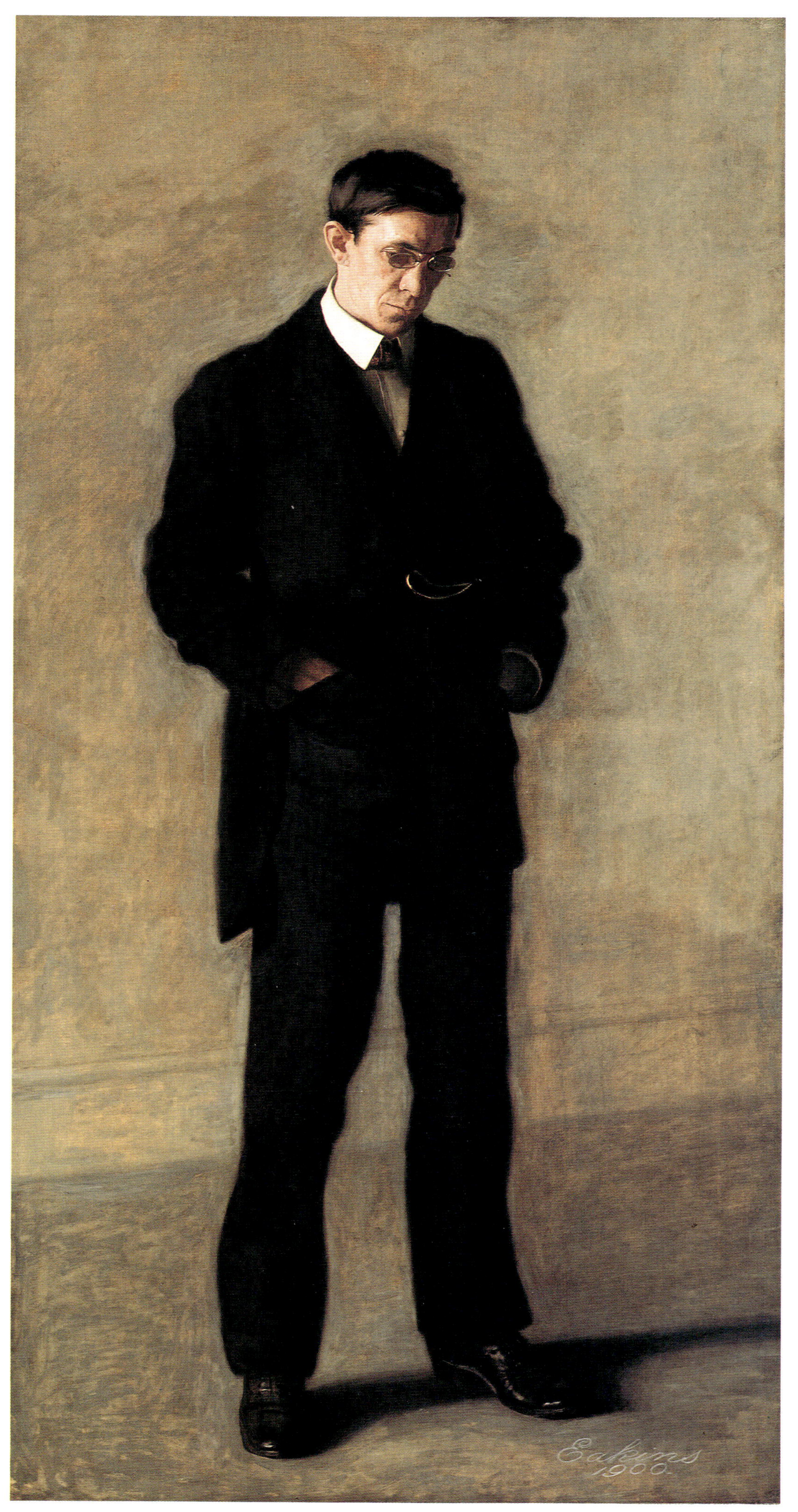
Eakins
1900.

Thomas Eakins
1844–1916

The Thinker: Portrait of Louis N. Kenton

Oil on canvas
82 x 42 in. (208.3 x 106.7 cm.)
1900
Signed and dated at lower right:
Eakins/1900
John Stewart Kennedy Fund, 1917
(17.172)

LIKE SO MANY ARTISTS of his time, Thomas Eakins came away from a pilgrimage to the Prado Museum in Madrid deeply impressed by the paintings of Velázquez, especially the standing full-length portraits of the king of Spain, the royal family, and the jesters. Manet, Sargent, Whistler, and Chase all experimented with the formulation evolved with such distinction by Velázquez. None, however, came as close as Eakins did to equaling the Spaniard's inspired grasp of the inner life expressed in a momentary pose and to fixing for eternity its revelation of the human essence. *The Thinker* was Louis N. Kenton (1869–1947), who was married for a brief period to the artist's sister-in-law. Eakins's profound knowledge of anatomy shows in the firm planting of the perfectly shod feet and in the complete correctness of the form and its reflective pose. Technical skills efface themselves in the service of expression, and style is indissolubly blended with content.

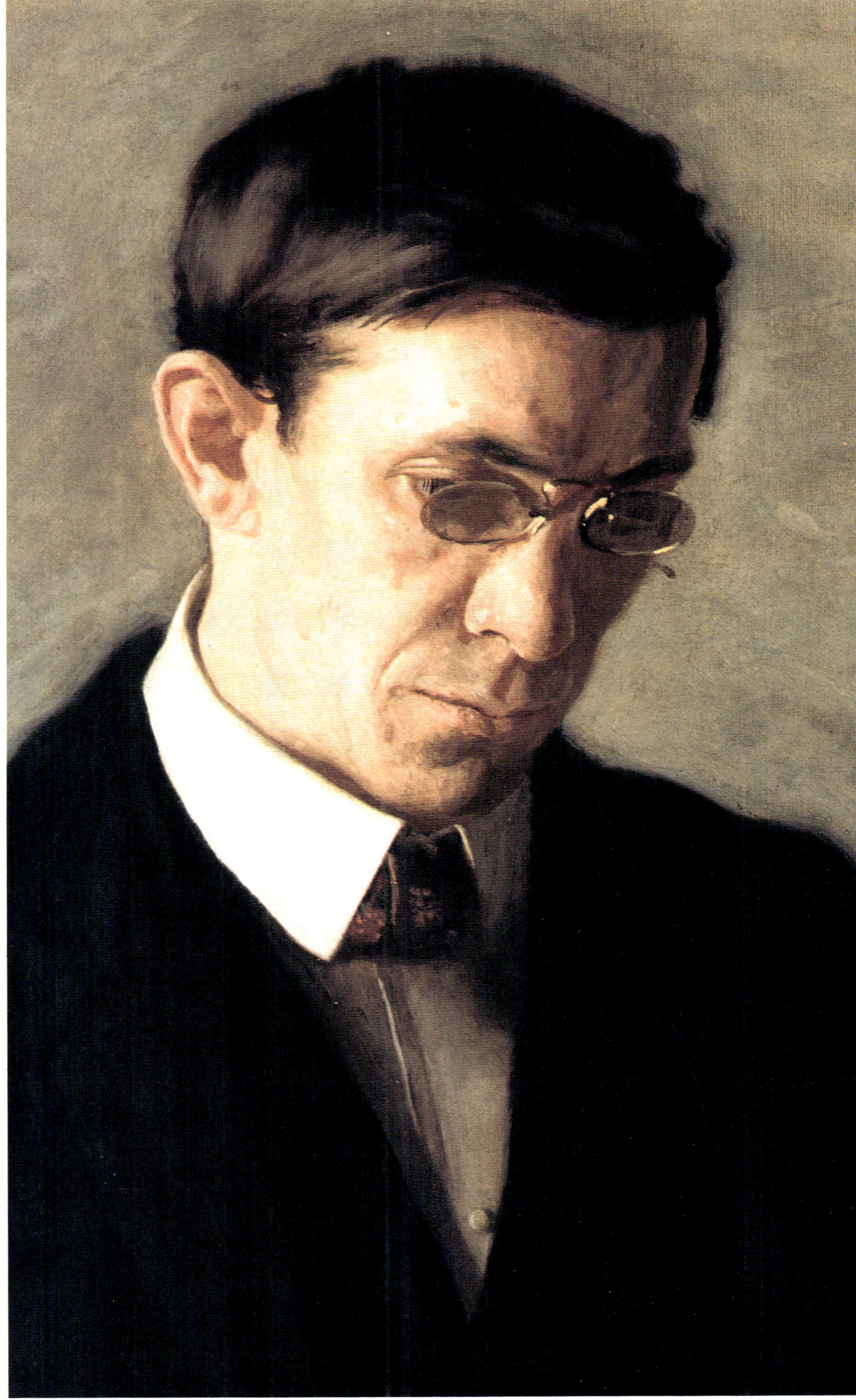

William Michael Harnett
1848–1892

The Artist's Letter Rack

Oil on canvas
30 x 25 in. (76.2 x 63.5 cm.)
1879
Signed and dated at upper left: WMH (monogram) ARNETT/1879
Morris K. Jesup Fund, 1966 (66.13)

WILLIAM MICHAEL HARNETT was the leading artist of the American school of trompe l'oeil, a style of painting conceived with the intention to deceive the eye into seeing a flat painted surface as having thickness and depth. In this picture, however, the idea of composing a grid of tape into which various objects are inserted seems to have come from another painter of this deception, John F. Peto, an example of whose work is shown on the facing page. Here, in this early work by Harnett, he has deliberately tried for an effect of flatness rather than for the solid three-dimensional quality of many of his later works. The pink tape forming the rack allows just enough give to hold in place some letters, a postcard, and a few scraps of paper bearing puzzling inscriptions. The grain of the wooden boards forming the background has been carefully delineated, and the slight shadows cast by the edges of objects have been subtly expressed. Many of the inscriptions remain unexplained, but a few clues suggest that the painting was commissioned by a member of the Philadelphia firm of C. C. Peirson and Sons, which dealt in hides. The other businessmen whose names are hinted at were probably involved in the wool and leather trades.

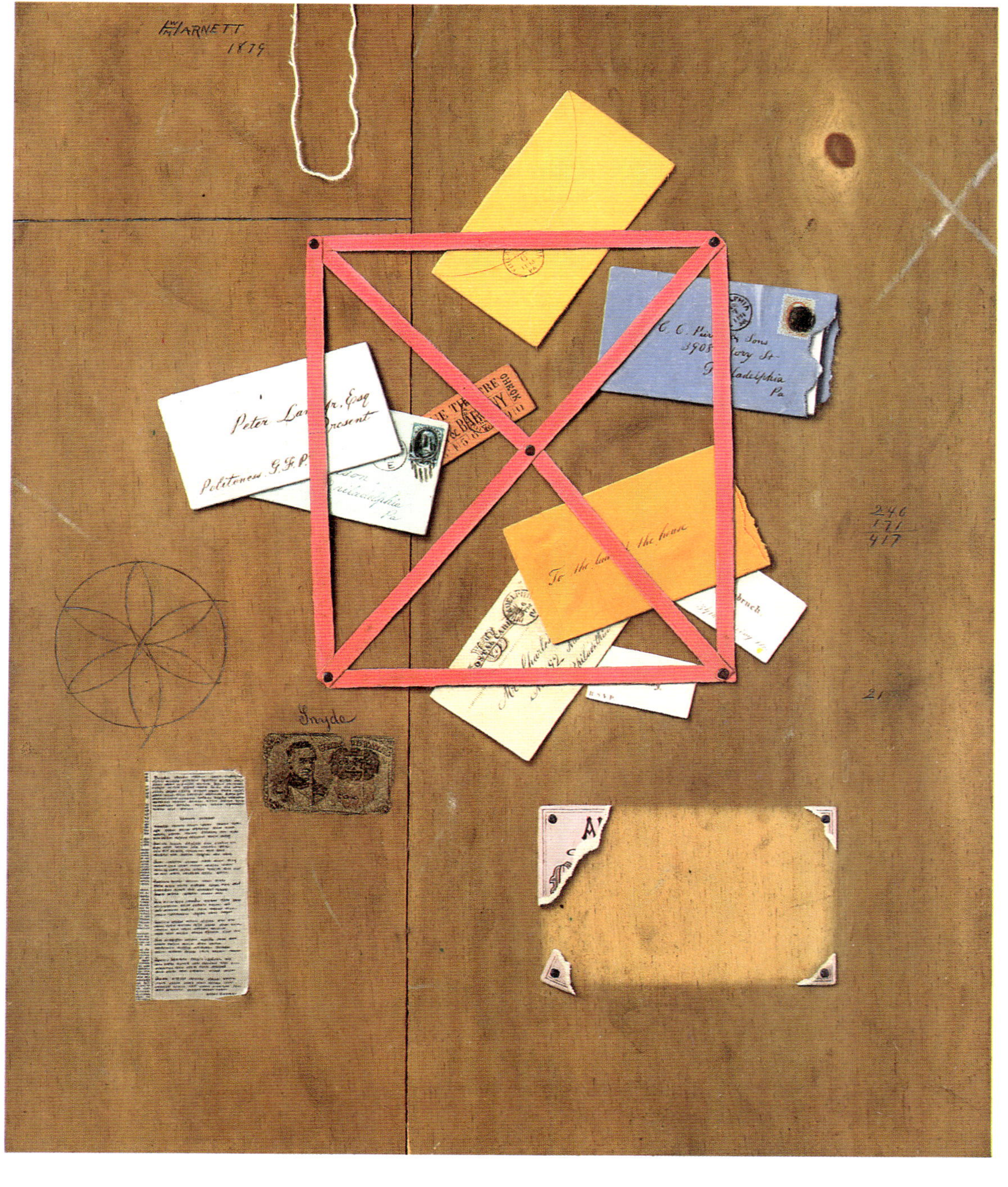

John F. Peto
1854–1907

Old Souvenirs

Oil on canvas
26¾ x 22 in. (67.9 x 55.9 cm.)
ca. 1881–1900
Falsely inscribed and dated at lower left:
WMH (monogram) ARNETT/1881
Bequest of Oliver Burr Jennings, 1968
(68.205.3)

A TYPICAL WORK by John F. Peto, another artist well known for his trompe l'oeil still lifes, this painting bears the false signature of William Michael Harnett. Actually this is a later version of the sort of picture that prompted Harnett to do rack paintings (facing page). Some of the objects stuck in the grid are dated or datable and provide clues to the years when the artist seems to have worked on this assemblage. The picture of Peto's daughter at the upper left was probably added over an earlier portrait around 1900, when she was about seven. The representation of objects, with their varying textures, is much less sharp and naturalistic than it is in the works of Harnett.

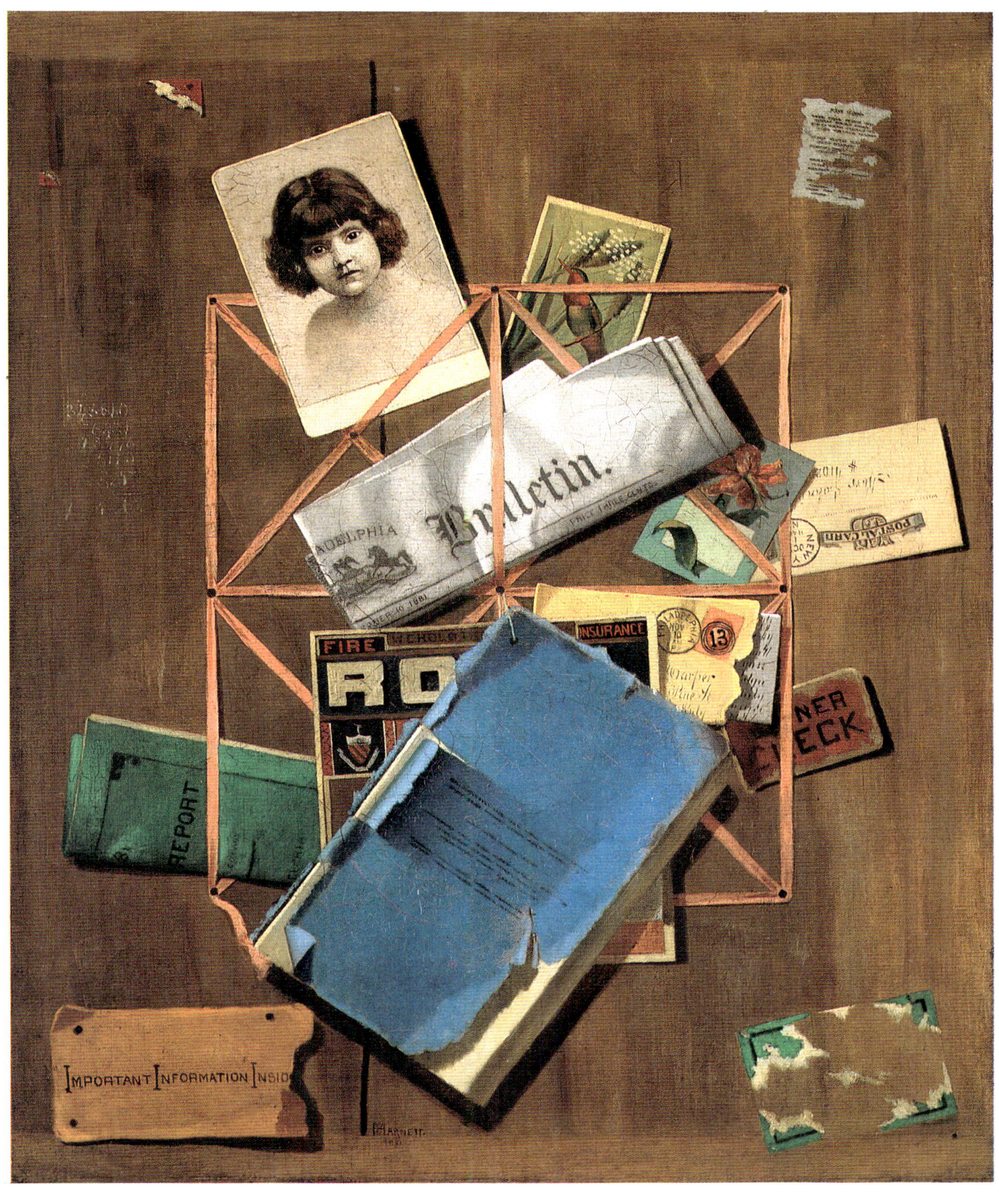

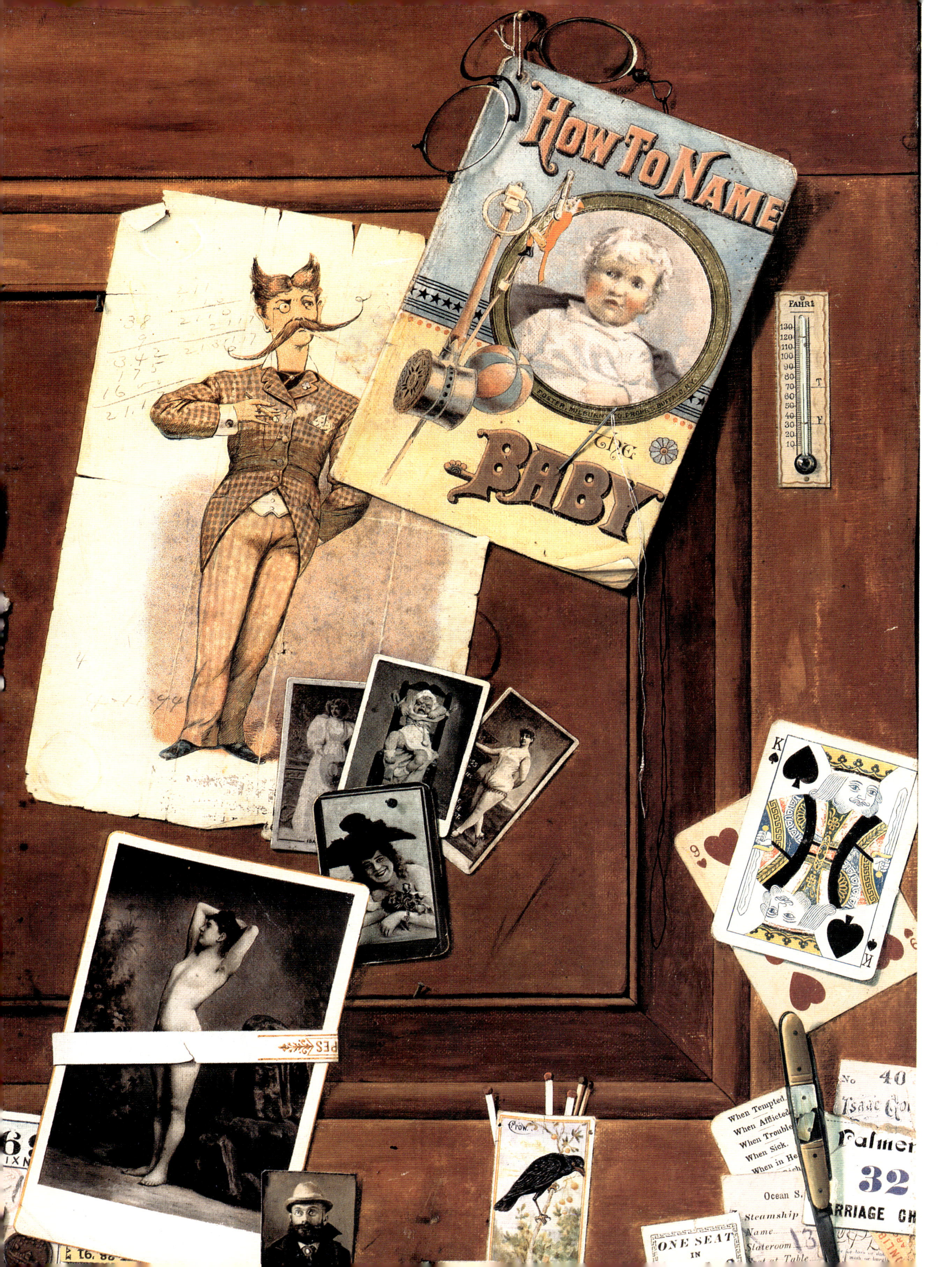
HOW TO NAME
THE
BABY
FAHR
ONE SEAT
Palmer
32
RRIAGE CH
When Tempted
When Afflicted
When Trouble
When Sick
Ocean S
Steamship
Name
Stateroom

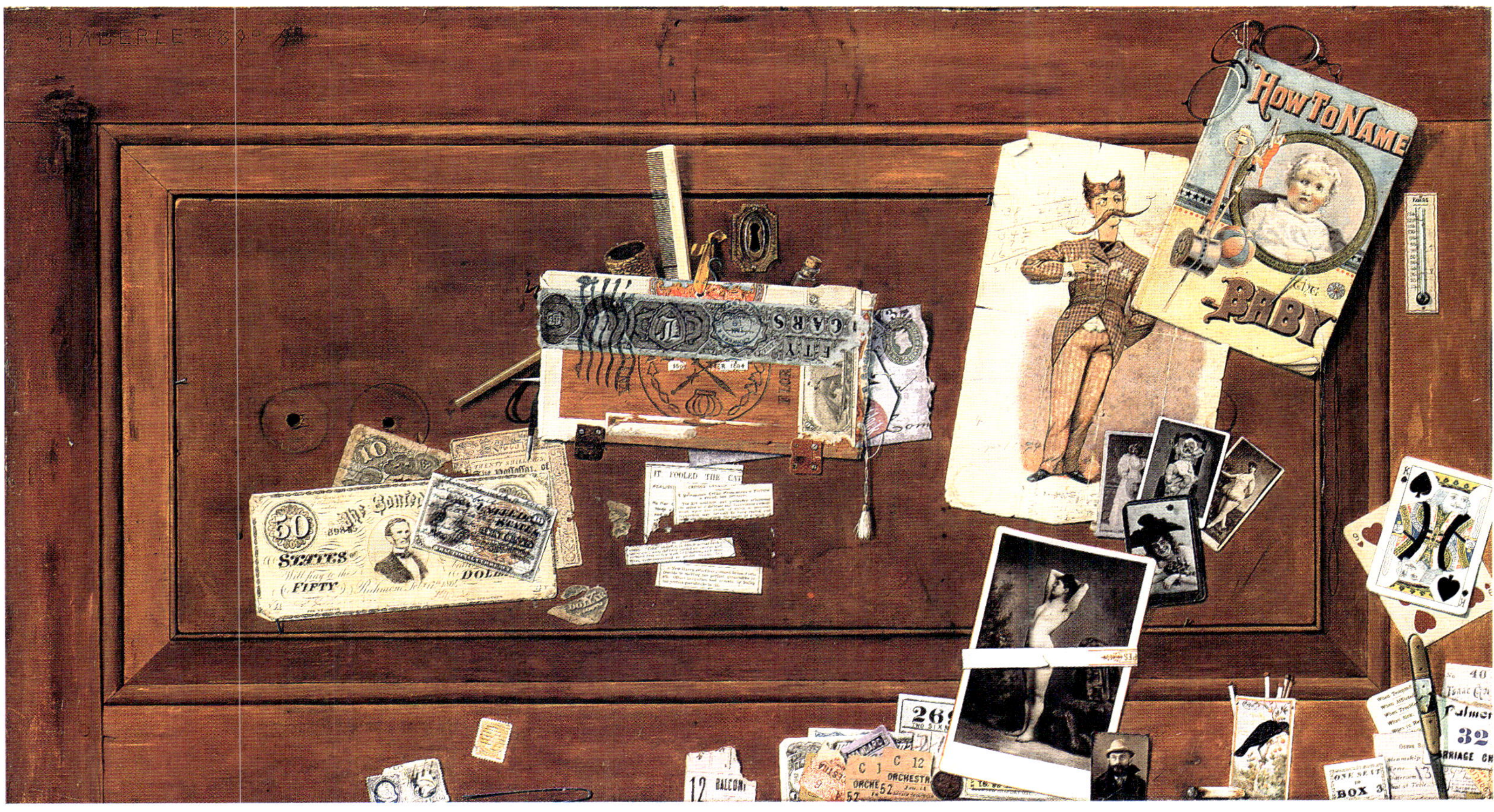

John Haberle
1856–1933

A Bachelor's Drawer

Oil on canvas
20 x 36 in. (50.8 x 91.4 cm.)
1890–1894
Signed and dated at upper left: HABERLE • 1890–94 •
Purchase, Henry R. Luce Gift, 1970 (1970.193)

JOHN HABERLE is generally regarded as one of the best of the American painters of trompe l'oeil. The artist's mastery of the craft was so complete that federal agents reportedly warned him to stop painting his representations of paper money. He brought to his still lifes impeccable technique and a sense of humor rare in paintings of this sort. *A Bachelor's Drawer* cannot be labeled autobiographical, yet certainly it tells a story. Some objects allude to a bachelor's freedom—theater stubs, playing cards, a pipe, and pinup girls; others suggest its termination—a paraphrase of the marriage service and a cartoon of a howling infant.

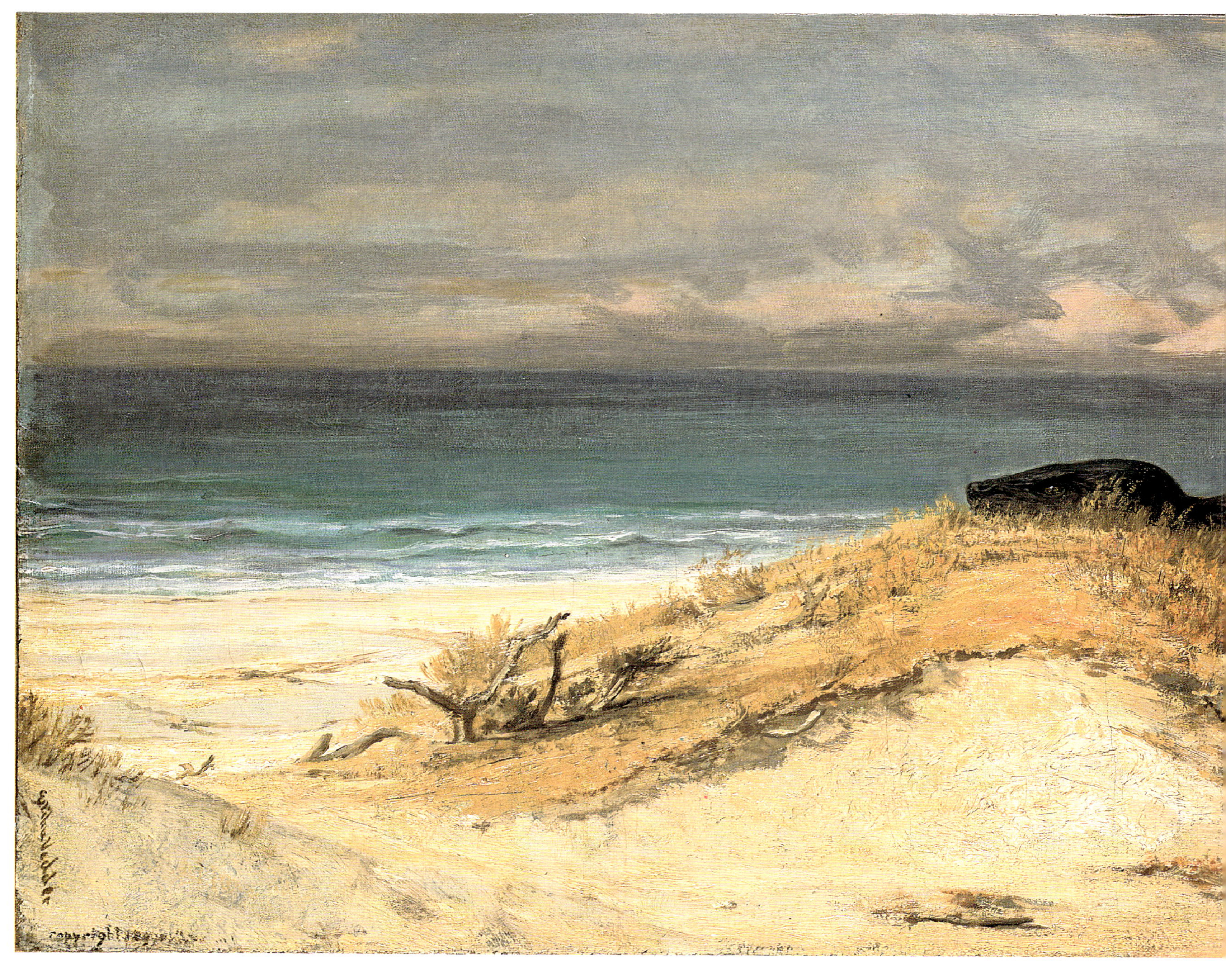

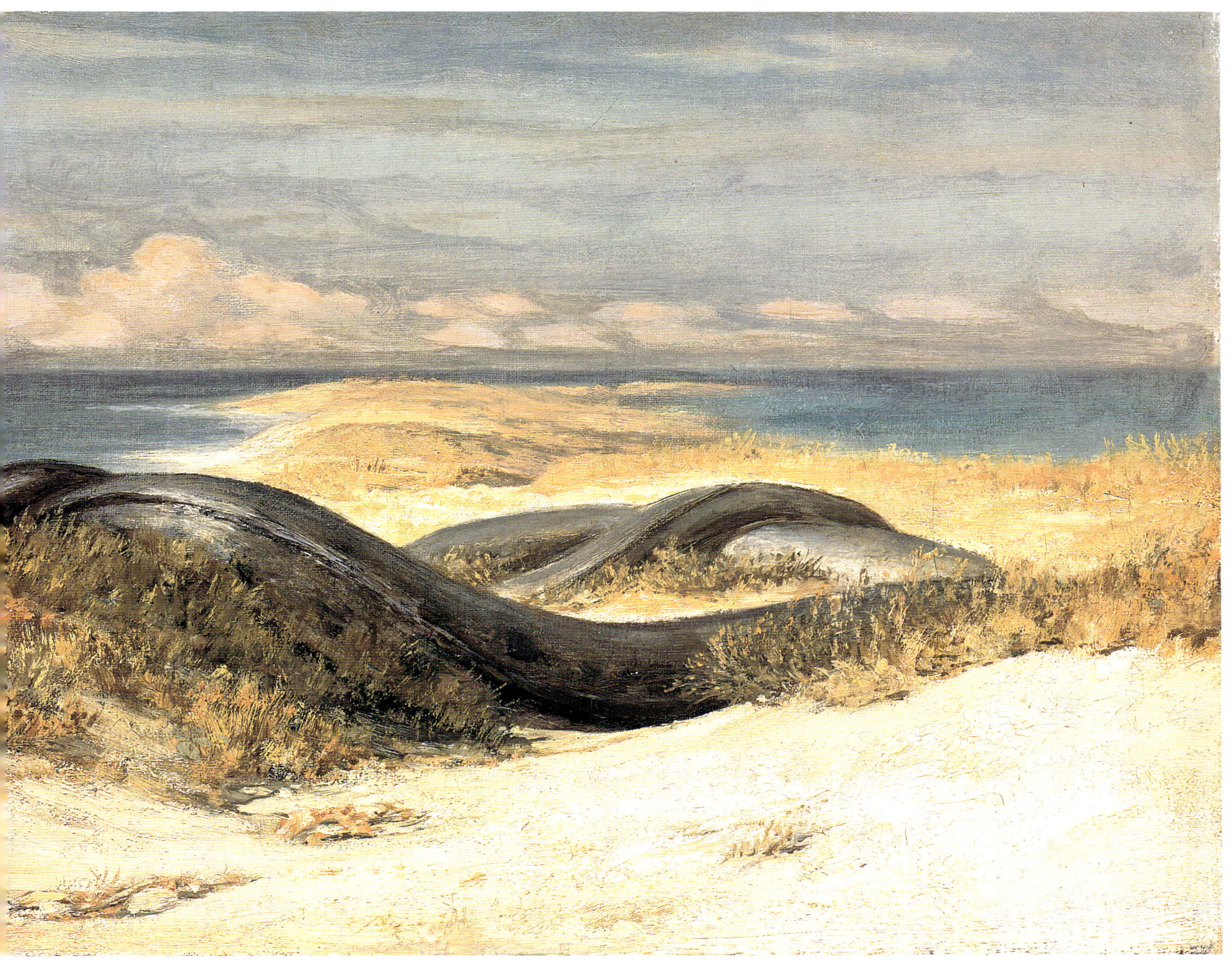

Elihu Vedder
1836–1923

The Lair of the Sea Serpent

Oil on canvas
12 x 30 in. (30.5 x 76.2 cm.)
1899
Signed, inscribed, and dated at lower left: Elihu Vedder [along left edge] / copyright 1899
Gift of Mrs. Harold G. Henderson, 1976 (1976.106.1)

THIS CURIOUSLY fanciful painting, bearing the date 1899, is actually the transformation of an oil sketch made in preparation for Elihu Vedder's larger painting of 1864, now in the Museum of Fine Arts, Boston. The picture in Boston has almost exactly the same composition, showing a huge, mythical creature burrowing into a hillock on a sandy shore. Here, in the Museum's reworking of the old sketch, the space allotted to sky seems considerably lessened, and the narrower strip of blue somehow increases the effect of distance and remoteness. The thick, coiled body is terrible in its size and potential destructiveness, but the mature Vedder thought it better to push it safely back from the spectator, and, in its harmonious, balanced setting of sea and sand, it now imposes no immediate emotional threat.

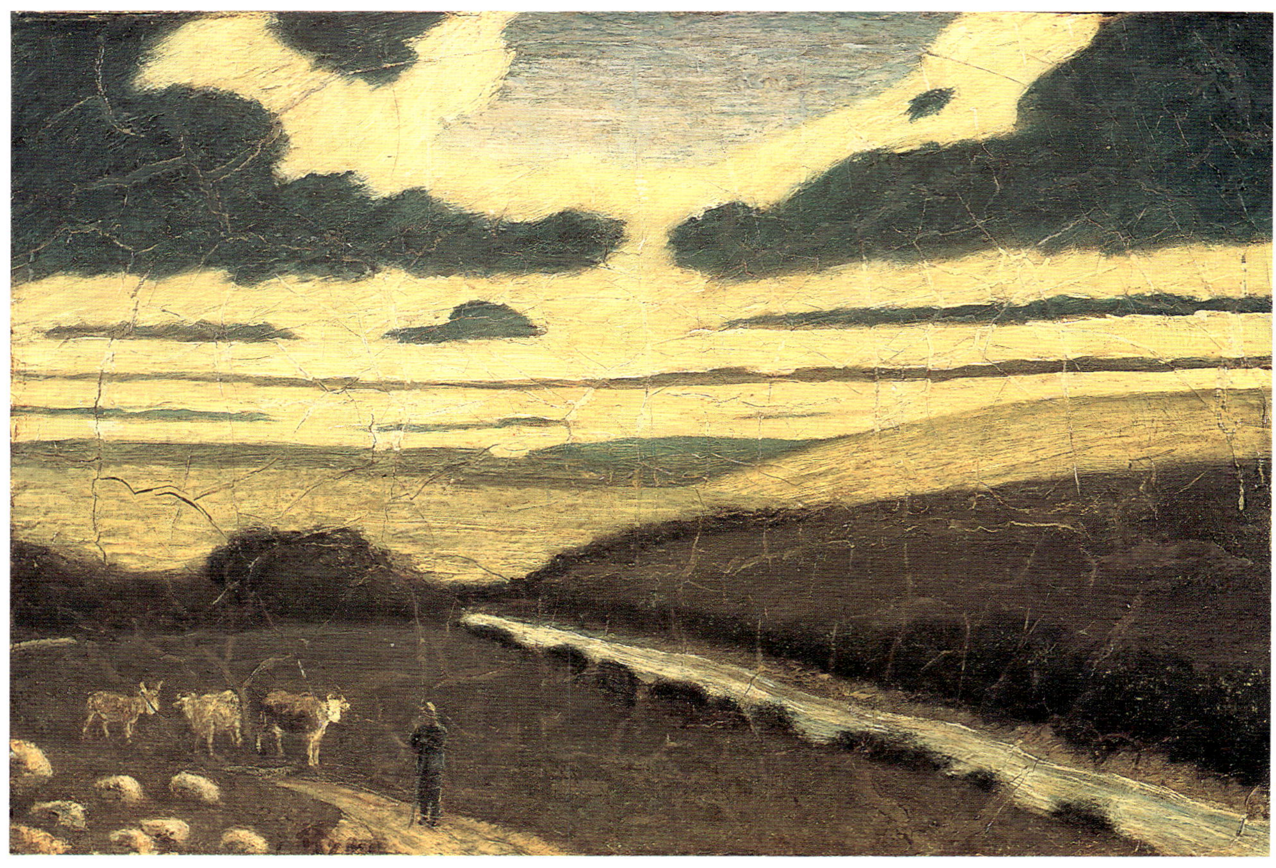

Albert Pinkham Ryder
1847–1917

Landscape

Oil on canvas (?)
9½ x 14 in. (24.1 x 35.6 cm.)
ca. 1897–1898
Signed at lower left: Ryder
Gift of Frederick Kuhne, 1952 (52.199)

AN ARTIST of unusual originality and independence, Albert Pinkham Ryder was shy and withdrawn. His subject matter, which was usually romantic and melancholy, is a modest adjunct to his powerful designs. He had very little training in painting and had a habit of reworking his pictures over a period of years, a practice that often led to a heavy buildup of pigment. This density of the painted surface, combined with his often unconventional and experimental techniques, has led in many cases to irreparable deterioration of the work. *Landscape* is more direct and understandable than many of his paintings, but it is overlaid, as most of them are, with a heavy mood. The little figure of the herdsman with his three cows, faintly recalling French landscapes of the Barbizon School, does not relieve the grimness of the broadly suggested countryside, but intensifies it by contrast. Ryder's whole preoccupation was with his design, and here, in this diminutive canvas, he has achieved a rare completeness of simplification. Pictures such as this by Ryder exerted a strong influence on twentieth-century American painting.

Ralph Blakelock
1847–1919

An Indian Encampment

Oil on canvas
37⅝ x 40⅝ in. (95.6 x 103.2 cm.)
Probably 1880s or 1890s
Signed at lower left, now partially illegible: R. A. Blakelock
Gift of George A. Hearn, 1906
(06.1269)

IN HIS EARLY TWENTIES, Ralph Blakelock, a native New Yorker, made a trip to the West that stimulated his interest in the American wilderness and Indian life and provided him with subject matter to which he would frequently return. In this painting, tiny figures of men and horses are intimately united with their setting in a rough clearing around the encampment. The trees recall works by the French Barbizon painters, especially Rousseau. The coarse textures of the trees and scrubby bushes are said to have resulted from Blakelock's curious practice of painting in thick layers that he later planed down with pumice stone. The effect of mystery and strangeness intended by Blakelock is partly due to this unusual technique.

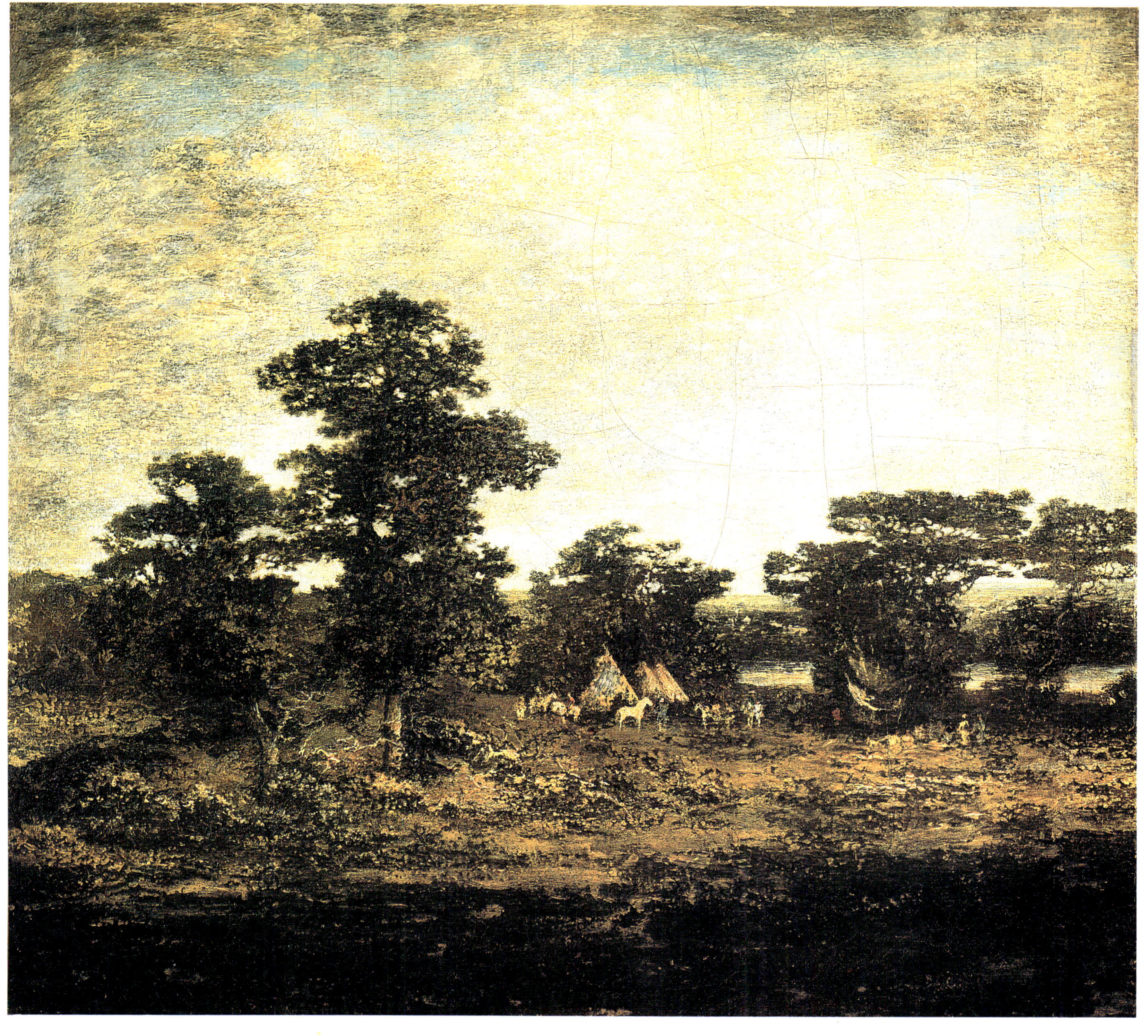

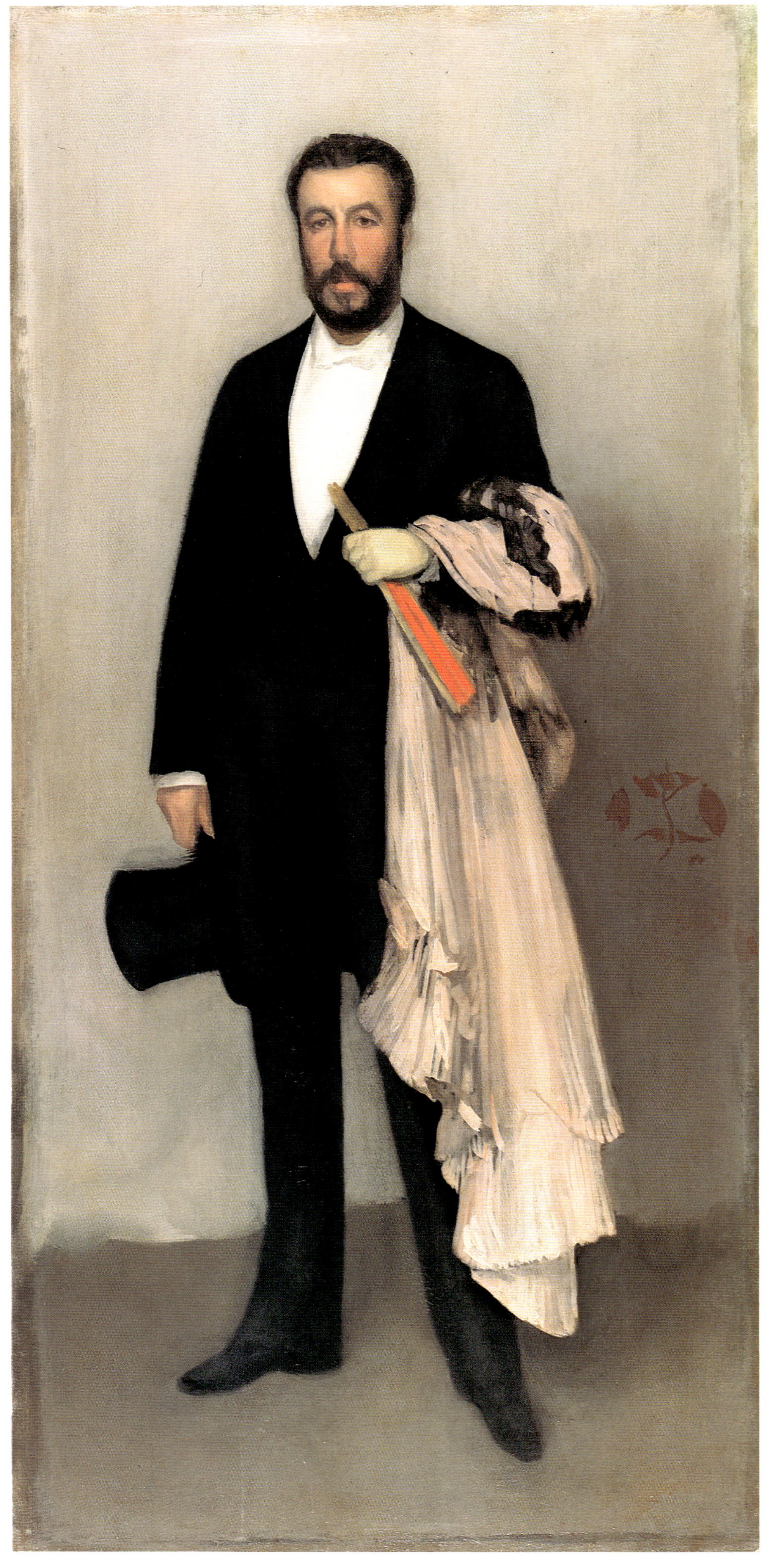

James McNeill Whistler
1834–1903

Arrangement in Flesh Color and Black: Portrait of Théodore Duret

Oil on canvas
76⅛ x 35¾ in. (193.4 x 90.8 cm.)
ca. 1883
Signed at right center with artist's butterfly symbol
Wolfe Fund, Catharine Lorillard Wolfe Collection, 1913 (13.20)

JAMES MCNEILL WHISTLER, like John Singer Sargent, was an American who lived and worked abroad. After some schooling in the United States, he went to Europe and spent about eight years in Paris at the very beginning of the Impressionist movement. Around 1863 he settled in London, which he made his home for the rest of his life. The subject of this portrait was a collector and an influential art critic in Paris, and the special champion of Manet. It was Manet who introduced Whistler to Théodore Duret (1838–1927), initiating a friendship that resulted in this painting, begun in London in 1883. It had been agreed that Duret, an elegant and sophisticated man of forty-five, should pose in evening dress. Whistler thought of all his paintings, even portraits, as arrangements of color schemes, and asked his subject here to bring to the studio a pink masquerade dress. A costumer in Covent Garden supplied the robe, which, along with the fan in Duret's white-gloved hand, suggests a masked ball and the lady he is escorting. The pink of the costume, the vermilion in the fan and the painter's butterfly signature, and the flesh tones of the man are finely orchestrated against the black suit and the rosy gray of the unrelieved background. Manet and Vuillard also painted Duret.

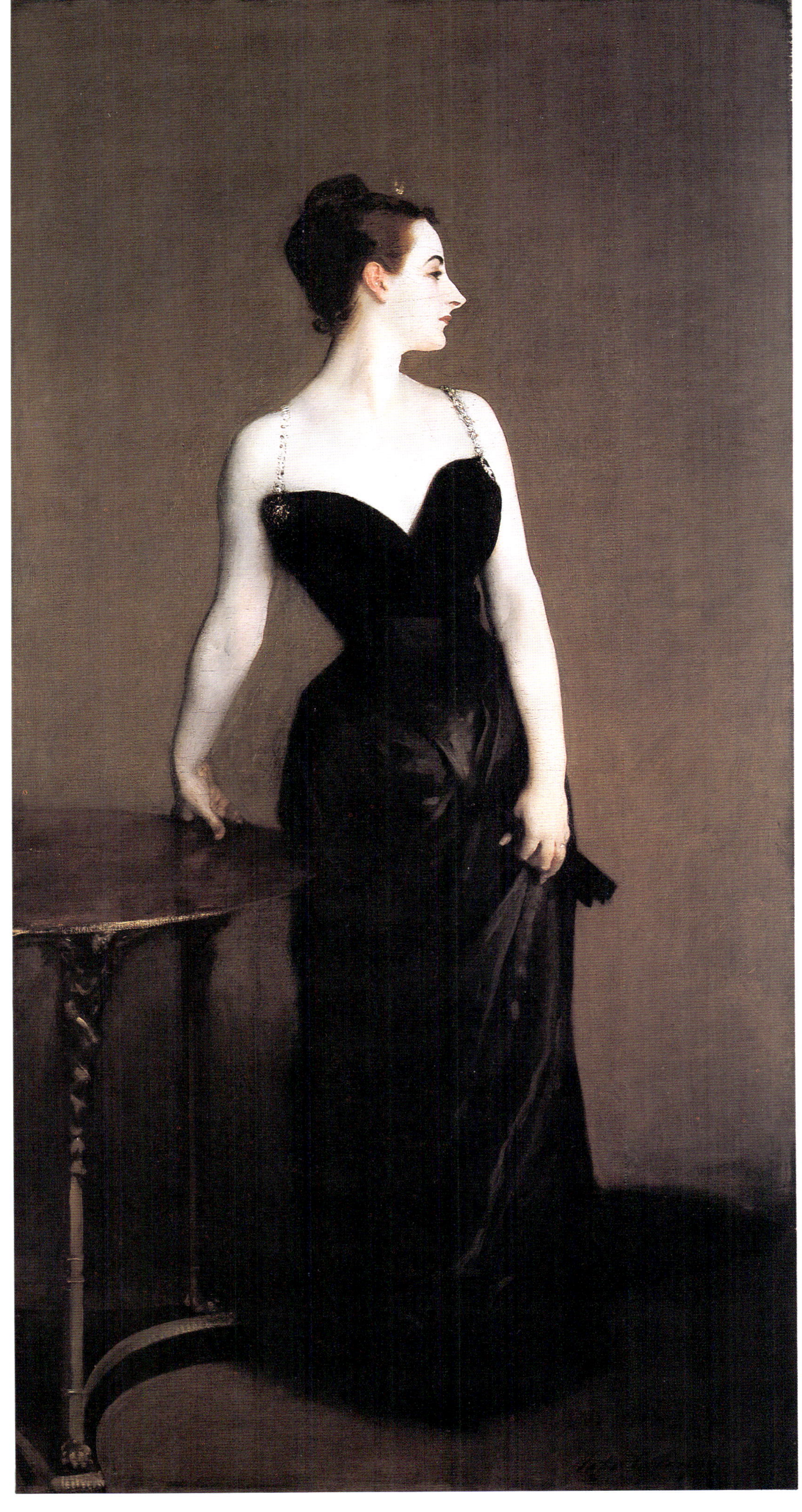

John Singer Sargent
1856–1925

Madame X (Madame Pierre Gautreau)

Oil on canvas
82⅛ x 43¼ in. (208.6 x 109.9 cm.)
1884
Signed and dated at lower right:
John S. Sargent 1884
Arthur Hoppock Hearn Fund, 1916 (16.53)

ONE OF THE MOST widely recognized American artists in his time, John Singer Sargent was born in Europe. He studied art in Paris and began his career there, moving to London when he was thirty, however, as a result of the uproar that arose over the showing of *Madame X*. He made numerous working visits to America, where he received many notable commissions.

This painting, the most famous of Sargent's early portraits, has a clear, sharp, linear design. The pronounced features are accentuated by the crisply drawn profile, and the silhouette sweeps down the graceful neck and over the shoulders and well-rounded arms. The subject (1859–1915) must have been as striking in real life as in the portrait. An American of Italian ancestry, she had been taken as a girl to live in Paris, where she married the banker Pierre Gautreau. She was twenty-five at the time Sargent painted her. When her portrait was exhibited at the Paris Salon of 1884, public and press were shocked by the shameless bodice with its delicate string of brilliants and by the violet tones of the copiously powdered skin. The stunning picture, which Sargent had expected to be his gateway to popularity and patronage, became instead a scandalous symbol of the lady's piquant reputation.

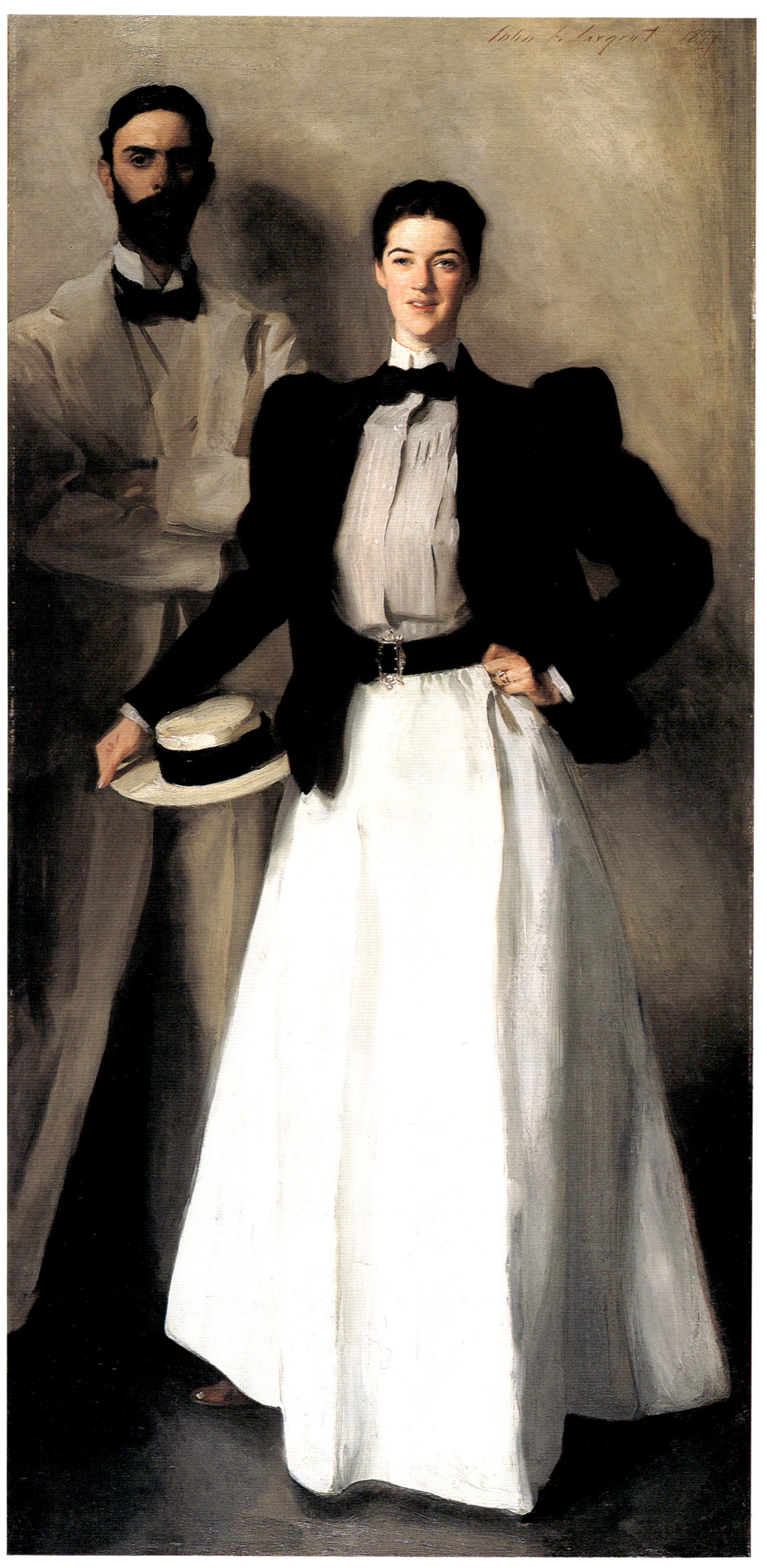

John Singer Sargent
1856–1925

Mr. and Mrs. I. N. Phelps Stokes

Oil on canvas
84¼ x 39¾ in. (214 x 101 cm.)
1897
Signed and dated at upper right:
John S. Sargent 1897
Bequest of Edith Minturn Phelps Stokes, 1937 (38.104)

JOHN SINGER SARGENT painted this double portrait two years after the couple was married. It was originally intended to show only Mrs. Stokes (1867–1937), posed, in the manner of a Van Dyck portrait, with a huge dog at her side. The Great Dane he wanted, however, was unavailable, and young I. N. Phelps Stokes (1867–1944) took its place. His portrait is rendered rather sketchily, in contrast to the vibrant clarity of the figure of the young woman. As always with Sargent, the drawing is superb and sure, the modeling, as in the sharp folds of the starched piqué skirt, firm and convincing, and the whole carried out with breadth and directness. A number of his portraits of about 1900 show the same exaggeration of height and slenderness, a mannered device that adds immeasurably to the effect of aristocratic elegance.

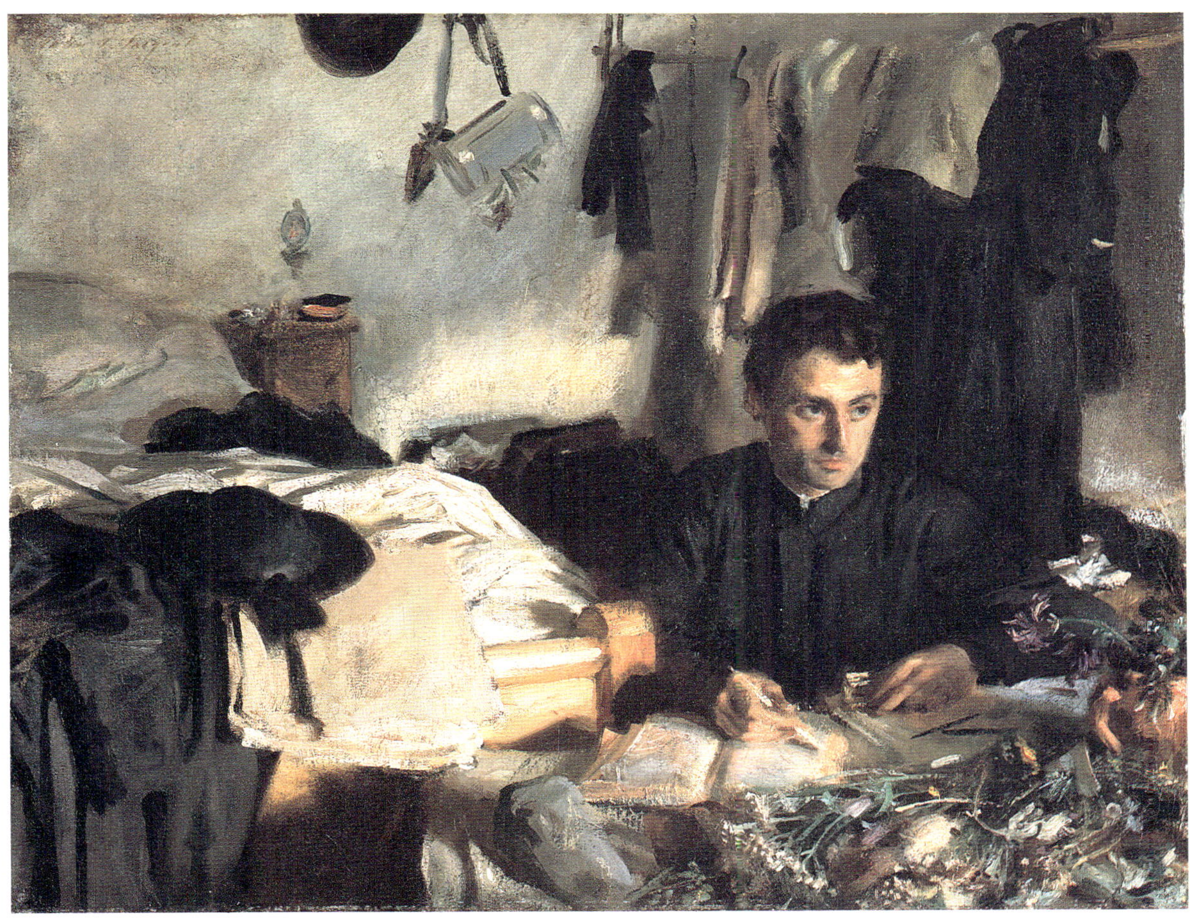

John Singer Sargent
1856–1925

Padre Sebastiano

Oil on canvas
22¼ x 28 in. (56.5 x 71.1 cm.)
ca. 1904–1906
Signed at upper left: John S. Sargent
Rogers Fund, 1911 (11.30)

THE CLERICAL COLLAR, the missal, and the broad-brimmed hat on the bed, and the specimens of flowers and plants spread out on the table in front of him, identify this gravely beautiful man as the "botanizing priest" John Singer Sargent painted between 1904 and 1906 on his summer holidays in the Italian Alps. A letter from the artist's sister Violet mentioned Sargent's meeting with the young priest, who, she added, held somewhat radical theological ideas and soon after left the Church and went to America. The picture's appeal lies in Sargent's characteristic gift for expressing his extraordinarily perceptive insights with bold and telling bravura. The head and shoulders of the sitter, who pauses in his note-taking for a moment of deep reflection, form a small island of serenity and quiet in a room jangling with disorder. Garments and laundry hang on a rack behind him, clothing is dropped on an untidy bed, and the table at which he works is cluttered and overflowing. All of this confusion of objects offered Sargent an opportunity for displaying his brilliant technique.

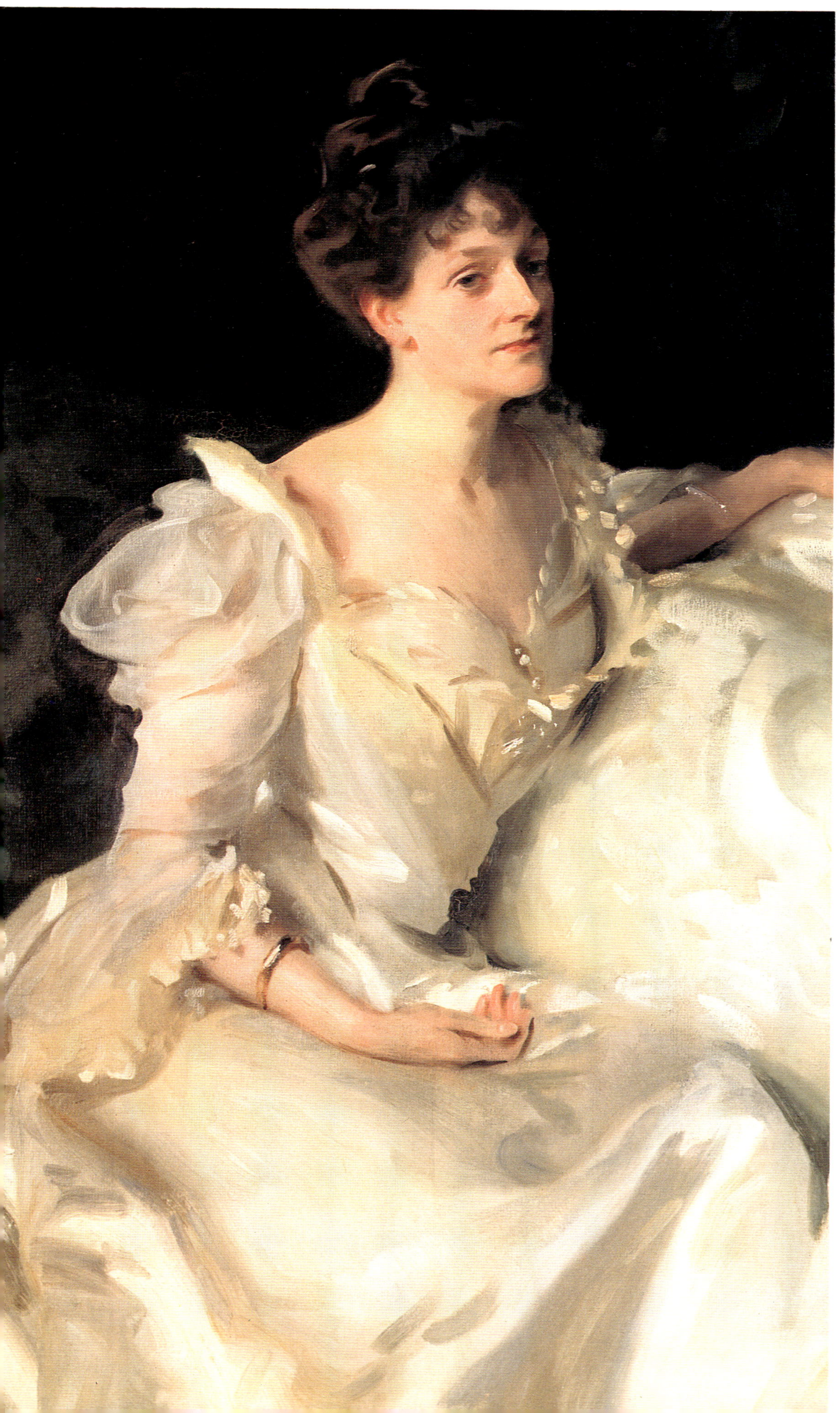

John Singer Sargent
1856–1925

The Wyndham Sisters: Lady Elcho, Mrs. Adeane, and Mrs. Tennant

Oil on canvas
115 x 84⅛ in. (292.1 x 213.7 cm.)
1899
Signed at lower right: John S. Sargent
Wolfe Fund, Catharine Lorillard Wolfe Collection, 1927 (27.67)

THESE PRETTY WOMEN, dressed in white and posed on a white sofa, suggest large white peonies. The subjects are set against the dark background of the drawing room of the Wyndham residence in Belgrave Square, London. Though Sargent preferred to paint portraits in his own studio, he apparently felt that the family setting, with George F. Watts's standing full-length likeness of the mother on the wall behind, offered a better foil for the group. All three were already married. Mary Constance, Lady Elcho, seated on the back of the sofa at the right, was thirty-seven; Madeline, Mrs. Charles Adeane, at the left, was thirty; and Pamela Tennant, later Lady Glenconner, beside her, was two years younger. The green-and-white color scheme is dazzling in its strong contrasts. It had been requested that the painter refrain from using any of the magenta and mauve tones that he especially favored. The paint is handled with utter facility, and the composition is impressively original. This painting, a sensation at the Royal Academy exhibition in London in 1900, assures Sargent a place with the great masters of American art.

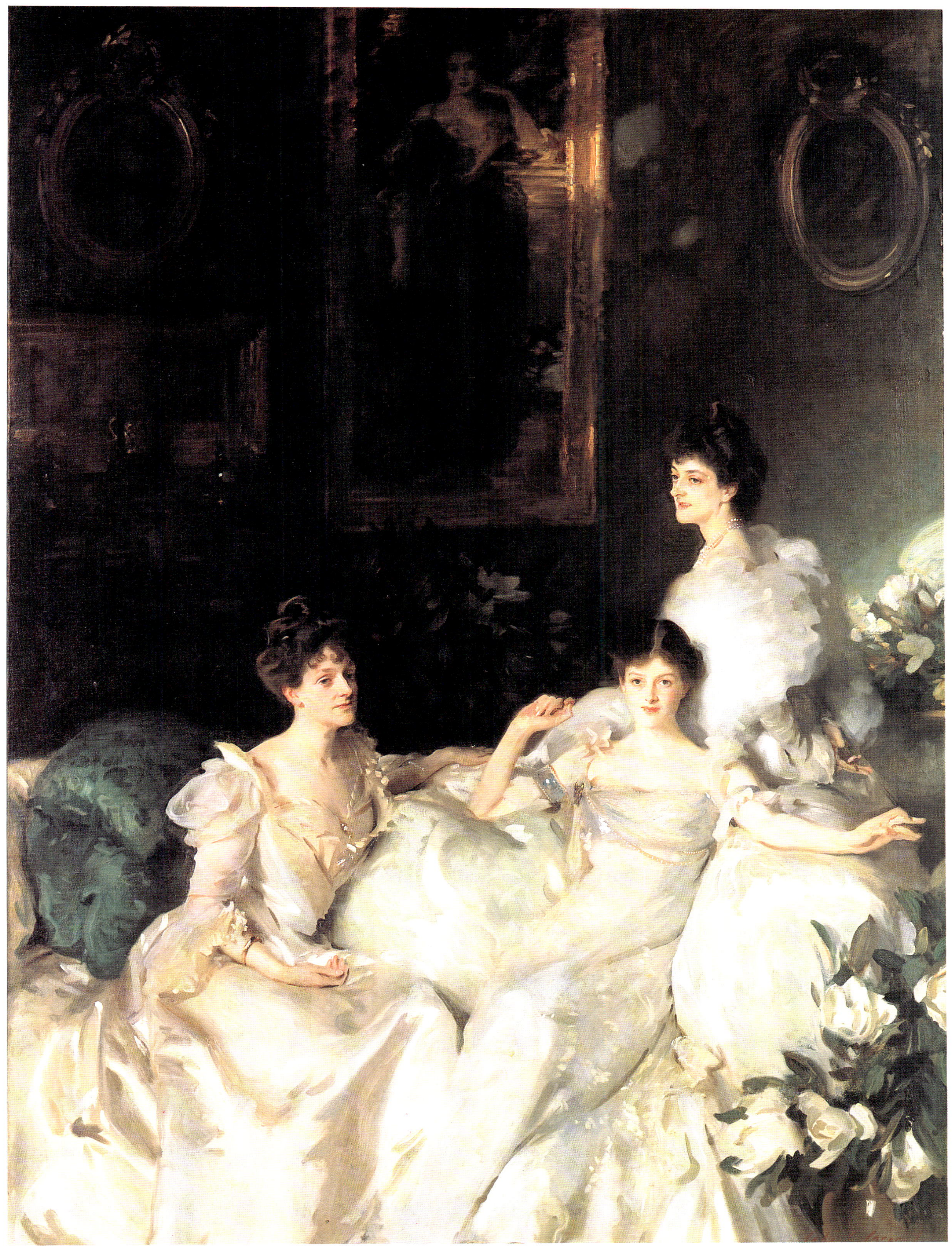

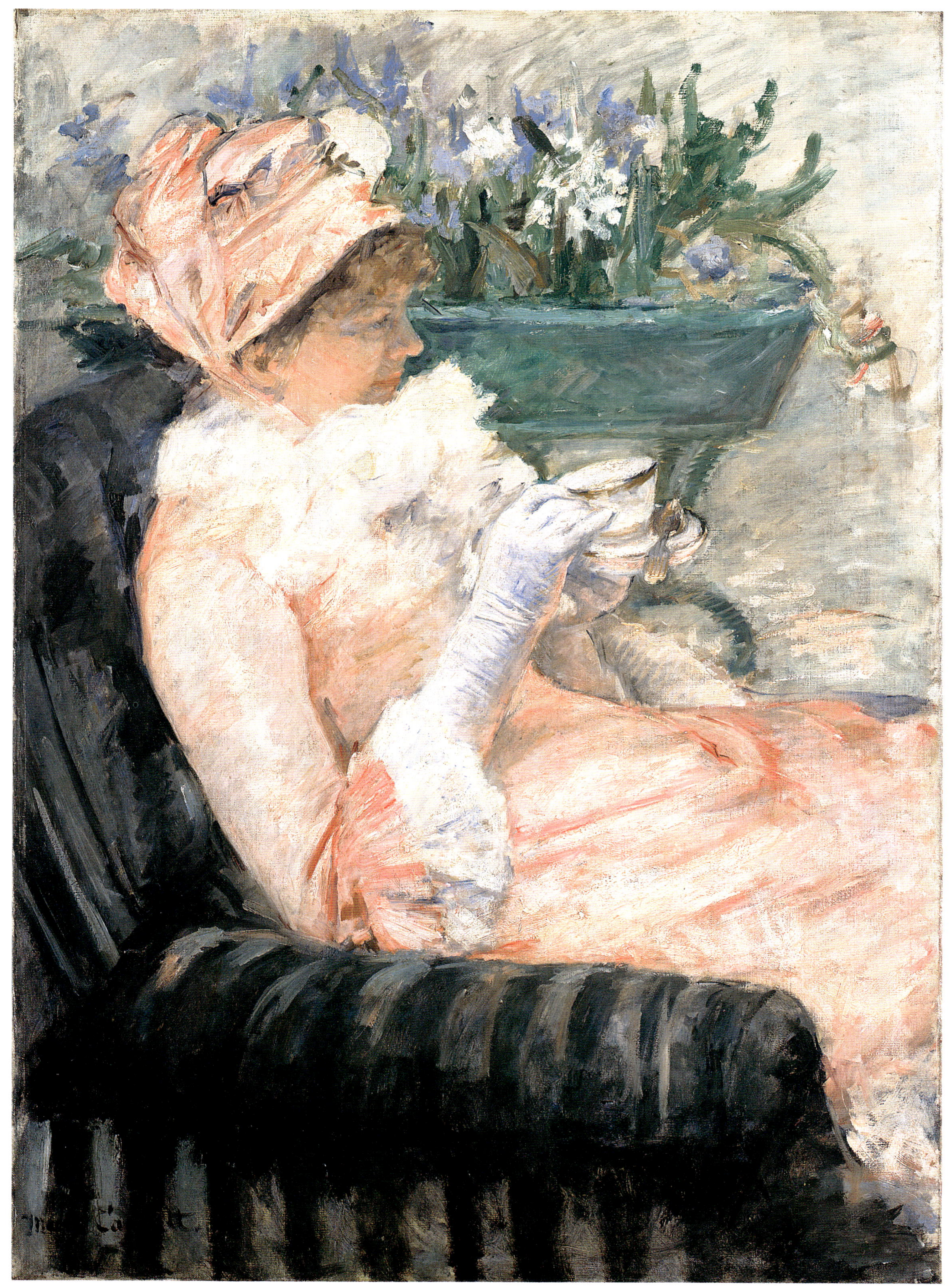

Mary Cassatt
1844–1926

The Cup of Tea

Oil on canvas
36⅜ x 25¾ in. (92.4 x 65.4 cm.)
1879
Signed at lower left: Mary Cassatt
From the Collection of James Stillman, Gift of Dr. Ernest G. Stillman, 1922 (22.16.17)

MARY CASSATT was an American artist who studied in Paris and spent most of her life there. In paintings such as this one she fully embraced French Impressionism: her brushwork is loose, and there are bright color contrasts and a general air of being true to daily life. This graceful picture of the artist's sister, Lydia (1837–1882), at tea and a painting of Lydia crocheting, also in the Museum's collection, were shown in the Impressionist exhibition of 1881 and praised for their grasp of Parisian elegance. A French critic admired the painter for capturing what he called "the cheerful tranquillity of an interior." The atmosphere of well-being is enhanced by the comfortable armchair and the white and blue-violet, certainly fragrant, hyacinths. The relaxed posture and the half-smile of the pretty woman combine in a peculiarly French way with the formal correctness implied by the hat, the white gloves, and the fine gold-banded china.

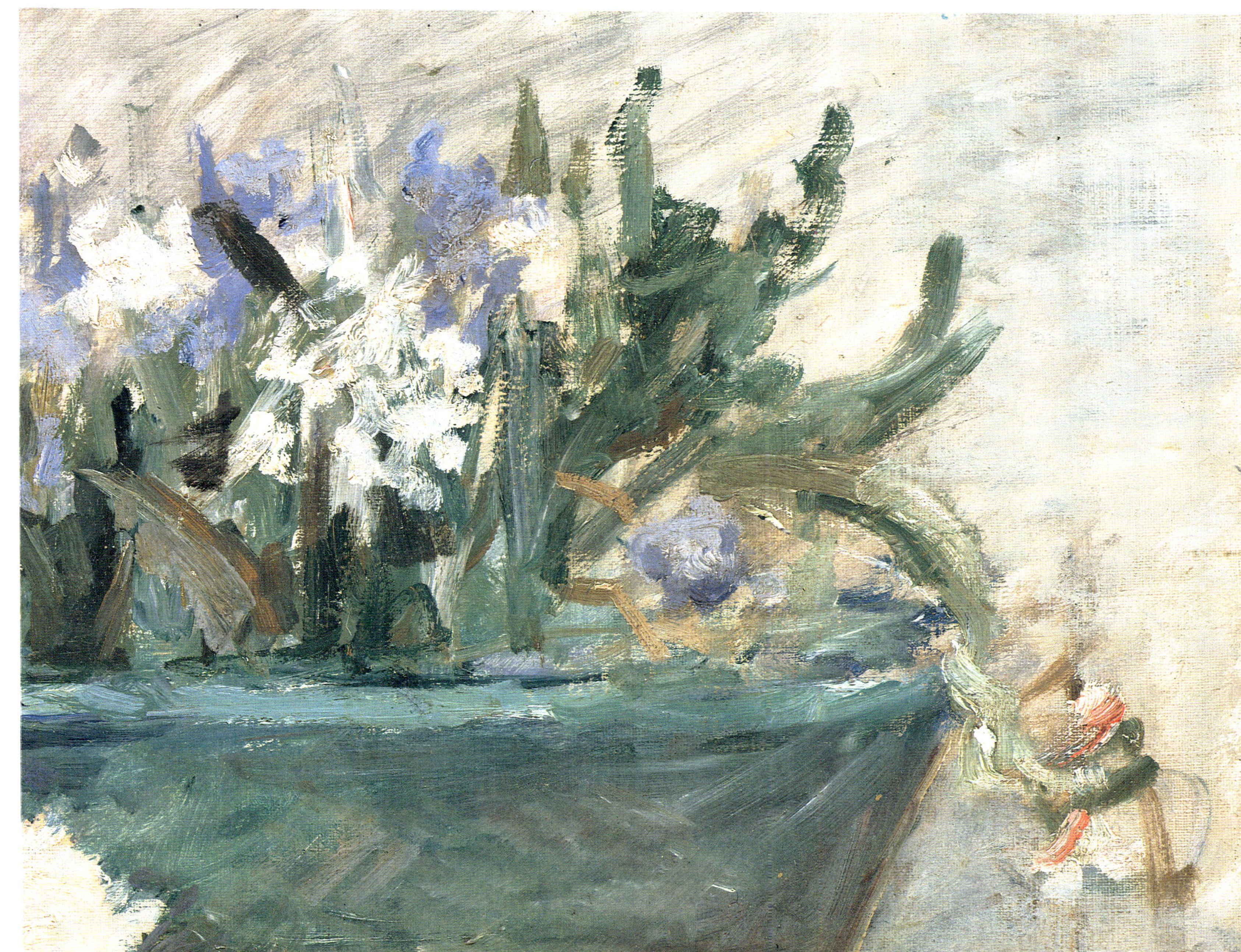

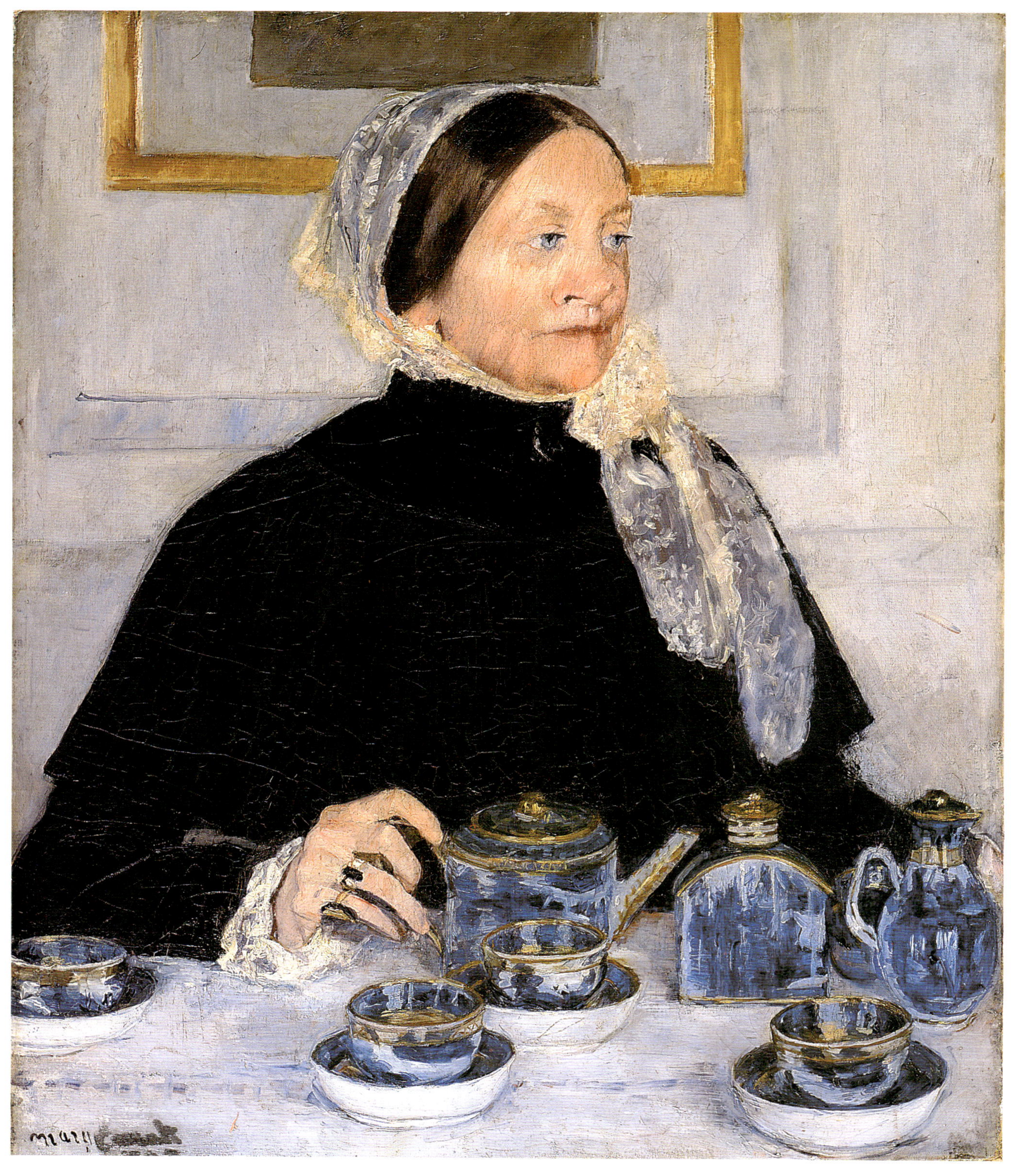

Mary Cassatt
1844–1926

Lady at the Tea Table

Oil on canvas
29 x 24 in. (73.4 x 61 cm.)
1885
Signed and dated at lower left:
Mary Cassatt/1885
Gift of the artist, 1923 (23.101)

DEGAS, a friend of Mary Cassatt's, considered this painting the very essence of distinction, but the family of the aristocratic (and slightly forbidding) sitter did not like it, and for almost thirty years it was shut away in a closet. The woman is Mrs. Robert Moore Riddle (d. 1890), a cousin of the painter. As in Holbein's portraits, character is revealed in the face, hands, and posture, while status is pronounced in the clothing, setting, and accessories. A blue color scheme is strictly maintained: intense in the tea service, deep in tone in the severely decorous navy blue dress, lighter in the wide, observant eyes and in the lining of the lace cap and ties, and palely shimmering on the tea cloth and the paneled wall. The gold frame of the truncated picture at the top is musically echoed in the bright rings of gilt that decorate the china.

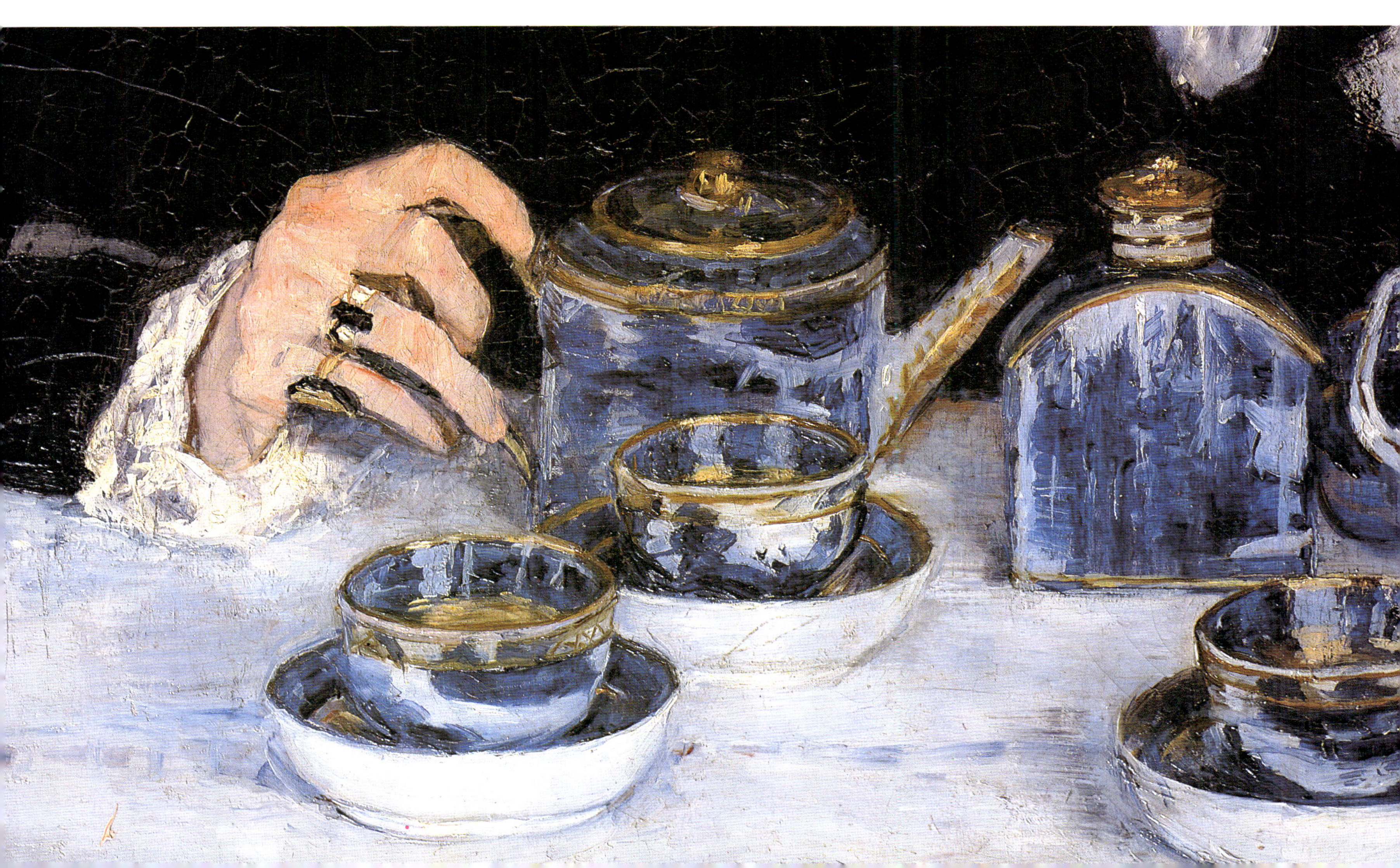

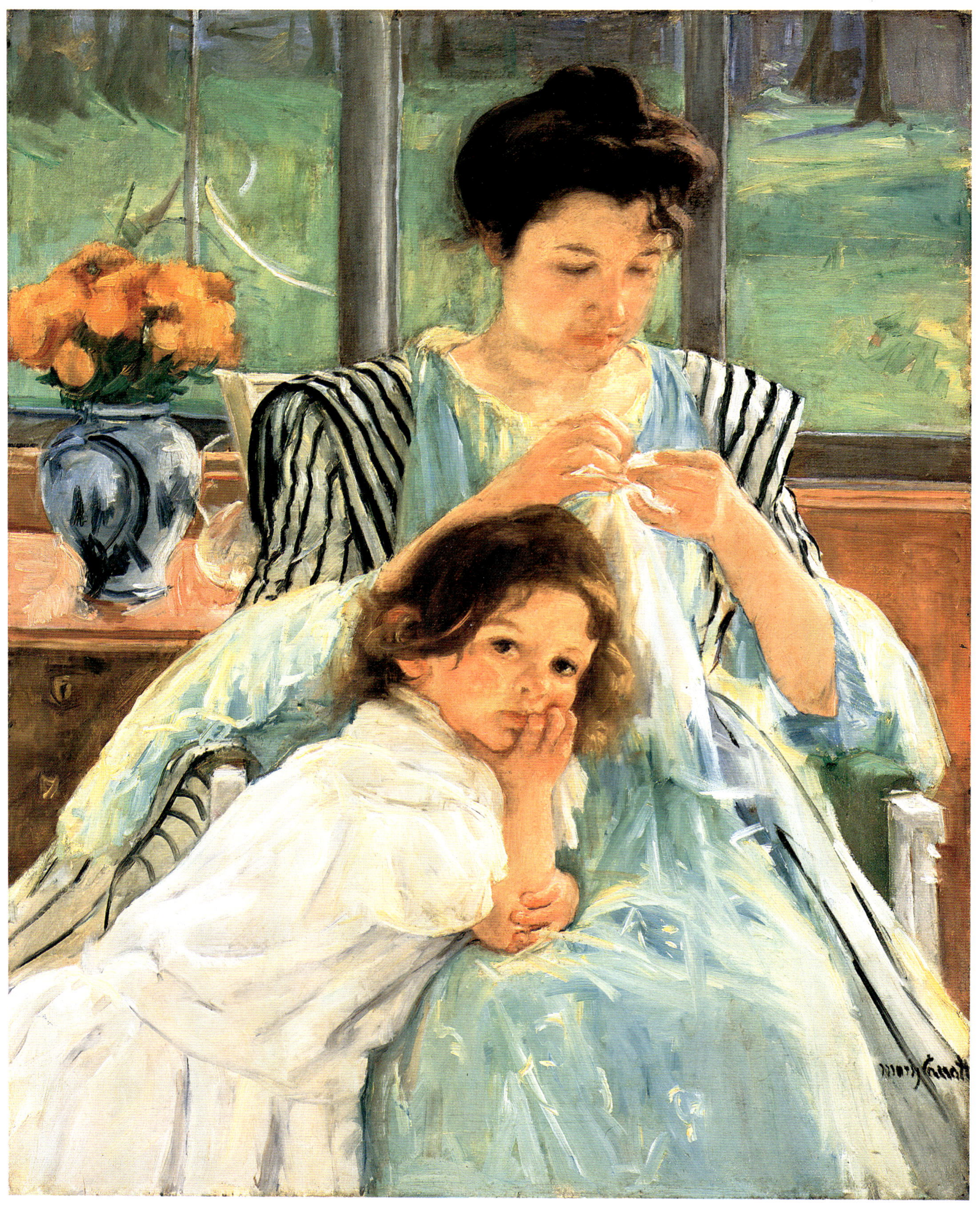

Mary Cassatt
1844–1926

Young Mother Sewing

Oil on canvas
36⅜ x 29 in. (92.4 x 73.7 cm.)
ca. 1900
Signed at lower right: Mary Cassatt
Bequest of Mrs. H. O. Havemeyer, 1929, H. O. Havemeyer Collection (29.100.48)

THE YOUNG WOMAN portrayed here as the industrious mother served as model for several of Mary Cassatt's pictures. Named Reine Lefebvre, she was a village girl who lived near the château Beaufresne, the country house in which Cassatt settled in 1894, in the neighborhood of Beauvais. Margot Lux, the child at her knee, was also from the village, and she, too, posed for Cassatt on many occasions. The wide window opening onto a lawn and park appears as a background in a number of Mary Cassatt's late works and is thought to have been part of the château's glassed-in room or conservatory. In the young woman's costume, the artist shows her special preference for the strong design of striped materials.

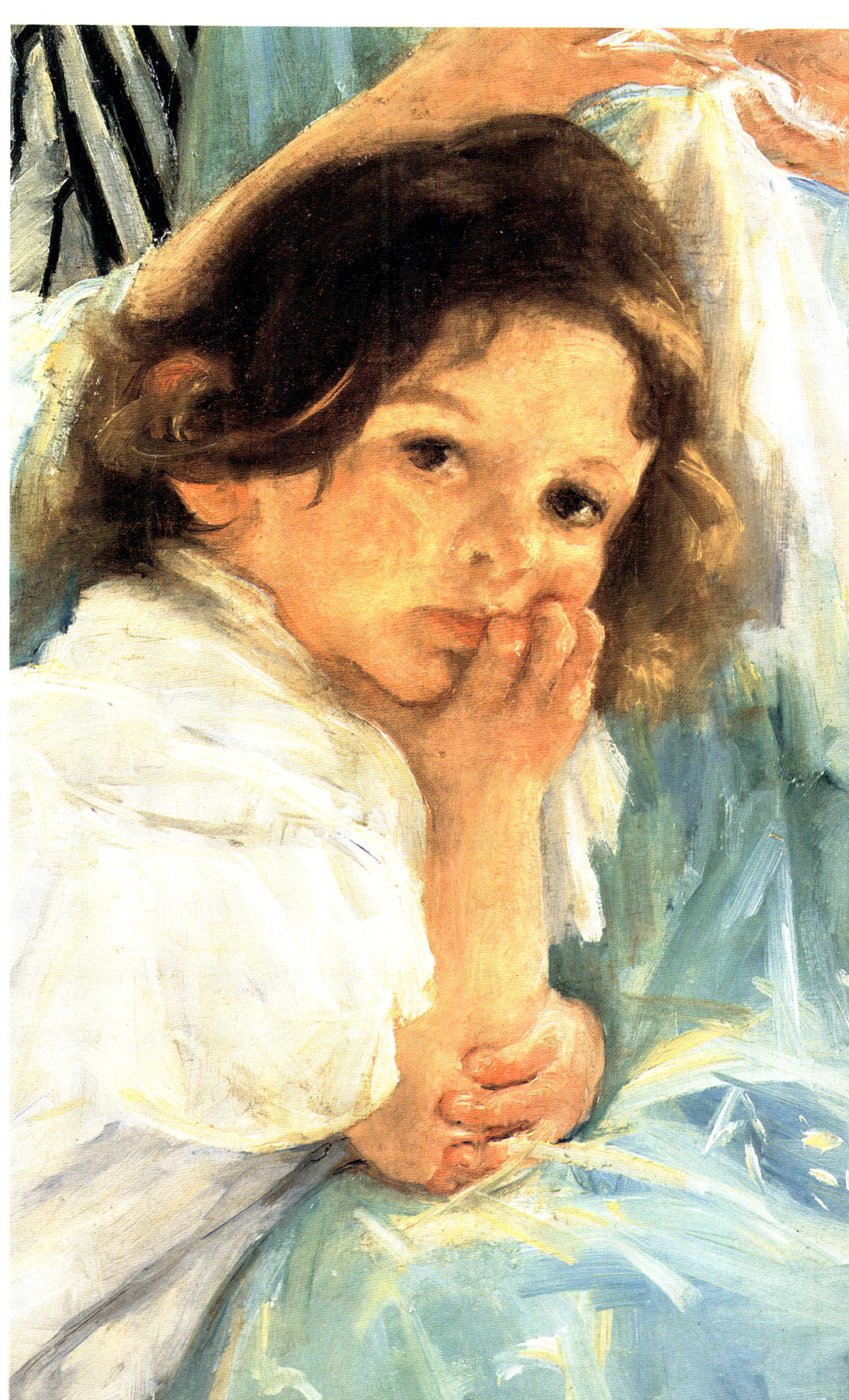

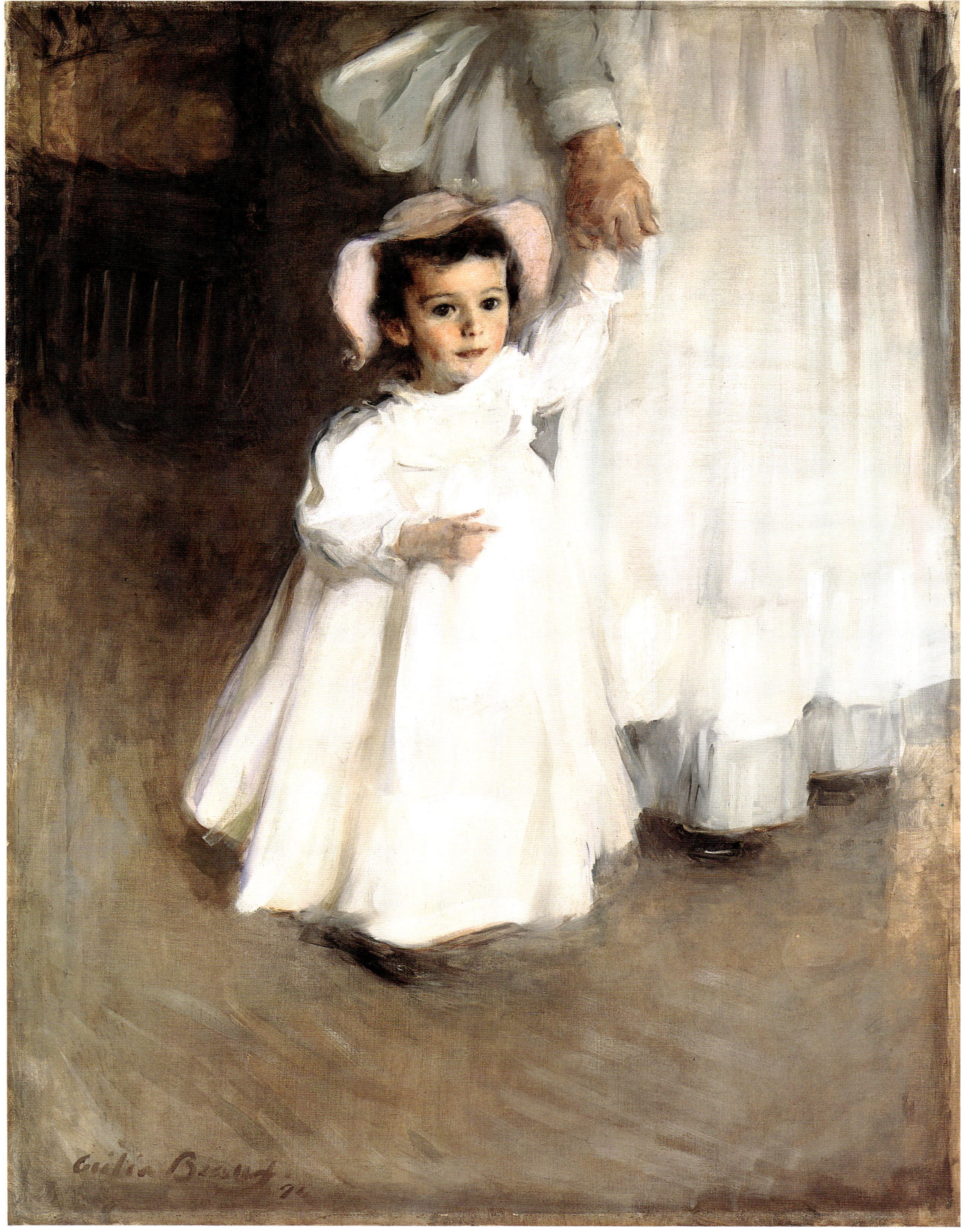

Cecilia Beaux
1855–1942

Ernesta (Child with Nurse)

Oil on canvas
50½ x 38⅛ in. (128.3 x 96.8 cm.)
1894
Signed and dated at lower left:
Cecilia Beaux/94
Maria DeWitt Jesup Fund, 1965
(65.49)

ERNESTA DRINKER, portrayed here at the age of two, was the artist's niece and favorite model. There is another portrait of her as an adult by her aunt in the Museum's collection. As in all Cecilia Beaux's paintings, the design and a clear estimate of what she meant to convey were equally and carefully considered. The dark-eyed little girl moves at her baby pace across a wide expanse of polished floor; she is like Velázquez's royal babies, dignified and at the same time vulnerable. The idea of showing only a part of the accompanying nursemaid here serves many ends. The hand to which the child clings becomes an abstract rather than a personal symbol of omnipotent protection and security, and the giant adult area of apron and uniform sets a scale for the tiny figure of the child.

John H. Twachtman
1853–1902

Arques-la-Bataille

Oil on canvas
60 x 78⅞ in. (152.4 x 200.3 cm.)
1885
Signed, dated, and inscribed at lower left:
J. H. Twachtman/1885/Paris
Morris K. Jesup Fund, 1968 (68.52)

JOHN H. TWACHTMAN had been studying in Paris for two years when he painted this subtle and moody river scene. In it, he has completely abandoned the dark palette and the richly loaded brushwork that characterized his style during his earlier years under the influence of Frank Duveneck and the painters of the Munich School. The aesthetic considerations of design and the disciplined, limited tonality that seem to have interested him most when painting this quiet, gray-green landscape clearly relate the picture to the oriental prints that exerted so strong an influence on French painting at this time.

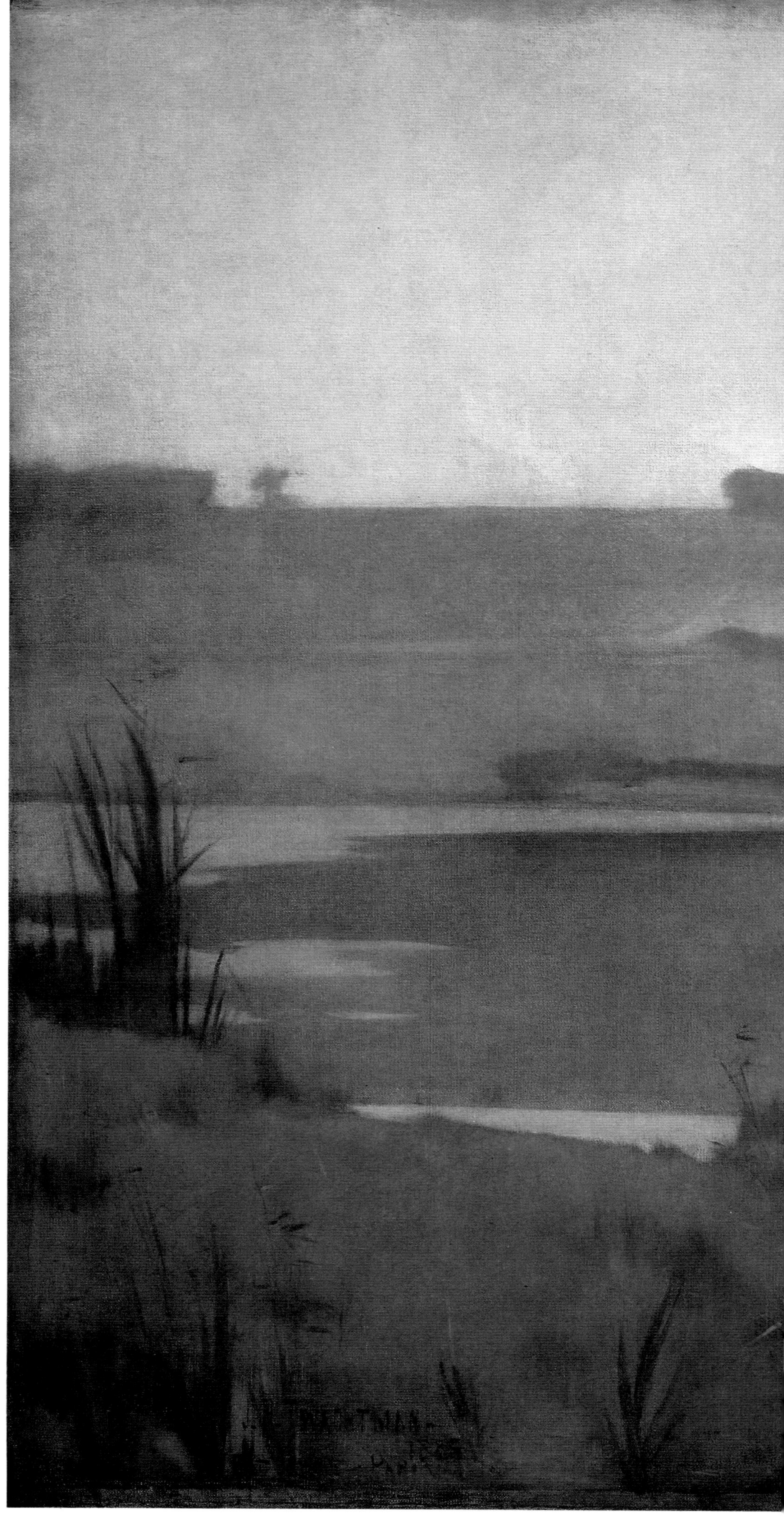

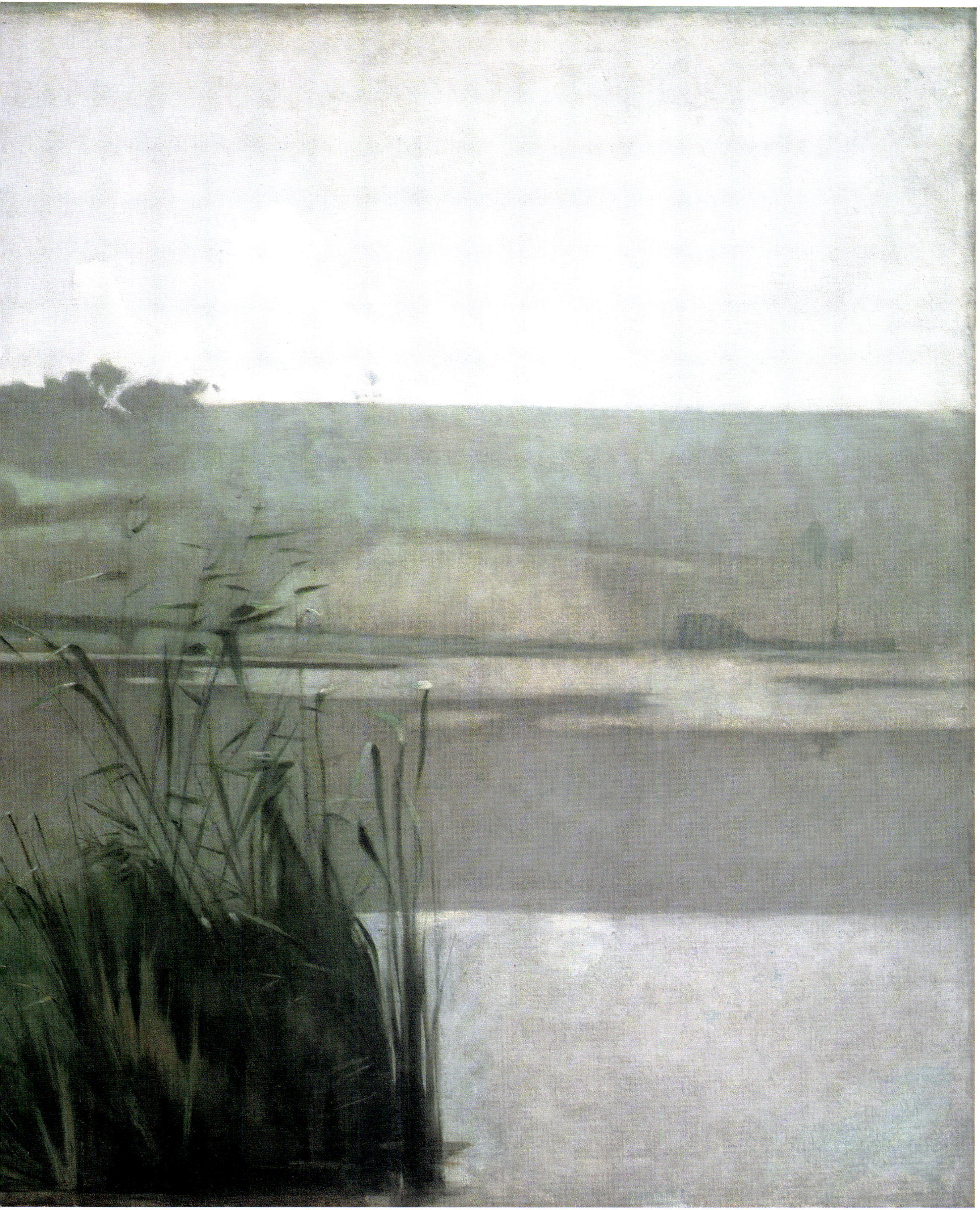

Theodore Robinson
1852–1896

A Bird's-eye View: Giverny

Oil on canvas
25¾ x 32 in. (65.4 x 81.3 cm.)
1889
Signed and dated at lower left: TH. ROBINSON—1889
Gift of George A. Hearn, 1910 (10.64.9)

THIS STRIKING VIEW, taken from high above the French village of Giverny, was painted after Theodore Robinson had met Claude Monet, who lived at Giverny. Monet's influence, which led Robinson toward the development of an Impressionist style, is more evident in the colors—the pinks and lavenders—than in the brushstrokes and paint surfaces, which are varied and controlled. Robinson shows his originality here in his overall two-dimensional design: the middle ground, in which he has stressed the shapes of the village buildings, lies between the spare, diagonal foreground and the parallel lines and level horizon of the distance. The combination of French influence with a strong expression of individuality makes this a notable example of American Impressionism.

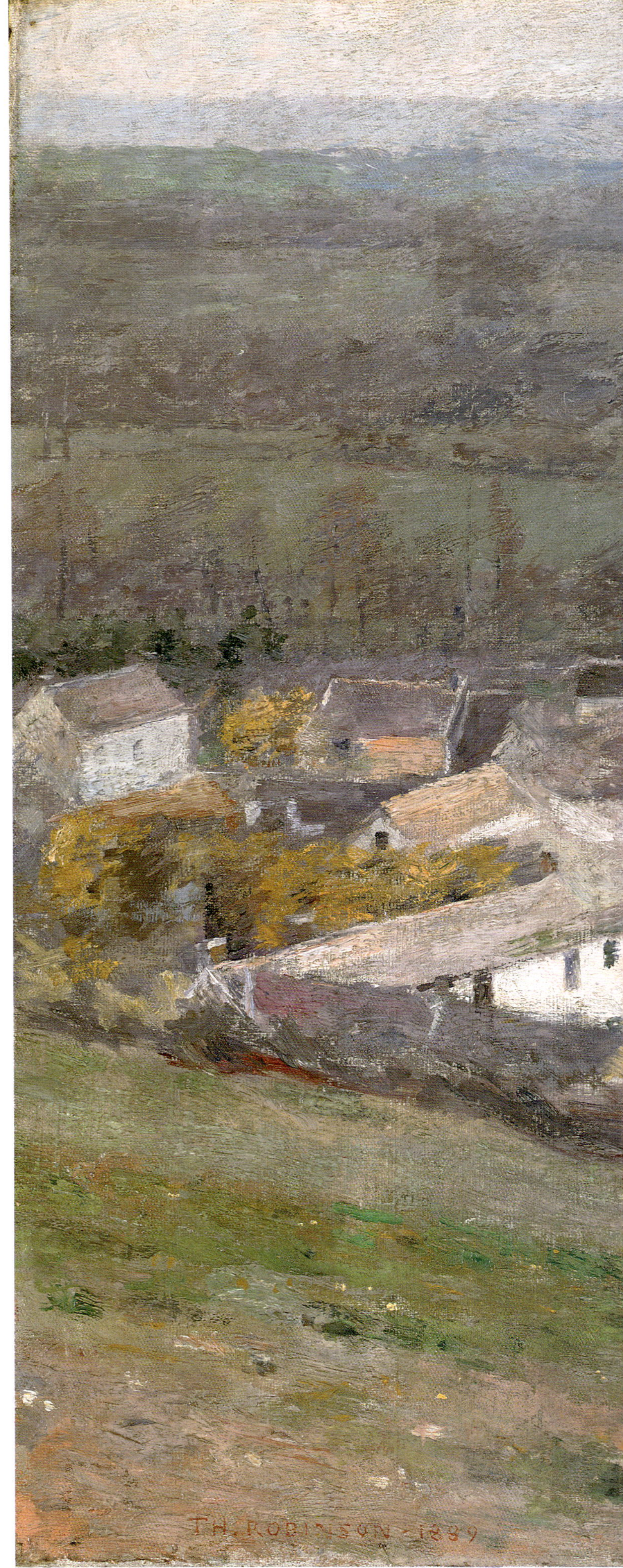

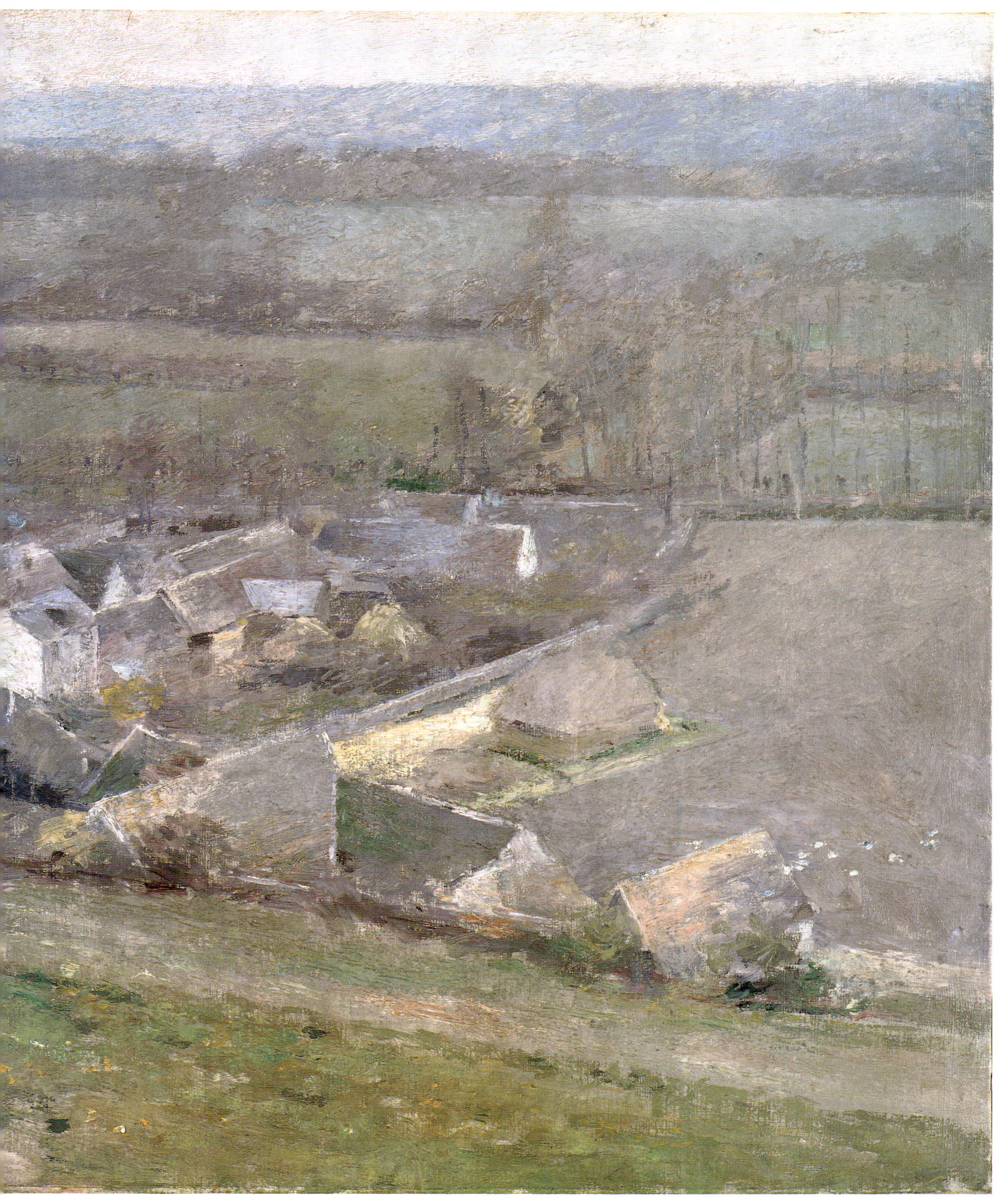

Homer Dodge Martin
1836–1897

View on the Seine: Harp of the Winds

Oil on canvas
28¾ x 40¾ in. (73 x 103.5 cm.)
1895
Signed and dated at lower right:
H. D. Martin 1895
Gift of Several Gentlemen, 1897 (97.32)

THIS LANDSCAPE of the Seine was painted more than seven years after Homer Dodge Martin returned from a long stay in France, and perhaps much of its lyrical beauty is due to the refining and crystallizing process that took place in the artist's memory of the French countryside during the intervening years. He took the unfinished painting with him when he went to live in Saint Paul, Minnesota, in 1893. By then nearly blind, he finished the work just two years before his death. The straight, slender poplars that are such a characteristic sight in the Seine basin were painted again and again by Claude Monet, but *Harp of the Winds* is different—it is a musical grouping in which the faint rustle of the tremulous trees expresses the whole light-toned landscape of the Ile de France that Martin treasured in his mind and had grown to love.

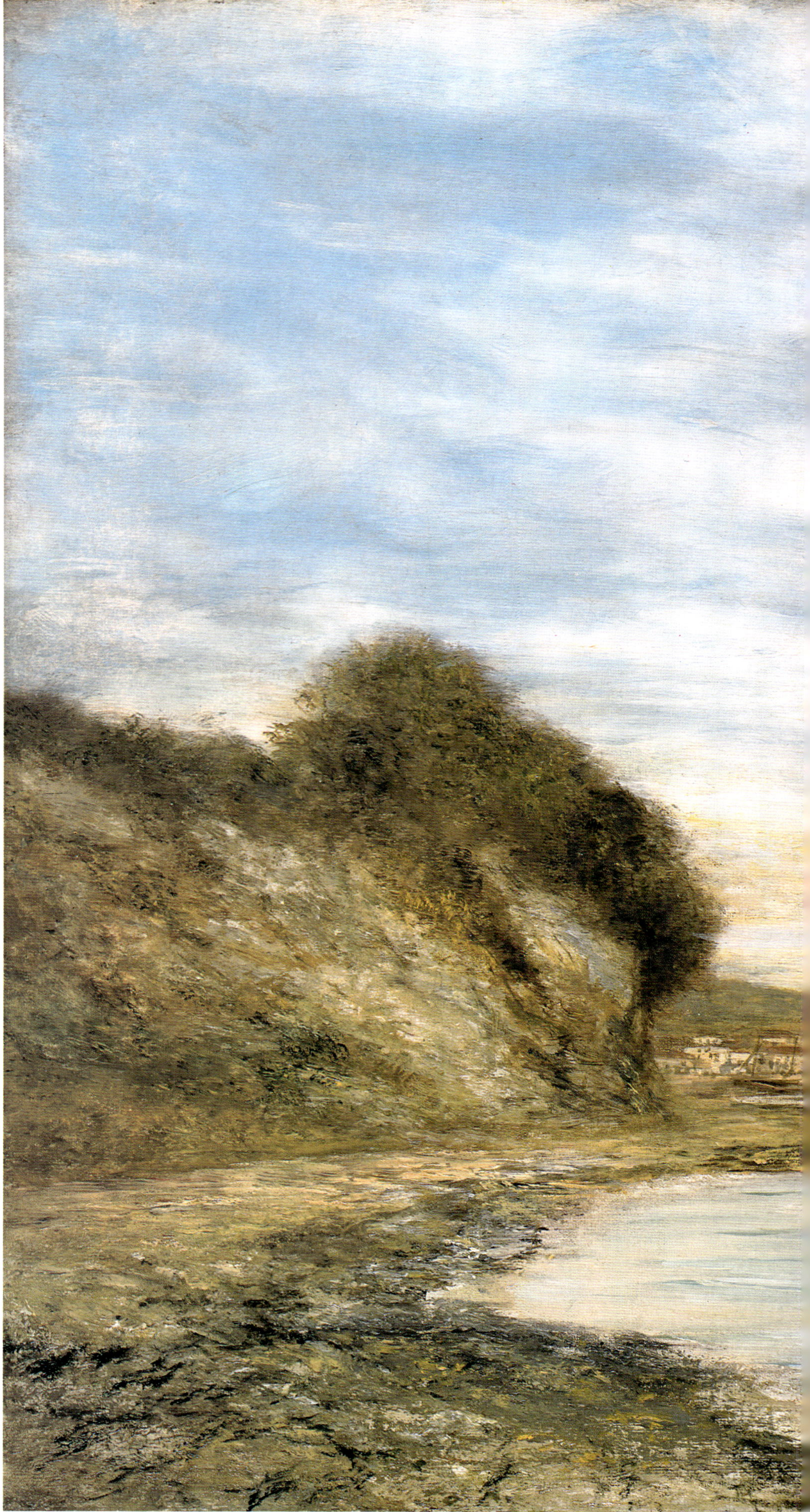

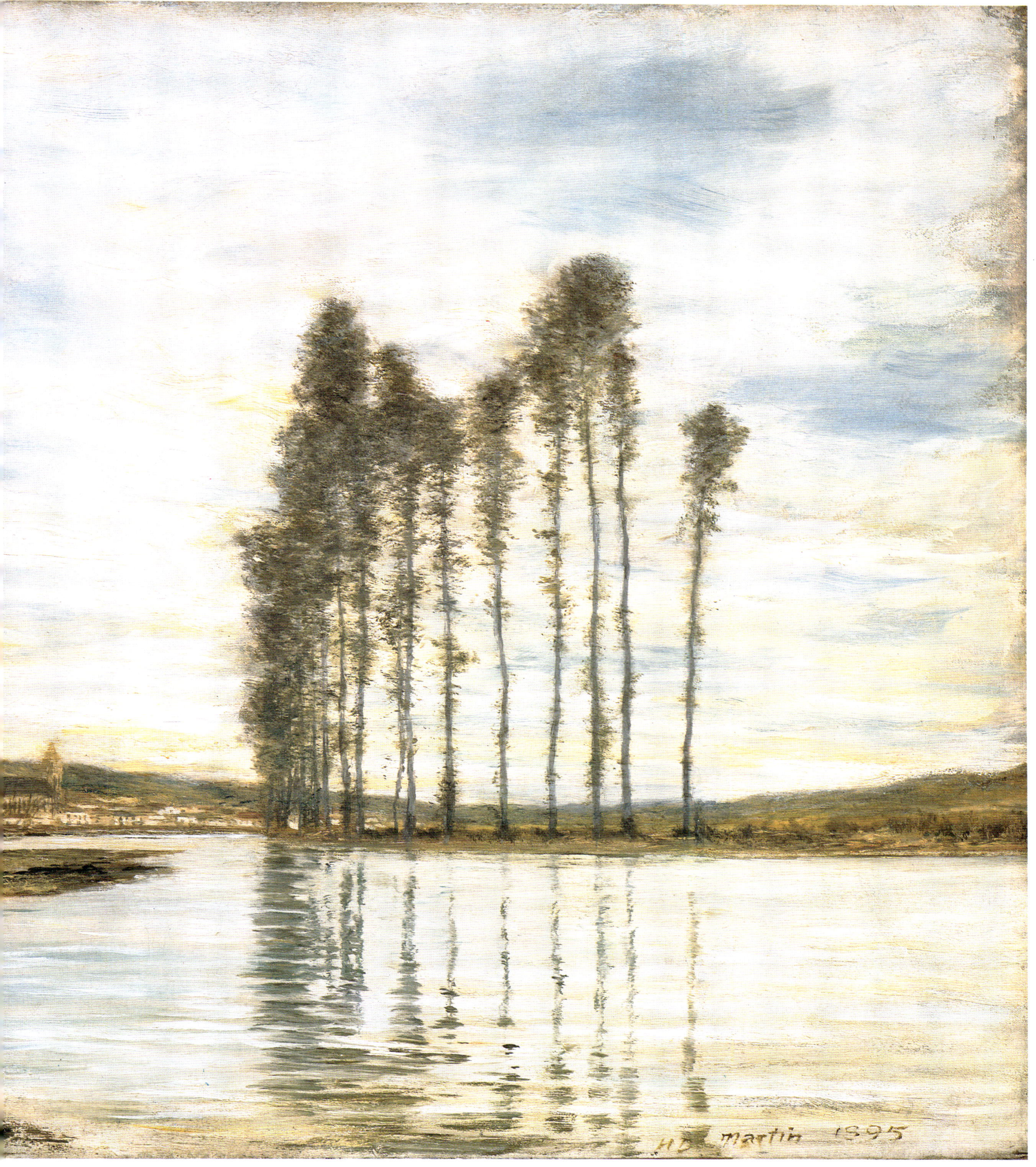
HD Martin 1895

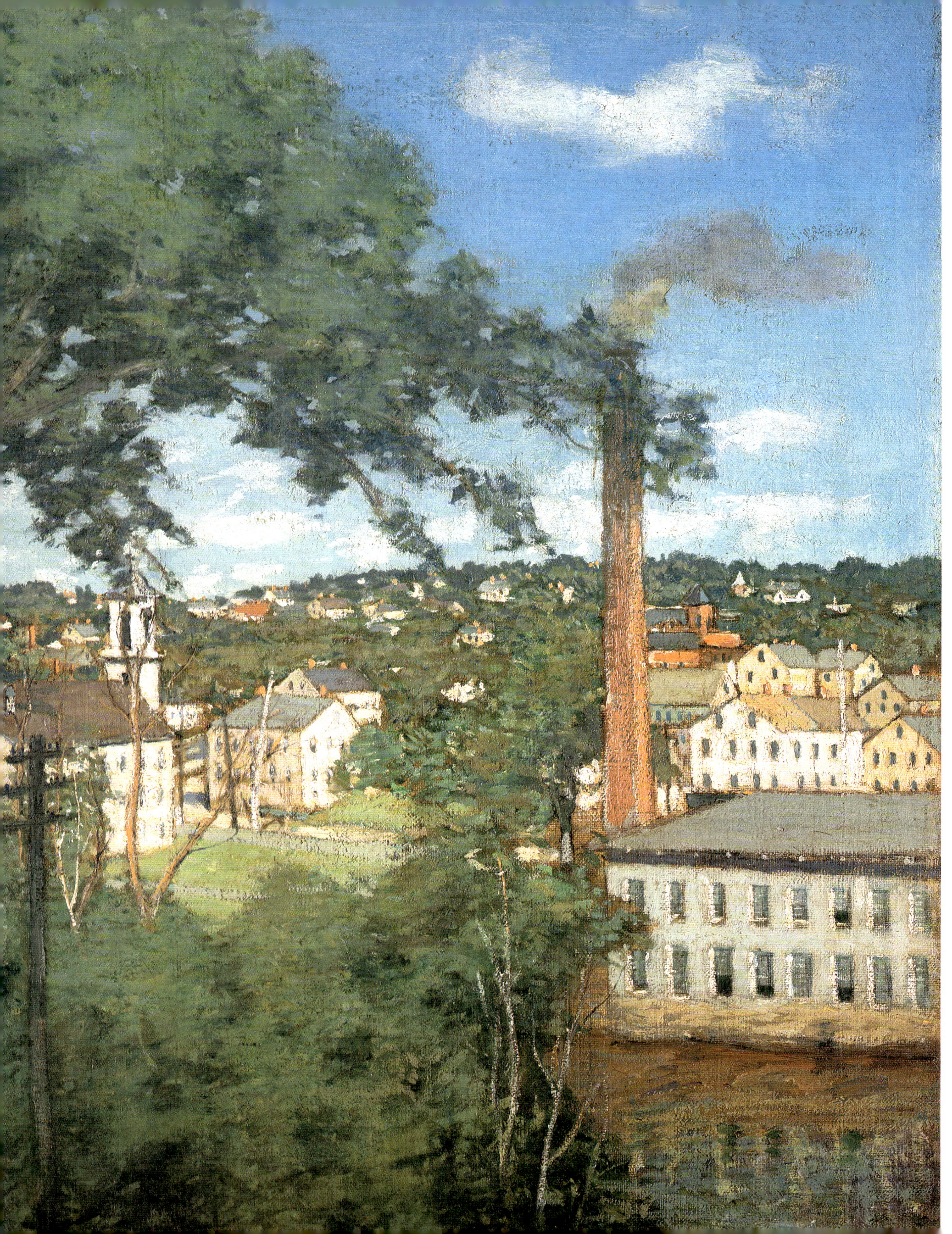

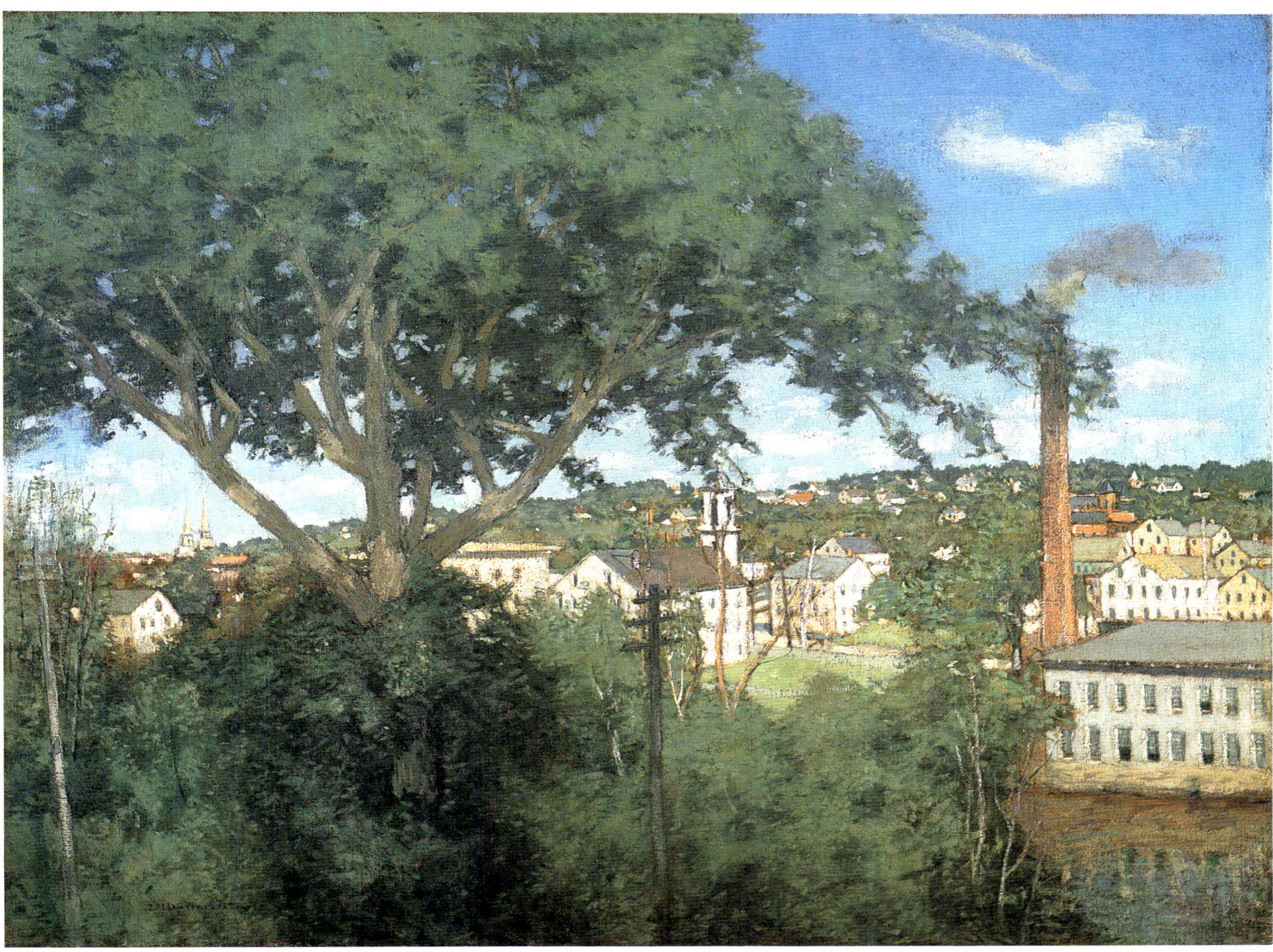

J. Alden Weir
1852–1919

The Factory Village

Oil on canvas
29 x 38 in. (73.7 x 96.5 cm.)
1897
Signed and dated at lower left:
J. Alden Weir 1897
Jointly owned by The Metropolitan Museum of Art and Cora Weir Burlingham, 1979
(1979.487)

J. ALDEN WEIR was the half brother of John Ferguson Weir and like him received his early training in painting from their father, an instructor at the United States Military Academy at West Point. In his twenties J. Alden Weir studied in Paris under the popular painter Jean-Léon Gérôme. It was probably at this time that Weir began to admire the paintings of the French artist Bastien-Lepage, to whom he remained devoted. He acquired Bastien-Lepage's famous *Joan of Arc* for the collector Erwin Davis, who later gave it to the Metropolitan Museum. Weir's first contact with the works of the Impressionists horrified him, but his antipathy gave way in the early 1890s, when he began to work in a style that, though basically his own, showed strong similarities to theirs. Ultimately Weir became a prominent representative of American Impressionism. The chief thing Weir and the French artists of the Impressionist movement had in common was their devotion to nature, and like the Impressionists Weir chose to work in the light of the outdoors. In the second half of his career Weir's color became lighter and his technique freer. He had always been dedicated to the study of nature and when he painted such pictures as *The Factory Village* (the village is Willimantic, Connecticut), landscape was the dominant theme, with man-made structures fitting into the wide expanses almost as subordinate elements in the scenes.

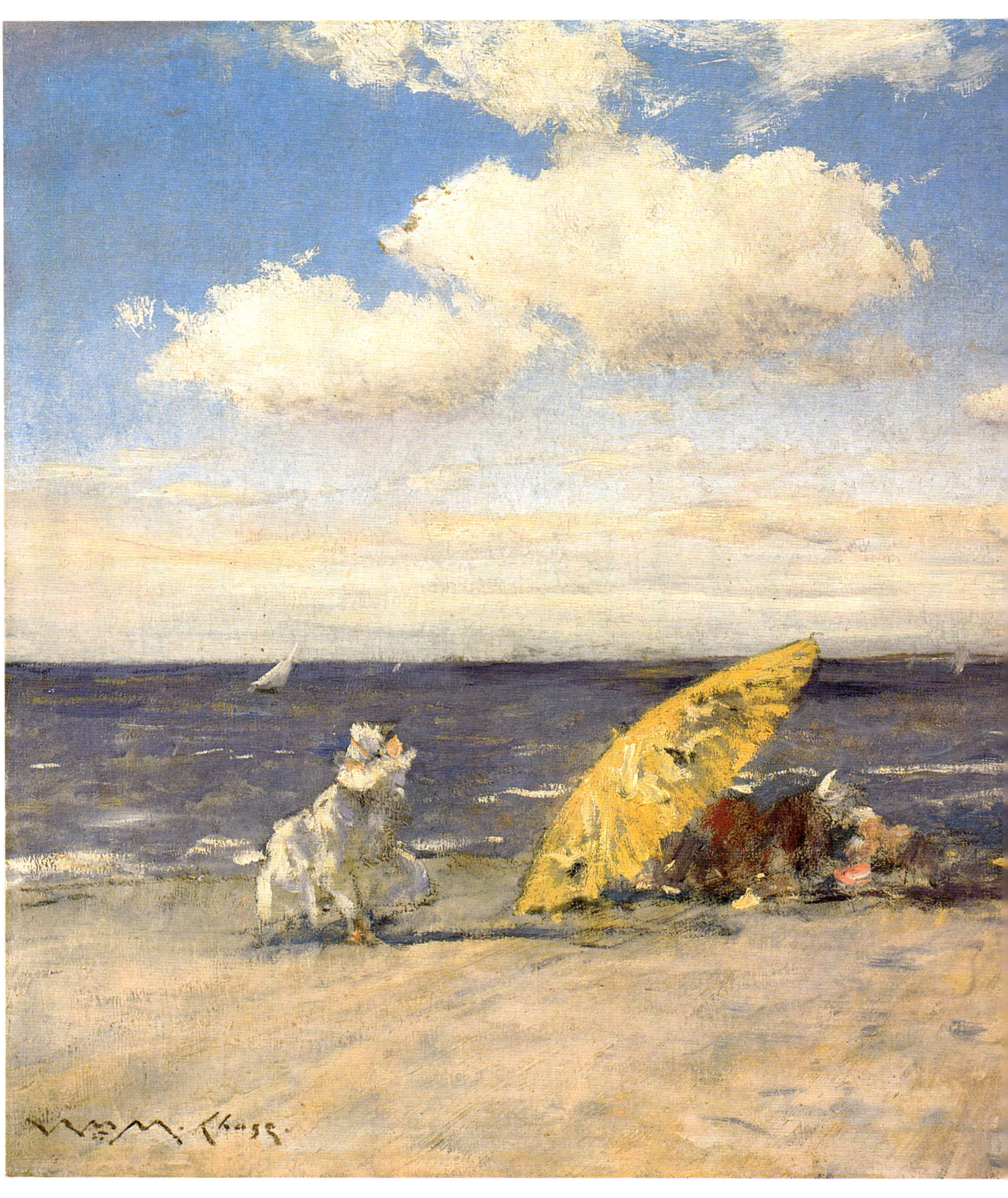

William Merritt Chase
1849–1916

At the Seaside

Oil on canvas
20 x 34 in. (50.8 x 86.4 cm.)
ca. 1895
Signed at lower left: Wm M. Chase; traces of a previous signature at lower right: Wm M
Bequest of Miss Adelaide Milton de Groot (1876–1967), 1967 (67.187.123)

AS A YOUNG MAN William Merritt Chase spent considerable time in Europe, studying at the Academy in Munich and traveling extensively. Back in the United States, he became a successful and highly respected artist and an important and influential teacher. In the 1890s, Chase conducted an outdoor art school at Shinnecock, Long Island, where he had a summer home. There he painted a number of scenes showing women and children on the sandy beaches around Peconic Bay. By this time, he had

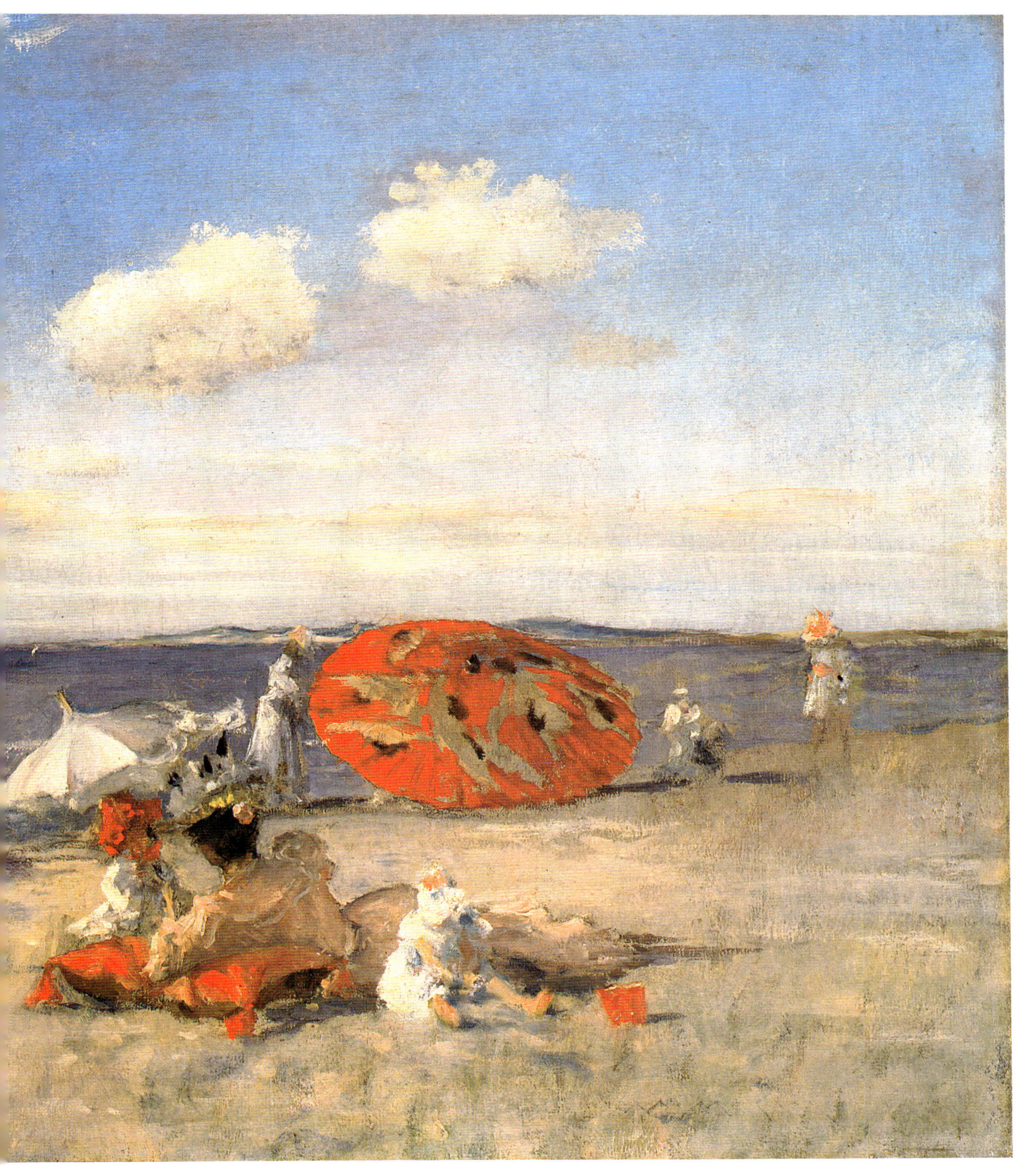

become a true devotee of French Impressionism, working in the open, using clear primary colors like the blues and reds in this picture, and always stressing the great, dwarfing expanses of sea, sand, and sky. This lively but delicate little scene actually owes less to Monet than to Eugène Boudin, who was famous for his paintings of the seaside in which the interest was equally divided between the foreground of fashionable figures and the pale, blue-gray atmospheric background.

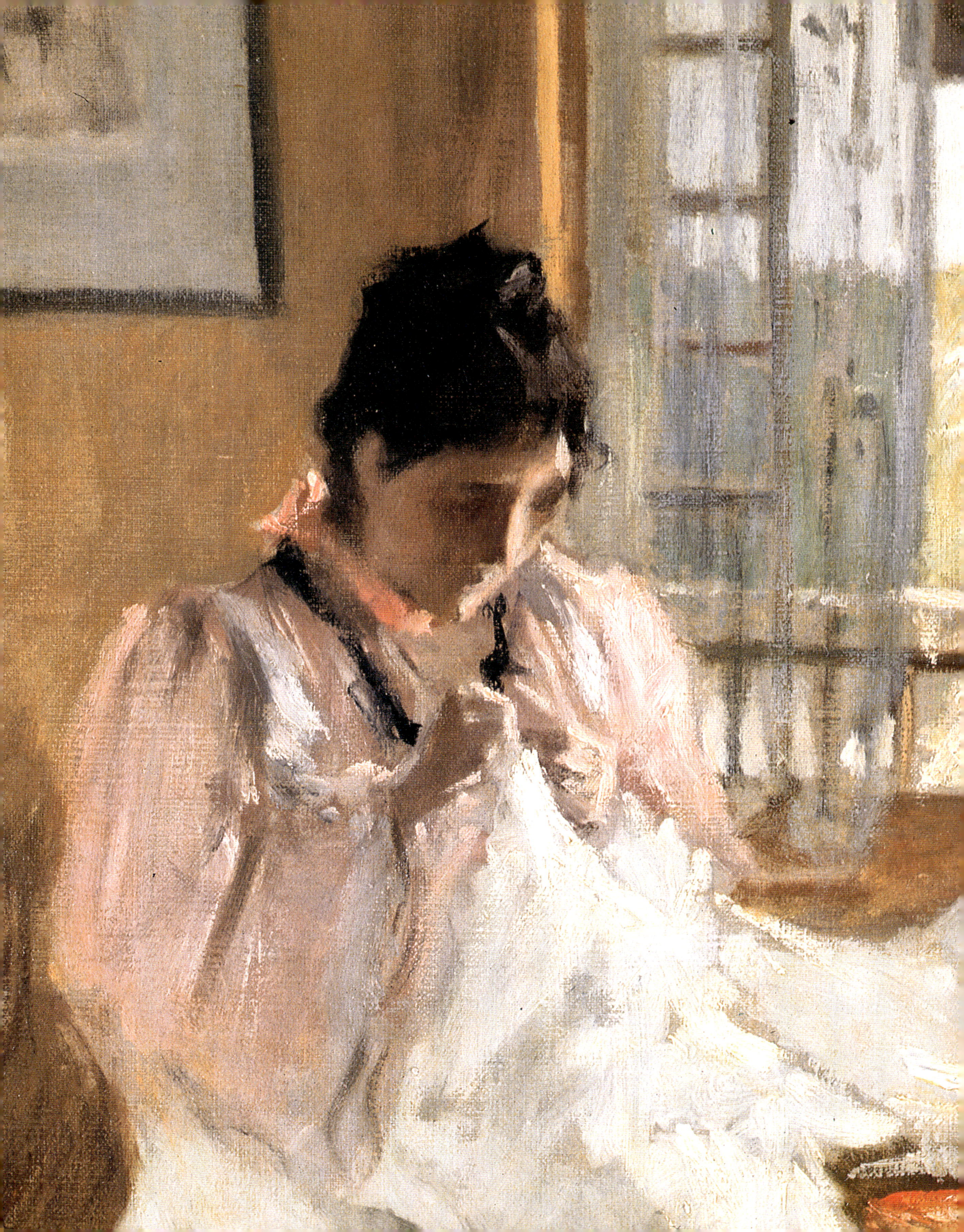

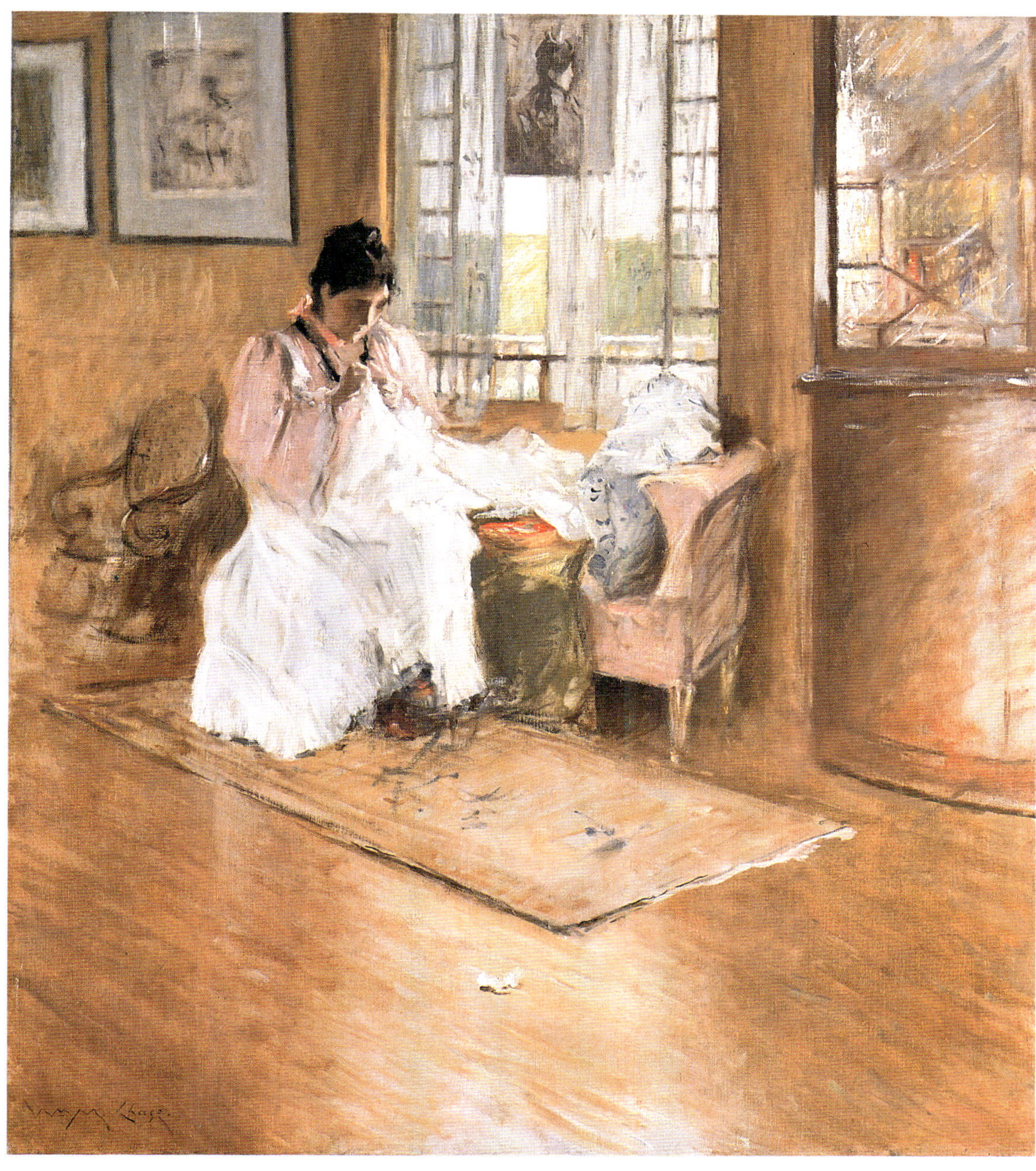

William Merritt Chase
1849–1916

For the Little One

Oil on canvas
40 x 35¼ in. (101.6 x 89.5 cm.)
ca. 1895
Signed at lower left: Wm.M. Chase
Amelia B. Lazarus Fund, by exchange, 1917 (13.90)

EARLY IN THE 1890s, William Merritt Chase commissioned the well-known architectural firm of McKim, Mead and White to design and build a summer home for him on Long Island that he called Shinnecock Hall. The setting of this picture is a bright room in his house, where his wife sews quietly by the window, probably fashioning baby clothes. The broad expanse of polished wooden floor occupying the entire foreground suggests good housekeeping and cleanliness and serves to isolate the gentle, absorbed figure from rude intrusion. This area of empty space and the diagonal lines of the rug and floorboards create a carefully planned and executed composition. The ordered life implied in the serene domestic scene, with its tasks and pastimes, is the subject of many of Chase's pictures during the last decade of the century.

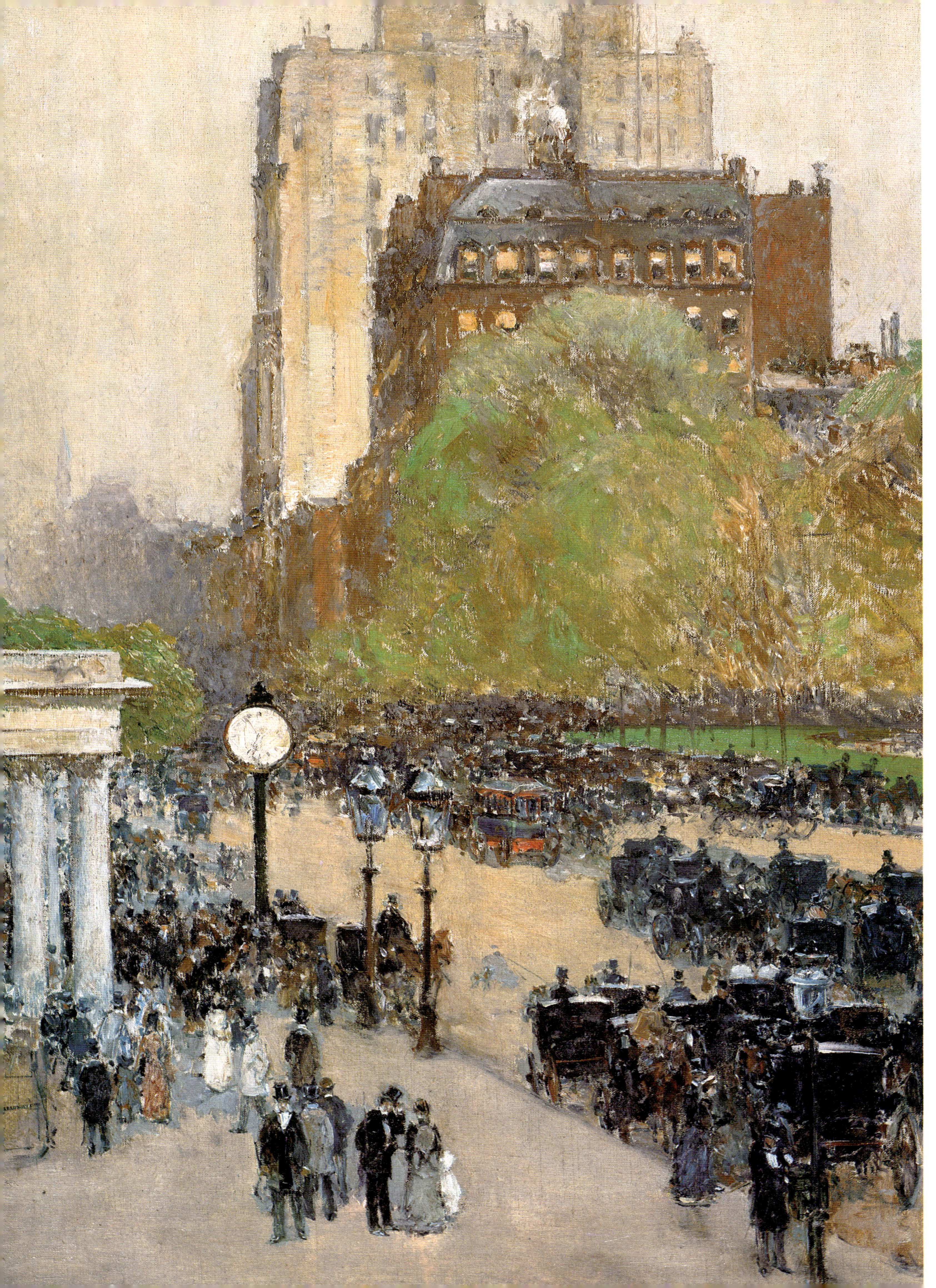

Childe Hassam
1859–1935

Spring Morning in the Heart of the City

Oil on canvas
18⅛ x 20¾ in. (46 x 52.7 cm.)
1890
Signed and dated at lower right:
(crescent) Childe Hassam. 1890
Gift of Ethelyn McKinney, in memory of her brother, Glenn Ford McKinney, 1943 (43.116.1)

THE SITE REPRESENTED in this picture is Madison Square in New York. The present title, its original one, characterizing the locale as "the heart of the city," indicates how steadily the center of urban life has moved uptown all through the twentieth century. When Childe Hassam painted the scene, Madison Square, established before 1850 between Fifth and Madison Avenues in the area north of Twenty-third Street, was a busy region, flourishing with trade and amusements, with fashionable hotels and restaurants. The artist, not long returned from a three-year stay in Paris, viewed this young and vigorous, typically American city with the same kind of affectionate scrutiny Monet and Renoir had applied to the boulevards and bridges of Paris. The foreground, though impressionistically painted, is relatively clear and detailed and set against a background of frothy spring green and vaguely delineated architecture.

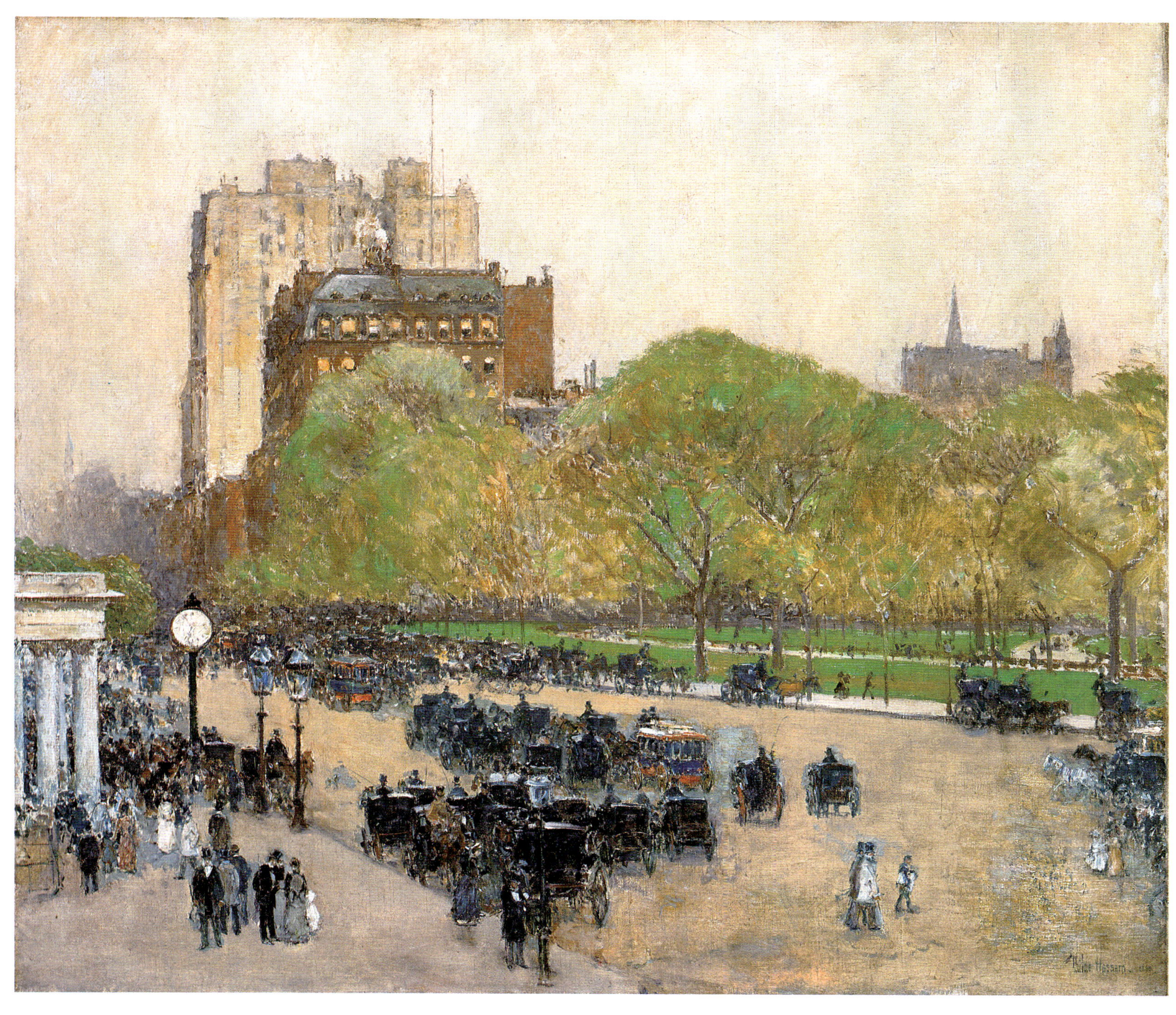

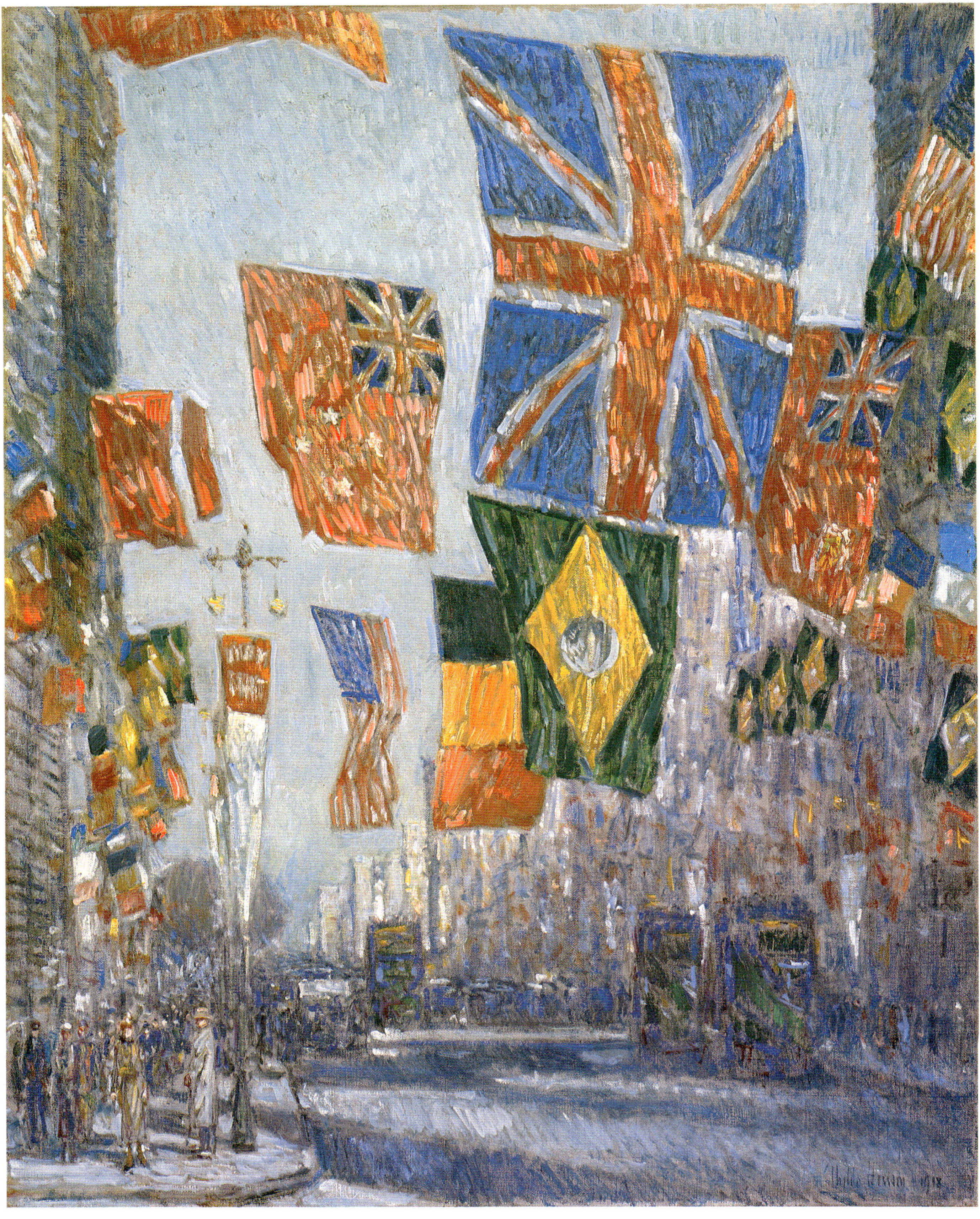

Childe Hassam
1859–1935

Avenue of the Allies, Great Britain, 1918

Oil on canvas
36 x 28⅜ in. (91.4 x 72.1 cm.)
1918
Signed and dated at lower right: (crescent) Childe Hassam—1918; signed, dated, and inscribed on reverse: CH (in a circle with a crescent)/1918
Bequest of Miss Adelaide Milton de Groot (1876–1967), 1967 (67.187.127)

DURING WORLD WAR I, Childe Hassam was among the most enthusiastic and dedicated of the patriot-artists. Between 1916 and 1918 his paintings kept a visual record of American involvement, first in "preparedness" and then in actual participation. One of a large group of flag paintings by Hassam, this New York scene celebrates the decoration of Fifth Avenue for the fourth Liberty Loan Drive, in the autumn of 1918, when each of the twenty-two allied nations had a specific block, brilliant with banners, devoted to it. Here, in the foreground, is the block between Fifty-third and Fifty-fourth streets, the block of the British Empire. Behind the Union Jack is the block of Brazil, and the vista looks to the north, toward the Belgian block and the upper reaches of Fifth Avenue. The scintillating color and the lively brushstrokes evoke the emotion of the last weeks of the conflict.

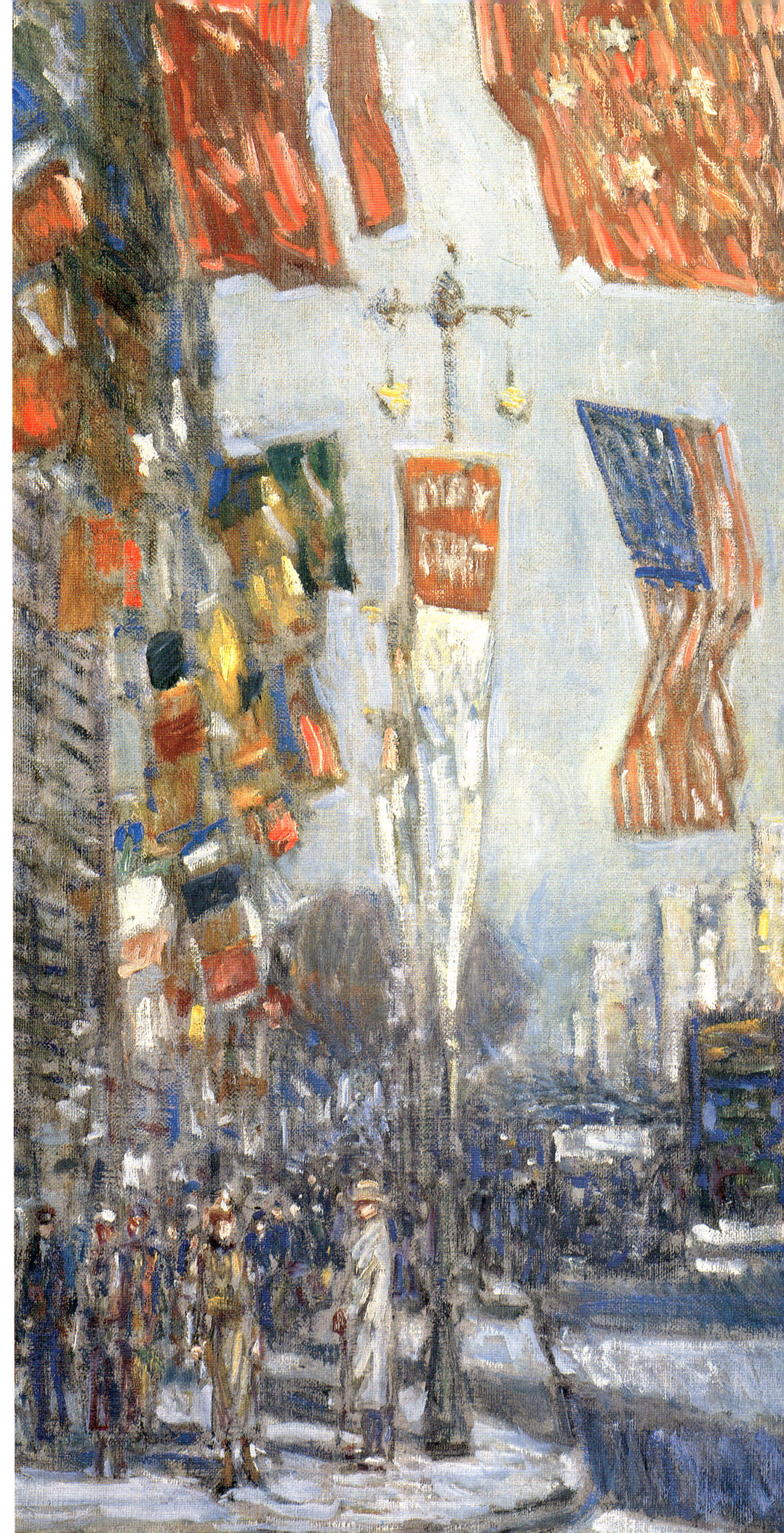

Edmund C. Tarbell
1862–1938

Across the Room

Oil on canvas
25 x 30⅛ in. (63.5 x 76.5 cm.)
ca. 1899
Signed at lower right: Tarbell
Bequest of Miss Adelaide Milton de Groot (1876–1967), 1967 (67.187.141)

AT ABOUT THE AGE of twenty, after an apprenticeship as a lithographer and some study in Boston at the School of the Museum of Fine Arts, Edmund Tarbell, like so many of his contemporaries, set off for Paris. There the Impressionists were approaching their eighth and final exhibition, and their fresh attitudes and revolutionary techniques made a deep impression on Tarbell and affected his way of painting. Their preference for working out-of-doors, their high-keyed palette, and their loose, rapid brushwork became characteristics of his style. Tarbell also admired the seventeenth-century Dutch painter Vermeer, whose quiet, light-filled rooms with their timeless images of solitary female occupants inspired many of his pictures. In this painting, a fashionably dressed, recumbent young woman, silent and motionless, is seen across a wide, polished floor on which the half light, filtering through a Venetian blind, creates a pattern of reflections. This would be a Dutch subject rendered in a French technique were it not for the flavor of innocently girlish and dreamy idleness that distinguishes the pictures of several other American painters at the end of the nineteenth century.

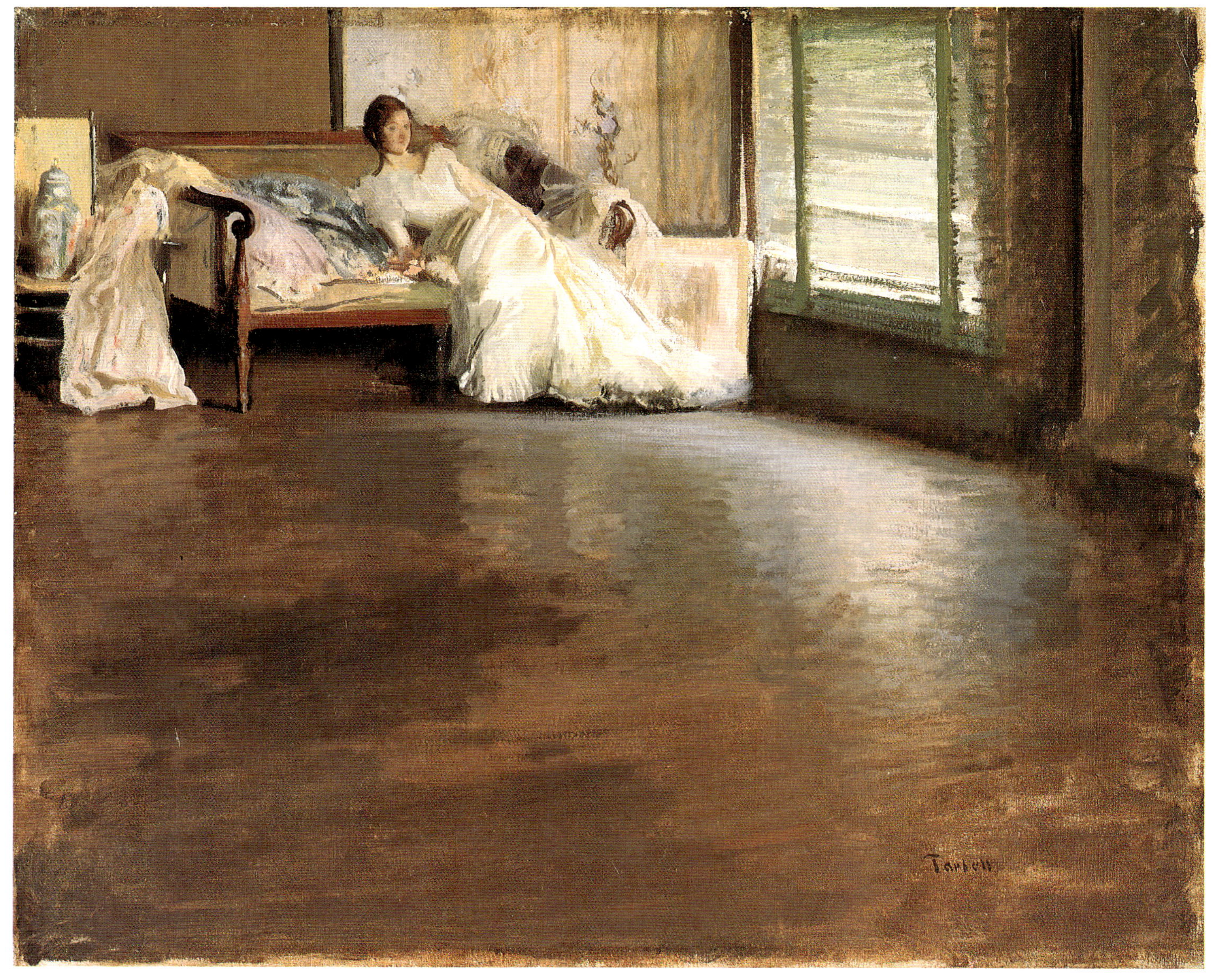

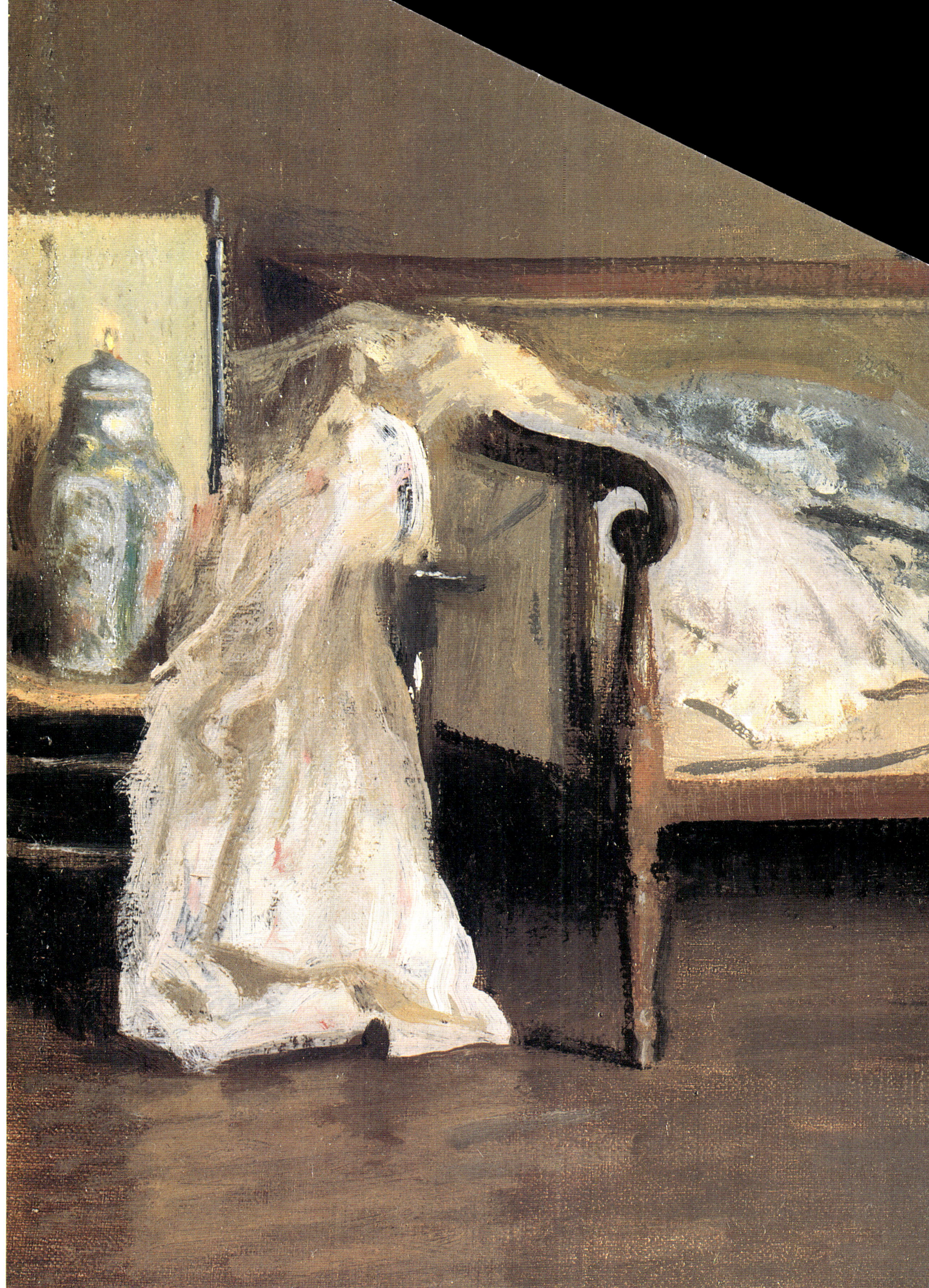

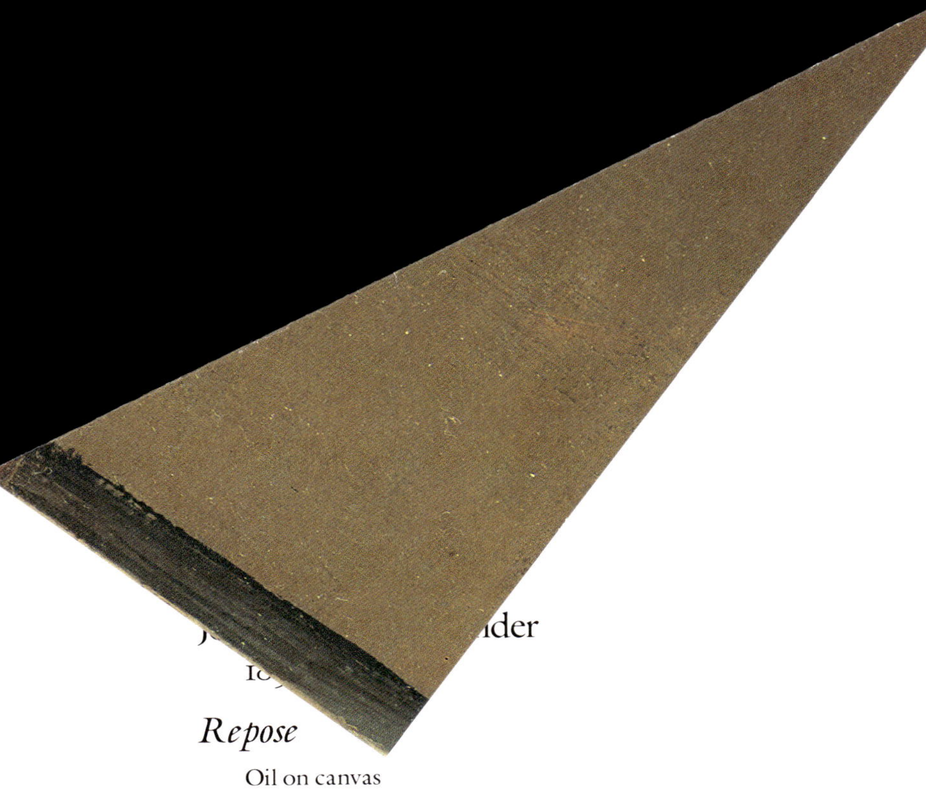

Repose

Oil on canvas
52¼ x 63⅝ in. (132.7 x 161.6 cm.)
1895
Signed and dated at lower right: J. W. Alexander 95—
Anonymous gift, 1980 (1980.224)

AS A YOUNG ARTIST John White Alexander spent four years in Europe, working at first in a thick, brushy style. After meeting with Whistler, however, he adopted a subtler, more delicate technique that characterized all his later work. He lived for ten years in Paris when he was a mature painter, and it was there that he painted *Repose.* It is one of a group of five pictures on the same theme that he sent to the famous Paris Salon of 1895.

Repose is a bold and highly original concept, in which a human figure, simplified and exaggerated, dominates an extraordinarily unified and compelling composition. The model is said to have been the American dancer Loïe Fuller (1862–1928), who was enjoying great popularity in Paris. She lies in calculated abandon on the massive cushions of a sofa. The long curves of the couch's drapery and the flowing fullness of her pale dress suggest the idea of a cradling, or swaying, dancer's motion, and carry on the rhythm of the dance even after the suspension of all physical activity. Her torso is sunk in the huge cushion and her legs are swathed in material, but the litheness and life of her muscle structure are wonderfully implied.

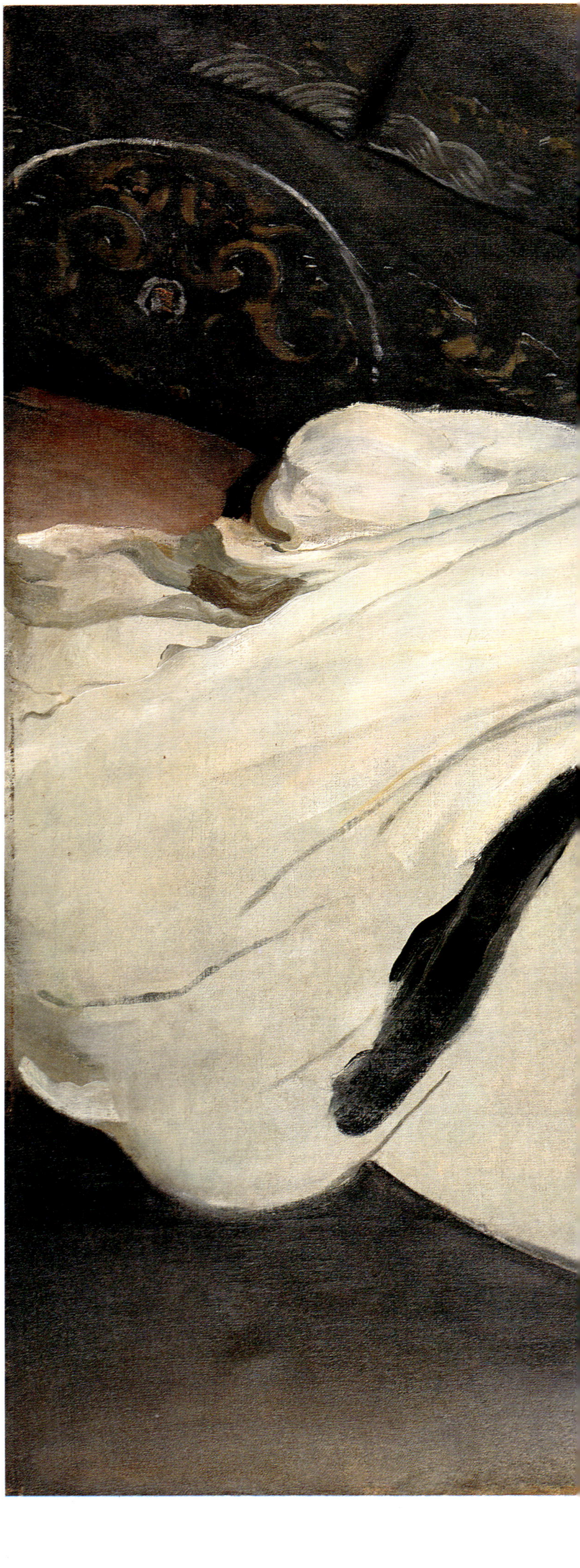

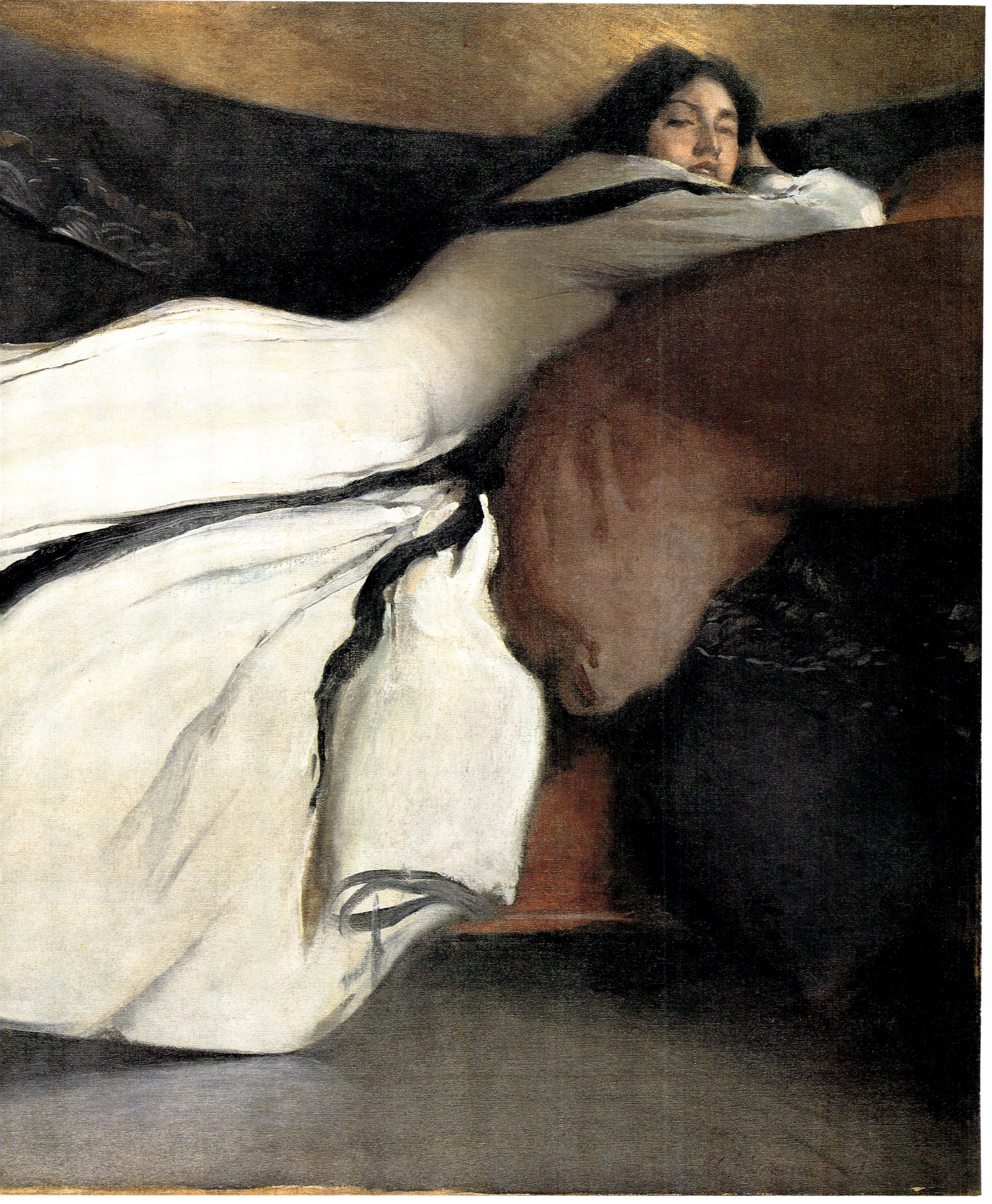

Abbott H. Thayer
1849–1921

Young Woman

Oil on canvas
39⅝ x 31⅝ in. (100.7 x 80.3 cm.)
ca. 1898
Signed at lower right: Abbott H. Thayer
Gift of George A. Hearn, 1906 (06.1298)

BESSIE PRICE (1879–1968), a young Irish servant, posed for this picture and for a number of Abbott H. Thayer's other paintings. In his many winged and allegorical figures, he quite naturally sought for ethereal expression and effect; here, however, he has not played down the wide, solid column of the model's neck, her broad shoulders, or her strong arms and hands. Her face has an open look of trust and inward serenity—the qualities of the idealized women so much favored in late nineteenth-century American art, and especially in the work of Thayer. It was usual in representing these women to invoke classical Greece and Rome, and, though Bessie's hair is not dressed in Greek fashion, her soft draperies, rendered with such skill, are a Victorian version of what was assumed to be classical costume. *Young Woman* won a gold medal at the Paris Exposition of 1900.

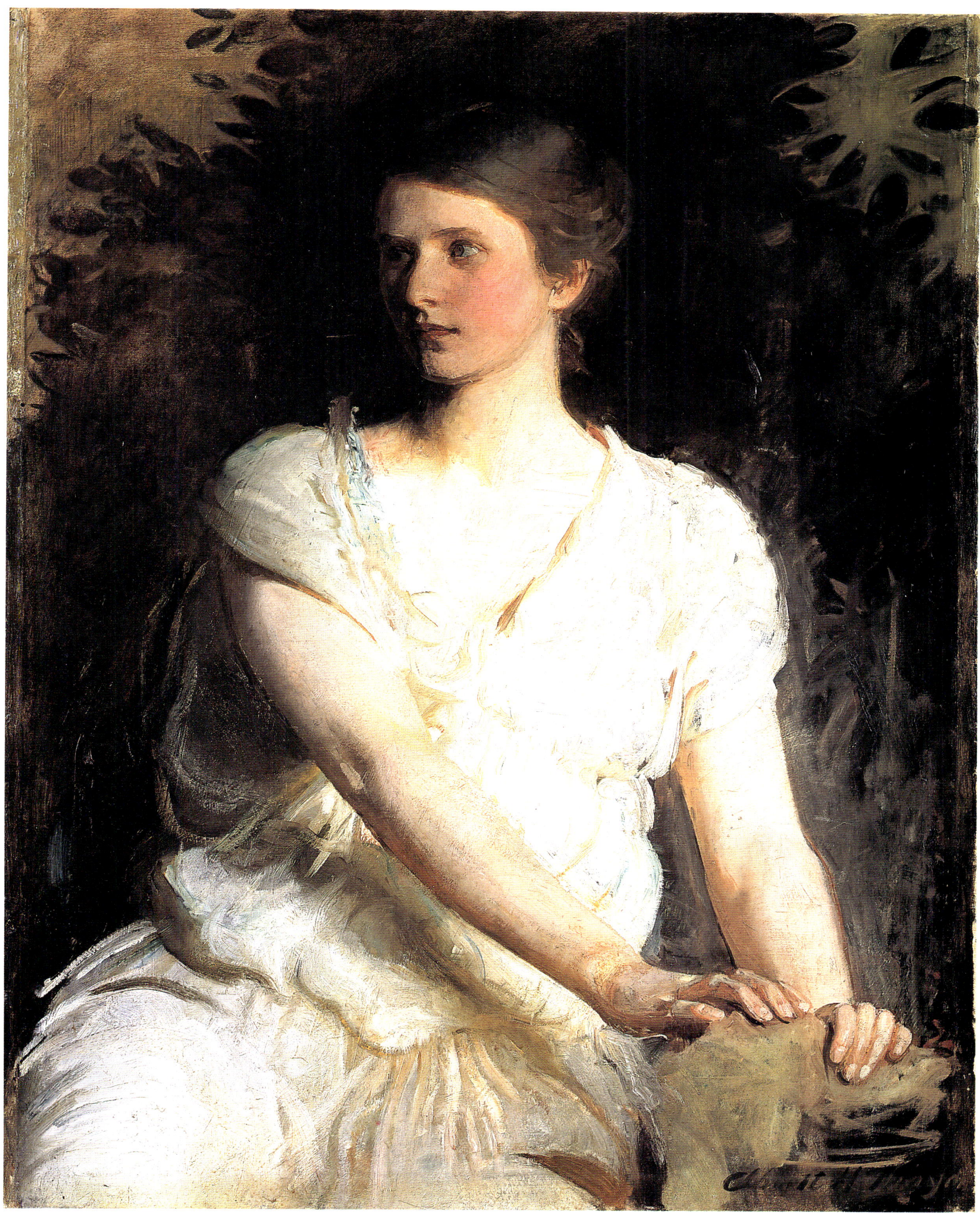

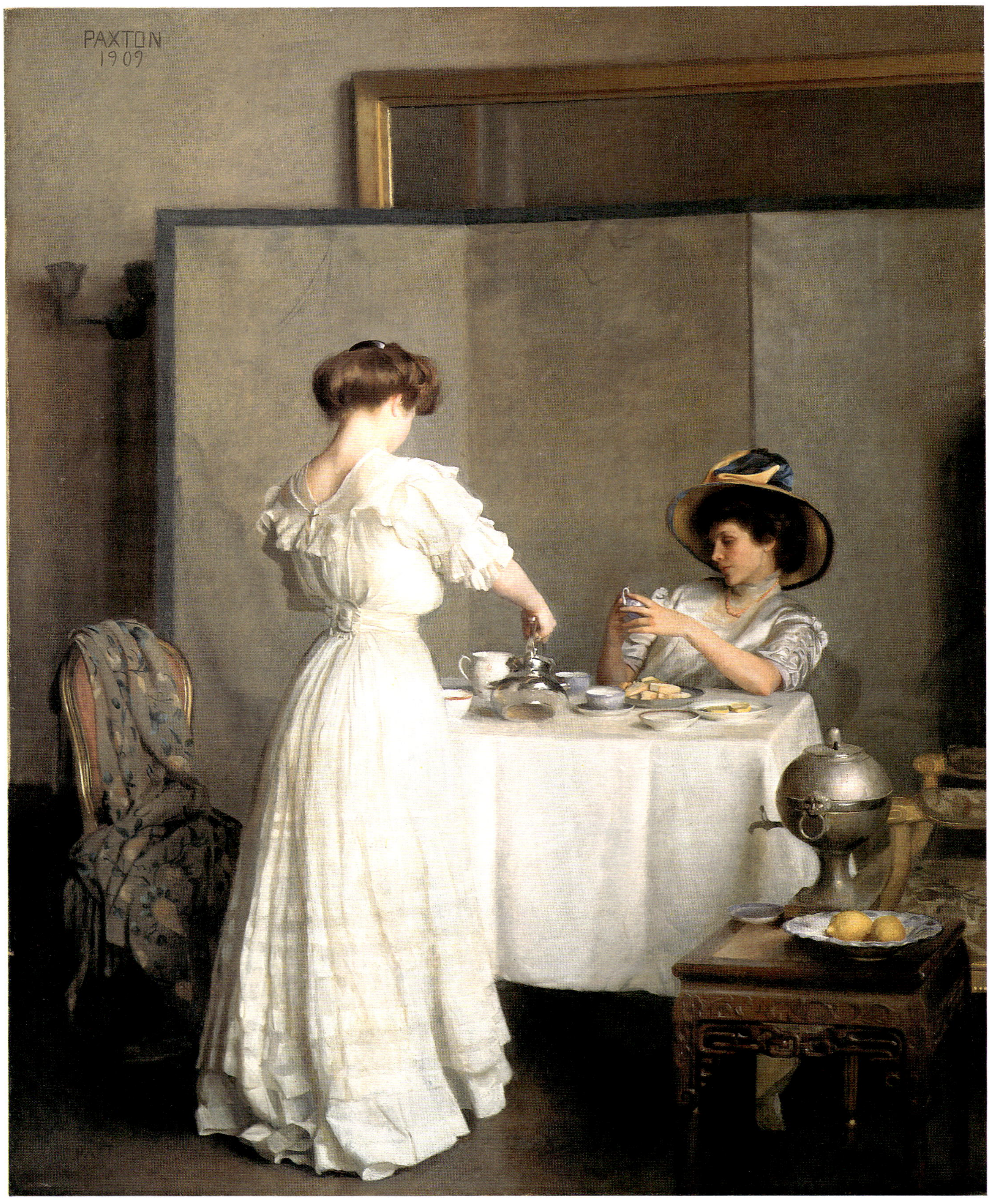
PAXTON
1909

William M. Paxton
1869–1941

Tea Leaves

Oil on canvas
36⅛ x 28¾ in. (91.8 x 73 cm.)
1909
Signed and dated at upper left:
PAXTON/1909
Gift of George A. Hearn, 1910 (10.64.8)

WILLIAM M. PAXTON grew up in Newton, Massachusetts, and, after a period of study in Paris, returned to Boston, where he spent most of his working life. He enjoyed great popularity as a portraitist. His smooth and finished way of painting was established early by a period of solid training under Jean-Léon Gérôme in Paris. He was also deeply impressed by the works of the French classicist Ingres. Paxton carefully depicted details and held true to accepted and conventional appearances of costumes, objects, and attitudes. These qualities make his anecdotal and genre scenes such as *Tea Leaves* incomparable records of the life of their time. These pictures were easy to understand and gave pleasure to large numbers of people, who could equate the figures and settings with their own experiences. The gentle and graceful ritual of tea drinking was an important part of social life well into the 1920s. It is interesting to compare Paxton's treatment of the theme with Mary Cassatt's on pages 154–57. Cassatt, who is equally circumstantial, is more intent on the aesthetic considerations of composition and structure. Both artists provide a wealth of detail, but while the Impressionist-oriented Cassatt manages to supply an aura of timelessness and accident to the scene, Paxton concentrates on the narrative of the attractive young hostess and her visitor, who tries to extract some meaning from the configuration in the teacup.

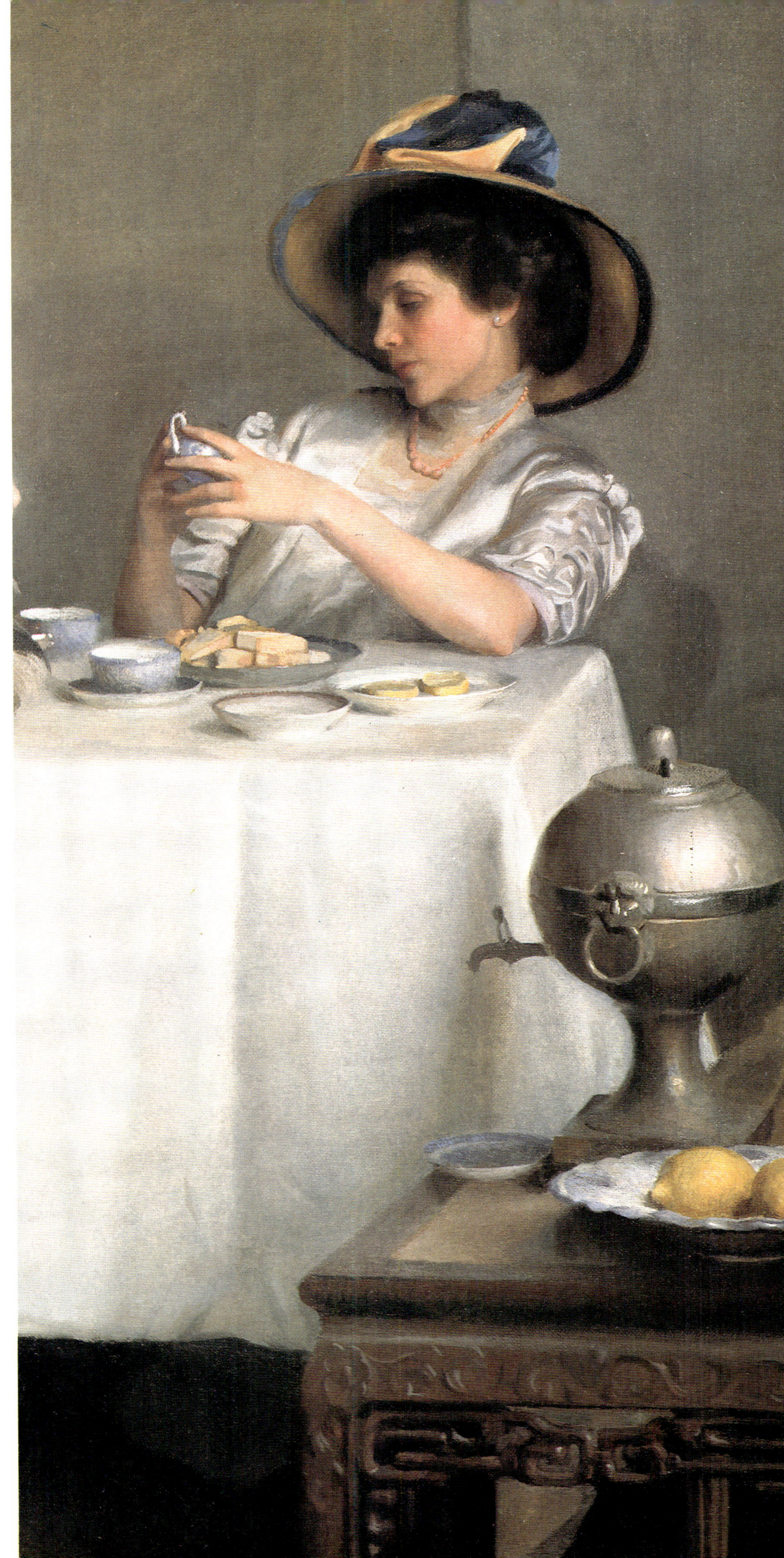

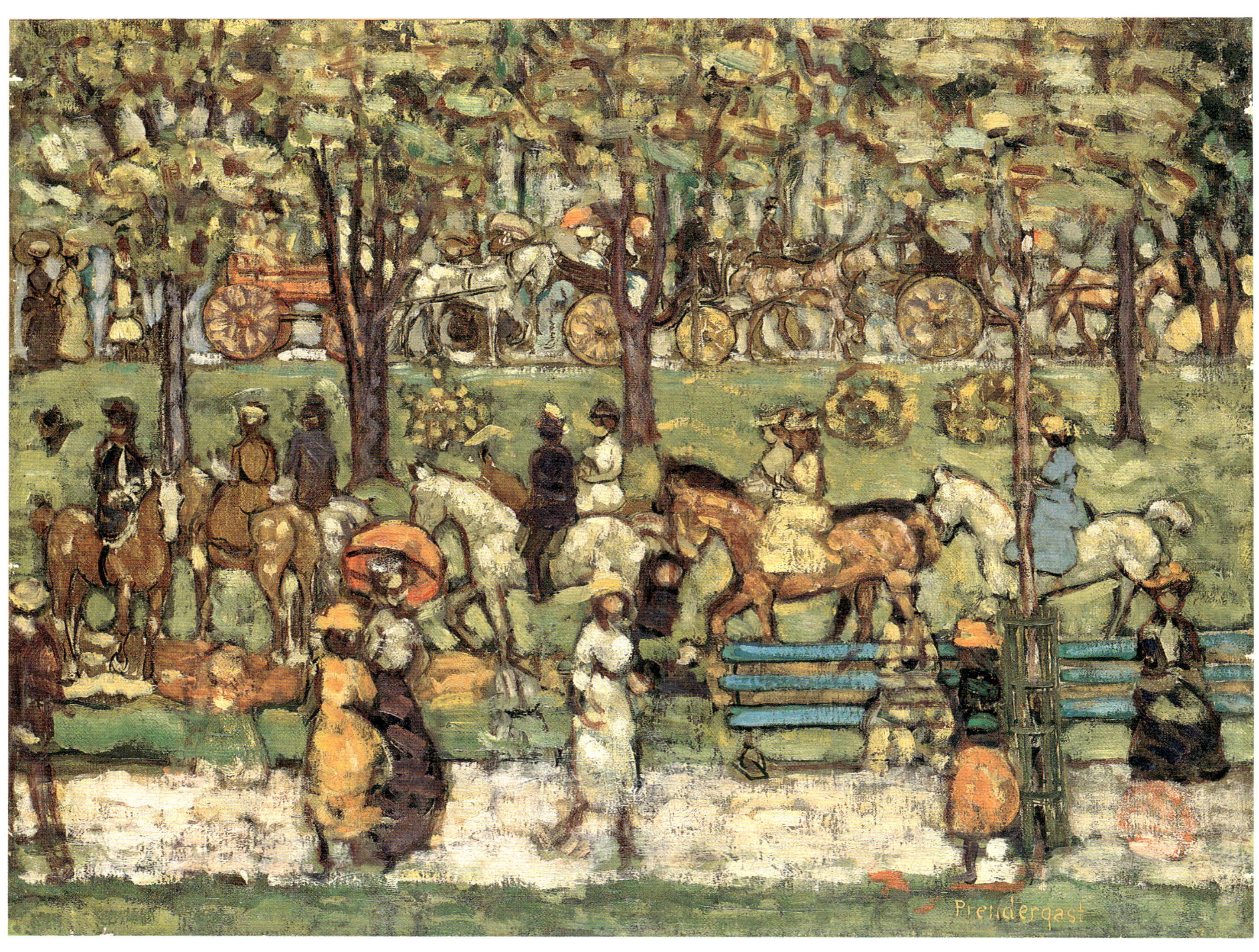

Maurice Prendergast
1859–1924

Central Park

Oil on canvas
20¾ x 27 in. (52.7 x 68.6 cm.)
ca. 1908–1910
Signed at lower right: Prendergast
George A. Hearn Fund, 1950 (50.25)

STUDIES IN EUROPE in 1886 and 1891 had brought Maurice Prendergast into contact with the work being produced in France by the Post-Impressionists. By the time he painted this scene, he had assimilated their styles and techniques into his own very personal and purely American interpretations. He was a member of the group of artists who named themselves The Eight when they first exhibited together in 1908, a group that included William Glackens, Robert Henri, George Luks, John Sloan, Everett Shinn, Arthur B. Davies, and Ernest Lawson. Sharing opposition to the accepted academic art of the day, they encouraged each other in their individual approaches, taking early twentieth-century American art into new directions. In *Central Park*, the verticals of the trees and of the slowly moving figures in the foreground cross bands of horizontals to form a flat, woven pattern. The painting recalls certain works by Gauguin (who also liked two-dimensional arrangements) and, to some extent, pictures by such Nabi artists as Vuillard. It seems likely that Prendergast submitted as well to the influence of the Australian artist Charles Condor and his English circle.

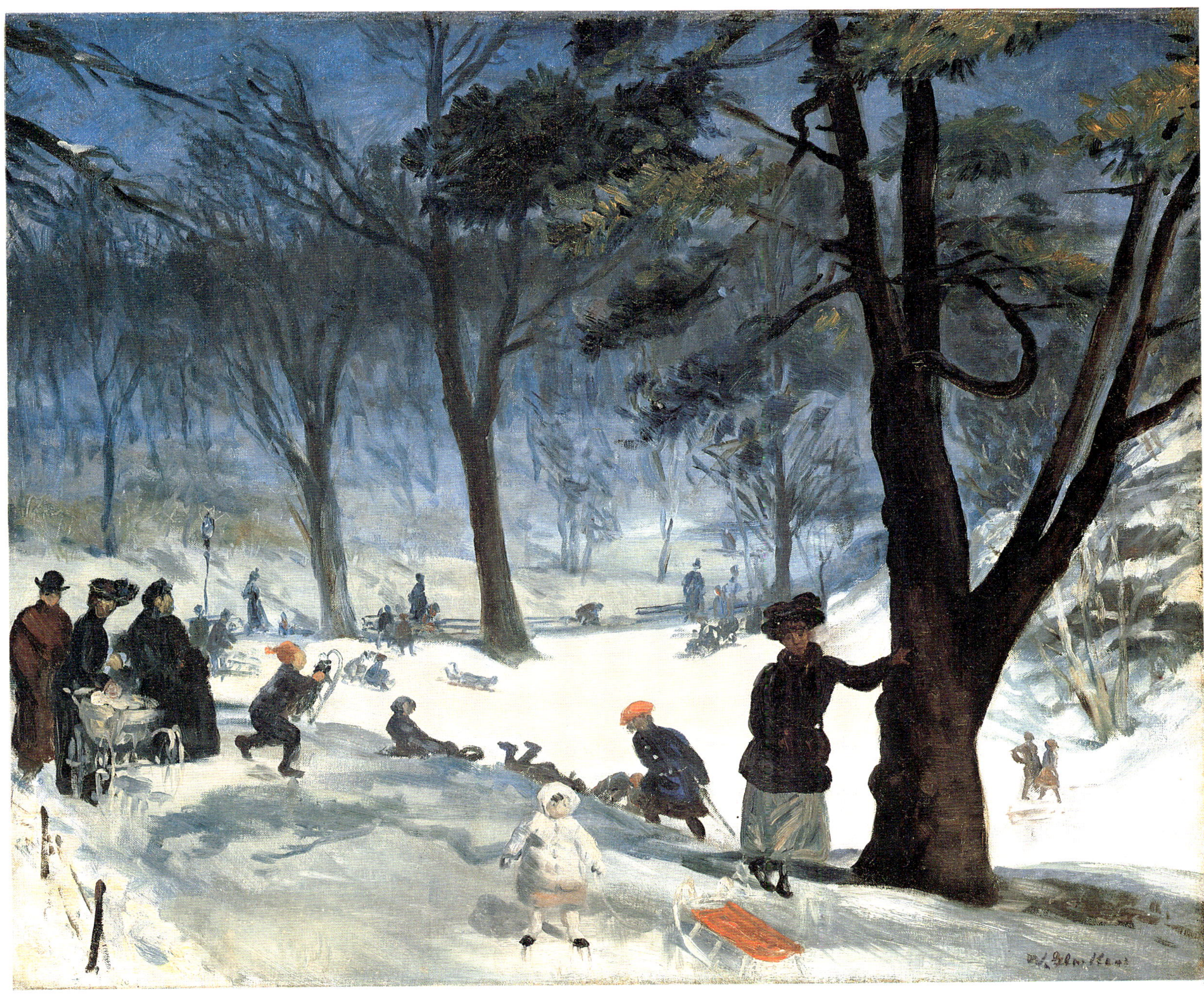

William Glackens
1870–1938

Central Park in Winter

Oil on canvas
25 x 30 in. (63.5 x 76.2 cm.)
1905
Signed at lower right: W. Glackens
George A. Hearn Fund, 1921 (21.164)

WILLIAM GLACKENS, a member of The Eight, was the only one of the group who was distinctly influenced by the French Impressionists. He was a cheerful painter and liked to record such scenes of recreation and city life as this lively view of children and adults enjoying Central Park under a blanket of snow. An accomplished illustrator, Glackens was a trained and experienced observer. His early pictures employ a broad, free brushstroke like that of his mentor Robert Henri, to depict in a shorthand technique anecdotes and everyday views. There is little detail but great vigor and sprightliness. Washington Square, where Glackens lived, also offered special opportunities to watch the daily scene, for the region around the great arch included both Greenwich Village and the aristocratic "old New York" of Edith Wharton.

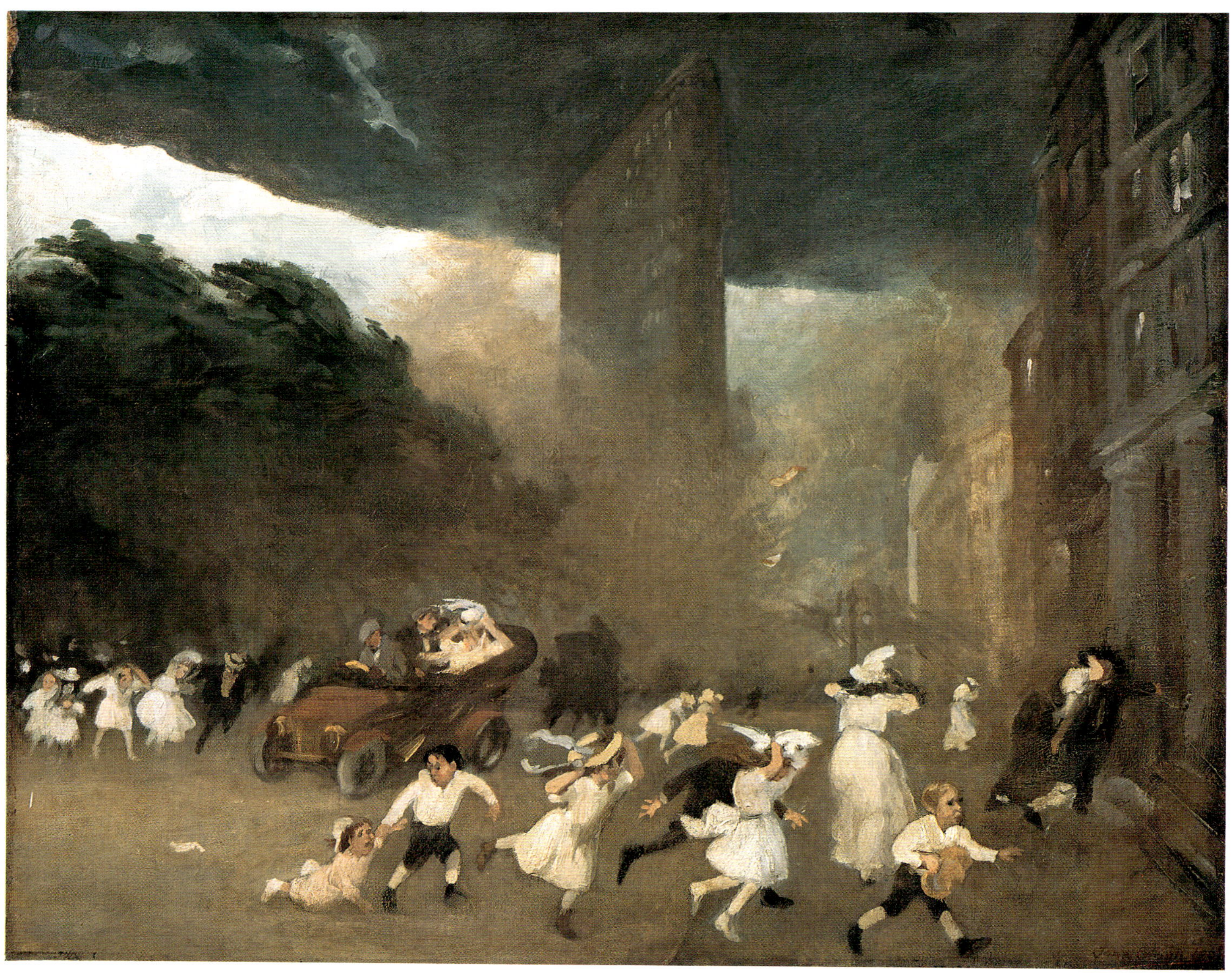

John Sloan
1871–1951

Dust Storm, Fifth Avenue

Oil on canvas
22 x 27 in. (55.9 x 68.6 cm.)
1906
Signed and dated at lower right:
John Sloan 1906
George A. Hearn Fund, 1921 (21.41.2)

AN ILLUSTRATOR and printmaker as well as a painter, John Sloan was acutely aware of the social structure of the life around him, and for a few years he was the editor of the radical magazine *The Masses.* As a member of The Eight, he was guided by Robert Henri, whose technique and choice of subject matter Sloan's work reflects. He never went to Europe and was severely critical of the formlessness he found in American Impressionism. His diary records a sudden storm of dust that blew up one afternoon on Fifth Avenue, near the Flatiron Building, which is pictured in the background of this painting. The panic of the people who found themselves threatened by the murky cloud is vividly expressed.

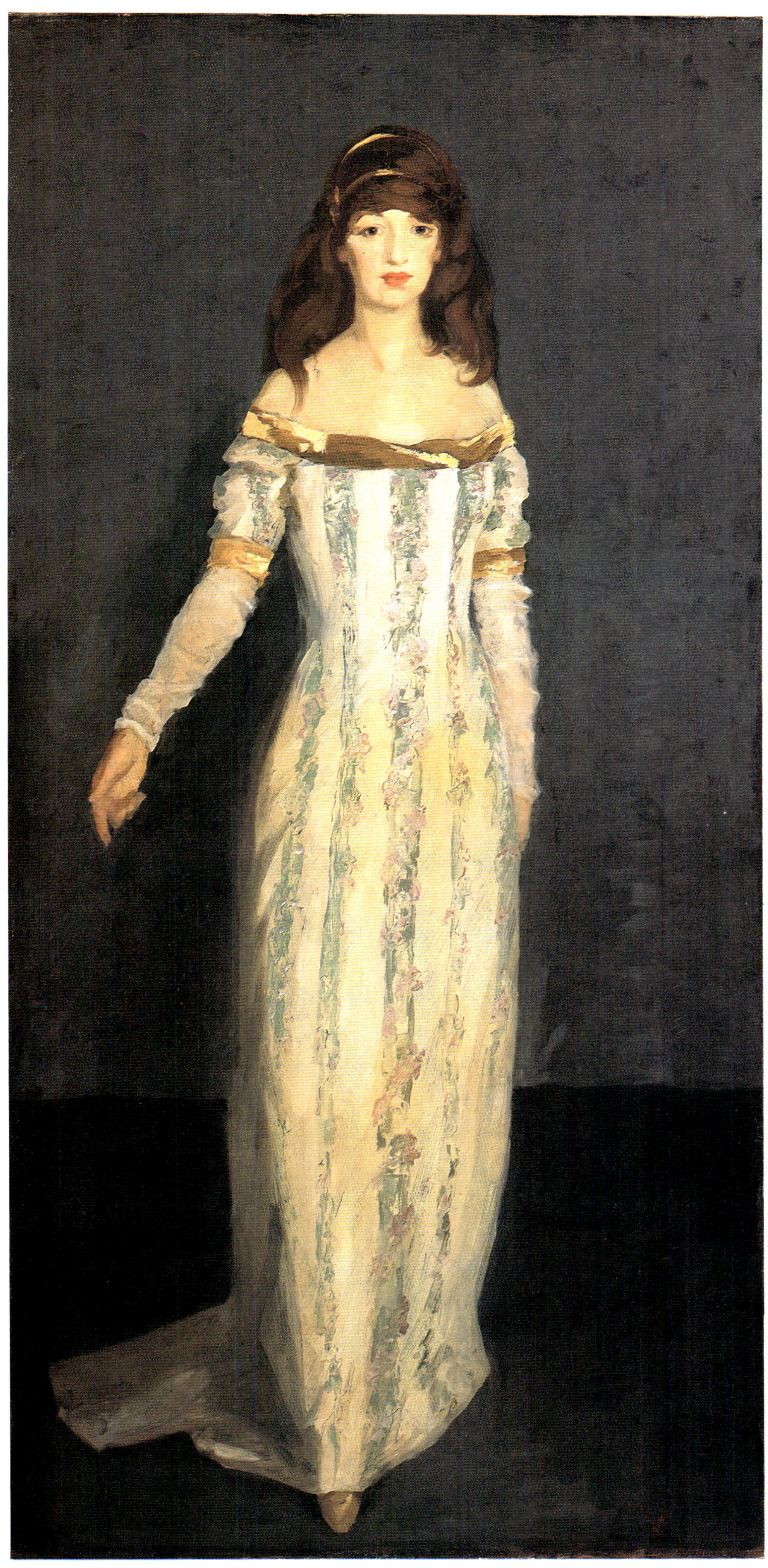

Robert Henri
1865–1929

The Masquerade Dress: Portrait of Mrs. Robert Henri

Oil on canvas
76½ x 36¼ in. (194.2 x 92 cm.)
1911
Signed at lower right: Robert Henri
Arthur Hoppock Hearn Fund, 1958 (58.157)

ROBERT HENRI, who painted this elegant and attractive portrait of his wife, also an artist, was one of the most progressive and influential teachers of the early twentieth century. A product of the Pennsylvania Academy of the Fine Arts, where the objective realism of Thomas Eakins was still a dominant force, Henri was the prime factor in bonding together the independent artists who exhibited jointly as The Eight. He established his own school of art in 1909 and the following year sponsored an important nonjury exhibition. A notable characteristic of his style was his emphasis on the texture of the paint itself, a technical preoccupation inspired by his admiration for Hals and Manet. This sensitive exploitation of the medium, stressed in his teaching, is evident here in the wonderfully suggestive treatment of the fabric of Mrs. Henri's dress.

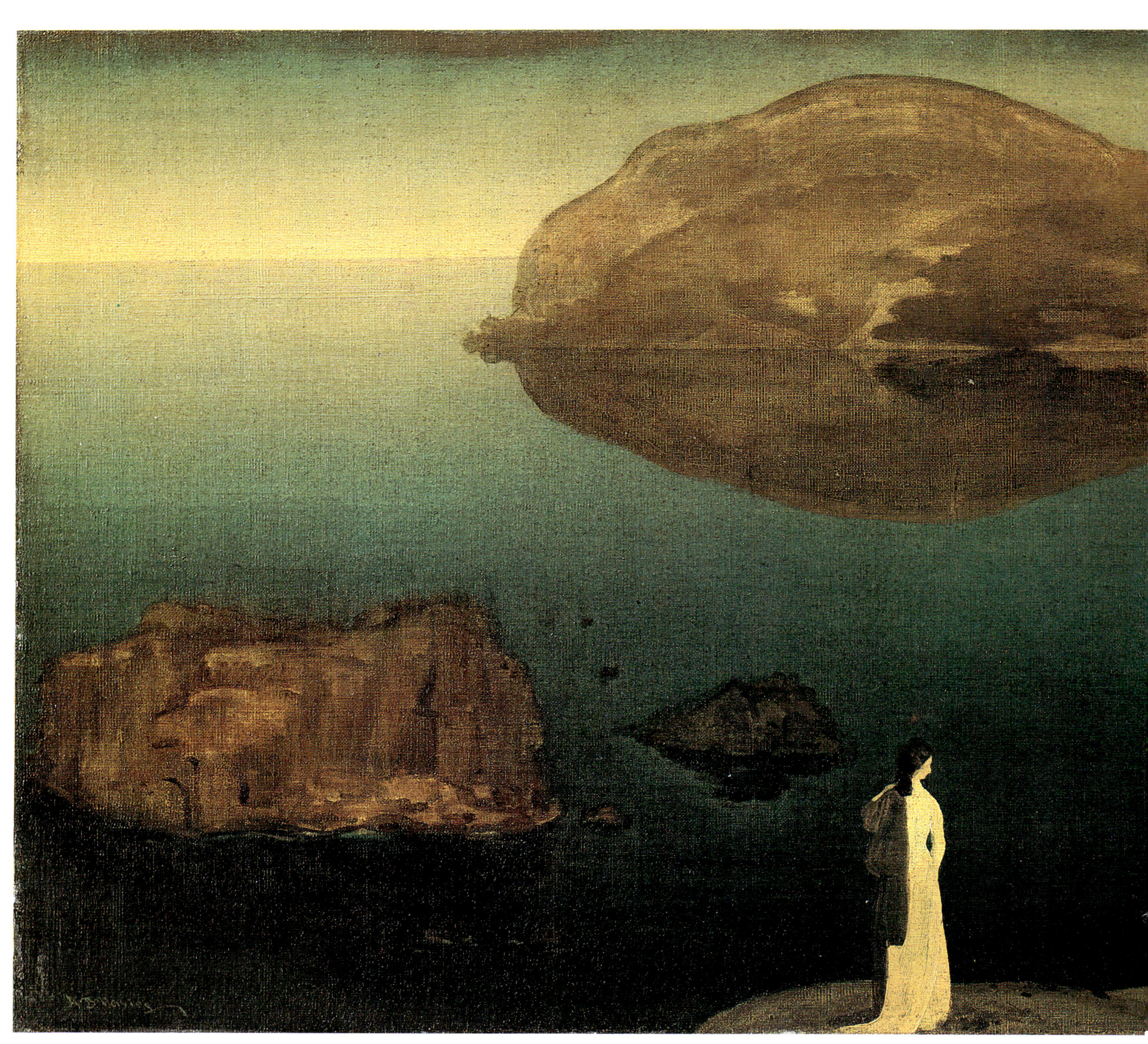

Arthur B. Davies
1862–1928

Unicorns (Legend—Sea Calm)

Oil on canvas
18¼ x 40¼ in. (46.4 x 102.2 cm.)
1906
Signed at lower left: A. B. Davies
Bequest of Lizzie P. Bliss, 1931 (31.67.12)

ARTHUR B. DAVIES himself chose the alternate title for this picture, but it is more generally known as *Unicorns.* Representational art here most nearly approaches the art of poetry, threatening to elude us completely if subjected to harsh and unimaginative analysis. Like a fairy tale, the painting is constructed from known factual realities: sky, sea, rocks, trees, human beings—all, however, crystallized in a trancelike unreality, timeless and silent. The journalist James Huneker, a friend of Davies, had written an essay the artist knew on the unicorn theme, identifying the mythical creature as the ideal and symbolic in art as opposed to the lion, which stood for realism. The horizontal format of *Unicorns* fosters a feeling of rhythmical progression, recalling Chinese painted scrolls; the pigment, thinly applied, with an effect of watercolor and ink rather than oil, enforces this similarity.

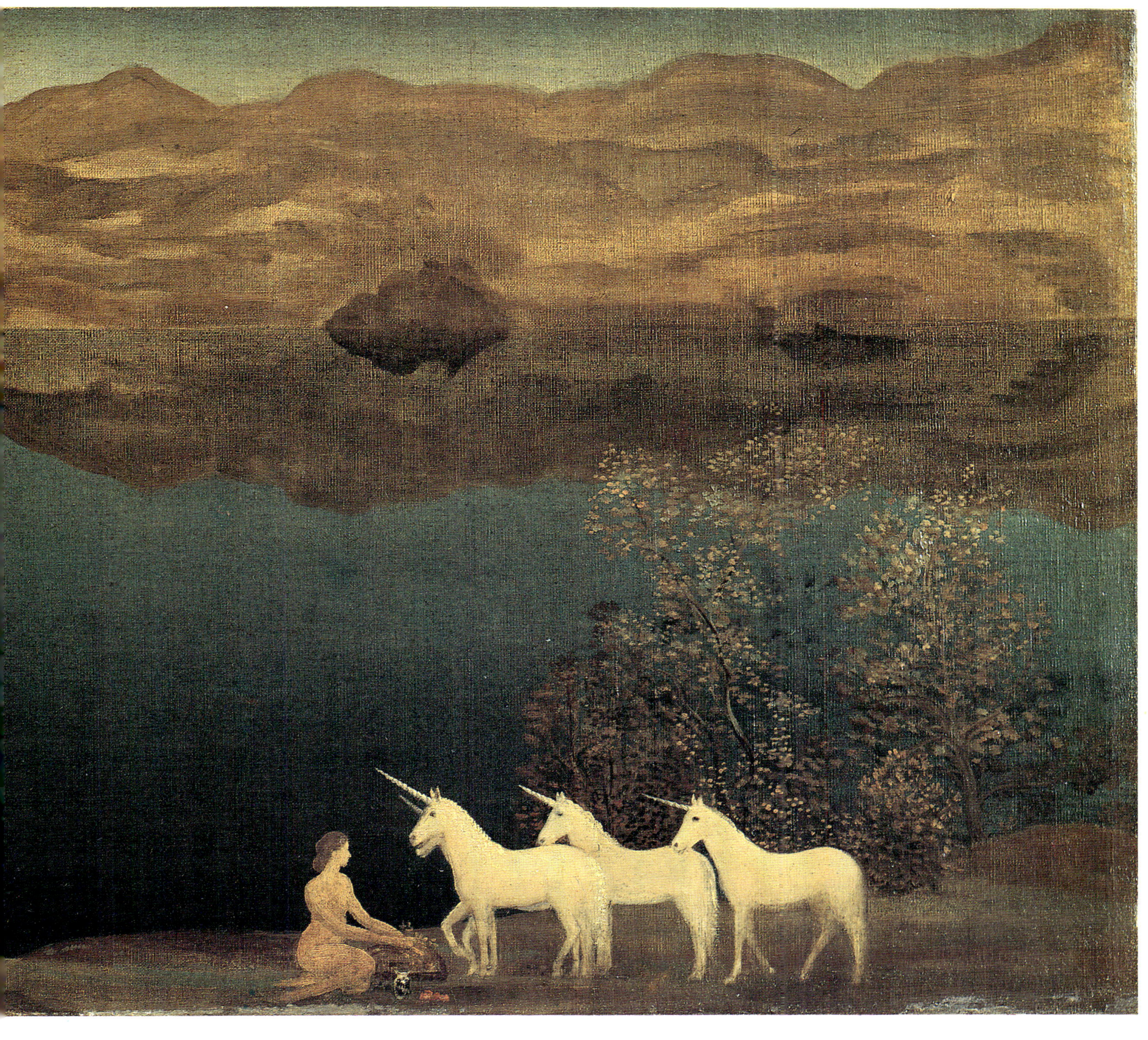

List of Illustrations and Selected Bibliography

Unknown American Painter

PAGE 13: *The Hunting Party—New Jersey*

Attributed to Pieter Vanderlyn (ca. 1687–1778)

PAGES 14–15: *Young Lady with a Rose*

Albert Ten Eyck Gardner, *American Paintings: A Catalogue of the Collection of the Metropolitan Museum of Art* (New York, 1965), vol. I, pp. 5–6. Mary Black, "The Gansevoort Limner," *Antiques* 96 (1969), pp. 738–44.

John Smibert (1688–1751)

PAGES 14, 16: *Francis Brinley*

H. W. Foote, *John Smibert: Painter* (Cambridge, Mass., 1950), pp. 64, 136. Albert Ten Eyck Gardner, *American Paintings: A Catalogue of the Collection of the Metropolitan Museum of Art* (New York, 1965), vol. I, pp. 3–4. R. E. Wood, ed., *The Notebook of John Smibert* (Boston, 1969), pp. 87, 104.

PAGES 14, 17: *Mrs. Francis Brinley and Her Son Francis*

H. W. Foote, *John Smibert: Painter* (Cambridge, Mass., 1950), p. 137. Albert Ten Eyck Gardner, *American Paintings: A Catalogue of the Collection of the Metropolitan Museum of Art* (New York, 1965), vol. I. pp. 3–4. R. E. Wood, ed., *The Notebook of John Smibert* (Boston, 1969), pp. 21, 87, 104.

Robert Feke (ca. 1708–ca. 1751)

PAGES 18–19: *Tench Francis*

H. W. Foote, *Robert Feke* (Cambridge, Mass., 1930), p. 66. Albert Ten Eyck Gardner, *American Paintings: A Catalogue of the Collection of the Metropolitan Museum of Art* (New York, 1965), vol. I, pp. 7–8.

John Wollaston (active 1733–1767)

PAGES 20–21: *Colonel William Axtell*

T. Bolton and H. L. Binsse, "Wollaston; An Early American Portrait Manufacturer," *Antiquarian* 16 (1931), p. 50.

William Williams (1727–1791)

PAGES 21–22: *Portrait of a Boy, probably of the Crossfield Family*

J. Biddle, "Collecting American Art for the Metropolitan: 1961–1966," *Antiques* 91 (1967), p. 485.

John Durand (active in America 1766–1782)

PAGES 21, 23: *Boy of the Crossfield Family, possibly Richard Crossfield*

C. F. Montgomery and P. E. Kane, eds., *American Art, 1750–1800: Towards Independence*, exhib.cat.(New Haven, Yale University Art Gallery, 1976), pp. 80–81.

Matthew Pratt (1734–1805)

PAGES 24–25: *The American School*

William Sawitzky, *Matthew Pratt, 1734–1805* (New York, 1942), pp. 6, 8, 10–12, 35–38. Albert Ten Eyck Gardner, *American Paintings: A Catalogue of the Collection of the Metropolitan Museum of Art* (New York, 1965), vol. I, pp. 21–22. J. D. Prown, *American Painting from Its Beginnings to the Armory Show* (Geneva, 1969), p. 38.

Benjamin West (1738–1820)

PAGES 26–27: *Omnia Vincit Amor, or The Power of Love in Three Elements*

G. Evans, *Benjamin West and the Taste of his Times* (Carbondale, 1959), pp. 77, 79–80. Albert Ten Eyck Gardner, *American Paintings: A Catalogue of the Collection of the Metropolitan Museum of Art* (New York, 1965), vol. I, p. 35. Helmet von Erffa and Allen Staley, *The Paintings of Benjamin West* (New Haven, 1986), pp. 138–39, 224, 232, 403–4.

John Singleton Copley (1738–1815)

PAGES 28–29: *Daniel Crommelin Verplanck*

B. N. Parker and A. B. Wheeler, *John Singleton Copley: American Portraits in Oil, Pastel, and Miniature with Biographical Sketches* (Boston, 1938), pp. 94–95. V. Andrus, "Copley's New York Visit," *MMA Bulletin* 8 (1949), pp. 264–65. Albert Ten Eyck Gardner, *American Paintings: A Catalogue of the Collection of the Metropolitan Museum of Art* (New York, 1965), vol. I, pp. 44–45. J. D. Prown, *John Singleton Copley* (Cambridge, Mass., 1966), vol. I, pp. 81, 115, 233.

PAGES 30–31: *Mrs. John Winthrop*

B. N. Parker and A. B. Wheeler, *John Singleton Copley: American Portraits in Oil, Pastel, and Miniature with Biographical Sketches* (Boston, 1938), p. 210. Albert Ten Eyck Gardner, *American Paintings: A Catalogue of the Collection of the Metropolitan Museum of Art* (New York, 1965), vol. I, pp. 46–48. J. D. Prown, *John Singleton Copley* (Cambridge, Mass., 1966), vol. I, pp. 89, 98, 116, 235.

PAGES 32–33: *Midshipman Augustus Brine*

J. L. Allen, "An English Copley," *MMA Bulletin* 2 (1944), pp. 260–62. Albert Ten Eyck Gardner, *American Paintings: A Catalogue of the Collection of the Metropolitan Museum of Art* (New York, 1965), vol. I, pp. 48–49. J. D. Prown, *John Singleton Copley* (Cambridge, Mass., 1966), vol. II, pp. 294–95, 345, 413. Alfred Frankenstein, *The World of Copley, 1738–1815* (New York, 1970), p. 150.

Ralph Earl (1751–1801)

PAGES 34–35: *Elijah Boardman*

Lloyd B. Goodrich, *Ralph Earl, Recorder for an Era* (Albany, 1967), pp. 61–62.

Charles Willson Peale (1741–1827)

PAGES 36–37: *George Washington*

Charles Coleman Sellers, "Charles Willson Peale's Portraits of Washington," *MMA Bulletin* 9 (1951), p. 152. Albert Ten Eyck Gardner, *American Paintings: A Catalogue of the Collection of the Metropolitan Museum of Art* (New York, 1965), vol. I, pp. 62–64. L. B. Wright, et al., *The Arts in America in the Colonial Period* (New York, 1966), p. 213.

PAGES 38–39: *Thomas Willing*

J. Biddle, "Collecting American Art for the Metropolitan: 1961–1966," *Antiques* 91 (1967), p. 485.

John Trumbull (1756–1843)

PAGES 40–41: *The Sortie Made by the Garrison of Gibraltar*

Eliot P. Richardson, *Painting in America: The Story of 450 Years* (New York, 1956), pp. 96–97. T. Sizer, *The Works of John Trumbull* (New Haven, 1967), rev. ed., pp. 2, 100–1, 138–39. Irma Jaffe, *John Trumbull: Patriot Artist of the American Revolution* (Boston, 1975), pp. 128–29, 131–38, 140, 148, 188, 208, 310, 318, 321–22. H. Cooper, *John Trumbull: The Hand and Spirit of a Painter*, exhib. cat. (New Haven, Yale University Art Gallery, 1982), pp. 56–62.

PAGES 42–43: *George Washington Before the Battle of Trenton*

Albert Ten Eyck Gardner, *American Paintings: A Catalogue of the Collection of the Metropolitan Museum of Art* (New York, 1965), vol., I, pp. 103–4. T. Sizer, *The Works of John Trumbull* (New Haven, 1967), rev. ed., p. 83. John K. Howat, "'A Young Man Impatient to Distinguish Himself:' The Vicomte de Noailles as Portrayed by Gilbert Stuart," *MMA Bulletin* 29 (1971), p. 339.

Gilbert Stuart (1755–1828)

PAGES 44–45: *Horatio Gates*

Lawrence Park, *Gilbert Stuart: An Illustrated Descriptive List of His Works* (New York, 1926), vol. I, pp. 340–41.

PAGES 46–47: *Matilda Stoughton de Jaúdenes*

C. M. Mount, *Gilbert Stuart* (New York, 1964), pp. 179–82, 349. Albert Ten Eyck Gardner, *American Paintings: A Catalogue of the Collection of the Metropolitan Museum of Art* (New York, 1965), vol. I, pp. 83–84.

PAGES 48–49: *Vicomte de Noailles*

John K. Howat, " 'A Young Man Impatient to Distinguish Himself:' The Vicomte de Noailles as Portrayed by Gilbert Stuart," *MMA Bulletin* 29 (1971), pp. 327–40.

PAGE 50: *George Washington*

C. M. Mount, *Gilbert Stuart* (New York, 1964), p. 378. Albert Ten Eyck Gardner, *American Paintings: A Catalogue of the Collection of the Metropolitan Museum of Art* (New York, 1965), vol. I, pp. 85–86.

PAGE 51: *James Monroe*

C. M. Mount, *Gilbert Stuart* (New York, 1964), pp. 311, 314. Albert Ten Eyck Gardner, *American Paintings: A Catalogue of the Collection of the Metropolitan Museum of Art* (New York, 1965), vol. I, pp. 96–97. John K. Howat and Natalie Spassky, *19th Century America: Paintings and Sculpture*, exhib. cat. (New York, MMA, 1970), no. 4.

James Peale (1749–1831)

PAGE 52: *Still Life: Balsam Apple and Vegetables*

J. L. Allen, "A Still Life by James Peale," *MMA Bulletin* 34 (1939), pp. 264–65. Albert Ten Eyck Gardner, *American Paintings: A Catalogue of the Collection of the Metropolitan Museum of Art* (New York, 1965), vol. I, p. 67.

Raphaelle Peale (1774–1825)

PAGE 53: *Still Life with Cake*

Albert Ten Eyck Gardner, *American Paintings: A Catalogue of the Collection of the Metropolitan Museum of Art* (New York, 1965), vol. I, p. 119.

Thomas Sully (1783–1872)

PAGE 54: *The Student*

E. Biddle and M. Fielding, *The Life and Works of Thomas Sully (1783–1872)* (Philadelphia, 1921), p. 287. Albert Ten Eyck Gardner, *American Paintings: A Catalogue of the Collection of the Metropolitan Museum of Art* (New York, 1965), vol. I, pp. 164–65.

Samuel F. B. Morse (1791–1872)

PAGES 54–55: *The Muse—Susan Walker Morse*

Albert Ten Eyck Gardner, "Samuel Morse and the Muse," *MMA Bulletin* 4 (1946), pp. 262, 267–68; *American Paintings: A Catalogue of the Collection of the Metropolitan Museum of Art* (New York, 1965), vol. I, pp. 190–2. James Thomas Flexner, *Nineteenth Century American Painting* (New York, 1970), p. 11.

Cephas Giovanni Thompson (1809–1888)

PAGES 56–57: *Spring*

Eliot P. Richardson, *American Romantic Painting* (New York, 1944), p. 48. John K. Howat and Natalie Spassky, *19th Century America: Paintings and Sculpture,* exhib. cat. (New York, MMA, 1970), no. 63.

Charles Cromwell Ingham (1796–1863)

PAGES 58–59: *The Flower Girl*

Albert Ten Eyck Gardner, "Ingham in Manhattan," *MMA Bulletin* 10 (1952), p. 252; *American Paintings: A Catalogue of the Collection of the Metropolitan Museum of Art* (New York, 1965), vol. I, pp. 206–7.

William Sidney Mount (1807–1868)

PAGES 60–61: *Cider Making*

B. Cowdrey and H. W. Williams, *William Sidney Mount, 1807–1868: An American Painter* (New York, 1944), p. 19. J. Biddle, "Collecting American Art for the Metropolitan: 1961–1966," *Antiques* 91 (1967), p. 485. S. P. Feld, "In the Midst of 'High Vintage'," *MMA Bulletin* 25 (1967), pp. 300–1, 304–5. Alfred Frankenstein, *William Sidney Mount* (New York, 1975), pp. 29, 61, 75, 102, 111, 202, 249, 421, 470, 483, 486.

PAGES 62–63: *Long Island Farmhouses*

J. Overton, "William Mount, Long Island Genre Artist," *Antiques* 41 (1942), pp. 46–47. B. Cowdrey and H. W. Williams, *William Sidney Mount, 1807–1868: An American Painter* (New York, 1944), p. 26. Albert Ten Eyck Gardner, *American Paintings: A Catalogue of the Collection of the Metropolitan Museum of Art* (New York, 1965), vol. I, pp. 248–49. Alfred Frankenstein, *William Sidney Mount* (New York, 1975), pp. 324, 479.

George Caleb Bingham (1811–1879)

PAGES 64–65: *Fur Traders Descending the Missouri*

H. B. Wehle, "An American Frontier Scene by George Caleb Bingham," *MMA Bulletin* 28 (1933), pp. 120–22. H. F. McDermott, *George Caleb Bingham, River Portraitist* (Norman, Okla., 1959), pp. 48–53, 279, 413. Albert Ten Eyck Gardner, *American Paintings: A Catalogue of the Collection of the Metropolitan Museum of Art* (New York, 1965), vol. I, pp. 251–52. E. M. Bloch, *George Caleb Bingham: The Evolution of an Artist* (Berkeley, 1967), vol. I, pp. 79–83, 85–86, 88, 110, 177, 256; vol. II, pp. 52–53. J. D. Prown, *American Painting from Its Beginnings to the Armory Show* (Geneva, 1969), pp. 83–84. James Thomas Flexner, *Nineteenth Century American Painting* (New York, 1970), pp. 104–5. Albert Christ-Janer, *George Caleb Bingham, Frontier Painter of the Missouri* (New York, 1975), pp. 22, 36, 48–49.

Thomas Cole (1801–1848)

PAGE 66: *A View Near Tivoli (Morning)*

Albert Ten Eyck Gardner, *American Paintings: A Catalogue of the Collection of the Metropolitan Museum of Art* (New York, 1965), vol. I, pp. 25–26. Matthew Baigell, *Thomas Cole* (New York, 1981), pp. 46–47.

PAGE 67: *The Titan's Goblet*

Albert Ten Eyck Gardner, *American Paintings: A Catalogue of the Collection of the Metropolitan Museum of Art* (New York, 1965), vol. I, pp. 226–27. J. D. Prown, *American Painting from Its Beginnings to the Armory Show* (Geneva, 1969), p. 65. James Thomas Flexner, *Nineteenth Century American Painting* (New York, 1970), p. 48. E. C. Parry, "Thomas Cole's The Titan's Goblet: A Reinterpretation," *MMA Journal* 4 (1971), pp. 123–40.

PAGES 68–71: *The Oxbow (The Connecticut River Near Northampton)*

Albert Ten Eyck Gardner, *American Paintings: A Catalogue of the Collection in the Metropolitan Museum of Art* (New York, 1965), vol. I, pp. 227–29. Barbara Novak, *American Painting of the Nineteenth Century* (New York, 1969), pp. 75–78. Lee Parry, "Landscape Theater in America," *Art in America* 59 (1971), pp. 58–60. Matthew Baigell, *Thomas Cole* (New York, 1981), pp. 54–55.

Asher B. Durand (1796–1886)

PAGES 72–73: *The Beeches*

J. Durand, *The Life and Times of A. B. Durand* (New York, 1894), p. 173. Albert Ten Eyck Gardner, *American Paintings: A Catalogue of the Collection of the Metropolitan Museum of Art* (New York, 1965) vol. I, pp. 210–11.

PAGES 74–75: *Thanatopsis*

J. Durand, *The Life and Times of A. B. Durand* (New York, 1894), pp. 174. Albert Ten Eyck Gardner, *American Paintings: A Catalogue of the Collection in the Metropolitan Museum of Art* (New York, 1965), vol. I, pp. 211–12. Barbara Novak, *American Painting of the Nineteenth Century* (New York, 1969), pp. 83–84.

Jerome B. Thompson (1814–1886)

PAGES 76–77: *The Belated Party on Mansfield Mountain*

"Outstanding Recent Accessions," *MMA Bulletin* 18 (1970), p. 399. "Picnics Long Ago; with Paintings by Artists of the Hudson River School," *American Heritage* 22 (1971), pp. 46–47.

Fitz Hugh Lane (1804–1865)

PAGES 78–79: *Stage Fort Across Gloucester Harbor*

John Wilmerding, *Fitz Hugh Lane, 1804–1865; American Marine Painter* (Salem, Mass., 1964), p. 63; *Fitz Hugh Lane* (New York, 1971), p. 181.

Emanuel Leutze (1816–1868)

PAGES 80–81: *Washington Crossing the Delaware*

Mark Twain [S. L. Clemens], *Life on the Mississippi* (1883; New York, 1951 ed.), pp. 318, 322. A. H. Hutton, *Portrait of Patriotism* (Philadelphia, 1959). John K. Howat, "Washington Crossing the Delaware," *MMA Bulletin* 26 (March, 1968), pp. 289–99. S. Kaplan, *The Black Presence in the Era of the American Revolution, 1770–1800*, exhib. cat. (Washington, D.C., National Collection of Fine Arts, 1973), pp. 44–46. B. S. Groseclose, "Washington Crossing the Delaware: The Political Context," *American Art Journal* 7 (Nov., 1975), pp. 70–78; *Emanuel Leutze, 1816–1868: The Only King is Freedom*, exhib. cat. (Washington, D.C., National Collection of Fine Arts, 1975), pp. 10–11, 13, 34–41, 43–47, 55, 57, 68, 83–85, 126. Natalie Spassky, *American Paintings in the Metropolitan Museum of Art* (New York, 1985), vol. II., pp. 16–25.

Martin Johnson Heade (1819–1904)

PAGES 82–83: *The Coming Storm*

Theodore E. Stebbins, *The Life and Works of Martin Johnson*

Heade (New Haven, 1975), p. 233, no. 110. Natalie Spassky, *American Paintings in the Metropolitan Museum of Art* (New York, 1985), vol. II, pp. 121–23.

Frederic Edwin Church (1826–1900)

PAGES 84–87: *Heart of the Andes*

Albert Ten Eyck Gardner, "Scientific Sources of the Full-Length Landscape: 1850," *MMA Bulletin* 4 (1945), pp. 59–65. David C. Huntington, *The Landscapes of Frederic Edwin Church: Vision of an American Era* (New York, 1966), throughout. Barbara Novak, *American Painting of the Nineteenth Century* (New York, 1969), p. 94. J. D. Prown, *American Painting from Its Beginnings to the Armory Show* (Geneva, 1969), p. 69.

Sanford Robinson Gifford (1823–1880)

PAGES 88–89: *Kauterskill Clove*

Albert Ten Eyck Gardner, "Hudson River Idyll," *MMA Bulletin* 6 (1948), pp. 223, 236. James Thomas Flexner, *Nineteenth Century American Painting* (New York, 1970), p. 81. Barbara Novak, "American Landscape: The Nationalist Garden and the Holy Book," *Art in America* 60 (1972), p. 53.

Albert Bierstadt (1830–1902)

PAGES 90–93: *The Rocky Mountains, Lander's Peak*

B. P. Draper, "Albert Bierstadt," *Art in America* 28 (1940), p. 62. James Thomas Flexner, *That Wilder Image: The Painting of America's Native School from Thomas Cole to Winslow Homer* (New York, 1962), pp. 295–96. Gordon Hendricks, *Albert Bierstadt: Painter of the American West* (New York, 1974), pp. 9, 90, 94, 113, 116, 134, 140–160, 179, 233, 258, 261, 277. Natalie Spassky, *American Paintings in the Metropolitan Museum of Art* (New York, 1985), vol. II, pp. 321–26.

Jasper Francis Cropsey (1823–1900)

PAGES 94–97: *The Valley of Wyoming*

S. P. Feld, "'Loan Collection' 1965," *MMA Bulletin* 23 (1965), p. 293. W. S. Talbot, *Jasper F. Cropsey, 1823–1900*, exhib. cat. (Cleveland Museum of Art, 1971–72), pp. 36, 43, 92–93. Natalie Spassky, *American Paintings in the Metropolitan Museum of Art* (New York, 1985), vol. II, pp. 190–92.

John Frederick Kensett (1816–1872)

PAGE 98: *Lake George*

E. H. Johnson, "Kensett Revisited," *Art Quarterly* 20 (1957), pp. 81, 82, 85–86, 90. John K. Howat, "John F. Kensett, 1816–1872," *Antiques* 96 (1969), p. 400. Natalie Spassky, *American Paintings in the Metropolitan Museum of Art* (New York, 1985), vol. II, pp. 34–36.

George Inness (1824–1894)

PAGE 99: *Autumn Meadows*

Leroy Ireland, *The Works of George Inness: An Illustrated Catalogue Raisonné* (Austin, 1965), p. 116; no. 475. Natalie Spassky, *American Paintings in the Metropolitan Museum of Art* (New York, 1985), vol. II, pp. 256–57.

PAGES 100–1: *Autumn Oaks*

George Inness, Jr., *Life, Art, and Letters of George Inness* (New York, 1917), pp. 229, 232–233. Leroy Ireland, *The Works of George Inness: An Illustrated Catalogue Raisonné* (Austin, 1965), p. 179, no. 729. Alfred Werner, *Inness's Landscapes* (New York, 1973), p. 84. Natalie Spassky, *American Paintings in the Metropolitan Museum of Art* (New York, 1985), vol. II, pp. 262–63.

Edward Lamson Henry (1841–1919)

PAGES 102–3: *The 9:45 Accommodation*

Elizabeth McCausland, *The Life and Work of Edward Lamson Henry, N.A., 1841–1919* (Albany, 1945), pp. 87, 112, 158. Natalie Spassky, *American Paintings in the Metropolitan Museum of Art* (New York, 1985), vol. II, pp. 559–61.

John Ferguson Weir (1841–1926)

PAGES 104–5: *Forging the Shaft*

Dorothy Weir Young, *The Life and Letters of J. Alden Weir* (New Haven, 1960), pp. 28, 71. Barbara Fahlman, "John Ferguson Weir: Painter of Romantic and Industrial Icons," *Archives of American Art Journal* 20 (1980), pp. 2–3, 5–8. Doreen B. Burke, *J. Alden Weir* (Newark, 1983), pp. 30–31. Natalie Spassky, *American Paintings in the Metropolitan Museum of Art* (New York, 1985), vol. II, pp. 568–73.

Winslow Homer (1836–1910)

PAGES 106–7: *The Veteran in a New Field*

James Thomas Flexner, *The World of Winslow Homer, 1836–1910* (New York, 1966), pp. 72–73, 82–83. John Wilmerding, *Winslow Homer* (New York, 1972), pp. 47–48. J. Grossman, *Echo of a Distant Drum: Winslow Homer and the Civil War* (New York, 1974), pp. 190–91. Milton W. Brown, *American Art to 1900: Painting, Sculpture, Architecture* (New York, 1977), pp. 496–97. Natalie Spassky, "Winslow Homer at the Metropolitan Museum of Art," *MMA Bulletin* 39 (1982), pp. 8–9; *American Paintings in the Metropolitan Museum of Art* (New York, 1985), vol. II, pp. 433–37.

PAGES 108–9: *Prisoners From the Front*

H. B. Wehle, "Early Paintings by Homer," *MMA Bulletin* 18 (1923), pp. 38–41. Lloyd Goodrich, *Winslow Homer* (New York, 1944), pp. 21–22, 26, 39, 50–51, 72. James Thomas Flexner, *The World of Winslow Homer, 1836–1910* (New York, 1966), pp. 70–71, 80–81, 107. John Wilmerding, *Winslow Homer* (New York, 1972), pp. 24, 43–44, 47, 49. J. Grossman, *Echo of a Distant Drum: Winslow Homer and the Civil War* (New York, 1974), pp. 114, 117–19. E. Parry, *The Image of the Indian and the Black Man in American Art, 1500–1900* (New York, 1974), p. 140. John Wilmerding, *American Art* (Harmondsworth, Eng ., 1976), p. 133. Milton W. Brown, *American Art to 1900: Painting, Sculpture, Architecture* (New York, 1977), pp. 496–97. N. Cikovsky, Jr., "Winslow Homer's Prisoners from the Front," *MMA Journal* 12 (1977), pp. 155–72. Gordon Hendricks, *The Life and Work of Winslow Homer* (New York, 1979), pp. 39, 58, 60, 64, 68, 73, 315. Natalie Spassky, "Winslow Homer at the Metropolitan Museum of Art," *MMA Bulletin* 39 (1982), pp. 8–13; *American Paintings in the Metropolitan Museum of Art* (New York, 1985), vol. II, pp. 437–45.

PAGES 110–11: *Eagle Head, Manchester, Massachusetts (High Tide)*

H. B. Wehle, "Early Paintings by Homer," *MMA Bulletin* 18 (1923), pp. 85–86. Lloyd Goodrich, *Winslow Homer* (New York, 1944), pp. 41–43, 51, 57. Albert Ten Eyck Gardner, "Metropolitan Homers," *MMA Bulletin* 17 (1959), p. 134; *Winslow Homer, American Artist; His Work and His World* (New York, 1961), pp. 184, 238, 247, 254. Lloyd Goodrich, *Winslow Homer's America* (New York, 1969), pp. 115–16, 129. Barbara Novak, *American Painting of the Nineteenth Century* (New York, 1969), pp. 174–76. John Wilmerding, *Winslow Homer* (New York, 1972), pp. 66, 85–86. Gordon Hendricks, *The Life and Work of Winslow Homer* (New York, 1979), pp. 78–81, 315. Natalie Spassky, "Winslow Homer at the Metropolitan Museum of Art," *MMA Bulletin* 39 (1982), pp. 15–17; *American Paintings in the Metropolitan Museum of Art* (New York, 1985), vol. II, pp. 449–53.

PAGES 112–13: *Snap the Whip*

Albert Ten Eyck Gardner, *Winslow Homer, American Artist: His Work and His World* (New York, 1961), pp. 146, 204, 250, 254. J. Gould, *Winslow Homer, A Portrait* (New York, 1962), pp. 123, 135, 183–84. John Wilmerding, *Winslow Homer* (New York, 1972), pp. 70, 87, 103. Gordon Hendricks, *The Life and Work of Winslow Homer* (New York, 1979), pp. 94, 316. Natalie Spassky, "Winslow Homer at the Metropolitan Museum of Art," *MMA Bulletin* 39 (1982), pp. 16, 20; *American Paintings in the Metropolitan Museum of Art* (New York, 1985), vol. II, pp. 468–71.

PAGES 114–15: *Moonlight, Wood Island Light*

Lloyd Goodrich, *Winslow Homer* (New York, 1944), pp. 142, 155, 187. Albert Ten Eyck Gardner, *Winslow Homer, American Artist: His Work and His World* (New York, 1961), pp. 220, 241, 248, 254. Philip C. Beam, *Winslow Homer at Prouts Neck* (Boston, 1966), p. 120. Gordon Hendricks, *The Life and Work of Winslow Homer* (New York, 1979), pp. 220–23. Natalie Spassky, "Winslow Homer at the Metropolitan Museum of Art," *MMA Bulletin* 39 (1982), pp. 24–26, 30; *American Paintings in the Metropolitan Museum of Art* (New York, 1985), vol. II, pp. 468–71.

PAGES 116–17: *Northeaster*

Albert Ten Eyck Gardner, "Metropolitan Homers," *MMA Bulletin* 17 (1959), pp. 132, 136; *Winslow Homer, American Artist: His Work and His World* (New York, 1961), pp. 127, 207–208, 241–42, 249, 254. J. Gould, *Winslow Homer, A Portrait* (New York, 1962), pp. 251, 263, 274, 283. Philip C. Beam, *Winslow Homer at Prouts Neck* (Boston, 1966), pp. 93, 139–40, 220. John Wilmerding, *Winslow Homer* (New York, 1972), pp. 164, 167. Gordon Hendricks, *The Life and Work of Winslow Homer* (New York, 1979), pp. 219, 223, 246, 315. Natalie Spassky, "Winslow Homer at the Metropolitan Museum of Art," *MMA Bulletin* 39 (1982), pp. 28–30, 35; *American Paintings in the Metropolitan Museum of Art* (New York, 1985), vol. II, pp. 471–75.

PAGES 118–21: *The Gulf Stream*

Lloyd Goodrich, *Winslow Homer* (New York, 1944), pp. 90, 158, 161–62, 186–87, 234. Albert Ten Eyck Gardner, "Metropolitan Homers," *MMA Bulletin* 17 (1959), pp. 132–33, 135–37; *Winslow Homer, American Artist: His Work and His World* (New York, 1961), pp. 34, 100, 211–13, 242–43, 247, 254. J. Gould, *Winslow Homer, A Portrait* (New York, 1962), pp. 272–73, 277–79, 286, 288. James Thomas Flexner, *That Wilder Image: The Painting of America's Native School from Thomas Cole to Winslow Homer* (New York, 1962), pp. 353–54. Philip C. Beam, *Winslow Homer at Prouts Neck* (Boston, 1966), pp. 169–73, 179, 241. John Wilmerding, *Winslow Homer* (New York, 1972), pp. 136, 170, 174–75, 200, 212. E. Parry, *The Image of the Indian and the Black Man in American Art 1500–1900* (New York, 1974), pp. 128, 169–70. Gordon Hendricks, *The Life and Work of Winslow Homer* (New York, 1979), pp. 196, 237, 240, 242–43, 248–51, 253, 265, 275, 315. Natalie Spassky, "Winslow Homer in the Metropolitan Museum of Art," *MMA Bulletin* 39 (1982), pp. 35–37, 39–42; *American Paintings in the Metropolitan Museum of Art* (New York, 1985), vol. II, pp. 482–90.

Eastman Johnson (1824–1906)

PAGES 122–25: *The Hatch Family*

James Thomas Flexner, *That Wilder Image: The Painting of America's Native School from Thomas Cole to Winslow Homer* (New York, 1962), p. 220. Alan Burroughs, *Limners and Likenesses: Three Centuries of American Painting* (Cambridge, Mass., 1936), pp. 169, 171. H. L. Peterson, *Americans at Home: From the Colonists to the Late Victorians* (New York, 1971), p. 143. Natalie Spassky, *American Paintings in the Metropolitan Museum of Art* (New York, 1985), vol. II, pp. 223–25.

PAGE 126: *The New Bonnet*

Alan Burroughs, *Limners and Likenesses: Three Centuries of American Painting* (Cambridge, Mass., 1936), p. 170. Natalie Spassky, *American Paintings in the Metropolitan Museum of Art* (New York, 1985), vol. II, pp. 229–32.

John G. Brown (1831–1913)

PAGE 127: *The Music Lesson*

Alan Burroughs, *Limners and Likenesses: Three Centuries of American Painting* (Cambridge, Mass., 1936), p. 168. H. W. Williams, *Mirror to the American Past: A Survey of American Genre Painting* (Greenwich, Conn., 1973), p. 180. Milton W. Brown, *American Art to 1900: Painting, Sculpture, Architecture* (New York, 1977), p. 533. Natalie Spassky, *American Paintings in the Metropolitan Museum of Art* (New York, 1985), vol. II, pp. 339–40.

Enoch Wood Perry (1831–1915)

PAGES 128–29: *Talking It Over*

John K. Howat, in Metropolitan Museum of Art *Notable Acquisitions, 1980–1981* (New York, 1981), pp. 55–56. Natalie Spassky, *American Paintings in the Metropolitan Museum of Art* (New York, 1985), vol. II, pp. 345–46.

William Morris Hunt (1824–1879)

PAGE 130: *Girl at the Fountain*

M. J. Hoppin, in *William Morris Hunt: A Memorial Exhibition*, exhib. cat. (Boston, Museum of Fine Arts, 1979), pp. 12–13. Natalie Spassky, *American Paintings in the Metropolitan Museum of Art* (New York, 1985), vol. II, pp. 201–3.

John La Farge (1835–1910)

PAGE 131: *Bishop Berkeley's Rock, Newport*

Natalie Spassky, *American Paintings in the Metropolitan Museum of Art* (New York, 1985), vol. II, pp. 403–5.

Thomas Eakins (1844–1916)

PAGES 132–33: *Max Schmitt in a Single Scull, or The Champion Single Sculls*

John Wilmerding, *A History of American Marine Painting* (Boston, 1968), pp. 225–26. Barbara Novak, *American Painting of the Nineteenth Century* (New York, 1969), pp. 191–93, 200. J. D. Prown, *American Painting from Its Beginnings to the Armory Show* (Geneva, 1969), p. 92. Gordon Hendricks, *The Life and Work of Thomas Eakins* (New York, 1974), pp. 64–65, 70–71, 333. John Wilmerding, *American Art* (Harmondsworth, Eng., 1976), pp. 137–38. Milton W. Brown, *American Art to 1900: Painting, Sculpture, Architecture* (New York, 1977), pp. 503–4, 573. T. Siegl, *The Thomas Eakins Collection* (Philadelphia, 1978), p. 53. Lloyd Goodrich, *Thomas Eakins* (Cambridge, Mass., 1982), vol. I, pp. 7, 81–83, 94, 107, 120, 165, 287. E. Johns, *Thomas Eakins: The Heroism of Modern Life* (Princeton, 1983), pp. 19–22, 23–37, 37–39, 40–45. Natalie Spassky, *American Paintings in the Metropolitan Museum of Art* (New York, 1985), vol. II, pp. 594–600.

PAGES 134–35: *Pushing for Rail*

Gordon Hendricks, *The Life and Work of Thomas Eakins* (New York, 1974), pp. 64–65, 75–83, 297, 333. E. Parry, *The Image of the Indian and the Black Man in American Art, 1500–1900* (New York, 1974), pp. 150–52. T. Siegl, *The Thomas Eakins Collection* (Philadelphia, 1978), pp. 24, 42, 45, 57–58, 63. Lloyd Goodrich, *Thomas Eakins* (Cambridge, Mass., 1983), vol. I, pp. 94, 107–8, 118, 199–200, 265, 270–71, 274. Natalie Spassky, *American Paintings in the Metropolitan Museum of Art* (New York, 1985), vol. II, pp. 594–600.

PAGES 134–35: *The Chess Players*

Barbara Novak, *American Painting of the Nineteenth Century* (New York, 1969), p. 204. Gordon Hendricks, *The Photographs of Thomas Eakins* (New York, 1972), pp. 9, 207; *The Life and Work of Thomas Eakins* (New York, 1974), pp. 96, 108, 111, 280, 333–34. John Wilmerding, *American Art* (Harmondsworth, Eng., 1976), p. 139. T. Siegl, *The Thomas Eakins Collection* (Philadelphia, 1978), pp. 22, 27, 43, 66, 102, 107. Lloyd Goodrich, *Thomas Eakins* (Cambridge, Mass., 1982), vol. I, pp. 67, 71, 100–2, 107, 111, 130, 200, 280; vol. II, pp. 106, 265, 187, 326. Natalie Spassky, *American Paintings in the Metropolitan Museum of Art* (New York, 1985), vol. II, pp. 600–5.

PAGES 136–37: *The Artist's Wife and His Setter Dog*

Gordon Hendricks, *The Life and Work of Thomas Eakins* (New York, 1974), pp. 128–29, 168, 174, 284, 332, 334. John Wilmerding, *American Art* (Harmondsworth, Eng., 1976), p. 140. Milton W. Brown, *American Art to 1900: Painting, Sculpture, Architecture* (New York, 1977), pp. 524–26. T. Siegl, *The Thomas Eakins Collection* (Philadelphia, 1978), pp. 27, 107, 113, 137, 156–57. Lloyd Goodrich, *Thomas Eakins* (Cambridge, Mass., 1982), vol. I, pp. 224–26, 235, 330–31; vol. II, pp. 165–67, 256, 274, 278–79. Natalie Spassky, *American Paintings in the Metropolitan Museum of Art* (New York, 1985), vol. II, pp. 613–19.

PAGES 138–39: *The Thinker: Portrait of Louis N. Kenton*

Barbara Novak, *American Painting of the Nineteenth Century* (New York, 1969), pp. 208–9. J. D. Prown, *American Painting from Its Beginnings to the Armory Show* (Geneva, 1969), p. 254. Gordon Hendricks, *The Life and Work of Thomas Eakins* (New York, 1974), pp. 246, 280, 282–83, 334. Milton W. Brown, *American Art to 1900: Painting, Sculpture, Architecture* (New York, 1977), p. 523. T. Siegl, *The Thomas Eakins Collection* (Philadelphia, 1978), pp. 30, 39. Lloyd Goodrich, *Thomas Eakins* (Cambridge, 1982), vol. II, pp. 179–82, 205, 256. Natalie Spassky, *American Paintings in the Metropolitan Museum of Art* (New York, 1985), vol. II, pp. 622–26.

William Michael Harnett (1848–1892)

PAGE 140: *The Artist's Letter Rack*

Alfred Frankenstein, *After the Hunt; William Harnett and Other American Still Life Painters, 1870–1900* (Berkeley, 1953; rev. ed. 1969), pp. 43, 51–53, 96, 108, 169. W. H. Gerdts and R. Burke, *American Still-Life Painting* (New York, 1971), pp. 135, 142. Doreen Burke, *American Paintings in the Metropolitan Museum of Art* (New York, 1980), vol. III, pp. 50–53.

John F. Peto (1854–1907)

PAGE 141: *Old Souvenirs*

Alfred Frankenstein, *After the Hunt; William Harnett and Other American Still Life Painters, 1870–1900* (Berkeley, 1953; rev. ed. 1969), pp. 5, 8, 17–19, 20–22, 51, 95, 108, 184. Doreen Burke, *American Paintings in the Metropolitan Museum of Art* (New York, 1980), vol. III, pp. 170–1.

John Haberle (1856–1933)

PAGES 142–43: *A Bachelor's Drawer*

Alfred Frankenstein, *After the Hunt; William Harnett and Other American Still Life Painters, 1870–1900* (Berkeley, 1953; rev. ed. 1969), pp. xv, 120–22. W. H. Gerdts and R. Burke, *American Still-Life Painting* (New York, 1971), pp. 152–53, 157. Doreen Burke, *American Paintings in the Metropolitan Museum of Art* (New York, 1980) vol. III, pp. 278–81.

Elihu Vedder (1836–1923)

PAGES 144–45: *The Lair of the Sea Serpent*

Elihu Vedder, *Digressions of V.* (Boston, 1910), p. 495. Regina Soria, *Elihu Vedder: American Visionary Artist in Rome (1937–1923)* (Rutherford, N.J., 1970), pp. 16, 37, 222, 225, 335. Natalie Spassky, *American Paintings in the Metropolitan Museum of Art* (New York, 1985), vol. II, pp. 514–15.

Albert Pinkham Ryder (1847–1917)

PAGE 146: *Landscape*

Doreen Burke, *American Paintings in the Metropolitan Museum of Art* (New York, 1980), vol. III, pp. 26–27.

Ralph Blakelock (1847–1919)

PAGE 147: *An Indian Encampment*

E. Daingerfield, *Ralph Albert Blakelock* (New York, 1914), pp. 16,

28–29. Doreen Burke, *American Paintings in the Metropolitan Museum of Art* (New York, 1980), vol. III, pp. 40–41.

James McNeill Whistler (1834–1903)

PAGE 148: *Arrangement in Flesh Colour and Black: Portrait of Théodore Duret*

Théodore Duret, *Histoire de J. McN. Whistler et de son oeuvre* (Paris, 1904), pp. 99–105, 153, 162; *Whistler*, trans. F. Rutter (London, 1917), pp. 10–11, 68–72, 102–3. John Rewald, *The History of Impressionism* (New York, 1946; 4th rev. ed. 1973), pp. 240–41. Denys Sutton, *James McNeill Whistler: Paintings, Etchings, Pastels and Watercolours* (London, 1966), p. 193. Roger Fry, *Letters of Roger Fry* (New York, 1972), vol. I, pp. 26, 28, 98, 307–8, 310–13. Hilary Taylor, *James McNeill Whistler* (New York, 1978), pp. 125–26, 129, 178. A. M. Young, et al., *The Paintings of James McNeill Whistler* (New Haven, 1980), vol. I, pp. 138–39. Natalie Spassky, *American Paintings in the Metropolitan Museum of Art* (New York, 1985), vol. II, pp. 385–92.

John Singer Sargent (1856–1925)

PAGE 149: *Madame X (Madame Pierre Gautreau)*

Henry James, in *Harper's New Monthly Magazine* 75 (1887), pp. 690–1; *Picture and Text* (New York, 1893), pp. 110–12. W. H. Downes, *John S. Sargent: His Life and Work* (Boston, 1925), pp. 12–13. E. Charteris, *John Sargent* (New York, 1927; reprint, Detroit, 1971), throughout. C. M. Mount, *John Singer Sargent: A Biography* (New York, 1955; 3rd ed. 1969), throughout. R. Ormond, *John Singer Sargent: Paintings, Drawings, Watercolors* (New York, 1970), throughout. Doreen Burke, *American Paintings in the Metropolitan Museum of Art* (New York, 1980), vol. III, pp. 229–35.

PAGE 150: *Mr. and Mrs. I. N. Phelps Stokes*

W. H. Downes, *John S. Sargent: His Life and Work* (Boston, 1925), pp. 41, 180–1. E. Charteris, *John Sargent* (New York, 1927; reprint, Detroit, 1971), p. 266. C. M. Mount, *John Singer Sargent: A Biography* (New York, 1955; 3rd ed. 1969), p. 448. R. Ormond, *John Singer Sargent: Paintings, Drawings, Watercolors* (New York, 1970), pp. 52, 169, 248. Doreen Burke, *American Paintings in the Metropolitan Museum of Art* (New York, 1980), vol. III, pp. 247–51.

PAGE 151: *Padre Sebastiano*

W. H. Downes, *John S. Sargent: His Life and Work* (Boston, 1925), pp. 60, 218–19. E. Charteris, *John Sargent* (New York, 1927; reprint, Detroit, 1971), p. 272. C. M. Mount, *John Singer Sargent: A Biography* (New York, 1955; 3rd ed. 1969), p. 470. R. Ormond, *John Singer Sargent: Paintings, Drawings, Watercolors* (New York, 1970), pp. 201, 255. Doreen Burke, *American Paintings in the Metropolitan Museum of Art* (New York, 1980), vol. III, pp. 261–63.

PAGES 152–53: *The Wyndham Sisters: Lady Elcho, Mrs. Adeane, and Mrs. Tennant*

W. H. Downes, *John S. Sargent: His Life and Work* (Boston, 1925), pp. 54–55, 188–89. E. Charteris, *John Sargent* (New York, 1927; reprint, Detroit, 1971), throughout. C. M. Mount, *John Singer Sargent: A Biography* (New York, 1955; 3rd ed. 1969), throughout. A. R. Tintner, "Sargent in the Fiction of Henry James," *Apollo* 102 (1975), pp. 129–31. Doreen Burke, *American Paintings in the Metropolitan Museum of Art* (New York, 1980), vol. III, pp. 253–57.

Mary Cassatt (1844–1926)

PAGES 154–55: *The Cup of Tea*

J. M. H. Carson, *Mary Cassatt* (New York, 1966), pp. 27, 30. Frederick A. Sweet, *Miss Mary Cassatt: Impressionist from Pennsylvania* (Norman, Okla., 1966), pp. 40, 61, 108–9, 137. Denys Sutton, *Apollo* 54 (1967), pp. 219–20. Adeline D. Breeskin, *Mary Cassatt: A Catalogue Raisonné of the Oils, Pastels, Watercolors and Drawings* (Washington, D.C., 1970), p. 51. N. Hale, *Mary Cassatt* (Garden City, N. Y., 1975), p. 166. Natalie Spassky, *American Paintings in the Metropolitan Museum of Art* (New York, 1985), vol. II, pp. 632–35.

PAGES 156–57: *Lady at the Tea Table*

J. M. H. Carson, *Mary Cassatt* (New York, 1966), pp. 59–60. Frederick A. Sweet, *Miss Mary Cassatt: Impressionist from Pennsylvania* (Norman, Okla., 1966), pp. 85–86, 92, 102. Adeline D. Breeskin, *Mary Cassatt: A Catalogue Raisonné of the Oils, Pastels, Watercolors and Drawings* (Washington, D.C., 1970), pp. 13, 80–81. Ellen J. Wilson, *American Painter in Paris: A Life of Mary Cassatt* (New York, 1971), pp. 119–23, 126, 138, 178. N. Hale, *Mary Cassatt* (Garden City, N. Y., 1975), pp. 120, 130–31, 165, 177, 258, 283. John Wilmerding, *American Art* (Harmondsworth, Eng., 1976), pp. 155–56. N. M. Matthews, ed., *Cassatt and Her Circle* (New York, 1984), pp. 174–76, 320–21. Natalie Spassky, *American Paintings in the Metropolitan Museum of Art* (New York, 1985), vol. II, pp. 638–42.

PAGES 158–59: *Young Mother Sewing*

Frederick A. Sweet, *Miss Mary Cassatt: Impressionist from Pennsylvania* (Norman, Okla., 1966), pp. ix, 139, 148. Adeline D. Breeskin, *Mary Cassatt: A Catalogue Raisonné of the Oil, Pastels, Watercolors and Drawings* (Washington, D.C., 1970), pp. 18, 166, 287, 306. Natalie Spassky, *American Paintings in the Metropolitan Museum of Art* (New York, 1985), vol. II, pp. 648–51.

Cecilia Beaux (1855–1942)

PAGES 160–61: *Ernesta (Child with Nurse)*

Cecilia Beaux, *Background with Figures: Autobiography of Cecilia Beaux* (New York, 1930), pp. 56, 348. H. S. Drinker, *The Paintings and Drawings of Cecilia Beaux* (Philadelphia, 1955), pp. 54–55. Doreen Burke, *American Paintings in the Metropolitan Museum of Art* (New York, 1980), vol. III, pp. 201–4.

John H. Twachtman (1853–1902)

PAGES 162–63: *Arques-la-Bataille*

Eliot Clark, *John Twachtman* (New York, 1924), pp. 20, 38–39. Doreen Burke, *American Paintings in the Metropolitan Museum of Art* (New York, 1980), vol. III, pp. 148–50.

Theodore Robinson (1852–1896)

PAGES 164–65: *A Bird's-eye View*

D. F. Hoopes, *The American Impressionists* (New York, 1972), p. 51. Doreen Burke, *American Paintings in the Metropolitan Museum of Art* (New York, 1980), vol. III, pp. 127–29.

Homer Dodge Martin (1836–1897)

PAGES 166–67: *View on the Seine: Harp of the Winds*

F. J. Mather, *Homer Martin: Poet in a Landscape* (New York, 1912), pp. 57–58, 60–61, 63, 76. James Thomas Flexner, *That Wilder Image: The Painting of America's Native School from Thomas Cole to Winslow Homer* (New York, 1962), pp. 331–32. Natalie Spassky, *American Paintings in the Metropolitan Museum of Art* (New York, 1985), vol. II, pp. 425–28.

J. Alden Weir (1852–1919)

PAGES 168–69: *The Factory Village*

Dorothy Weir Young, *The Life and Letters of J. Alden Weir* (New Haven, 1960), pp. 194, 199. Doreen Bolger Burke, *J. Alden Weir: An American Impressionist* (Newark, 1983), pp. 19, 218–19, 228, 235.

William Merritt Chase (1849–1916)

PAGES 170–71: *At the Seaside*

Doreen Burke, *American Paintings in the Metropolitan Museum of Art* (New York, 1980), vol. III, pp. 91–92.

PAGES 172–73: *For the Little One*

Richard J. Boyle, *American Impressionism* (New York, 1974), pp. 202, 204. Doreen Burke, *American Paintings in the Metropolitan Museum of Art* (New York, 1980), vol. III, pp. 92–94.

Childe Hassam (1859–1935)

PAGES 174–75: *Spring Morning in the Heart of the City*

Doreen Burke, *American Paintings in the Metropolitan Museum of Art* (New York, 1980), vol. III, pp. 353–56.

PAGES 176–77: *Avenue of the Allies, Great Britain, 1918*

Doreen Burke, *American Paintings in the Metropolitan Museum of Art* (New York, 1980), vol. III, pp. 353–56.

Edmund C. Tarbell (1862–1938)

PAGES 178–79: *Across the Room*

Frederick W. Coburn, "Edmund C. Tarbell," *International Studio* 32 (1907), p. 8. Doreen Burke, *American Paintings in the Metropolitan Museum of Art* (New York, 1980), vol. III, pp. 438–39.

John White Alexander (1856–1915)

PAGES 180–81: *Repose*

Julie Anne Springer, "Arts and the Feminine Muse: Women in Interiors by John White Alexander," *Woman's Art Journal* 6 (no. 2, 1985–86), pp. 6–7.

Abbott H. Thayer (1849–1921)

PAGES 182–83: *Young Woman*

Nelson C. White, *Abbot H. Thayer: Painter and Naturalist* (Hartford, Conn., 1951), pp. 76–77, 80, 210–11. Doreen Burke, *American Paintings in the Metropolitan Museum of Art* (New York, 1980), vol. III, pp. 100–2. Ross Anderson, *Abbott Henderson Thayer*, exhib. cat. (Syracuse, Everson Museum, 1982), pp. 68–70, 139.

William M. Paxton (1869–1941)

PAGES 184–85: *Tea Leaves*

Ellen Wardwell Lee, *William McGregor Paxton, 1869–1941, Member of the National Academy*, exhib. cat. (Indianapolis Museum of Art, 1979), p. 159.

Maurice Prendergast (1859–1924)

PAGE 186: *Central Park*

Doreen Burke, *American Paintings in the Metropolitan Museum of Art* (New York, 1980), vol. III, pp. 339–40.

William Glackens (1870–1938)

PAGE 187: *Central Park in Winter*

Ira Glackens, *William Glackens and the Ashcan Group: The Emergence of Realism in American Art* (New York, 1957), p. 20.

John Sloan (1871–1951)

PAGE 188: *Dust Storm, Fifth Avenue*

Bruce St. John, *John Sloan* (New York, 1971), pp. 33, 47, 146.

Robert Henri (1865–1929)

PAGE 189: *The Masquerade Dress: Portrait of Mrs. Robert Henri*

William I. Homer, *Robert Henri and His Circle* (Ithaca, 1969), pp. 146–48.

Arthur B. Davies (1862–1928)

PAGES 190–91: *Unicorns (Legend—Sea Calm)*

Phillips Memorial Gallery, *Arthur B. Davies: Essays on the Man and His Art* (Cambridge, Mass., 1924), pp. 10, 15, 41, 62. B. Wright, *The Artist and the Unicorn: The Lives of Arthur B. Davies (1862–1928)* (New City, N. Y., 1978), pp. 36, 115–18. Doreen Burke, *American Paintings in the Metropolitan Museum of Art* (New York, 1980), vol. III, pp. 423–24.